DELVING INTO DIFFERENT
LITERARY TERRAINS

SUBHAJIT BHADRA

TRUE SIGN
PUBLISHING HOUSE

Published by True Sign Publishing House
Address: SY. No. 21/2 & 21/3, Sonnenahalli,
Krishnarajapura, Bengaluru,
Karnataka - 560049 India
E-mail: truesignbooks@gmail.com
Website: www.truesign.in

Delving Into Different Literary Terrains

Author: Subhajit Bhadra

ISBN: 978-93-5584-978-6

First Edition: 2023

CONTENTS

Contesting The Grand Narrative: "A Critical Reading of Jayanta Mahapatra's Poetry"

Subhajit Bhadra

The aim of this paper is to show how Jayanta Mahapatra's poetry contains grand narratives and centre stages the interplay of various mini narratives. If India is considered as the macrocosm then Odisha becomes the microcosm in Jayanta Mahapatra's poetry and this paper makes an attempt to reveal the various layers associated with Odisha in his poetic oeuvre. Jayanta Mahapatra's poetry is extremely rich, evocative and powerful and the poet refuses to believe in the validity of any grand discourse or narrative. The Indian novelists writing in English have been more or less preoccupied with grand discourse or narratives of nation, identity, nationality, etc and contemporary Indian English novelists like Salman Rushdie, Shashi Tharoor and Kiran Desai have dealt with grand narratives in their respective creations. Salman Rushdie and Amitav Ghosh have exhibited an extraordinary anxiety to depict India in a large canvas in novels like Midnight's Children and The Shadow Lines that also reveal their consistent engagement with concepts like nation, identity and nationality. Compared to these stalwarts, the Indian English poets have maintained a low profile and the poetry of Nissim Ezekiel, Jayanta Mahapatra, Arun Kolatkar and Agha Shahid Ali have exhibited an awareness to bring to light a few particular mini-narratives in their poetic work. Ezekiel had given priority to Bombay in his poetry, Mahapatra has been consistently preoccupied with Odisha, Arun Kolatkar with Maharashtra and Agha Shahid Ali had immortalized Kashmir in his poetry. Though the central argument of this paper is derived from theoretical assumptions, yet there has been a sustained attempt to maintain consistent engagement with Mahapatra's poetry.

Both post-modernism and post-colonialism have been preoccupied with mini narratives and revealed a concern to give voice to the socially, politically and economically oppressed lot. Post-modernism is a specific literary and cultural movement that swept the shores of Europe during the second half

     Delving Into Different Literary Terrains

of the 20th century and subsequently consolidated its position within the academic realm by 1980s. Post-modernism has often been viewed as a thorough departure form modernism or a phenomenon arriving after the demise of modernism. But looked at from a critical point of view, post-modernism is neither a total break away with preoccupations or concerns of modernism, nor it is a radical movement logically followed by the death of the former; rather post-modernism critically re-examines the central ideals of modernism as it also questions some of the major ideas of the modernists. The modernists valorized concepts like progress, civilization, enlightenment, etc. but the post-modernist questioned the validity of such "grand narratives" in a post-war and post-holocaust European world. As Jean-François Lyotard convincingly argues in his seminal work **The Post Modern Condition: A Report on Knowledge:**

"Simplifying to the extreme, I define post-modernism as incredulity towards metanarratives. This incredulity is undoubtedly a product of progress in the sciences; but that progress in turn presupposes it. To the obsolescence of the metanarrative apparatus of legitimation corresponds, most notably, the crisis of metaphysical philosophy and of the university institution which in the post relied on it." **(Lyotard 1979, XXIV)1**

Lyotard's comment had stimulated the intellect of a generation of readers, critics and academicians across the world to think anew. In fact, Lyotard's argument so convincingly signaled the demise of grand narratives that literary and cultural activists appropriated his powerful theory to meet the challenges of their respective disciplines. In this context Tim Woods succinctly comments in his major book, **Beginning Postmodernism:**

"In other words, knowledge in the post-modern era can no longer be legitimated or sanctioned according to the great 'narratives' that have shaped western knowledge to the date, like notion of progress embedded in Marxism, or the release form unconscious trauma harboured by Freudian theory. Indeed, Lyotard regards such narratives as violent and tyrannical in their imposition of a 'totalizing' pattern and a false universality on action, events and things." **(Woods 2010, 20-21)2**

According to the tenets of post-colonial theory as espoused by Homi K. Bhabha, there are two types of representation – the pedagogic and the performative and it should be taken into account that these two modes of representation take place in the context of nationalistic discourse. The theory of nation and nationalism becomes grand narratives and within the domain of post-colonial theory and critics, there are a few critics who instinctively distrust such fanfare about nation that threatens to become a grand narrative. The concept of one grand nation tires to subdue other mini narratives and some of the post-colonial critics have challenged such theorization. The great narrative threaten to marginalize the mini narratives and in this context John McLeod argues:

"It is through the performative aspects of nationalist discourses that difference returns from within to challenge the homogeneous nation with its unified people and myths of origin, as the marginalized people of the population are granted an opportunity to intervene in the production of the nation's representative of itself to itself." **(McLeod 2007,119)3**

Post-colonial criticism/theory enables one to come to terms with the marginal voices which otherwise cannot articulate anything because of the domination of grand narratives. Post-colonial criticism questions the validity of western notion of progress, civilization, enlightenment and it provides a convenient scope to re-examine nationalist history anew. Post-colonialism has found fault with colonial historiography and many post-colonial writers and intellectuals write histories and the history of the nations putting aside the dominant and oppressive colonial history. In the wake of subaltern studies, intellectuals and writers like Ranajit Guha, Dipesh Chakravarty, Patha Chatterjee, Sumit Sarkar, Gayatri Chakravarty Spivak, Shahid Amin and others have attempted to re-write Indian history from an insider's perspective. Gayatri Chakravarty's seminal essay, **"Can the Subaltern Speak?"** argues the need for giving voice to the socially subjugated, oppressed and marginalized people. But post-colonial critics have often shown a tendency that has resulted in the marginalization of the subjugated voice. In this context Elleke Boehmer argues:

"Post-structuralist and/or post-colonial critics as Ajaz Ahmed has argued, 'Third World Literature' as a coherent field of knowledge, defined by unitary forces of history, such as nationalism or anti-colonial struggle." **(Boehmer 1995, 246)**

Jayanta Mahapatra's poetry brings to light the subjugated and oppressed voices and he always makes an attempt to contest the validity of grand narratives in his poetry, instead he gives priority to the depiction of Odisha as a microcosmic locale in his poetry. Jayanta Mahapatra does not write for professional reasons because writing for him is not only an aesthetic pursuit, but also a means to remain alive in a vibrant way. He has exhibited an awareness regarding the value of space in poetry and for him, Odisha symbolizes the past, present and future and it is precisely in this context one can argue that he, as a creative artist has dealt with mini narratives of Odisha in his poetry. For a poet, language is not merely an instrument to write but also the very essence of his/her identity. For a poet the clash between speech and silence enhances his/her sensibility and Mahapatra's own remark in this context is appropriate:

"And I would say we are only faced with a silence which words have brought us ultimately to all the words we thought were grand exercises of imagination, fusing the imaginary with reality. This silence is not just a stock character of mystery, or a knowledge, a knowledge that is always provisional." **(Mahapatra 2004, 22)**

Mahapatra struggles against this silence and continues to write poems of high aesthetic merit, his poems bring to light the deplorable plight of ordinary individuals, the misery and agony of common people, the acute poverty that taints sacred human relation, the hopeless condition of the socially underprivileged and the erosion of human values. Mahapatra was born in Cuttack and grew up in a lower middle class family. He had his upbringing in a narrow rural community. Mahapatra's poetry exhibits an extraordinary desire to depict Odisha in the midst of chaos, poverty, physical and spiritual degeneration and Odisha is not merely a space/ place in Mahapatra's poetry rather Odisha turns out to be a significant trope for him.

Mahapatra gives importance to ritual in his poetry and in **"A Rain of Rites,"** he talks about it:

"The rain I have known and traded all this life is thrown like kelp on the beach.

Like some shape of conscience I cannot look at, a malignant purpose in a nun's eye. "

The poetic persona here talks of an ordinary encounter with rain and this occasion works as a catalyst for creating a mosaic of images to bring to light the dark mood of the speaker. It is an intensely appealing subjective poem where an individual's response determines the texture and structure of the poem. Bijay Kumar Das rightly points out in this context:

"The landscape of place around the poet is the parameter of his life and faith and perhaps unalterable as his own body." **(Bijay Kumar Das 2001,9)**

Jayanta Mahapatra puts emphasis on the description of the so-called minute entities of nature and human life that is often neglected by the other Indian writers writing in English. Mahapatra is not bothered about the description of grand narratives, he is rather enamoured of small entities which he depicts through the piling up of a few striking images.

> "Swan sink wordlessly to the carpet
> miles of polished floors
> reached out
> for the glass of voices
> There are gulls crying everywhere
> and glazed green grass
> in the park with the swans
> folding their cold throats"

Both post-modernist and post-colonial critics distrust grand narratives and give voice to the socially oppressed as they depict the deplorable plight of poverty-stricken common people who lack the basic essentials of life. In **"Hunger,"** Jayanta Mahapatra makes an ordinary fisherman the protagonist of the poem; that fisherman is virtually a non-entity in a greater context. Mahapatra's fisherman reminds one of William Wordsworth's, **"The Leech Gatherer"** and **"The Solitary Reaper."** Mahapatra does not merely reveal his sympathy for the plight of the poor fisherman, he also makes the readers feel for the fisherman who does not hesitate to offer his own daughter as a prostitute to mitigate his hunger. The poetic persona is awestruck when the fisherman makes an abrupt and candid offer:

"I heard him say: My daughter, she's just turned fifteen...Feel her. I'll be back soon, your bus leaves at nine. The sky fell on me, and a father's exhausted wile. Long and lean, her years were cold as rubber. She opened her wormy legs wide. I felt the hunger there, the other one, the fish slithering, turning inside."

The poet talks about two different types of hunger in this poem – one is physical hunger and the other is sexual hunger. The poet also provides a vivid picture of poverty of the fisherman in this poem that brings to light a typical concern of both the post-colonial thinkers and the post-modernists – the concern for the marginalized and oppressed.

"In the flickering dark his hut opened like a wound. The wind was I, and the days and nights before.Palm fronds scratched my skin. Inside the shack an oil lamp splayed the hours bunched to those walls.Over and over the sticky soot crossed the space of my mind."

The concern for the simple and the "small" helps one to situate Mahapatra in the assembly of those Indian English poets who do not display any anxiety to come to terms with grand narratives. Mahapatra talks about "sad houses," "small screams," "boat" and "lake" in his evocative poem, **"Her Hand"** which brings to light his fundamental concerns as a poet.

> "As a boy I learned to come in
>
> by the back door. Sad
>
> houses now, clean and leaning
>
> against one another, full of sleep.
>
> My old rag elephant is
>
> smothered with small screams.
>
> From the dark surface,
>
> waving like grass –
>
> when the last boat crosses the lake."

In **"The Abandoned British Cemetery at Balasore,"** Mahapatra challenges the grand narratives of history and expresses his sympathy for the alien soldiers who died meaninglessly. The poet does not want to disturb history, he simply watches "the ruins of stone and marble," "any yet," he is "awed by the forgotten dead." Post-colonial critics clamour for the need to revive historical memory and to retrieve the voice that had not only been subdued, but also stifled.

The speaker of the poem mourns the death of common soldiers and he also laments the loss of identity that was caused by the war as a large number of soldiers died without being identified properly. The war caused havoc and it also led to the spread of disease and the poetic persona feels disgusted with the machinations of the Empire which is expressed in the following lines:

> "Of what concern to me is a vanished Empire?
>
> Or the conquest of my ancestors' timeless ennui?
>
> It is the dying young who have the power to show
>
> What the heart will hide, the grass shows no more."
>
> **(The Abandoned British Cemetery at Balasore)**

Similarly, "the cries of fishermen" disturb the poet in "the captive air of Chandipur-on-sea" and he listens to the "music" of what the world has lost. G.J.V Prasad rightly points out about Mahapatra:

"This transcendental poet is also a poet of Orissa.... This is clear in all his poetry and even more so in relationships, his epic attempts to write a long poem which would embody the myths of his culture – the history, mythology and legends of Orissa." **(Prasad 1999, 97)**

In Jayanta Mahapatra's poetry the subjective "I" becomes more important than the fate of a nation, he as the poet of individual subject experiences and that is why he can see the sky growing "lonelier with cloudlessness". In all these poems of Mahapatra the locale is Odisha and he repeatedly digs the native soil to bring out the essence of his creativity. In the poem, **"The Vase,"** the poet brings to light the conflicting realities that take place on an ordinary day and he provides an almost graphic description of these passing images:

<blockquote>
"But each day

we watch the sifts come and go,

watch the still – slender, leasing where

who shuffles down the crowded road and finds out

that the middle-aged ma surreptitiously following her."
</blockquote>

Mahapatra is nurtured by the organic world of his surroundings and he is firmly rooted in the soil and setting of Cuttack which is a microcosm of the macrocosm India. Mahapatra's heart reaches out to the poor women workers who toiled hard to maintain their livelihood. Mahapatra depicts the toil of four women labourers mending a road at two o' clock in a hot summer afternoon.

<blockquote>
"As four women workers rule the hot tar

On to the pitted face of the road.

Soon, it will be late in the afternoon and their

the mangled lepers will shuffle along, going home,

their deplorable looks." **(Again one day walking by the river)**
</blockquote>

Mahapatra depicts the plight of an old woman who can barely walk and the authentic picture of real suffering softens the hearts of readers. The following lines from the poem, **"Bazaar, 5 P.M. Orissa"** brings to light Mahapatra's compassion for the suffering lot.

<blockquote>
"An old woman prostrates herself

to the day's last sun

the crawling mass of people on its knees
</blockquote>

carrying her upward, through a tight suffering

that fells the sun, measuring

the darkness break out of her shrouded shrine. "

(Bazaar, 5.P.M. Orissa)

Puri occupies a pivotal place in Mahapatra's poetry and the poverty and plight of the leprosy patients is effectively brought out by the poet in the following lines:

"At Puri, the crows

The one wide street

lolls out like a giant tongue.

Five faceless lepers move aside

as a priest passes by.

And at the streets end

the crowds thronging the temple door,

a huge holy flower."

(Taste for Tomorrow)

The poems **"Dawn at Puri"** and **"Main Temple Street, Puri,"** Mahapatra again reveals his consistent preoccupation with common incidents, subjects and dejects. In **"Dawn at Puri"** he talks about the sad plight of the widows and leprosy patients.

"her last wish to be cremated here

twisting uncertainly like light

on the shifting sands." **(Dawn at Puri)**

From the above discussion it becomes transparent that Mahapatra as a poet contests the validity of any grand narrative and instead gives priority to the foreplay of various mini- narratives which is a continuous concern for both the post-modernists and post-colonial critics.

Works Cited

Boehmer, Elleke, 'Colonial and Post-colonial Literature, Migrant Metaphors,' Oxford: OUP, 1995

Das, Bijay Kumar, The Poetry of Jayanta Mahapatra, New Delhi: Atlantic Publishers, 2001.

Lyotard, Jean-Francois, The Post-modern Condition: A Report on Knowledge, Manchester: Manchester University Press, 1979.

McLeod, John, Beginning Post-colonialism, Manchester: Manchester University Press, 2007.

Mehrotra, Arvind Krishna, The Oxford India Anthology of Twelve Modern Indian Poets, New Delhi: OUP, 2003

Panja, Shormishtha. (ed) "Many India's Many Literatures, New Critical Essays', New Delhi: Worldview Publications, 2004.

Prasad, G.J.V., 'Continuities in Indian English Poetry, Nation Language Form,' Delhi: Pencraft International, 1999.

Woods, Tim, Beginning Post-modernism, New Delhi: Viva Books, 2010.

An Astounding Narrative

REVIEW OF THE BENGALI NOVEL, "KHOMA KORO HE PROBHU"
Written by Rupak Saha,
Published by Deep Prakashan, Kolkata. Price: Rs: 300.
The novel was published in 2013

By: Subhajit Bhadra

In the realm of contemporary Bengali literature, Rupak Saha has carved a niche for himself. Though he is basically recognized as a sport journalist, yet his imaginative fiction has earned applause from critics and general readers. He has shown his expertise in the genre of sports journalism, short story and novel. In the field of Bengali sports journalism, Moti Nandy was a pioneering figure and Rupak Saha followed in his footsteps. But that doesn't mean that he was a servile imitator. He had an independent aura that had enabled him to move into different parts of the world to cover various sports events. His fictional range was also astounding and the book under review reveals his trademark traits as a novelist.

The book under review is titled, **"Khoma Koro he Prabhu"** (Forgive, Oh God) is based around the life of the saint Shri Chaitanya who was one of the foremost religious and social reformers of India during the Later Medieval Period. Chaitanyadeva originally belonged to Nabadwip but later on he migrated to Orissa, especially to Puri because of the fear of religious persecution from the Muslim rulers of the region. Rupak Saha started his novel, "Khoma Koro he Prabhu" (Forgive, Oh God) published in 2013 in such context and made a wonderful mixture of history, myth and contemporary life. This novel is basically a result of painstaking research about Chaitanya's life but Rupak Saha doesn't merely show his erudition to exhibit his learning or to take the readers by awe and fear. He has shown that a good research- based novel can also be a highly interesting one as the contemporary setting of the 21st century gives it another dimension. There is dearth of good research-based books, particularly novels on Chaitanyadeva and this emptiness has been somehow filled up by Rupak Saha and that is also one of the reasons why he deserves credit.

Saha has exhibited a successful blending between subject matter and style and these complement each other. Saha has been able to impart polyphonic voice to the novel in the Bakhtinian sense of the term. The dialogic discourse manifests itself in the novel as Saha waves a tapestry of rich narrative. The basic theme of the novel is the mystery of the disappearance of Chaitanyadeva during his time. There is a group of researchers who believe that Chaitanyadeva was murdered by Oriya people as he was bringing a large section of people under his fold because of his reformative zeal.

Many people in Orissa could not tolerate him because they believed that Chaitanyadeva was responsible for the degradation of religious and political life in Orissa.

Rupak Saha chooses four major characters from contemporary 21st century and their names are Gora, Jaydeep, Upasana and Purandar. Gora initially appears as a Dalit leader who wants equality and democratic rights for the Dalits and that is why he has joined a political unit and this fact created some distance between Gora's mother and him.

As the novel proceeds we find the metamorphosis of Gora from a political leader into a religious avatar. Many people take him to be the reincarnation of Chaitanyadeva as he bodily resembles the saint and performs a few miracles that trigger off a huge group of followers to take him into their custody. There is also a group in Orissa which does not like anyone to go for research regarding Chaitanyadeva's life and it is precisely this group that wants to murder Jaydeep and Upasana who are researching about Chaitanyadeva. They are initially followed by the professional murderer Purandar who, however, understands later on that he has been pushed into doing wrong things or has been used as a toy. He does penance and atones for his crime by saving the lives of Jaydeep and Upasana a number of times.

The novel is full of details about Chaitanyadeva's life but Rupak Saha makes an aspect very transparent - and it is that anybody who does any research about the great medieval saint would run the risk of being eliminated. The glaring example of this fact in the novel is the brutal murder of Upasana and the mysterious death of Sushovon and a few other good people who wanted to unearth Chaitanya's life and the reason of his death. Jaydeep and Upasana are co-researchers and fall into love with each other but before they get married, Upasana is murdered. Upasana's friend Swati consoles Jaydeep but to remind him of pragmatic affairs appears futile. Rupak Saha makes a very curious, interesting and mysterious case study regarding the transformation of Gora from an ordinary individual into a great saint who is even revered by the Chief Minister of the State.

The characters in the novel have motivation of their own and each works according to his or her design. The four major characters live out their predestined lives and there is no escape route for them. The novel divides the characters into two specific groups - one group reveres Chaitanyadeva and another wants to take revenge upon people who show any minute interest on Chaitanyadeva's life.

There is intense political rivalry and different groups including foreigners take active role in the narrative of Chaitanyadeva's life. Rupak Saha's credit lies in the fact that he transforms an ordinary narrative into extraordinary heights through a prefect blending of fact and fiction. Saha dramatizes the narrative but he is never out of control. Rupak Saha ends the novel on a passive note but there is transformation and mystery till the very end. Rupak Saha has shown that Chaitanyadeva's life, death and the mystery of his being is still relevant today. Kudos to Saha for constructing such an interesting novel. This novel must be translated into English and various other Indian languages to make it available to a wide spectrum of readers.

An Engaging Research Work

A Review of Periodical Press and Colonial Modernity:
Odisha /1866 to 1936
Written by Sachidananda Mohanty
Review done by: Subhajit Bhadra Asst. Professor P.G Dept.of
English Bongaigaon College, Bongaigaon Pin: 783380 Assam,

Mobile: 9957858903
Email: subhajit.bhadra@gmail.com

Sachidananda Mohanty is a renowned academician and scholar who is recognized in both India and abroad for his formidable contribution towards serious research work.

The book under review titled **"Periodical Press and Colonial Modernity"** provides a detailed survey of the rise and decline of the periodicals in colonial Odisha since 1866 to 1936 and shows how the advent of **Utkala Deepika** and **Utkal Sahitya Samaj** brought about the concept of colonial modernity through writings inspired by western enlightenment. Mohanty also shows how these periodicals sometimes resisted colonial modernity and ushered in alternative/vernacular modernity. Mohanty begins his book with a quotation from James Mill and he presents before readers what the legendary filmmaker of India, Shyam Benegal termed "unreliable cultural memory." He writes about the contemporary period of e- publishing and internet and says that the concept of periodical literature must acquire new meaning or else it will be forgotten and relegated to the backdoor. **Periodical Press**, according to Mohanty, reached its zenith during the 19th century. Mohanty relates it to the structure of university system and he also traces its link to the advent of capitalism and a new leisured class. Mohanty shows how journals became invaluable archives for academic professionals and administrators in course of time. The term, 'periodical' encompasses a wide spectrum and Mohanty states that it is a colonial import. These periodicals of Odisha reached out to a non-specialized and non-technical audience. During the Victorian Age periodicals reached to the middle class and Mohanty cites examples of various British periodicals to clinch his point.

Internet has added a new dimension to knowledge system and the concept of the periodical press has not been able to dissociate it from such straightjacket. Mohanty argues that except in Kerala and Bengal there has not been much effort to document the rise of the periodical press during the Raj and Odisha was no exception.

That is why Mohanty has to undertake painstaking research to unearth the history of the periodical press in Odisha during a stipulated period. Mohanty provides a detailed account of socio- economic background of colonial Odisha and states that British rule in Odisha was indirect. Mohanty proves that Utkala Deepika's advent can be directly traced to the terrible famine in Odisha in 1866. The oppression in form of taxes was great and Mohanty raises the question regarding the bearing of economy on the nature of colonial modernity practiced by colonial state. Mohanty tries to link up periodical press with colonial modernity. High modernism of colonial masters was highlighted with great rhetoric of progress and superiority of the west. Resistance to colonialism came in the form of vernacular/alternative modernity and in this context the periodical press of Odisha played a significant role.

By highlighting the lives of the editors of **Utkala Deepika** and **Utkal Sahitya Samaj** – Gourishankar Ray and Biswanath Kar, Mohanty wants to contextualize vernacular/alternative modernity. Mohanty proclaims that his study begins with the birth of the periodical in Odisha in 1866 and closes with the advent of Odisha as a separate province in 1936. Mohanty says that colonial modernity in Odisha came in the form of rich cameos. English education and rhetoric of progress were the central projects of colonial discourse. Mohanty writes as an insider with a whole gamut of Odisha scholars who had prepared a ground for him to plunge deeper into his research. The book is short, containing just 126 pages but every line adds to an existing body of knowledge and research. There is not a single page in the book where the readers do not find glimpses of Mohanty's erudition.

In the recent times when post-colonial critical theory has gained prominence, academicians like Mohanty would naturally turn his attention towards concepts like colonial enterprise but his specialty lies in the fact that he has been able to localize his vision. Odisha is Mohanty's motherland

and it is where he searches the advent and root of alternative modernity through the rise of the two periodicals that he discusses in the book. Mohanty exhibits the scholastic and rigour of a deft academician in this book. His wide range of reading in different fields enriches the text and the readers are provided with reason and logic at every page. **Utkal Sahitya's** inaugural issue speaks of a balance between tradition and modernity which reminds one of T. S Eliot's essay, **"Tradition and Individual Talent"**. Mohanty cites the example of writers like Fakir Mohan Senapati, Radhanath Ray, Chandramohan Maharana and Radhanath Rao who stand for " Bhasha tradition." The book is very informative and we come to know about many forgotten details regarding Odiya life and culture - for example, Mohanty remarks that the first missionary schools were set up in Cuttack in 1822. Mohanty makes it clear that it is due to the " widespread dissemination" of missionary literature in Odiya"- such as the parable, morality play, miracle play, essay, novel and tract were internalized in the native soil. Mohanty documents the journal recordings of Rev. C. Lacey which brings to light the attempt of the missionaries to convert the natives. Mohanty shows how along with the rise of colonial modernity, the periodicals gave rise to vernacular/ alternative modernity.

Female education became an important concern during that period and the periodicals contributed towards such goal. Mohanty refers to Bankim Chandra Chatterjee's essay regarding female education published in **"Bangadarshan."** Mohanty also posits his argument in the context of the intellectual difference between Rabindranath Tagore who supported everything "new" in contemporary life and Chandranath Basu who was a conventional man bound to the street socio- religious dogma. The way Mohanty makes a parallel comparison between Bengal and Odisha is really commendable. Mohanty has not only researched through studying books, but he has also taken recourse to archival findings. Mohanty shows how in Odisha by the first of the 20th century the concept of the new woman was being debated in **Utkal Sahitya, Mukura** and other journals by Sailabala Das, Sarala Devi and Pratibha Devi. Fakir Mohan Senapati made it explicitly clear in his fiction that reading periodicals was a must for domestic couples.

That is how Mohanty selectively points out the validity of periodicals in the 19th century and 20th century Odisha. On the other hand, a female poet like Sushila wrote an instructive poem regarding the female education in Odisha and Mohanty relates it to the rise of the vernacular/ alternative modernity in Odisha. Mohanty gives the citation from a periodical titled **"Grahalaxmi"** and comments how female education was resisted by a section of native population. Mohanty comments that Fakir Mohan Senapati questioned the validity of western historiography and upheld the virtue of oral history and that is how he threw a challenge to the dominant modernity project by highlighting the importance of alternative modernity. The first chapter of the book deals with the history of the **periodical press** in Odisha. The theme of filial ingratitude brought about by baneful western education is also discussed in the context of writings of Fakir Mohan Senapati. Mohanty charts out the growth and decline of the periodical press in Odisha in the first chapter. Mohanty makes it apparent that the East India Company and the missionaries were responsible for the birth of the periodical press in India and Odisha was no exception. The second chapter deals with the lives and ideology of the two editor's respectively **Utkala Deepika and Utkal Sahitya Samaj** and their contribution to the society. The third chapter deals with the print journalism and Odiya modernity while the fourth chapter discusses Utkal Sahitya and colonial/alternative modernity. Issues like patronage are also discussed in the book at great length but basically the book brings to light a forgotten chapter of the intellectual and cultural/literal history of Odisha. The book is written in a lucid style and Oxford University Press deserves praise for bringing out such an interesting volume.

Kudos to Mohanty for writing such a book which does not pretend to be a dry academic work full of critical jargons.

An Intimate Conversation With Subodh Sarkar

Q 1) Every poet internalizes the truth from his or her quest for life, search for life and perceptions of life and then continuously advances towards his own way of art. How will you explain the fact from your life of poems, personal life and the equation of your perception of your life? How important are your childhood and the later life in this regard?

Answer: Mr. Bill Gates once said, "It's not your fault to be born poor, but it is your fault to die as a poor man." I was born in a very poor family. My father, a poor school teacher was driven away from the erstwhile East Pakistan and he fled away to settle in Krishna Nagar. We could hardly have two square meals a day. I saw my mother managing to have the remaining mounds of rice which would be left out at the bottom of the utensil after having fed all other members of our family. With a smiling face, she would say, "Go to school. Study well. Get me a good 'saree' when you get a job." But my father died a premature death due to cancer during my childhood. We, the six brothers and sisters in all became really helpless and were brought to the margin of starvation. Nobody stood by us during that period. Our relatives moved away from us. The most surprising event was that a kind of stubbornness developed in me. Didi, my elder sister managed to have a broken harmonium and would sing the songs of Rabindranath Tagore very nicely. I would often say to my Didi, "Please sing the song once again for me, "Everyone has gone to the garden in the full moon night." In that worse situation, the 'Geet Bitan' of Tagore became my Bible. The Naxalite movement started in Krishna Nagar during that period. We had to go across the dead bodies in order to reach the school. I saw handmade bombs in the school bags of our classmates. We would be rebuked by the elders as we would go to enjoy the sunset by the edge of a forest. "Never visit here. If you come, remember not to come in the evening." I was scared. But the sunset could really be enjoyed fully only in the evening. Perhaps, I could not have joined the community of writers if I had not passed through such a phase of life during my childhood. Nobody advised me to write. Nobody allowed me to sit beside adorably. Being hard-pressed by poverty, when an adolescent picked up weapons in his or her hands, I picked up the 'Geet

Bitan'. During my boyhood, I could sing 500 songs without seeing the song book. My mother was very angry with me. One evening, I was singing the song as loudly as I could, "You came but you did not come." My song having finished, my mother who was scourging the utensils, said, "You engage in tall talks when you don't have the money." I could have said to my mother had she been alive. "Today, I am also a Bill Gates. Could a person become a Bill Gates if the person had to struggle from the point from which I had to struggle?"

Q 2) What is your opinion regarding T.S. Eliot's view that a modern poet builds a poetic world based on tradition? How far can Mr. Subodh Sarkar be considered a modern or post-modern poet on the perspective of the evolution of Bengali poetry?

Answer: Who am I to say that I am a modern poet? There is really nothing to be called as post-modern. I don't believe in this. The definition of modernity dates back to the days of the Mahabharata. Is Mr. T.S. Eliot as modern as Homer ? Are we necessarily modern if we have cell-phones and laptops on our hands? I sometimes feel while I read the ancient texts that a 5000-year-old Subodh is lying within me. He is my look alike, he has beard like me, he is sitting having put on jeans and T-shirt like me. He also talks and sends SMSs through , but the hieroglyphics is open before him. It has still not become readable. I shall call a poet 'modern' if he or she can translate the hieroglyphics. As if an electric wire passes through all the unlimited machineries of modern life - a loud laugh passes through like electric current. T.S. Eliot only wanted to say about that laugh. Sitting within unlimited machineries is what we call 'tradition'.

Q 3) In many poems of yours, it can be perceived by the readers that there is an attempt to represent the depth of life in a light mood and in the said life of Mikhail Bakhtin, it has been represented in the most forceful way. How will you analyze this style of discourse in poems?

Answer: At the end of each moment of grief, each hour of suffering, each kind of failure, I can see a small container and restrained laughter is lying hidden in it. Grief is the mother of all poems - there can be no two opinions about that. I search for that container at the end of every poem. I can't bear the tears from the eyes. I don't like a person sitting being overwhelmed with grief. Once I said to a beggar near the Taj Bengal hotel, "Can't you go inside and snatch your food? What's the use of sitting in front like this?" I wrote about this in my poem, **"Tears from Eyes."** When dangers appear on its feet at my home then I speak out to the danger, "Just sit on my chair.

Have tea. I shall talk to you when you cool down." The most dangerous moment for a man is his hunger or his inability to eat. Throwing away that danger under a banyan tree in my childhood, I crept in Kolkata. Reaching Kolkata, I felt that I was in a greater danger than before. Visiting Delhi, I realized the intensity of the danger was greater still. A person moves from one kind of danger to another, from one kind of wonder to another, from one type of love to another in his or her own life. Should we not laugh then? Should we leave our acts of cutting jokes? I have the habit of taking up any serious subject in a lighter vein. I have shaken the chins of personalities from Gautam Buddha to Fidel Castro in my poems. Actually, the presence of blasphemy is more prominent in my psyche than that of a true worshipper. Perhaps for that reasons my poems are twisted, rough and chaotic.

Q 4) The description of sexuality is found to be written openly in many of your poems and in some other poems there are mentions of the physical love which is the favourite of the present generation. Again, there are elements of satire on the duplicity and show off's of the society in some of your poems. How will you explain the value systems of the present generation and the dangers evolving out of it?

Answer: Should a writer have the responsibility of explaining those things? I don't think in that way when I write poems. In reality, I think about the matters that I don't write on. It takes some time to decide what to write and what not to write. Duplicity or falsehood is an important part of my life. I have much regards to those who always speak the truth; but the persons who has inherent bad qualities, in whom there are a queer mixture of honesty and duplicity are the subject matters of my writings. There are stories and characters in my writings - as such I regret before the poems. I can't write without mentioning about the characters. It may be Mussolini or my teacher. I shall inflict pains on him or them. I shall surely say to a evil person, "You are a bad person." I don't spare even myself in that matter. I like to satirize myself. I like to hide my grief with a cap of happiness. But sometimes I feel that I should manage a revolver and shoot on my head.

Q 5) As there is co-existence of black and white, light and darkness in life, so there are mixtures of polished and unpolished words in your poems. One can find an effortless, yet sensible use of English and Hindi words in your poems. Your dexterity in this field comes to surface through your choice of subject matters and the use of language. Again, this can be said that you have freed the language of the Bengali poems from artificiality and widened its scope. What is your opinion about this?

 Delving Into Different Literary Terrains

Answer: I have no words of my own - I am a slave to the sound wave that flows and extends from a fish market to a university classroom. I have never felt ashamed of using any word till today. No word is either polished or unpolished for me. Both the words like 'Om' and 'Son of a Pig' are holy words for me. A word is created from the depth of life. The words are the symbols of our feelings even though there may be good or evil things in their depths. The English and Hindi words used by me are found to be used randomly in the Bengali poems of today. "Why should they be not used after all? Can you tell me how many Hindi words are used by an auto-wallah? There is a mosaic of Hindi, English and Bengali words in his language. How can I escape from that? Why should I escape at all ? "

Q 6) You have written some narrative poems which resonate with the echoes of condemnation against social exploitation. Can a poet portray the sketch of a single personality set in two different poles? Does the nectar of creativity that arise out of ceaseless struggle between inner psyche of a poet with that of the outer sphere of the society simply beautiful or society-oriented?

Answer: The persons' who write love poems all his or her life also have a responsibility. The question is who is responsible and to whom. I don't believe in the fact that a poet becomes a great poet once he has a sense of responsibility. There is no relationship of responsibility with writing. This question has often been raised in West Bengal and it comes even now. As a priest has a responsibility, a Communist has a responsibility, a Gandhian has a responsibility, a poet, too, has a responsibility. Why should it be considered a pre-condition for writing poems? When I go through a nice poem, I like to bow down my head near the feet of it. I don't question about the responsibility of the poet. The question of my consciousness that has arisen, I have a clear view that an unconscious person also can write good poems. One can write good poems without having proper knowledge of monetary policies, socialism or market policies. On the other, it is often dangerous to understand these concepts. Then the essence of a good poem evaporates. According to me, a piece of poem is as holy as a piece of white paper. There is no need to stigmatize that by showing much consciousness. We should not think that the poets are only conscious creatures in this world while others are not. A beggar is also a conscious person. Even he knows who will offer him alms and who will not. A kind of great madness is required for writing poems. One should write poems in an open mind keeping the principles of economic, social and market policies in their pockets. The more I grow up, the more I understand that composing poems is a very difficult task. The kind of craziness I had in my younger days has been replaced by philosophical undertones.

Q 7) Many of the readers of your poems may have felt that one of the chief themes of your poems is love and unconditional love. Your poetic soul is devoted to the selfless love - that love which has got wealth of heart and warmth of life. They deal with that kind of love in which the black shadow of the materialistic world has not fallen. What is your opinion about this?

Answer: Let me tell you in easy terms or language that love poems is not my cup of tea. The best of all the love poems in Bengali have already been written by Sunil Ganguly. The lover will come out of his grave to listen to 'Nira's poems' composed by him. None of my poems turns out be a true love poem. I have no regret for this. I shall feel myself rewarded when my poet stands by the threshold of a thatched house of a family in the Sunderbans, after being ravaged by a storm. If my poems are found to be lying in the pocket of a boy called Aakash Mahato, then I shall feel that I have received the Academy awards. If my poems are found to shine in the corners of the eyes of a black lady of Mathabhanga, that will be my best love poem. As I don't read my self-composed poems, so if someone tells me to choose from, then I shall choose the 'Nira's poems' by Sunil Ganguly.

Q 8) In some of your poems, there is a rebellion against urbanization and there is a keen desire to preserve the rural value-system. How and why do these two-dimensional conflicts in your poems or in your mental world strike your mind?

Answer: Let me tell you something about my hypocrisy here. I am used to a typical urban life. If we make use of the Metro Rail service everyday, if we use cars, if we use laptops, and also use it for spread of the town, then nothing than a piece of paper will be left. I grew up in Krishna Nagar. I could reach Kolkata in about two and a half hours time. I started to write from Krishna Nagar but I would remain in Kolkata in my own imagination. The city that I landed after my first travel by air was New York City. It appeared to me while walking through the Manhattan that, "It is my own city. I would love to live here. Having landed my feet in London, I felt that I had been in this city for long. I saw this city through the pages of Charles Dickens. Therefore, I am really an urban poet." Going to any village, I never felt that I had gone there to live. I like the villages for hardly two days. I like the shade under a banyan tree for a couple of days. But the hypocrisy lies in the fact that I want that the entire world should go back to the villages.

 DELVING INTO DIFFERENT LITERARY TERRAINS

There will be no video parlours, newspapers or radio there. Much in the same way as Homer once recited the poems having called in 5-6 students. Like the way sage Valmiki once started to compose the 'shlokas' sitting by a riverside. I do imagine taking everyone to such a place. Nobody speaks like this besides the mad ones. There are occasional stories of madness and mad characters in my poems.

Q 9) One of the most memorable lines of your poem is 'as poem is a basement of history'. There are signs of hatred and revenge against the different representative 'entities' of the state. In this connection , a quotable line is, "Never before the police resembled as much as a widow." In the perspective of your own poetic world and the world poems, how will you analyze your poems?

Answer: Having twisted the ears of the police, I wrote many poems. It is easy to criticize the police - people love it. Who builds up the police? The state does it. Actually, the police are made to act as per our choice. We want that police should accept the hush money, so they accept the bribes. The police does evil work as we want them to do. We seem to forget the fact that the police have their own houses, own parents. The police are good so long as it works in our favour. The police will surely have to be considered bad by us if they go against us. The U.S.A. will be good when it will do work in our favour, when the same country will pick up your sons and daughters, then the U.S.A. is to be considered bad. The main reason behind my calling the poems as 'a basement of history' is that such perceptions do not have a market rate, the opinions that do not hit the headlines of the news, the symbols that are ignored by people are the subject-matters of my poems. The entire world condemned the U.S.A. when it visited Vietnam. But on that day the Jupiter laughed. It makes me laugh today to note that the Vietnamese people who came from the basement of history have spread themselves out in different parts of the U.S.A. - they are now being offered a royal treatment. Who could have thought that the historical situation would change so much within a span of thirty years? Who could have thought the persons whom the masters of America once brought from Africa in chains or as slaves would send one of them to the 'White House'? I was taken aback when I visited Russia recently. There were many rape cases, murder cases and snatching incidents there. People have become very greedy there. The present Russia is crowded with people with costly cell-phones, night-clubs and women with scanty dresses. Where are the next generations of the Russian writers with whose ideas we have grown up? I don't normally consider such big incidents, my point of consideration are those small incidents and call them as 'the basement of history' which are normally ignored by people.

Q 10) The relationship between men and women is shown to be a metaphor of an everlasting flow in your poems. The ease with which you uphold this invincible and plain truth through your artistic portrayal is really enviable. I am eager to know regarding this from you in detail.

Answer: I can't simply see a woman as a woman only. I watch how she is crossing her gender. According to me, gender is a check-post, a borderline. Two guards are standing there with AK-47s in their hands. I like to see women driving cars, driving aircraft and ruling countries very much. I like to watch a woman smoking cigarettes very much. I have never liked the idea of a stereotyped woman. I grew up along with my three elder sisters. Out of the three, two of them did not yield to poverty, on the other hand, they managed to stand in their own feet with honour and entered the world of service with dignity. I like working women - whether they are those who carry bricks on their heads or the ones who would sit before the computers. There are mentions of women of varied professions in my poems. Their relationships with their men have also been discussed in my poems. I think that the men-women relationship is like a big mine. We can get many golden ornaments if we go inside it.

Q 11) A poem and its ideology is integrally related. Have your ideologies as a person influenced your poems? How far do you think that an ideology has widened or compressed the poetic world of a poet?

Answer: It is good to have an ideology. Everything feels empty without this. It makes us feel that there is no support, it also makes us feel that our feet are not on the ground. But it should not be considered as be all and end all. My ideology is my own. There is no use to blow the trumpet on this. It is better to leave an ideology if it destroys the essence of poetry. Why can't a person leave his ideology if someone else can hoodwink immortality for the sake of poems. I shall give more marks to those poets who had thought of not to attempt to write some poems due to the presence of an ideology, can write poems having kept that ideology aside. I shall not award marks to the 'fundamentalists'. The problem with an ideology is that it does not know how to honour another ideology. Why shall I not be able to call them good poems if those are written by others beyond my notions of an ideology? I don't like to adorn the poems with ornaments. I have never tried to clad a poem with a 'Banarasi saree'. This does not necessarily mean that I shall not tell them good poems if they are decorated by anyone. A bare-bodied person clad with a towel looks as attractive as 'suited-booted' Amitabh Bachchan.

Q 12) You have been devoted to the art, literature and philosophies of the East and the West for long. That is why the references to Derrida, Foucault, Kafka, Camus and Lorca are used with ease in many of your poems. Where can you find the similarities and the differences between the philosophy of life and the poetic philosophy of the Indian and the Western poets?

Answer: One of the faults of my poems is the fact that I more global than local. Among all my contemporaries and my followers, it is in my poems that one can find the mentions of America, Israel, Iraq, China and Afghanistan more than anyone else. It is also true that I have been writing a collection of poems on Gujarat. According to me, the countries need not be geographically separated. They are not separate entities. Recently, I wrote a book of poems on Delhi. I live myself within an entire human life. Many people do like me. My entire world is spread out from my toothpaste to my laptop - and I am an ordinary citizen of that world. I get equal shocks and feel the heart-burn if some untoward incident takes place either in Lalgarh or in Guatemala. The friend from New Jersey who rings me up daily is a part of my family, I get the impression of grief at my residence in Tollygunge area if there is any grievous incident in his family. A human life is no longer attached to a country only. Therefore, to say it in a very simple and natural way, despite the fact that my poems are written in Bengali, but they have the audacity to cross the threshold or barriers of a language.

Q 13) You are an Editor of a well established journal called **'Indian Literature'** of Sahitya Academy' right now. How will you analyze the importance of translated versions of the texts in the context of the spread of Indian literature and for bringing Indian literature closer to world literature?

Answer: This is one of the dreams I have. Translation is a big dream. Poems cannot be translated by anyone without a dream. It was due to the dream of Mr. Buddhadeva Bose that even Baudelaire could be converted into a Bengali poet. As there are many signs of glory in the forehead of Indian literature, in the same way, it is really shocking not to find very good translated versions of books from one language into another. We get the translated texts from all over India for our journal **'Indian Literature'**. We select some of them and publish them. In recent times, some kind of awareness has been growing. It was not there earlier. The Sahitya Academy has a dominant role in the matter of translations. In recent times, there is a growing trend of discussion regarding Indian literature even in the western world. It has been observed that the world famous publishers like Penguin Books are coming forward to publish the translated texts. But there is a dearth of good translators and the good translators of poems are very rarely found. Jibanananda Das was fortunate enough to get a high profile translator like Mr.Clinton. B. Seely.

Q 14) How will you look into the increasing aggression of English language and the problems of the Indian languages arising out of it as a poet in Bengali?

Answer: Books written in English are the tools to dominate the dynamics of power, it has become easier to catch the market if the books are written in English. On the other hand, the students of IITs have put aside their tools and they are trying their hands on writing books. I have heard that Mr. Chetan Bhagat has a good market share. Will it be such that people will start writing in English only leaving aside the languages like Bengali, Assamese and Marathi, etc. Are those days coming near? I am afraid. The Indian languages are so rich that the writers in English will not be able to imagine. Salman Rushdie is my favorite writer but I don't consider him a sensible person when he said and wrote that best literature from India is being written in English. I have condemned it; I will never forgive him for selling this idea to the west. If Indian literature is properly translated, India will win. But I don't think my dream is coming true. The post-colonial writings we championed as 'empire writes back` in India are now hungrily eating up the vitals of Indian literature in languages. We are in the war with English. After 30 years India will be Ireland. Do we know any Irish writer writing in Irish Gaelic? None of our children will read Bengali. Amitav Ghosh will survive in the world as a Bengali writer, not Sunil Gangopadhyay.

   Delving Into Different Literary Terrains

An Unsuccessful Fantasy And Some Spoiled Characters

Translated by Subhajit Bhadra

(Based on an Assamese story called 'Eta Byartho Fantasy Aru Kisu Nawshta Saritra' from the collection of short stories called 'Jaatra Enekoiye' by Prarthona Saikia)

He once said this to her. She heard the saga of his desire and that special song and without wasting time any further, she called him 'crazy as you were' and burst into peels of laughter.

The breeze that had spread the sweet-smelling scent from the wild flowers at once caught their attention. Suddenly, Himangshu became exuberant, " Oh you all, (Clapping his hands with force, he took a deep breath) the smell is simply fantastic."

(Dragging Shahjahan nearer to him, he patted on his back) "Friend, let's go and seek the source of the scent."

Shahjahan did not utter anything. Bowing his head down, he sat on a rock lying on the edge of the hilly road.

Seeing the indifference and inattentive reactions of Shahjahan despite the warm proposal from Himangshu , Pranjal and Hiranya came beside Himangshu.

They even looked insipid in comparison with Himangshu. But they were, at last, ready to go with Himangshu. When Himangshu, Pranjal and Hiranya went farther scaling the sides of the small hillock, Bhaskar, Shahjahan and Kartik Dutta sat on the rocks lying on the edges of the road. Shahjahan became restless after having torn away the bunch of leaves lying by the road. He offered a proposal to Bhaskar in a hurried manner:

"Let's go back , brother Bhaskar." He knelt down like a small boy near Bhaskar looked upto his eyes as if he were begging for his mercy.

Bhaskar gave the last puff to the fag end of the cigarette and looked at Shahjahan's eyes. A small line of laughter was visible on one corner of his lips. He said in an unclear voice:

"Is death so easy ?"

He did not go up the hills with Himangshu and others . He knew. He had known about their plans very well. But he was also unavoidably busy. He had many things left to do ! He became busy once more. He thought, which book should he lay his hands on - Das Kapital ! Oh no. he would listen to Suman's songs – that special song and read out the poems of Phalguni Roy. He turned on the music system. He took the poems of Phalguni Roy on his hands...he started reading....

Many works are still left - still left to read the thieves' journals

The world is still left to be seen through the spectacles of Manik Banerjee

Still left to ride the newly coloured tram causing the death of Jibanananda Das

Still left to get hooked up with a woman with a smooth pair of thighs

Still left to sit with folded knees by the silent graves of Michael and Henrietta

On top of the flowers of grass spread all across

Many works are still left to be done.

Himangshu climbed down carrying a bunch of wild flowers in his hands. Pranjal and Hiranya also followed him. Everyone's face was brightened with smiles. Himangshu felt doubly encouraged. His rough voice was coming like the falls of the small hillock being obstructed by rocks on its way down.

" Oh dear ! A bunch of flowers... they must be some kind of orchids. Have a look, here !"

Himangshu quickly passed on the bunch of flowers in the hands of Shahjahan. Shahjahan unwillingly smelt the violet flowers. A strange kind of smell entered his nose.

He shrank his nose.

"Oh shit ! the unwanted smell of this bunch..."

Everybody seemed to roar while laughing. At the end of the laughter session , Hiranya forwarded a bunch of white flowers before everyone with pride which he had brought hiding at his back. The air was soon filled up with the scent of wild flowers which seemed to madden Himangshu a while ago. With a gloomy face, Shahjahan looked furtively at the bunch. A bunch of 'gutimali' flower was visible in Hiranya's hands.

"Fie ! such a bad smell this is !" He put his hand on the nose. Having sat opposite to her, he smoked out his cigarette and looked at her. Being sentimental, she sat gravely and quietly with a bitter face like a 'bashful and speechless new bride.'

" Hello dear ! Will you listen to a song ?" he asked with a deep tone and feeling. She did not utter a single word. He opened the window of the room facing the north. Showing the 'sotiana' tree lying by the room , he said---

" I told you about this tree, dear."

She uttered a word 'ish' and she sprang up from where she was sitting and shut the window forcefully. She looked at him angrily and said:

'How crazy you are !'

She was listening to the song repeatedly in the walkman. She took away the cassette from him by force. After having listened, she rewound and listened to it again.

'Hang, hang yourself , Dipali Mahato

The towel is lying on the branch of the tree

Whose shameful daily activity drove you to tie the knot on your neck .'

The dead bodies of the four daughters

Kept close to the tree

Now, Dipali is observing the branches of the banyan tree...'

When she left her body lazily on the bed, the voice of Kabir Suman rang up in her ears and when she tried to sleep keeping her eyes shut, the image of a helpless mother lying close to the 'sotiana' tree, came up before her eyes.

"To hell with democracy ! Voting, Minister, M.L.A. President and people; there seems no existence of people in the democracy." Himangshu spitted.

"For that reason... for that reason only we wanted to fight against this system." Hiranya said so removing the large dangling locks from his forehead "but what's the benefit ? Before we could dream of breaking the system , all the documents having details of our modus operandi reached the hands of the system-keepers , shit !" Pranjal became really excited.

Shahjahan began in a slow voice:

"Look brother, Himangshu ! I told you this earlier also that there is no use dreaming of breaking the system. If we can do something special being within the system...."

" Leave your leftist propaganda of the student movement. Those bloody hounds call ourselves as naxalites, and condemn us as escapists....and themselves act as dogs loyal to their masters, they drag the feet of those who fly the flag of democracy high...all...all of them are no better than young ones of pigs.."

Everyone remained silent till Himangshu cooled down. Sipping his third peg of whisky, Bhaskar seemed to say to himself:

"Meaningless....simply meaningless . In reality all these words have no base at all. Some abstract principles.......democracy, socialism all are meaningless....!"

With a long yawn, Himangshu said:

" For that sake , friends ! We made elaborate arrangements for that sake only."

"But brother Himangshu, hiding this way, have we really..." Pranjal covered Hiranya's face without allowing him to speak any further—

"I have also thought about this. But, is it worth dying without doing anything substantial ?.. There will be no change even if we die ! Therefore...."

"Go , and live free from this moment..... Why should you lay down your lives listening to this Himangshu ? You should not. Better you continue to live. Everyone has got the right to live...like those nocturnal bats.....I've just told you about my decision." Himangshu would die.

Because he had no interest to live . He was very much worthless and helpless ! Himangshu emptied the remaining amount of whisky at a single draught and stared at the bottle.

Sitting in a corner, Kartik Dutta, too, stared closely at the fire. Looking at the fire shining in his glass, he told slowly ---

"Death has become a necessity. I have also felt it like Himangshu. We could do really nothing. There's really none who could make us free from the bondage

! We couldn't simply untie ourselves. The globalization had kept people amused. We had realized, observed, heard. But could do nothing. It's better to die than to live as inert, speechless, sightless like a dead man ! Let me accept it..."

None had spoken anything for a long time. Himangshu and comrades continued to sit around the burning fire in the hilly forest. Sometimes the sound of wild insects could be heard from a distance. When the burning fire was beginning to turn ash, Pranjal lightly massaged his eyes and stood up. He took away the bottle of remaining whisky forcibly and prepared a peg for everyone. Throwing two pieces of firewood into the source of the fire, he almost shouted:

"Cheers ! Then this happens to be our last night."

Everyone stood up one by one. Everyone held his glass in his hand and advanced towards Pranjal's glass. A 'ting' sound could be heard. Before the sound finished its echoeing, everyone shouted:

"Cheers !"

Then, the next dawn was not too far away.

He kept a close look to the 'sotiana' tree through the window. Sotiana was a firewood tree. He buzzed in his mind and laughed. Lighting a new cigarette, he continued to look at the tree. Suddenly it crossed his mind that Himangshu and his men had been hanging from the branch of the tree. They were united as they had some desire and unwillingness in common. They had a common desire even now also. All of them wanted to die together. He also wanted to.

But he did not want to die by jumping from the peak of the hillock, but by hanging from the 'sotiana' tree. Like the mother described in Suman's song. Like the mother failing to look after the children, fed poison to her children and she died by hanging in the 'sotiana' tree ! ...he remembered her. Even she was there with Himangshu, Pranjal and others. She joined them as soon as she left the left-wing students organization. Even her father's administration could not bind this freedom-loving girl. During the election , she aptly and wholeheartedly canvassed against her father in different areas of the constituency. Her father only won the elections most of the times and she cried as loudly as she could putting her hands on her head or forehead. On the day prior to the election date, her father would distribute carfuls of money, clothes and mosquito nets in front of her eyes and showed his supremacy. They did not tell her about their decision to commit suicide....only a few days ago , she divulged a 'master-plan' to them. She told about their positions in the forthcoming election ! ...and she added that she believed that a revolution would take place one day. People would come down on the streets putting off their shirts of the globalization....could my dream go in waste! She would never know the reason behind his death or that of Himangshu and his comrades ! They had nothing to write about themselves !.. Should he write something to her ! – he thought. Specially at least from his side... No, he would not write anything to her..he would rather commit suicide before it was morning... The sun was about to rise in the east.

They did not utter a single word while they were coming down the hilly terrains. They walked as if they were habituated. None of them had the enthusiasm to talk or to have eye-contacts with one another. They came down to the nadir of the barbarism from the zenith of the civilization. All of them were naked or coverless. Having reached the peak of the hillock , they were unable to face death and they fled away from there like timid individuals .

They once desired to get ready to jump and fly the air from the hilltop. Himangshu cried, "Good bye, friends."...The sun that looked like the yolk of an egg gradually brightened before their eyes..... a flock of birds flew in.....the hilltop was echoing the sound of the birds. The birds seemed to defy the height of the hill and gliding along deeper and deeper in the sky. The height of the hill seemed nothing to them. Himangshu stayed back as also Pranjal, Hiranya and Shahjahan. Bhaskar was static. Then, Kartik Dutta also stepped back. After sometime all of them did the same – Pranjal, HIranya and Shahjahan. Himangshu dragged back Bhaskar with a force. Himangshu murmured with his dry lips, "We'll fight till the end of the pain."

Himangshu could really understand that he had wanted to cover his weaknesses. The talk seemed to be really unnecessary.

Sitting under the 'sotiana' tree, he also felt it -- unnecessary....death was unnecessary. What's the meaning—of dying at one's own will ! There were a lot of reasons to continue living..... he had still to understand how the society got divided into classes.....how men were divided in the name of communities.... of countries. Only Heaven knows how much was left to be known, understood, seen....nothing could be done with regard to them and the pain..for which kind of pain he would own death as 'means'....was he really helpless like the mother ! No, no....time was still there. He had much time to hope for a positive change. At least time should be there.......like her dream....and the most importantly, he had a life to live...keeping aside the society and the country....both she and he had a separate life.......

He sat on the grasses under the 'sotiana' tree. He dreamt a dream in the sunshine of the morning.....an unsuccessful fantasy was hanging in the 'sotiana' tree. All his words made inroads into her mind , like that mother , my mind wanted to swing from the 'sotiana' tree rather than leading a 'meaningless' life...She again pressed the 'play' button on her walkman again...she listened to the song and remembered his lines simultaneously... she thought for whom death was very much necessary-- for that mother or for her. All of a sudden she thought that death was necessary for herself only....at a young age , she collected funds for the students' organization in the box made of cardboard...actually she started to weave her dreams.... but when she grew up , she found that the political equations under the cover of the students' organization were different from her ideals...She left the organization when she felt that those were all gimmicks under the banner of the leftist ideologies....she came across Pranjal and others.... she held public meetings against her father in every election....seeing dried and gloomy face of mother, she could not leave her home also. Her father became indifferent to her....in every election, her father made her realize how unsuccessful she was...and even after that....and after that she expected a full-fledged revolution...no , no she was mistaken...in reality she had nothing besides loneliness, failure, etc. She was defeated. She was badly defeated...and for that reason, death became essential for her..yes, according to her , it was better for her to hang from the 'sotiana' tree than leading a meaningless life...

She switched off the moving ceiling fan. She drew out a white side-cloth from somewhere and dragged the table right under the fan...she placed a chair on top of that...for a moment she thought about him...then afterwards the mother.....that special song of Kabir Suman rang up in her ears...the 'sotiana' tree lying to the north of her room appeared before her eyes....

She lay hanging.

Contesting The Grand Narrative:- A Post-modernist Reading Of Anita Desai's, In Custody

Subhajit Bhadra

The aim of this paper is to provide a post-modernist reading of Anita Desai's novel **In Custody** (1984) in light of the fact that the text contests the validity of any grand narrative and prioritizes the interplay of various mini-narratives. **In Custody** is an extremely rich and powerful text that seeks to validate the typical post-modernist assumption that stubbornly refuses to believe the authenticity of "grand" or "meta" discourses. The Indian novelists in English have been historically preoccupied with "grand" discourse or narratives of nation and nationality and contemporary Indian English novelists like Salman Rushdie, Amitav Ghosh and Arundhati Roy , Kiran Desai have dealt with these twin "grand narratives" in a grand canvas in their respective creations. Salman Rushdie and Amitav Ghosh have exhibited an extraordinary anxiety to depict India in a large canvas in novels like **Midnight's Children** and **The Shadow Lines** which also reveal their consistent engagement with concepts of nation, nationality and nationhood. Compared to these stalwarts, Anita Desai has rather maintained a low- profile in her writing career and **In Custody** remains a major achievement in the creative oeuvre of Desai as it wonderfully brings to light the subtle interplay of a number of "mini-narratives" and for the sake of critical convenience, I have identified three such narratives within the texture of the novel. These are :- (a) The narrative of space/place (b) The narrative of pain and anguish and (c) The narrative of language. Though the central argument of the paper is derived from theoretical assumptions in light of a particular theoretical paradigm, yet there has been rigorous attempt to maintain consistent engagement with the text.

The publication of **In Custody** fetched great critical acclaim for Anita Desai and the rich nuances of the novel____ have provided convenient scope to the critics to analyze the hidden layers of the text from multiple perspectives. R.K. Gupta rightly argues in his book **The Novels of Anita Desai: A Feminist Perspective:-**

"Thus the technique of characterization used by Anita Desai in the novel holds a great significance besides all the novels characterized prior to the novel." **(Gupta 2002:218)**

In Custody brings to light the tremendous prowess of Desai as a novelist and compels a sensitive reader to plunge deeper into the layers of subletting nuances that make the text both engaging and absorbing.

Post-modernism is a specific literary and cultural movement that swept the shores of Europe during the second half of the 20th Century and subsequently consolidated its position within the academic realm by 1980s. Post-modernism has often been viewed as a total departure form modernism or a phenomenon arriving after the demise of modernism. But looked at from a critical point of view, post-modernism is neither a total break with the preoccupations or concerns of modernism, nor it is a radical movement logically followed by the death of the former; rather post-modernism critically re-examines the central ideas of modernism as it also questions some of the major ideas of the modernists. The modernists valorized concepts like progress, civilization and enlightenment, but the post-modernists radically questioned the validity of such "grand narratives" in a post- World War and post-Holocaust European World. As Jean-Francois Lyotard convincingly argues in this seminal work, **The Post-modernism Condition: A Report On Knowledge.**

"Simplifying to the extreme, I define post-modern as incredulity towards meta-narratives. This incredulity is undoubtedly a product of progress in the sciences: but that progress in turn presupposes it. To the obsolescence of the meta-narrative apparatus of legitimation corresponds, most notably, the crisis of metaphysical philosophy and of the university institution which in the past relied on it."**(Lyotard, 1979:XXIV)**

Lyotard's comments in that book have stimulated the intellect of a generation of readers, critics and academicians across the world to think anew. In fact, Lyotard's argument so convincingly signaled the death of "grand narratives" that literary critics and cultural activists also appropriated his powerful theory to meet the challenges of their respective disciplines. In this context Tim Woods succinctly comments in his major book **Beginning Postmodernism.**

"In other words, knowledge in the post-modern era can no longer be legitimated or sanctioned according to the great 'narratives' that have shaped western knowledge to date, like notion of progress embedded in the Enlightenment or the notion of social liberation through history embedded in Marxism, or the release form unconscious trauma harbored by Freudian theory. Indeed, Lyotard regards such narratives theory as violent and tyrannical in their imposition of a 'totalizing' pattern and a false universality of actions, events and things."**(Woods 2010, 20-21)**

Anita Desai's, **In Custody** contests the validity of "grand narratives" both texturally and structurally and centre stages the subtle interplay of the three mini- narratives that I have identified in this paper. **In Custody** vividly brings to light the frustrations, disappointments and desolation of a college teacher, Deven who teaches Hindi to his average students and as Deven accepts his friend, Murad's offer to interview the great Urdu poet, Nur and subsequently fails in the endeavour, Anita Desai brilliantly displays the subtle play of mini-narratives in the novel that speaks eloquently of the novelist's post-modernist concern both at the thematic and technical levels. The novel is an independent genre and critics, academicians and theoreticians have attempted to grasp with its riddles, nuances and mysteries as an art form in their own ways. The Russian thinker, Mikhail Bakhtin was the harbinger in this realm as he was one of the earliest critics to grasp the limitless possibility of novel as a genre and during the later half of the last century critics and theoreticians put increasing emphasis on the aspect of narrative in context of the novel as an independent art form. In this context, Shlomith Rimmon-Kenan forcefully argues.

"Narration is in no way restricted to literature.

In order to make sense of experiences, people consciously or unconsciously, audibly or inaudibly tell stories to themselves as well as to others. Narratives are governed by a dual time-scheme owing to the ontological gap between the succession of signs and the temporality of events," **(Kenan 1983, 147)**

In Custody foregrounds the mini-narrative of space/place negotiated through the subjective position of Deven and Murad who bring to light the differences and dichotomy of interpenetration between various realms of existence. Deven inhabits a small place/ space called Mirpore that seems to both contain and constrain his existence but he also seeks to escape from the limitations of such crippling locale. The chance encounter with Murad, his friend who lives in the great metropolitan city of Delhi releases a new possibility for Deven but that very possibility is mired not only in disaster, but also in a new realization about one's own existence. Murad approaches Deven with an enticing and enchanting offer of interviewing

     DELVING INTO DIFFERENT LITERARY TERRAINS

Nur, the greatest living Urdu poet whom Deven eulogizes beyond measure and this in turn opens up a new avenue for Deven to renew his existence in terms of a spatial encounter with the great city of Delhi. Murad initially tempts Deven with the lure of city life as he tells his friend –

"We're going out to lunch. We're going to lunch in the best restaurant in your great city." **(In Custody 10)**

Murad's tone reveals a sarcastic and even ironic tinge when he obliquely attacks Deven who has restricted his life to the suffocating surroundings of Mirpore.

"A full-fledged lecturer in a college, an important citizen of Mirpore and still can't afford a whole packet of cigarettes? You seem to be where you were in your college days." **(In Custody 10)**

Deven too realizes the reality of his life but he has somehow found a safe refuge within the limitations of his space/place and in an ironical narrative twists the readers to get a glimpse of how that space/place shrinks further.

"Recoiling from them, Deven made his way down the passage to his classroom and arrived at the desk beside the blackboard as if at a refuge, panting with exertion and relief." **(In Custody 11)**

Irony becomes a potent figurative device for the post-modernist writers and Desai moulds this specific instrument to her purpose in this densely textured novel and I would like to emphasize here that Anita Desai is not a self-avowed post-modernist, rather my reading of her fiction is post-modernist. Stuart Sim convincingly argues:

"We move on now to consider how that spectrum of response is communicated across the range of discourses and intellectual disciplines we have identified – in other words, to post-modernism, the case for and against ... Irony and crises , we will see, can be interpreted in a wide variety of ways for a wide variety of uses." **(Sim 2002:13)**

The way Deven negotiates with space/place also determines his living standard that he tries his level best to hide from Murad but fails miserably. Desai's narrative again assumes ironic mode when the two friends decide to take food.

"It must seem very mean in comparison with the restaurants of Delhi but he could not possibly afford a meal in Kwality or Gaylord, the two best restaurants, both air-conditioned and exorbitant ... and perhaps it was not a bad idea to show Murad that he was not at all well off..." **(In Custody 13)**

Desai posits the conflict of Deven's existence in terms of the dichotomy between two different spaces/places, in this context represented by Mirpore and Delhi. To Deven, Mirpore symbolizes disappointments, stagnation and defeat while Delhi epitomizes hope, mobility and triumph but as the novel proceeds we find how these fixed associations are not only subverted, but also crushed. As Deven journeys towards Delhi, the narrative encapsulates a changing trajectory of the ordinary protagonist's mind.

"The bus left Mirpore behind. It came as a slight shock to Deven that one could so easily and quickly free oneself from what had come to seem to him not only the entire world since he had no existence outside it, but often a cruel trap, or prison, as well, an indestructible prison from which there was no escape."**(In Custody 19)**

The post-modernists have been consistently engaged with the idea of space/place and it is a fact that the first discipline to claim the attention of post-modernism was architecture. In other words, post-modernism came into existence as a reaction against the uniform architectural framework upheld by the modernists and since then space/place has remained a major concern for the post-modern thinkers. Christopher Butler argues in this context:

"All this promiscuous adaptation can perhaps be seen most clearly in the relationship of post-modernist architecture to the heroic modernism that preceded it. A citational hybridity is typical of much post-modernist work."**(Butler 2002:89)**

Delhi contains the great treasures and triumph of history, but Mirpore remains a mere apology to such grandeur__ of history and it is suggested in the text that the inhabitants of Mirpore fail to appreciate the sublime.

"History had scattered a few marks and imprints here and there but no one in Mirpore thought much of them and certainly gave them no honor in the form of special signs, space or protection." **(In Custody 20)**

The distance between Mirpore and Delhi is not merely suggested in terms of geographical paradigm, but also in terms of attitudinal framework of the inhabitants of Mirpore and it should be taken into account that Delhi is viewed through the gaze of Mirpore in this novel and not the other way round.

"Others merely passed through, peering out of smeared train windows and wondering how much longer it would take to Delhi, or reaching out to buy oranges, lengths of sugarcane, dry gram or the particular sweet for which Mirpore was known." **(In Custody 22)**

Thus the mini narrative of space **In Custody** remains inconclusive and open-ended, a typical post-modernist symptom and this also acts as a counter to the general representation of India on a grand canvas by many Indian novelists writing in English.

The narrative of pain and anguish find manifestation through the consciousness of three important characters of the novel – Deven, the frustrated college teacher, Murad , the irritated and anxious editor of a run-of-the-mill Urdu magazine and Nur, the mere apology to his earlier grand self. Deven knows the limitations of his existence, but he finds it very difficult to confront the ridicule of others directed towards his economic status and that is why he feels a sense of anguish when Murad obliquely satirizes him.

"He could not bear to think of Murad flashing those brightly colored teeth in another derisive grin and saying, 'Oh, still a two-cigarette man?

Why should Murad not pay for the lunch after all?" **(In Custody 12)**

Deven is quite reluctant to strike a literary deal with Murad who has often cheated him in the past and this reluctance converts it into a grievance against Murad.

"It was true that he had never paid Deven for the book reviews he had printed in an issue six months ago or for the poem he had accepted and was to publish in the next one." **(In Custody 12**)

Murad edits an average Urdu magazine that does not do well in the market and he finds it increasingly difficult to maintain the expenses. He knows that very few readers subscribe to his magazine and his frustration and anguish are vividly brought to light in his encounter with Deven.

"Worries, worries, worries. And where are the readers? Where are the subscriptions? Who reads Urdu any more?" **(In Custody 15)**

Deven's life is just a mundane routine devoid of any sign of grandeur or sublimity and he has learnt the art of living with his disappointments and frustrations. However, the proposal of interviewing the living legend of Urdu poetry, Nur opens up a new vista of existence for Deven but his anguish manifests itself as he realizes that he is financially incapable of rising up to the demands of such a magnificent encounter.

"It was sadly disappointing to him that he was not traveling up to Delhi on this important occasion in style more suited to a literary man, a literary event. **(In Custody 25)**

Urdu happened to be Deven's first love but he chooses Hindi to cater to his professional demands and he finds it very difficult to convince Nur about the validity of his choice as he is trapped in an ironic situation that enhances Deven's anguish further.

"I am – only a teacher, sir, … and must teach to support my family. But poetry – Urdu these are – one needs, I need to serve them to show my appreciation. I cannot serve them as you do –" **(In Custody 43)**

As Deven gets an intimate glimpse of Nur's day-to-day life a tragic realization dawns upon him and he gradually accepts that Nur is a dead genius now and the once great poet's fading intellect is capable of only occasional firework, not of sustained brilliance. Nur is surrounded by sycophants interested in grand feast and free alcohol, average woman who are the custodians of the old poet's miserable existence and casual visitors who fail to appreciate his aesthetic prowess. Deven's anguish intensifies as he realizes that his enthusiastic venture has turned out to be a disastrous misadventure.

"He could not waste the day and return to Mirpore without having accomplished even so much, nor could he face Murad again without showing himself capable of having made such an attempt. Yet, his hopes of a dialogue about poetry in the centre of all this garishness began to seem, even to him, quite grotesque." **(In Custody 50)**

Nur has been the great cultural icon for Deven and he has always venerated the great poet. Deven thinks that Nur is an infallible grand genius and his anguish increases when he confronts the bitter gap between the ideal image of Nur and the sordid reality.

"What was this conviviality of steamy femininity that found him a figure of fun and even reduced the aged and revered figure of the poet Nur to a pathetic old cushion that spit out old stale cotton?" **(In Custody 83)**

Nur himself realizes the depth to which he had fallen and he feels totally shattered but he is incapable of transcending the limitation of this miserable trap. He suffers intense pain and anguish as he attacks Deven whom he thinks to be just another visitor with vested interest.

"Another looter? Raider? Thief? Poor as I am, must I have the rags torn off my back by these vultures who can't wail till I die? Allah – oh Allah." **(In Custody 87)**

Deven feels like an absurd being that somehow makes an attempt to fill up the empty space of his life with something substantial and he realizes that it is really a daunting and difficult task. Albert Camus powerfully pointed out about the plight of the absurd hero:

"The absurd is his extreme tension which he maintains constantly by solitary effort, for he knows that in that consciousness and in that day-to- day revolt he gives proof of his only truth which is defiance." **(Camus 1942:55)**

The bitter truth that emanates from Deven's encounter with Nur makes his heart heavy with intense pain and grief and Anita Desai brilliantly evokes that trauma in the following narrative.

"He felt it inside him like an empty hole, one he had been string at all his year, intimidated by its blackness and blankness. Even his attempt to fill it with a genuine and heartfelt homage to a true poet... had been defeated ... It was one more blow, and perhaps the bitterest of all." **(In Custody 128)**

The image of a cage poignantly captures the tragedy of Nur's existence and Deven's heartfelt pain is vividly evoked as he too finds himself trapped.

"Being an illustrious poet had drawn people to the zoo to come and stare at him but Nur had not escaped from his cage for all that – he was trapped as Deven was even if his cage was more prominent and attracted more attention. Still, it was just a cage in a row of cages. Cage, cage. Trap, trap." **(In Custody 31)**

In order to pursue his project with Nur, Deven takes extended leave from his college, neglects his familial obligations, convinces the college authorities to provide financial assistance, buys a damaged tape-recorder, manages to get hold of an inexperienced assistant, cajoles the old poet to give his best, bribes the woman who behaves like the custodian of Nur's existence, pleads Murad to grant him more time and yet fails miserably in his endeavour.

"It was a fiasco. There was no other word for it. Disbelievingly, Deven had the first tape removed, the second tried and then the third and the fourth. The cardboard carton that held them seemed bottomless, there were so many" **(In Custody 173)**

Desai's credit lies in the fact that both Deven and Nur enact their pain and anguish rather than merely expressing that. The narrative evocatively captures the anxiety, anguish, pain, grief, desolation and desperation of

Deven, Nur and Murad who authenticate the validity of their traumatic existence within the nuanced resonances of the text. The anguish and pain of these characters emanate from their inability to distinguish between reality and ideal construction. Carl Gustav Jung rightly points out in this context –

"We must always bear in mind that despite the most beautiful agreement between the facts and our ideas, explanatory principles are only points of view, that is, manifestations of the psychological attitude and of the a priori conditions under which all thinking takes place." **(Jung 1960:6)**

The third prominent mini-narrative that **In Custody** deals with is the narrative of language that subtly brings to light the hidden layers of hostility lying dormant which often fail to manifest themselves because of the predominance of other grand discourses or narratives. Deven teaches Hindi not because of love, but because of professional obligations; Murad brings out an Urdu magazine both out of love and professional obligations, Nur writes Urdu poetry because it is both his vocation and identity and Siddique teaches Urdu out of compulsion. Murad articulates his anguish regarding the deteriorating status of Urdu in post-independence India.

"Yet, like these vegetables, it flourishes, while Urdu – language of the court in days of royalty – now languishes in the back lanes and gutter of the city.**(In Custody 15)**

Nur is not merely a great Urdu poet, in fact he is one of the custodians of the Urdu language and he feels greater pain to realize the bitter position his language occupies in the contemporary scenario.

"How can there be Urdu poetry when there is no Urdu language left? It is dead, finished. The defeat of the Mughals by the British threw a noose over its head, and the defeat of the British by the Hindi-wallahs tightened it. So now you see its corpse lying here, waiting to be buried." **(In Custody 42)**

Language defines identity as it constitutes one's very being and the collapse of a language also signifies the death of a particular socio-cultural ethos. Language carries within it a living socio-cultural tradition, a living community and in fact, a living ontological dynamics. Highlighting the value of language R.L. Trask succinctly points out:

"Without language, we could hardly have created the human world we know. Our development of everything from music to warfare could never have come about in the absence of language. More than any other single characteristic, then language is what makes us human." **(Trask 1995:1)**

The conversation between Nur and Deven glaringly portrays the pathetic condition of the great language which is also undoubtedly one of the richest languages of the world. More than the indifference of general people, it is the lackadaisical treatment of the Indian Government coupled with faulty policies that have relegated the status of Urdu. Nur angrily voices such discrimination when he says.

"Why such treatment of Urdu, my friends?

Because Urdu is supposed to have died, in 1947. What you see in the universities – in some of the universities, a few of them only – is its ghost, wrapped in a shroud." **(In Custody 56)**

The narrative acquires a symbolic dimension when Desai provides a glimpse of Siddiqui's residence that some how mirrors the deplorable condition of the language he teaches.

"Eventually, he had edged his way through and now stood in the wide, graveled driveway, looking up at the dilapidated villa and the recognizable , yet unfamiliar figure of the title professor of Urdu seated on the terraces."**(In Custody 163)**

It is not only that the language has lost its prestige and glory, in an ironical narrative twist, Desai also choreographs how the custodians of the language have also been dwarfed and become deplorable and desolate.

In conclusion, it may be convincingly argued that Anita Desai's, **In Custody** exemplifies post-modern concerns without making any explicit claim to do so. The novel is so densely textured and structured that it contests the validity of all grand narratives and rather facilitates the subtle interplay of various mini-narratives that both enhance and contribute to the aesthetic appeal of the text. Peter Barry rightly points out:

"For the post-modernist, by contrast, fragmentation is an exhilarating, liberating phenomenon, symptomatic of our escape from the claustrophobic embrace of fixed systems of belief. In a word the modernist laments fragmentation while the post-modernist celebrates it." **(Barry 1995:84)**

Anita Desai's, **In Custody** makes an attempt to liberate the readers "from the claustrophobic embrace of fixed systems of belief" by contesting the validity of grand narratives and celebrating the subtle interplay of mini-narratives.

Works Cited

Barry, Peter, Beginning Theory: An Introduction to Literary and Cultural Theory, Second Edition , Manchester and New York: Manchester University Press, 2002.

Butler, Christopher, Post-modernism: A Very Short Introduction, Oxford: OUP, 2002.

Camus, Albert, The Myth of Sisyphus, trans. Justin O'Brien and James Wood, London: Penguin Books, 2000.

Desai, Anita, In Custody, New Delhi : Penguin Books, 1984

Gupta, R.K, The Novels of Anita Desai: A Feminist Perspective, New Delhi: Atlantic Publishers, 2002.

Jung, Carl Gustav, On the Nature of the Psyche, trans. R.F.C. Hull, London and New York Routlegde, 1969.

Kenan, Shlomith Rimmon, Narrative Fiction, Second edition, London and New York : Routledge, 2002.

Leotard, Jean-Francois, The Post-modern Condition: A Report On Knowledge, Manchester: Manchester University Press, 1979.

Sim, Stuart, Irony and Crisis: A Critical History of Post-modern Culture, UK and USA: Icon Books UK, Totem Books USA, 2002

Trask, R.L.,Language : The Basics, Second Edition, London, New York: Routledge, 1999

Woods, Tim, Beginning Post-modernism, New Delhi: Viva Books, 2010.

Subhajit Bhadra worked as an Assistant Project Scientist in IIT-Guwahati and is a freelance writer and literary critic. He has published articles, reviews and interviews in **Indian Literature, The Assam Tribune, The Sentinel, The Times of India, Dainik Dainik Jugoshankha** (a Bengali daily and monthly), besides little magazines like **Malancha, Srot, Jololipi.** He writes short stories and poems in Bengali. His poems have been published in **Nandan** - a reputed Bengali magazine from Kolkata in a special issue on **'21st Century Bengali Poetry: a Beginning'**. He is currently writing a book on Ramayana as part of a commissioned project assigned by the South Asian Ramayana Research Centre, Guwahati. His area of specialization includes American Literature, Post-colonial Literatures in English, Partition Literature, Twentieth Century European Literature, Indian Writing in English, and Indian Literature in Regional Languages.

It is hereby declared that this article is completely original and has not been published anywhere else - either in parts or in whole.

Subhajit Bhadra

Cricket

(Based on a Hindi short story called 'Cricket' by Akanksha Parey)

I have not yet understood why people become so obsessed with 'cricket-fever' while they are scared of real fever. When this fever begins to spread, then even the best of the best of people seem to go crazy. Therefore, it was the charisma of cricket that this town without multiplexes had gone mad. They were so crazy that they would ask about a solitary public water-supply pipeline, 'Did the pipe hit a sixer ?' Then the other man in front would reply, 'No brother, it seems that the pipeline will cross a century of being without water before it is restored.' The boys would sit to eat in the kitchen and tell their mothers , ' Why upon earth are you bouncing the 'roti' on the platter like a bouncer ?' Mother would reply, ' Before your father arrives here and gets you clean-bowled, just eat it and get lost.' On the whole, it was time the cricket-loving people considered Sachin Tendulkar as a God incarnate. Cricketing legends like **Sunil Gavaskar, Kapil Dev** and **Krishnamachari Srikanth** were getting retired as players and Tendulkar was rising like a hero. The small suburban area which people knew as Sripuram, had been suffering from acute shortage of water those days. Boys felt utterly irritated for this water because they had to exhaust all their energies on that hand-pump which had not been working properly. Or else, they had been waiting for the drops of water to fall from the one and only government pipeline. Problem occurred due to the fact that it was not considered fair for the young sisters to fetch water from a universal water-pump and the cause of the anger was that they could not actively cooperate with their share of patriotic feelings. When the entire country seemed to take a long dip into the river of vitality and waving the tricolor vigorously and the rest of the inmates of the neighbourhood in whose houses horse-powered submersible pumps were installed, gathered and were glued to the screens before the Dilruba Paan Centre , the Municipal Complex and in the yards of Sri Rambabu Sahay M.A. M.L.A. to see **Sourav Ganguly, Sachin and Sreenath** comfortably, while some of the others were bound to utilize the time in arranging for water. All of a sudden, many government officials of the sub-division caught malaria or typhoid while trying to strike a balance between their powers and their situation in the offices. The half of the lecturers of the suburban college were either laid up with breathing problems or someone's child fell seriously ill. It was not evident from the way in which people were on leave if the fever in their children would come down before the end of the 'cricket-fever'. Only one Motiya Langar was there in the village who would sit on his bed listening to some unintelligible things from his age-old radio. Then a war was going on against Pakistan in a place called Kargil or perhaps Karagil. The son of Motiya Langar was preparing for the war. Langar was busy in the thought of his son who was an ex-soldier who was awarded 'Shourya Chakra'(an army medal offered to the armies for the outstanding display of courage in the war-front) by the President. But the persons who were shouting 'war-war', had no real time to waste for this meaningless discord. When someone saw Langar battling it out with his cacophonic radio-set, then they would ask, "What's up, Langar ? Are you not going to watch television today ?"

Then Langar would smile and say,"My son Ganesha has gone to join the war. So I am trying to learn what is going on there at the front."

"Which war is going on right now, Langar ?"

"He is fighting against Pakistan."

"Oh! that's a regular affair. What's so new in that ?" Then Langar would not argue with anyone and sat quietly turning off the radio till everyone moved off.

Among the three places where the television sets existed, the crowd that huddled in Rambabu Sahay's place was of a different type. Actually all wanted to go to his place because he had a TV set which at once reminded us of the brand having a catchword – 'Neighbours' envy, owners' pride' and wherein one could find the blue jerseys exactly looking like blue as Kerry Francis Bullmore Packer had wanted them to be. Then Sahay babu would keep himself pinned to his easy chair and would rock on it until the pressure of the crowd increased. Then he would drag the television cover made of crochet knitting and say very stylishly facing the crowd, "Got to save it from dust, you know. It's so dusty here that the T.V. set will stop functioning properly within a day or two." People had to put up with his mannerisms and attitudes once they watched the T.V. programmes over there, so people would prefer to take shelter together in large numbers beside the Dilruba Paan Centre than anywhere else. Nobody was denied permission to watch the orange-coloured portable T.V. set kept in the Dilruba Paan Centre . On the contrary, Raju, the shopowner, never liked the off-seasons of cricket. Be it the crucial period of Tendulkar only a few runs short of a century or the players of Australia or Pakistan taking it on the Indians, hitting fours and sixes and making the Indian attack look like an ordinary one, people sitting there would naturally be under stress and due to the stress, they would smoke one or two bidis or the moneyed people would show off their higher choices and would empty a plastic sachet into their mouths - were the common features of the people present there. That cricket season might not be making him a multi-millionaire like Tendulkar or Ganguly, but it was enough for him to raise his standard of living . If anybody would come to his shop, he would act as if he were trying to wipe off the area with a piece of napkin and he would say, "I am so lucky that you have stepped in here. Sometimes I see you and the next moment I see my locality." Such a mind-blowing act of him would please anybody and the empty square before his shop would remain 'housefull'.

That was a real bad time for Indian cricket. The crucial month of 'cricket fever' was over. Nothing had happened within the entire month in the way the entire country wanted it to be. The shining trophy was gracefully taken away by another country. Sripuram was lost into a vast pool of sorrow. Nobody could really understand what to do as the festival of cricket ended all of a sudden. Another dream was also shattered just as the dream of cricket. A news reached that the scheme of a flyover through Sripuram which had been in the pipeline for a long period of time, on which there would be shining white lights like those of the foreign countries, would not be passing through Sripuram any further. Had the flyover passed through here, then heavy vehicles would have passed through that area and Sripuram would have found a place in the road-map of India. India lost the game under the captaincy of Tendulkar , on the other hand the captaincy of Mr. Sahay was also at stake. So, Mr. Sahay was trying to offer other attractive baits to the people of the sub-urban areas. The general election was knocking at the door and the level of blood-pressure of Mr. Sahay was soaring as high as the Mount Everest. But as it often happened, God was very merciful, as during the days of Lilawati and Kalawati , Sri Satyanarayan would take a round, likewise he sent his brother-in-law to a neighbouring big city. The brother-in-law arrived and as soon as he got off the bus in the bus-stand he at first glanced at the place where a team of twelve or thirteen boys, diggng three de-shaped stumps into the ground, were hitting a small fruit-ball with a bat which was generally used for beating the clothes while washing them. That ground belonged to the **Government Arts P.G. Science College**. The boys did not look very serious , but they were playing cricket very seriously. At first the brother-in-law thought that it would be wise to walk upto the boys and gather some knowledge from there. He, too, was an expert in this field while he was living in the city. Though he did not play then, but he would definitely play it on the players and the game. When he reached home then the brother-in-law who would put on black glasses all the time, noticed that his brother-in-law's face looked weird as if he had lost everything. He did not ask for the cause of that as his sister who was lost in the thoughts of her husband like a 'disprin' tablet fully dissolved in water, told him straightway," He has been waiting anxiously for the flyover for a long time. Now you can see for yourself how he is getting withered away like a fried stuff. The election is round the corner and on the other hand , there is no solution either for water-problem or for the flyover. Brother, I don't know what is lying in store for us this time." The elder brother heard the remarks of her sister and his forehead showed three wrinkled lines of his anxiety. His mind started to move faster than 'chetak' the horse. The man with a big mole on his face, whose colour was like a dried piece of firewood and having unmanageable moustache chanted some hymns into the ear of the M.L.A. brother-in-law resembling the features of tall and thin palm tree and it seemed to her wife as if God appeared before him as if a farmer saved his dying crops at last by spraying pesticides. Then, as usual, incidents got mixed up with coincidences and coincidences helped in accomplishing great tasks. The incident was such that a simple daughter of a distinguished father was loved by a young man of this suburban locality who was away to a big town for further studies. Though he went for studies, but he was so much obsessed with cricket he managed to find a place in the college cricket team and after much struggle, he started making a mark in the world of cricket.

Therefore, this coincidence gave birth to this story. Had there been no town as this one then perhaps the girl would not have been there, and had not been that girl there the story would not have been possible. The girl was the lonely heir and lived in the same neighbourhood. There lay a unique similarity in the choices of that town-bred girl and the suburban boy. That was cricket. The girl was a die-hard fan of cricket and the young man of Sripuram became a fan of this girl. The girl was very simple by nature. Simple as she was, she spent most of her time in college canteens instead of attending the classes. Telling lies at home, she went to enjoy picnic, if her boyfriends' called her over the phone in front of her mother, she would say, "Sudha, How are you ? Yes, I went to attend the class today and I read all throughout last night." In this way she could converse with her boyriends for hours together. She had another special quality. She loved all the producers and the directors of Mumbai cine-world, so she went to enjoy all their movies from **'Maa Kasam Badla Loonga' down to 'Koyla', 'Raakh', 'Aag' and 'Badla'** to fill in their coffers. Then she was keen to enjoy the cricket matches and. Therefore. she went to watch them too often. She could remember and tell the scores of many of the matches played. She knew most of the players of all the major teams of the cricketing fraternity very well. Her girlfriends would call her 'mad' and she would go round the entire bazaar to buy a poster of Sourav Ganguly. If she got some time besides these two of her major activities, then she would spend time to read her books. She was an avid reader of the magazines like **'Manohar Kahaniya,' 'Satya Katha' and 'Griha-Shobha'**. She used to be so much exhausted with these non-scholastic activities that she had no real interest to devote some time for the insignificant Bachelors Degree. Her mother would say,"Beti, the days of the examination are fast approaching. At least read something." She would reply positively and engulf herself in a mysterious story. It was her third year in the first year degree courses of her college. Yet, she was a woman with a great heart.

One day her father who would wear clothes that resembled his grey hair, put a black sunglass of Ray Ban and a time-piece or watch in his pocket resembling that of Gandhiji , woke her up and told her that he was chosen as the President of the State Cricket Board. The girl kissed her father out of extreme happiness even without washing her face and could only manage to say, 'I love you, Daddy.' She got up and rang up that imaginary 'Sudha' whose real name was Dinesh as given by his parents. This was the boy who lived in the same neighbourhood of the Dilruba Paan Centre with the symbol of an arrow piercing into a red-coloured betel-leaf. He grew up listening to radios in the beginning and later by watching at the Dilruba Paan Centre. Cricket was always a part of the living of this boy. He came to study in the college of the town and perhaps by sheer luck he got a place in the cricket team of the college. He developed the friendship with the girl in the cricket field , when he saved the prestige of the college by hitting two big sixes. The girl rang him up saying that her father had become the President of the Cricket Board . The boy replied that he had known it already. When the girl wondered about his prior information, then the boy told her that he had a habit of reading the newspapers daily and he had seen the photo of her father on the front page of the newspaper that morning. Thereafter

     DELVING INTO DIFFERENT LITERARY TERRAINS

the girl assured him that she would talk to her father regarding him, so that he might get a fair chance to chase his dreams.

Then the boy and the girl would meet each other regularly and the boy told her that he was poor , and so she should not try to develop friendship with him. The area which he lived in was still backward , where the brides had to cover their heads with the sarees. The girl replied in a stereotyped 'filmy' way ," I am ready to take up any trouble for you." Thereafter the girl forced her mother and bought four kameezes along with the veils and one day she applied a layer of red paint to decorate her feet. Showing her feet, she said, "I really love to wear red paints on my feet." Then the boy named Dinesh and the girl named Ranjita started mixing up with each other more frequently. The boy wanted to say, "Come on friend, you make me feel bored." Then the girl would say more energetically, "Do you know what my father said , he proposed to call Kapil Dev to dine with him." When the boy would say, " Friend, just leave me alone," that very moment , in an unprecedented way the girl would say,"You know, the marriage ceremony of the daughter of the selector of this term is going to be married soon and I need to go to the market to purchase a new dress to attend her marriage ceremony ." The moment the boy would be uncomfortable with his choice of the girl , that very moment he would remember that Ranjita's father had become the President of the Cricket Board. One day, he told the girl in a 'filmy' way that (although he did not want to tell this to the girl but he was bound to say that he loved her more than anybody else in the world, that necessarily meant that the girl was his first love) he wanted to do away with his second love and that was cricket. The boy wanted to imitate the emotional face of a new film-actor, but he could not imagine a new actor, so he made a mixed impression of Dilip Kumar and Rajendra Kumar and told her that his father was then not in a position to provide extra money to pursue his ambition. His career would get a setback had anything not done at the right earnest. The girl embraced him, kissed his head and assured him that she would surely talk with her father regarding him. The boy reached his ten feet by twelve feet room and glanced once with a note of hope on all the posters of the cricketers glued to his wall and he brought out a bottle from his back-pocket and brought in a glass.

Since the bridge was not going to be erected, the people could realize that he would have to try some other ways to woo the voters. People who lived in the houses by the roadside and those who could convert their houses in such a manner that they could easily be transformed into hotels, inns or small tea-stalls, were facing a very tough time all of a sudden. The fathers of the 'Road-side Romeos' started thinking seriously about the future of their sons , the boys were forced to think seriously about any job they could lay their hands on. Before this, the boys did nothing more than drawing the figures of some ladies in the walls of the toilets of the one and only Government Arts & Science College, and writing vulgar words in a neat handwriting. They were a sort of happy-go-lucky fellows. But their fathers wanted them either to study or think about a job seriously. A group at the bus-stand , some at the railway station, some at the school and some others at the Kannaujialal Arts & Science College were fatigued and depressed. Their sorrows were so deep that even the recognition from the government to Jitu Jaiswal in the form of a three-cornered badge could not make them feel better. The Professor of Physics would be called ' Oye, civilized beast! ' at the top of their voices and the lady teacher who taught Zoology would be called 'Dumdami Mother', but even such bitter and disdainful remarks did not give the boys any sort of mental peace. That day was a holiday, so , in order to avoid useless scoldings of their fathers, the sons took away the bats for washing clothes from Mory and reached the college playground. In that right time of the day, a boy who would wear sunglasses even during the night, and who would try his best to hide his swollen skin by buttoning up the shirt with a lot of difficulties, appeared on the scene. The brother-in-law of the M.L.A. had an high voltage idea to make his brother-in-law re-elected as an M.L.A. and the Kanaujilal Cricket Academy emerged with that end in view. This academy seemed to woo the heart of the boys and their hearts were at once filled up with utter happiness and satisfaction. This academy might or might not have become beneficial for the boys, but one thing was for sure, that the boys had the opportunity to pass off their time.

So, the practice was on instead of studies. The boys tried heart and soul to get themselves admitted into this academy and later to become a part of the cricket team. They collected money and gradually the cloth-washing bats were replaced by the actual bats. The pads. the gloves, the stumps, etc. became available and the boys shone in their new white dresses. Presently the boys started dreaming to become a Tendulkar or a Ganguly. Those were the days when they were at the seventh heaven of happiness. The pitches even seemed to be built in the air. The boys had indeed their feet on the ground, since there was no such magic till date to make them walk in the air, but their attitudes showed that they would walk in the air. The practice was going on in full swing. During that period, if anybody became depressed or thought how they could play in the midst of such talented players, then Dinesh's name would be immediately announced because he was playing good cricket on behalf of the Champion Cricket Club and perhaps he could go to play the **'Ranji Trophy'** matches , and from there he could get the chance to wear the blue jerseys painted with the picture of a fluttering tri-colour and on which the word, 'Sahara' would be written. All these were taking place only due to the conscious efforts of the brother-in-law, who once arrived at the suburban area without a reason. Gradually, he came to learn about Dinesh and he went to the nearby town to meet him. He got some 'weightage' due to the brother-in-law. The brother-in-law left no stone unturned to make them crazier about cricket and to make them 'youth icons'. The practices of the boys were going on quite nicely. The election-time was just knocking at the door. The high-voltage idea of the brother-in-law made the army of the boys to favour the ex-M.L.A. When the boys would be away from the cricket fields, then they would go out to distribute some free materials to the voters. The boys were given the responsibilities to warn the people and to start canvassing about their leader in an open jeep fitted with big loudspeakers. The urban boys were sweating it out in the stadium ground for the upcoming tournament while the suburban boys were working really hard for the elections.

At mid-day just before the commencement of the match, there was a call from Ranjita to the boy who was listening to a song from the, 'Vividh Bharati' – "Look, what I have become, Oh faithless, in your love." The boy could not hear the call of the landlady due to the high volume of the song and for this reason the landlady had to come downstairs to meet him. The structure of the landlady was such that it seemed she could be used as a unit of weight to measure the weight of an elephant. The door was opened with force all of a sudden without a knock and the secret was also revealed that the boy would put on his underwear only inside the room. The landlady glanced at the boy and said with a note of annoyance , "You have a call. There is someone called Ranjita on the line."

"Aunty, could you tell her that I'll ring her up later ?"

"If you're so worried, then why do you distribute the phone number to anybody and anywhere? Now, let's go upstairs. I've put her on hold."

The dreams might have been pinkish in colour , but that 'dream-house' was painted in green. There was a high-walled fencing made of buried bamboos and it was painted in green. There was a big and black gate. A man wearing blue uniform, who was popularly known as a gate-keeper, stopped him there.

Later the boy told stammeringly that Ranjita had called him. After sometime he found himself comfortably seated on a soft-cushioned sofa. The sofa was so soft that he had to put in some extra effort to get up from the sofa and to say 'namastey' to a man clad in white-clothes.

"Ranjita was saying that you play cricket. Is it true?"

"He does not simply play . He plays it really well."

"Ranjita told me that you wanted to have a membership of the club?"

"Papa, he met uncle Tilak in this regard."

"Ranjita was saying that you manage to bowl well?"

"Papa, he is an all-rounder of our college team."

And there followed many other such questions beginning with 'Ranjita was saying.....' and their replies were being given by the daughter of the father instead of the boy. That was the first day in his life when the boy had his food using a table and a chair and he knew it for the first time in his life that the rich would not pour 'ghee' into 'dal' , sugar into the custard and salt into the vegetable curry. But he was happy with the tasteless items , because the man in white not only confirmed his membership with the champion club but he was also assured to have a place in the team for an important match to be held in the coming month. Some selectors were supposed to arrive there, who were 'good friend' of the black man clad in white apparel. The boy came back home almost flying in and put his mouth on the oil-stained pillow and tried to believe that he had really returned from such a rich man's house. In that crazy moment, he forgot that he had soiled the one and only good shirt that he possessed.

The boy was playing for the **Champion Cricket Club.** In the evening edition of the **Duniya Times** , he was praised twice and a small interview of him was published. The boy became a 'hero' among his friends. He could realize that his days of putting on the blue jerseys were drawing near. An important match was about to take place. The selectors were pressurized to stay away from giving opportunities to the newcomers. The brother-in-law had the responsibility to ensure that no one got a second opportunity elsewhere from this 'Cricket Academy'. The brother-in-law came to the town and met with the black man dressed in white garments. It was decided that a match would be held between the urban and the suburban boys. So that the suburban boys would keep quiet for a few days as also the selectors could say that matches were held for them for the convenience of their selection process.

 DELVING INTO DIFFERENT LITERARY TERRAINS

The next day was an important one. The match would decide the fate of the boys. A group of eleven enthusiastic suburban boys came to the town. The girl was adamant that she would feed the boy with the 'prasad' from the temple. The boy refused to do that but the girl did not pay heed to it and rushed into the ten by twelve feet room putting her maroon-coloured salwar-kurta on. In that humid afternoon the entire colony was as silent as a beaten-up child. The boy quietly opened the gate and let her in.

In the morning , the boy came to the ground with a panache. He had the suburban cricket team in front of him. All of them were his friends but each of them played like his enemies. The girl was clapping loudly. The boy introduced her with the boys of the sub-urban team before the commencement of the match. "So many brother-in-laws?" The girl shamefully winked at him and said,"You naughty." The boy remarked enthusiastically after a long time. The match was a great tussle between the two teams. It resembled the great battle of the Mahabharata. The urban boys were hitting and the suburban boys were on the verge of a crushing defeat. Neither the batting nor the bowling seemed to be effective. The suburban boys tried their level best but they had to accept the defeat. The boy was declared the match-winner. "These cheats have purchased the umpires," a permanent member of the Jitu Kalali's team raised this protest.

"Come on, nothing like that really."

" It seems as if you knew how everything came about," the dissatisfaction seemed to increase gradually.

"Haven't you seen the father of the girl. How his eyes were fixed to the boy. I feel he set every thing for his daughter only."

"Bullshit, we could not do anything. Try to impress the daughter of the rich and have the match pre-fixed." The bitterness paved the way for finding out the justification of the match. Jitu Kalali was not present there, but that did not make any difference. The Budh Park, which was popularly known as 'Buddha' in Delhi had, in one of its corners, a man ready with the salty Bengal grams, grated raw onion pieces and the 'English' addictive liquids and the buzzing sounds could be heard. The plastic glasses ,when emptied, were being thrown up in the air and so they were not being emptied. The night was gradually setting in and so was the revelry.

"It's a no-moon day today," someone said philosophically. Others started laughing loudly.

"Bull-shit, our future has darkened like a moonless night. What shall we do now?"

They came out with limping pairs of legs. " Relax, I only asked someone the way to the New Delhi railway station."

"Am I your servant ?"

The departing scene was being picturized in the gate of the garden. A small red car was making sounds to indicate that it was ready to go. But the person with blowing hair, flexible body and white complexion was not ready to go. The honey complexioned boy was repeatedly requesting the girl to go away," Please go away , it is already nine p.m. You know how tense the match was. I feel extremely tired. I'd like to sleep...please, please, try to understand." The more the word 'please' would be uttered , the more the beauty seemed to flourish and grow. "Friend, the boys belong to my suburban locality, I need to visit them without fail. Otherwise they may think that as my team has won the match, so I haven't gone to meet them."

Destiny came forward to meet them. The way the unruly mob might not know which words of whom would destroy the town, much in the same way a crazy voice shouted " Look, how he has stuck to that girl. Does that ruffian think himself to be a 'hero' by defeating us? The boy is showing off under the active support of the father of that girl." That show-off was converted to a lesson for them. The boys became ready to play another match. The soft body of the boy was turned into a pitch. The girl saw 'so many brothers-in-law' with closed eyes and in the agony of pain. The girl limped while she was trying to get up. Her soft hands touched the trophy kept on the bonnet of the car. The lid of the trophy fell on the ground bouncing twice like a dead ball. There was a rolling sound of its fall and everything became quiet thereafter.

Dilip Simeon's Revolution highway

Dilip Simeon's first novel, **Revolution Highway** is a significant attempt in the domain of Indian writing in English as the author deals with the naxalite movement that shook the Indian state during the late 1960's and early 1970s and the after-effects or implications of that movement as the members once associated with naxalism indulged in serious contemplation based on retrospective hindsight. There was a commonplace allegation against the Indian writers writing in English that they generally ignored local issues in their writing as compared to their counterparts who wrote in regional languages and **Revolution Highway** acted as a counter to such allegations as Simeon's novel dealt with the origin, implications and impact of the naxalite movement on a large canvas which was considered by many a typical subject to be dealt effectively only by regional writers. However, Dilip Simeon also makes an attempt to place the naxalite movement within the larger historical context of the revolutionary movement in different geographical locations of the world during the 1960s and that is how the novel acquires an international dimension. The novel prioritizes the gradual expansion of the **Naxalite Movement** through the trials and tribulations of three protagonists from different socio-cultural and linguistic backgrounds – Pranav, Mohan and Rathin as they initially succumb to the revolutionary rhetoric of Mao and Charu Majumdar, the chief architect of the Naxalite Movement in West Bengal but later on become aware of the pitfalls and limitations of the movement which failed to create any definite impact except West Bengal, Kerala and certain parts of the Northern Indian region. There is a conscious attempt to understand the implications of the naxalite movement from a retrospective perspective as the novel captures the disappointments and disillusionment of the associates who once actively participated in the grand dream of eliminating class enemies, building a corruption-free society and upholding the great ideals of Marx. The novel provides a severe critique of the naxalite movement as it brings to light the pain and pathos of a generation of brilliant youths who killed and died without any valid cause or reason, the anguish of the helpless parents as they were mute spectators to the destruction of their sons and daughters, the ruthless domination spearheaded by Siddhartha

Shankar Ray and carried out by Tapan Mukherjee in West Bengal, the clash between ideological commitment and personal emotions and the gradual dissidence within the naxalites themselves regarding larger international historical developments. The novel deftly deals with the implications of the American invasion into Vietnam and its after effects, the war between India and Pakistan caused by the liberation of Bangladesh, the rise of Pol Pot regime in Cambodia and the role of China and U.S.S.R. to safeguard the interests of Pakistan and India respectively.

Simeon exhibits subtle narrative dexterity as the narrative framework not only shifts across time, but also across different geographical spaces and throughout the novel there is a juxtaposition of the elite and popular discourses. Modernists made a serious attempt to uphold the elitist discourse in their works but with the advent of post-modernism popular culture gradually gained prominence and Dilip Simeon's novel provides foreplay of such popular discourses within its textual universe as he incorporates lines from numerous popular Hindi songs, refers to a number of popular Hindi movies of that time and famous English songs of the 1960s that appealed to the passionate feelings of the youths. Simeon deserves kudos as he has done meticulous research for the novel – a fact that can be corroborated by the many newspaper clippings that he attaches to many chapters, a few transcripts of radio interviews about important historical upheavals and perceptive details that brings to light hitherto unknown facts about the activities of the **Anushilon Samiti** in pre- Independence Bengal. **Revolution Highway** gives enough space to the conflict between America and Vietnam, which has not been previously dealt with by other Indian novelists writing in English and in this context one is reminded of the American novelist, Kurt Vonnegut's, **'Slaughterhouse-Five,'** that brought to light the shattering magnitude of American violence in Vietnam. Two great historical figures – Karl Marx and Mahatma Gandhi emerge as potent but absent figures in the novel as the believers and non-believers of their ideologies grapple with the relevance and implication of their views from a contemporary perspective and in this connection, I was reminded of Derrida's, **'Spectres of Marx'** which argued how even the detractors of Marx were haunted by his ghost.

Dilip Simeon has created aesthetics of polyphonic discourses in the novel and this sometimes becomes a flaw as the readers are distracted and an objective assessment of **Revolution Highway** from the generic perspective has to be quite guarded. Great writers like Leo Tolstoy and

Thomas Mann had dealt with greater historical issues in their novels like **Anna Karenina, War and Peace and The Magic Mountain** and all these novels prioritized free-interplay of numerous discourses but the discourse was never imposed from outside as it emerged from the conflict and clash of the characters' destiny and actions. The author of **Revolution Highway** could have exhibited more restraint regarding the imposition of several discourses which sometimes impinges upon the narrative from outside and readability suffers in the process.

However, Simeon has shown remarkable prowess in handling language in **Revolution Highway** as the novel provides satisfactory examples of appropriation of the English language by an Indian author, (that begins with Raja Rao's **Kanthapura**) a fact that can be authenticated by the mention of words like "anudder"(another), "piss-taul" (pistol), "genwin" (genuine), "udder" (other) which are also interesting puns. Simeon is a widely read person and his vast erudition in different disciplines of knowledge gets reflected in the novel and this is spontaneous. Though Simeon's novel is a politically charged one where larger historical and social issues predominate, yet it is a relief to come across such sentence that also reveals the inherent literary merit of the novel. "Loneliness is the discrepancy between what you are and what you might have been."

The titles of different chapters chosen by Simeon consciously echo other titles – one interesting example is **"The Accidental Death of a Communist"** which echoes the title of the celebrated play by the Italian Nobel Laureate, Dario Fo. **"The Accidental Death of an Anarchist"** looked at from this angle can be considered a post-modern novel as it incorporates within its fabric intertextuality, narrative playfulness, free play of popular culture and a mixture of the sublime and trivial.

The novel also raises important concerns regarding the role of women within the context of the naxalite movement in particular and revolutionary ideal in general and the articulation of women's anguish is filtered via the consciousness of Maya and Divya.

The epilogue juxtaposes the resolution of both the public and personal matrixes as the novel ends with a life-affirming tone and **Revolution Highway** is both a significant and interesting addition to the canon of Indian writing in English as it deals with a crucial phase in Indian socio-political history in a broad canvas.

As The Night Deepens
A Bengali Short Story By

Pracheta Gupta

Translated by Subhajit Bhadra

The doctor remained silent for a while. Then he lifted his face and said, "Stop studying at night. Don't read at night."

Frightened, I replied, "How can that be possible, doctor? Old habits die hard. This habit of studying deep into the night has stayed on since my college days. Life will take turns if I give up the habit."

The doctors are usually sparing in laughing. As if their personalities will take a beating if they do so. Sometimes patients get to their nerves if they watch a doctor smile too often. They talk unnecessarily more than what is needed. My doctor laughed a little. Perhaps he enjoyed my frightened face.

"You are mistaken, Swapanbabu. You are no longer a college student now. You are a teacher. You teach in a school, don't you? You can't have the same lifestyle you once had in the college . This will be quite out of place with you at present. It is not possible too."

With a nod, I said, "I don't keep myself awake till late at night these days, doctor. I remain awake till it is one or one-thirty at night. That's it. Then I retire to my cozy bed." I paused a little. "This is not true at all. Sometimes it becomes two also. It depends on the subject-matter of the book. This decides how long I shall keep myself awake. The more the topic becomes interesting, the deeper into the night, I'll stay up." Keeping this matter a secret, I laughed reluctantly: "I have got no trouble of sleeplessness. I am that sort of guy who sleeps as soon as my head touches the pillows. I sleep continuously for six to seven hours. I don't even wake up in the middle."

I thought that the doctor would take up this matter lightly, watching me smile. Will he cancel his previous suggestion of not waking up late into night reading books. Or at least he would partially cancel his suggestions.

But things did not happen that way. The smiling face of the doctor became at once serious. Lowering his face, he spoke out, "All I can say is that you need to do away with this habit. You need to be early to bed at night. It is better for you to sleep at ten. But you can't do it overnight. Let it be eleven for the time being. Try it out. It is equally important when you sleep and for how long you sleep. Having gone to bed, you can listen to some light music and that's it. Nothing more than that. You do not seem to have major trouble inside your body, Swapanbabu. You have a bit of a digestion problem. Acidity is developed from that. You seem to be stressed up, though that's not too much, but I feel that it is due to your overstay in the night. This may lead to multiple physical ailments if you do not change this habit right now. Now, you are young. You can change yourself you like. This will turn into insomnia later. Then you will have to remain awake all night."

To speak the truth, I did not accept the offers of a job or two when I learnt that I needed to wake up early in the morning. It was not possible for me to leave my house as early as seven or eight in the morning. I felt on the top of the earth when I got the job of a school teacher in Palashpur. The school started at eleven. One could be attached to bed till 9 a.m. It was no harm if one lay on the bed till it was nine-thirty. It was hardly a fifteen minute cycle ride from the place where I lived right then.

"How can I leave an age-old habit so easily, doctor? Besides...besides, I don't get much time these days. A considerable amount of time is spent at the school."

The doctor seemed to be a little irritated. Then, lowering his face, he uttered, "Bad habits should be given up."

Having two days leave, I came to Kolkata. I had some trifling work to do. Having finished, I came to see the doctor. It was not that there was dearth of doctors in Palashpur, but one could rely on a well-known doctor. If I knew that the doctor would advise me to sleep early to get rid of indigestion and belching, then I would not visit here. The doctor scribbled a prescription on a piece of paper and handed it over to me.

"Here you are. I prescribed one medicine for digestion problems and the other for sleeping troubles. Have the tranquilizers only when there will be acute sleeping problems. Else, don't take them. Follow my directions for a few months. Be early to eat and bed at night. Wake up early in the morning. Have a morning walk daily, There are plenty of trees there, aren't they? It is not as polluted as Kolkata. You will feel more agility and freshness in a few days. You will get the results within a short time. I bet the problems of indigestion, headache and waking up till late night will be over."

I did not have much trouble in waking up till late night. But it was useless to make it known there. I got up from the chair nodding my head like an obedient patient. I had to catch the train to Palashpur in the afternoon. I had to resume my school duties from the next day. I was a new employee, so there was hardly any room for any sort of negligence. To top them all, I liked the job very much.

The doctor told me that it would take a couple of days to cure. It, however, did not take too long to get over my ailments. My problems like indigestion, belching, headache and stomachache vanished within three days. I continued the act of reading till late night hours with renewed vigour and enthusiasm. There was no problem at all.

The problem occurred on Saturday. Saturday night to be exact.

It was hardly half past twelve at night. It had been drizzling outside continuously for quite some time. The rain was beating down neither too hard nor too soft. One would become habituated to continuous rainfall. One could hardly differentiate the sound of the raindrops then. It would become a normal sound then. I would take up books on different subjects at night. I would pick up the book that I liked the most. I did exactly the same on the Saturday night. I was deeply engrossed in the book. Suddenly I felt out of sorts. I had a little uncomfortable feeling. I thought I had fallen ill once again. Lifting my face from the book, I waited for some time. Nothing seemed to trouble me then. There was no problem in my body. I poured my mind back to the book. It was really an interesting book. It was about mesmerism. In other words, it was a book based on the power of human attraction. I was deeply involved in the contents of the book. The secrets of the art of mesmerism lay in three secret skills of vision, touch and will-power. One who would master the three arts very nicely, could become a great master in this art.. The book dealt with countless number of ways to mesmerize others. Dr. Mesmer, Dr. Braide, Mr. Libon, Mr. Burnheim, Prof. Binny were some of the famous practitioners.. Some of them used electrical waves on the body; some held a source of light near the forehead, while some others commanded something. The procedure of Dr. James Esdaile was apparently strange. The President surgeon of the Viceroy of Calcutta appointed him. He built a hospital to cure the patients with the power of mesmerism. The patient would be laid down on a bedstead in a dark room. Then he would induce the patient to sleep by blowing on his or her eyes and head. The patient would be operated upon as and when he slept. How strange it was!

I paused after having read up to this point. The uncomfortable feelings set in again. Then, I could feel that the uneasy feeling was not of any internal origin. It was external. I seemed to feel uneasy as if someone stood at my back. I could slightly feel the breathing in and out on my shoulder. This was coupled with the coarse sound produced by the friction of the pieces of clothes. "Who's there?" I turned back.

Nobody was there. There was no possibility of anyone being there. Who would be there in my bedroom at such late hours at night? I looked at the door. The door was shut. I would bolt the door for a few days when I arrived at this house for the first time. Then afterwards, I would not do so. Suddenly I thought one day, "Why do I bolt the door when the entrance gate of the house is locked?" The entrance gate was not only locked, it was chained up too. It was, therefore, meaningless to bolt the door of my bedroom. There was another door at the back of the house. It was a door type window. It had double locks in it. Heaven knows how long it had been locked. The locks had been rusted. There was a story of the possession of this house. Having arrived here, I spent a few days at a hotel near the station. It was not a good hotel at all. It was obvious that I would not find a good hotel at a place like Palashpur. The food items served were worse than the hotel itself. I had a firm belief that my problem of indigestion originated from there. I had no other option to stay. I could not speak out my problems of accommodation to other teachers. They would laugh at me and call me 'a Babu from Kolkata.' So I started searching for a rented house vigorously. I could somehow manage to cook for myself. I could cook dal, rice and fish curry. I needed a somewhat civilized place to live in. I told one or two persons, "Inform me if you have found one." After ten days, a staff of the hotel came forward to inform me. His name was Ganesh. One evening he arrived at my room when I returned from the school. He said to me, "There's house. Will you see it?"

I told him," I won't see if there's too many people or if the area is overcrowded. I can neither stay near the station nor near the market place. I feel suffocated even at this place of yours. I find the rattling sound of the trains and all sorts of unwanted noises. These trouble me till night. I can hardly concentrate on books here.

Ganesh said, "The house is a little way off the town, sir. You need to cross a lake to reach there. Its surroundings are not crowded at all. I know that you study deep into the night. I think this will stand you in good stead."

I said. "What's the rent?"

Ganesh said, "The owner of the house lives in Kolkata. I'll tell him to arrive here on Sunday if you give your consent. Let him come, talk to you and show you the house. The rent will be finalized then. It will hardly be too much. The house has been closed for the last five years."

I said, "Closed? For five years? Why? Doesn't anyone stay there?"

Ganesh paused a little. Then, lowering his head and voice he added, "No, sir. They stayed five years back. The owner used to stay there with his wife and daughter. Thereafter...thereafter they closed the house and shifted to Kolkata. Now they prefer to offer the house on rent. Otherwise the house may be dispossessed by them. But, there's none here to have such a big house on rent. One Nantu takes care of the house here on behalf of the owner. I met him in the market two days ago." He said, "Ganesh, the owner wants to offer this house on rent now. Inform me if you have one. I shall also leave this place and settle in my native village. I would be better if I can do something with it before my departure."

Being excited I asked, "How many rooms are there?"

Pausing a little, Ganesh resumed, "It's a one-storied house. He will give the entire house on rent."

I was a little shocked and said, "The entire house! Oh my God!"

Lowering his voice, Ganesh said, "If the rent isn't too high, then, what's your difficulty? It will be good for you. You will get the entire house on rent, sir."

I said, "What shall I do with the entire house, Ganesh? I am a single person. I don't need more than one room."

Scratching his head, Ganesh said, "Today you may be a bachelor. Tomorrow, you may have a family. Then you will need more space. You will be benefitted if you arrange for this beforehand, sir."

Laughing a little, I said, "Forget what will happen in future. Should I take such a big house on rent for future?"

Ganesh uttered, "It will be an excellent place for your studies. No one is going to disturb you over there. Moreover, it's better to remain single than to be with someone."

I could realize that Ganesh was trying to force me to take the house on rent. I frowned a little. I said, "What's the matter, Ganesh? Is there any problem with the house? Come on, speak out the truth."

Ganesh was awestruck. He paused. Then he said, "No sir, why should there be any problem with the house? I informed you as you had been in search of a house. If you don't like it, then, leave it. I shall inform you if I get another one."

I could not avoid the house though Ganesh gave me an option. To speak the truth, I could not resist the temptation. I was fully excited to think that I would live in a big house in a quiet atmosphere without any trouble. To speak the truth, the assumption of Ganesh of having a family life soon, couldn't be overlooked also. At home, they had been pressurizing me to get married soon. I came to learn that my mother had started to search a suitable daughter-in-law secretly. I did not say anything. I had some serious thought about marriage. Will any woman prefer to see me studying till late night hours? Nobody will. Then I would not marry too. She should not only be beautiful, but she should also be able enough to adjust with my bad habit.

One day I accompanied Ganesh to see the house. I offered to take the house on rent within three days also. The owner of the house was Mr. Dhananjay Sanyal. He could not arrive there from Kolkata due to his physical ailments. Nantu detailed everything on his behalf. He wanted me to talk to Mr. Sanyal. It seemed that the gentleman was a bit serious by nature.

"Swapanbabu, why have you taken such a big house? You could have got a room near the market area or the station. The rent also would have been less."

Smilingly, I said, "I was searching such a house so that I could stay away from the hustle and bustle and live a quiet life."

Pausing a bit, the gentleman said, " The surrounding of my house is really calm and quiet. I built this house willingly to stay a little away from the town. Nowadays, there is too much hustle and bustle in the suburban areas than in big cities. I, however, decided to dispose of this house. But Sritama's mother did not agree."

I asked curiously, "Who is Sritama?"

Pausing a bit on the other end of the telephone, Mr. Sanyal said, "She's my daughter."

I said, "I can't pay you more. Perhaps you know that I am a school teacher....but I liked your house very much indeed."

Mr. Sanyal said, "Don't worry about the house rent. I am telling Nantu all about this. He will tell you everything. Pick up all your belongings and come here."

I could hardly think that he would be ready so easily. In a vague tone, I said, "Thank you very much."

Mr. Sanyal said, "May I ask you one thing, Swapanbabu?"

Curiously I said, "Please go ahead."

"Will you not feel uncomfortable to live in a big house alone in a quiet atmosphere?"

Being awe-struck, I said, "Where's the problem? I wanted to have a quiet place indeed. This place may be a little far away from the markets and shops....what's there in it? I have a bicycle. What else may be the problem?"

Perhaps the man on the other end of the telephone stopped a little. In a low and quivering voice, he said, "No, I am not talking about that difficulty. I thought you might be afraid..you hail from Kolkata......"

I laughed a bit. I said, "What's the fear? Did you mean of thieves and robbers? There's really nothing with me to be robbed off."

In a murmuring voice, Mr. Sanyal said, "That's great."

The old man Nantu moved around the house and showed me the entire house. Showing the window type door, he said, "Would you like to have the key to this door? This is the backyard of the house. There are bushes there and a boundary wall at the end."

I did not take the key. What shall I do with this door? Who will pass through that door? The more the doors and windows are opened, the more they need to be shut. It had been three months since I entered this house. I became oblivious of the window-door. Not only the door, I did not even take the small room lying by the staircases. Apprehending a regular and vigorous routine of dusting, I did not take that room. I heard that there were old chairs, tables, books and a broken table-fan there. The room had remained closed for a long time. There was a grill door attached to a wooden frame on the staircase. It could be said for sure that it was really impossible for anyone to enter the house after unlocking so many locked doors.

Then? The thieves and robbers would not stand at my back in the bedroom.

A water-bottle lay on a corner of a table. I drank water from that. I wondered why there was an extraordinary sensation. I didn't know why I had felt that someone was standing at my back! Could there be so much hallucination? It might be possible. It was possible that my body had been tired internally. So, I might have felt that way.

Having closed the book of mesmerism, I stood up. I forgot everything as I slept after switching off the lights. I slept longer and woke up the next morning. I forgot the uneasy feeling of the last night.

I could remember that just after two days.

I was reading a book on 'Palash' flower. Its title was 'Palash-Katha'. Many things were described about the flower. Perhaps this matter attracted me the most as I read after having arrived at Palashpur. I was utterly surprised as I went through the lines. So long, I knew that 'Palash' flower was very beautiful to look at. I also came to learn that it had multiple qualities besides its good looks. In France, the 'Palash' flower is known as ' Aare-un-llokoyan.' I said to myself, "Wah. I need to remember the name." The school students would be much amused if they were told so. The moment I drew the pen on the table to scribble the name on the corner of a piece of paper, I felt that someone walked past the opened door of my room. Even in darkness, I could see that it was a woman. I was frightened. The table clock was indicating that it was ten minutes past one. That meant that it was one. My clock ran faster by ten minutes.

I had never believed in ghosts. I left my chair and stood up. Leaving the room, I came to the dining room outside. I switched on the light there. I saw what I had expected. There was nothing there. There was none there. The empty room seemed to wake up suddenly when I switched on the light. I came to my bedroom. I sat at the table. Last Saturday, I felt uneasy. Having switched off the light, I slept. I decided that I would not sleep like that on that day. I should keep myself awake a little longer. Such a feebleness of mind was unacceptable to me. One should not yield to such a situation also. I read 'Palash-Katha' for half an hour more. Then I went to sleep.

On other days, I would sleep immediately after switching off the lights. But, on Saturday, I did not feel like sleeping. I changed sides on my bed restlessly. When I dozed a little, I felt that someone had stood near my bed. She wore bangles on her wrists. Some tinkling sounds were coming from the bangles.

I searched for Nantubabu on my way to school the next day. I could not get him. He had already gone to his native village. While returning from school, I thought that I should ring up Mr. Sanyal. But immediately I thought what I was doing. Why should I ring up the owner of the house? What should I ask him for? Who walked around your house at night? What is the problem of your house? Fie upon me. There must be a limit to foolishness. I was angry with myself. Should I keep telling this from person to person that I was terrified on two occasions at night? Shirking off everything from my head, I came back home and took a nice bath. I cooked rice, dal and egg-curry and relished them happily. Then I sat down with the morning newspapers. The house was free from troubles indeed. There was none to disturb once anyone would enter. The noises of the moving vehicles would not come as it was a little way off the main road. Only the sounds of the crickets would come once the window was opened at night.

Besides the news of murders and robbery cases, some good news could also be found. Some interesting news could be found. I was deeply engrossed in such kind of news. A retired teacher donated all his savings to the school. It was a nice thing to think over. Would we ever do that? I thought it was impossible. The biography of such a person should be there in the textbooks of the children. Such news would refresh anyone's mind. In such a pleasant state, I could feel that someone was walking! Someone was walking silently inside the house. Removing my eyes from the newspaper, I sat straight. Who was walking?

Who it was? It would not be wise to leave the chair and wake up just as I did the other day. I got up slowly. I ensured that there should be no sound of the chair. I heard the sound of walking once more. Was it a cat or any other animal? I went straight to the door very carefully. I decided not to switch on the light on that day. I waited in darkness till I could bear it. It was hardly a moment or two.

I could see the woman in darkness. She was wearing salwar-kameez. A veil was attached round her neck. She disappeared into the room by the staircase.

I could not remember how long I stood having bolted my bedroom door.

I told Nantubabu that I had no need of all the keys of the big house. But I kept the entire bunch of keys from him. Next morning, I drew out my drawer and took the bunch of keys to open the door of the room that lay by the staircases. I opened the room. One should correct the errors by oneself if they were committed earlier. Therefore, I decided I should see the room by myself. Having opened the door with a creaking sound,

I discovered myself on a heap of dust. The room was filled with broken items all over. This could truly be called a godown. There were tables and chairs on one side. Some books were lying on the table. Having crossed the broken suitcase, the sewing machine and the harmonium, I went near the table. When I opened one exercise book, a layer of dust covered my hands. The pages turned yellow and crinkly. I turned over the pages. With the help of a faint light that came through the door, I found that it was an exercise book on history. The handwriting seemed womanish. On the cover page, the name Sritama Sanyal was written. She was the daughter of Mr. Sanyal! Was this the study room of Sritama indeed ?

I tried to behave normally in school. But I failed. A sense of uneasiness had already crept in my mind. Then, I could feel that everything was not my hallucination. There were some problems with the house. What was the problem? I decided that I would meet Ganesh after the school hours. Ganesh might know this. I went straight to the old hotel on the bicycle. Ganesh was not there. He had gone to Kolkata. He would return the next morning. The Manager of the hotel could perhaps apprehend something from my grim face. He said, "What's wrong, sir? Is there any trouble?"

Controlling myself, I replied, "No, nothing happened. I thought I would talk to Ganesh regarding the house-rent. Let it be. I shall come tomorrow or the day after. Now, I feel that it would have been better if I could lower the house rent a little......"

"Please have a seat. Have a cup of tea."

I said, "No, thanks. Let me get back home."

The Manager did not pay heed to my words. He forced me to have my seat. He fetched tea and 'samosa' for me. Once he said, "Is everything fine in Mr. Sanyal's house?"

I was startled. Did the man know something about the house? He might know. He was a local fellow, after all. Should I ask? No, let it go. It would be a foolish act if I did so. Everyone in Palashpur would know it. I would become an object of ridicule. Everyone would call me a timid teacher from Kolkata. I was timid indeed. There was no worth expressing my uneasiness over what I had seen at night on two occasions.

With an artificial smile, I said, "Why should I pray? Why should it not be alright? It's a nice house indeed."

Biting on the 'samosa', the Manager said, "It's okay if everything is nice. Have the 'samosa' please. Else it would get cold."

Returning home, I could feel that the Manager hid something from me. What was it?"

I heard the piece of advice of the doctor for the first time. Leaving my habit of reading after my meal, I went to sleep. I took a sleeping pill also. There was really a hidden stress inside my body. Why could a man see a woman in an empty house? What was the harm if I could follow the doctor's advice for a day or two? Heaven knew why I locked the door of my bedroom after a long time on that day. Even I bolted the door nicely. Looking on the roof of the dark room I thought that the members of my own house would be ready if I talked about marriage at that time. These were the troubles of being alone. The problem meant a hotchpotch of everything. Even my habit of studying at night would also come to an end. It was; therefore, better to have a life-mate. Thinking so, I slept within a while.

I could not say when I woke up at night. Through the gap of the door, I saw that some light was there. This was the light from a bulb. How could there be light at late hours at night?

I did not know how I got down from the bed and opened the door. When I stepped into the parlour, I saw that the light was coming from the room lying next to the staircase.

For a moment, I felt weightless. I would surely fall down. Holding on to the door, I controlled myself somehow. It took a long time to come back to my senses from that spell. Thereafter, I thought that I must have put the switch on while locking the door the other day. What else could there be? I said to myself, "That's what it is. That was surely the case." Gaining strength on my feet, I walked to the room.

Not only the room was lit, even the door was put ajar. Through the gap, I noticed that an innocent teenage girl was reading sitting at the table and on the chair. She was moving sideways while reading.

I could not remember what happened afterwards. Losing all my strength, I fell on the floor. While I was falling down, I could somehow realize that somebody held me lightly. Who was it? I came back to my senses the next morning. I found myself lying on the floor near the room by the staircase. The door of the room was locked as I had done the other day. While getting up I realized that strangely enough, I did not receive any severe injury. Keeping myself as quiet as possible, I got out of the house. I wanted to meet Ganesh anyhow.

 DELVING INTO DIFFERENT LITERARY TERRAINS

I could not meet Ganesh. He had not returned from Kolkata. Then I pressed the Manager for some information. He gave a detailed description of everything. It was a simple and small story.

"At first, I thought I would tell you about the house when I came to learn that you were going to shift there. Then I thought, let it be. You might have thought I had told you for my own benefit. You might have thought I wanted to hold you back. But I have not heard anything foul about the house."

Pressing my teeth hard, I said, "Tell me the story, please."

Sritama, the daughter of Mr. Dhananjay Sanyal was not only ravishingly beautiful, she was also equally good at studies."

I asked, "Was...it means..?"

The Manager said, "Yes, she was. She used to read much. She used to keep herself awake till late at night like you. One day, a good marriage proposal came. The boy belonged to a well-to-do family in Kolkata. They had three houses in Kolkata. Sritama was noticed at a marriage party and she was liked too. She was not of a marriageable age. Her parents, however, could not resist their temptations. At first, they tried to make her realize it. Then they forced her. But she was adamant. She decided not to marry but to continue her studies. This resulted in a regular family trouble. Sritama warned them that she would either fly away or hang herself. At last, she committed suicide with her veil instead of a rope."

I remained silent. The Manager said, "But there is nothing uncanny about the house. Mr. Sanyal can't help selling the house only because it bears a memory of their daughter. May be he can sell it one day or else it will lie in the same way if a crazy people like you prefers to stay alone....."

Having finished his speech, the Manager smiled a little.

I went back home riding slowly on my bicycle. The moon rose. It spread its light everywhere. Even Sritama's house was well-lit. I would change it the next day. I had told the Manager that I would like to come back to the hotel. The shops and the market area lay too far away. It was becoming increasingly difficult for me. I had to search for a new house after a few days. But I would get the room by the staircase cleaned before I left. All the dust had to be cleaned. A little girl read till late hours at night. Should that room be so dirty?

Fish Of A Dead River

Translated by Subhajit Bhadra

(Based on an original Manipuri story by Dr. Smriti Kumar Singha and its transcreation into Bengali by Sri Subhajit Bhadra)

It was a Sunday morning. Rajen woke up from sleep and looked at the wall clock. It was nine forty in the morning. By caressing with his hands gently from his forehead to the top of the head, he realized that the middle portion of his head was hairless. As if it was a widespread field. Why should it not be? Should the age be the same during his transition from a clerk to a superintendent? He gave a few sips on the lemon tea left for him by Sima and rushed to the verandah. He lit a cigarette and sat hurriedly on an easy-chair. As soon as he sat, the visible fats of his body bounced and like the jolts of an earthquake, it took a little time to settle down. He heaved a sigh of tiredness. Umm, the scent could be felt even then. Truly. After all, it was a brand for the army. Moreover, his dose was a little heavy last night. Earlier he had time to hide this from Sima by sealing his mouth with betel-leaves and tobacco after having a peg of whisky. But these days the bottles lay awake all the night on the table in his bedroom. It had been long since Sima issued a no-objection certificate . She had developed her standards of late.

Offering a long puff to his cigarette, Rajen looked in front. The heat of the sun had gone up. The water of the lake in the front was shining. As if it were a veil worn by a female dancer in a night club. The lake really meant the curved portion that was formed as the river called the Rukmini lying in front had changed its course. Water could be available all throughout the year as both its mouths remained closed, but it had no current. Not even during the rainy season. A dead river. The water of the dead river looked as clear as distilled water if it was seen from above, but one and a half feet below, there lay a kingdom of the algae--- which was beyond imagination.

A cluster of quarters, offices, shops stood on either side of the lake. It was not a very old story. It was simply a village a few years back. The area was

     DELVING INTO DIFFERENT LITERARY TERRAINS

transformed into a town as soon as a few government offices and factories were set up here. The signs of a village were still visible till the other day. As for example the man sitting with a fishing-rod under the simul tree a little way off. He was as black as a buffalo. A tall man. His hands and feet were very strong. A bait would always be attached to his fishing-rod. An infallible bait made of indigenously brewed wine. Rajen would always observe this hunter. It was a real mystery to think how he managed to catch the big fishes ! A young man sitting under the 'simul' tree was asking something to him. Perhaps he had been transferred here of late. Offering a puff to the cigarette with utter happiness, Rajen could hear their conversations.

"No bait is there, I see. Do the fishes get hooked into it?"

"Yes, they do. The bigger ones got food and had gone deeper inside and the lake was covered with algae in such a manner that it would be very difficult to find out the dead bodies of people once they fell into it. Once in a while they would float on removing the layers of algae. When there was a flow of current...."

"Current! What do you mean ?"

"Now, in fact, the river is dead. Earlier the Rukmini river would flow past here with a curve. When the mouths of the river became narrow, then a few government employees and some wicked persons sealed the mouths immediately and changed the course of the river. Therefore, the Ima Rukmini became sentimental and moved off."

" Oh, I see. Then this did not happen long ago."

"No , no. Not even fifty years. The silvery fishes would dance on the crystal clear waters of the flowing current. There were no algae at all."

" Sweeping can be done now."

"Sweeping! The man with the fishing rod looked at the young man with his large and round pair of eyes."

"Then sweep. Young person's like you can be up and doing and can get a move on. Just try to make the current of the Rukmini flow in this direction if you can."

'Right'. Dropping the ashes of the cigarette in the ash-tray, Rajen said, " The youth power, Come forward."

'Right'. Rajen would repeat this word in his speech as a student-leader some twenty five years ago. The real meaning of the word became evident then—the man with the fishing-rod was talking like a philosopher.

Once a student leader, Rajen started to deliver a speech in his own mind-- Clear the algae. All types of algae. The ones that can be found in the lakes, drains and also the ones that get stuck to the fencing of the houses. Sweep off all the algae. The ones that are hanging like a piece of cotton right under my eyebrows....

Rajen threw away and contorted the cigarette in the ash-tray out of excitement.

"Oh darling, do you hear ? Get up and wash your mouth. It is already ten o' clock."Sima told this appearing in the verandah.

"Umm." Rajen was still sitting on his easy-chair. After a while, Sima said, "Today is a holiday. You can easily teach your son a little. Altogether...."

"Why ? Is his tutor not coming these days ?"

"Tutors are different . Piku becomes extremely happy if you discuss the lessons."

"Does he really become happy?" Rajen sat straight. Having sat, he saw that Piku, his ten- years-old son, stood on the threshold of the door with a book and looked at him. Piku read in class five. Both his eyes shone like the aparajita flower. He was a meritorious student. He had a self-acquired knack for studies.

He would certainly be something if guided in a proper way. But he would not get his father all the time. Actually Rajen would not allow him to come closer . His bad habit should not touch the little angel—he thought so. Sima had an opinion that the drunkards could never adore their wards ."..foolish..." Smiling a little, Rajen gestured his son to come near him. Piku came rushing in and sat on his father's lap.

"Let me check your maths."

" It's not Maths. It is on our morality."

"Morality ? You mean Moral Studies, eh... "

Rajen looked at Sima with swelling noses and a little gaping mouth. He came back to senses when Piku's hair touched his chin.

"Oh Piku, go now. Your mother will make you understand all these."

"Not at all, I can't do it." Sima told so turning off her face.

"Why not? You had education as one of your subjects in your graduation programme. You taught in a private school before entering into the job. Even though you may forget, but giving a little try will...."

 DELVING INTO DIFFERENT LITERARY TERRAINS

Sima looked at Rajen before he could finish off his sentence.

"Okay, Piku. Don't worry ..." Rajen spoke stammeringly. "I'll arrange for another tutor for you from tomorrow. He will teach you the subjects like literature, moral science, etc. Today you go." Piku entered inside a room carrying a book with a gloomy face. Immediately afterwards, Rajen charged Sima, "Have you gone mad ? Shall I teach Moral Studies ? Would you like to put me to utter shame in presence of my child ?"

"Why can't you ? You're also a graduate."

"It's all right."

"Just try to imagine, what a trace of morality is still left in this father who accepts bribes, who is a drunkard and a characterless person to be worthy of teaching moral studies ? It had been twenty five years since I accepted bribes to touch the public files, I tell at least a hundred lies en route to the office and back, how the same father can advise his son not to tell lies. Don't do any injustice. It will be great sin. Mahatma Gandhi, Vivekananda..et all.......bullshit..."

" It's enough. Don't ever shout like that. It would have been better if you had told the meaning straightway instead of offering sermons like that."

"I could. I could do it twenty five years ago."

"I know why you can't."

"I feel. One can tell a thousand lies to others but can't be a liar to oneself."

The sometime ideal student-leader Rajen was utterly depressed with himself at heart. Keeping quiet for a while, he continued, "Shall I not be ashamed of myself before my son when I shall tell all these stories based on moralities or principles for a better living, and he will accept it gladly? After all, I respect my son."

"Me too," Sima spoke out.

"Therefore, never tell me to teach my son. I shall appoint a few more tutors if needed."

Saying so he went to the bathroom with his fatty body.

All the old thoughts would rush in Rajen's mind when he would be alone in a quiet bathroom. Actually the solitude was the permanent address of the memory. A home address. Looking at his own image in the mirror while brushing his teeth, Rajen thought—what he was and what he had become of late. He had been suffering from an excruciating pain of life having worn a mask of 'duplicities'. His childhood memories of the village flashed upon his mind. He remembered his search for dried cow-dung from field to field, hopping and jumping from road to road. He could remember his school days of biting the seeds of lotus and carrying a slate in his armpit. The affection he got from everyone for being meritorious as he was. He could remember his college days. Students' organization, movements, jail, boycotting of examinations, road-blockade. The first meeting with Sima, an unrestrained love story, his madness for an early marriage—he could remember everything. Everything was almost alright until the marriage took place. An ideal floated before his very eyes. The marriage was done but what about the job! He stepped into the world of corruption as he was searching for a job. All his ideals were shattered into pieces. He had to sell a plot of his land for getting a job. Then money became a be-all and end-all for him. He started squandering money on the excuse of extreme poverty of his family. Then he had his sons and daughter. The thatched house in the village was converted into a pucca building. Gradually, his land and property also multiplied. He managed to have T.V. , fridge, car, promotion and a service to Sima. The more such consumer goods entered into their houses, the more their happiness got dried up proportionately. It looked as if they developed life-style diseases for evading the income-tax and letting people know that they had enough money. Sima developed melena while Rajen had a cardiac problem. Even their children gave no relief to them. These days children would enjoy with their father's money, would be happy to move on motorbikes , and would always remain busy in talking to others over cellphones. But they would feel ashamed to disclose the identity of their fathers. People might laugh to know about their father's department. Their self-respect might be hurt. His eldest son was a brilliant boy. But he was spoiled outright. He took to wine, hemp and drugs. He would not admit Rajen as his father. His daughter also let him down by committing a shameful incident. He heaved a sigh of relief by somehow managing to keep her in the village. Let it be. But that could not put an end to her earning a bad name. But whenever Rajen would go to the village, he would deliberately donate a thousand or two for occasions like Literary Society, public meetings, clubs, pujas, the Bihus, the Eids, etc. and could manage to earn a good position. Therefore, nobody could speak anything clearly against him. Had it been the case with another person, then it would have been different. He had to shell out a huge amount from his pocket to put an end to the unending gossips. How could he marry off his children if he

     DELVING INTO DIFFERENT LITERARY TERRAINS

had not kept a good relationship with the society! Again, he also needed a sound social platform after his retirement. He did not have too many days left for retirement. Above all, his youngest son Piku just resembled his elder brother during his childhood -- studious and meritorious. But if he would go to the dogs when grown-up, ush, this was his last hope. Oh, what a day had come about. The father could not control his own son! If he would ask a question on the face, then? There were reasons to feel scared about. The entire generation had become weak. Could there be no way out to be really free from the tentacles of corruption? Was there any superman who could sweep everything off? No, it was not there. All had been corrupt. The hydra-headed monster of corruption could be found even in the tiniest social molecules. There was no healthy environment to breathe in fresh air. Oh, what a life it was then!

Heaving a deep sigh, Rajen came out of the bathroom. He sat beside the dining table and sipped off the tea made for him by Sima . The bitterness of his mind was soon transmitted into the tea.

"Where's Piku?"

"He sat on the verandah with a gloomy face a while ago."

"Piku, Piku. Sima came out from the verandah."

"Where he may have gone? He was right here."

"To which direction? Has he gone towards the lake? If he slips and falls into the lake water! You seem to take no care of the boy at all." Being frightened, he pushed aside the cup of tea and crossed over the verandah to come to the yard with Sima.

"Oh mummy—mummy—Oh daddy....."the voice of Piku could be heard from the direction of the lake. "Come sharp. See for yourself."

"What happened ? What's wrong ?" Sima went ahead running followed behind by panting Rajen.

"Look there . A huge fish has come out of water today. Wow!!" Piku started clapping and jumping out of enjoyment. It was really so. Being awestruck, Rajen and Sima noticed the fish was really taking breath on the surface of the water. It swept off the algae that had stuck to its tail. There were black spots all over the body of the silvery fish.

"It's good enough. It could come out at last. It could at last come up sweeping off so much algae." Rajen muttered those words. The man with the fishing-rod started to move his infallible bait just in front of its mouth. But the fish never seemed to notice that . Sometimes it dovetailed , sometimes it stood up and sometimes it played in a circular motion due to utter happiness for his freedom from the algae,

Suddenly it produced a narrow and a temporary current with tremendous velocity in the dead river with the help of his back fin and moved off to a long distance.

"Bah !" Rajen became fully excited with emotional outburst. Looking at the temporary current produced by the fish for a while, he spoke out to Piku, "Come Piku. You told me to teach something, didn't you ? Come on. Let's go now."

Interview Of Harekrishna Deka
By Subhajit Bhadra

S.B: It is believed that every child is a prospective adult and every adult nurtures within him/her a lost child. Childhood as a formative phase of life is always important in case of any individual human being and it becomes significantly special in the life of a writer. Looking back, how much do you think your childhood has shaped as a human being and as a writer?

HKD: As a child one begins his imaginative adventures through the magical world of fairy tales, nursery rhymes, etc and one looks at the world with a sense of wonder. For a child, his/her entry into language is exciting as he or she learns to express their experiences of the surrounding through a communicative medium. As a child, I was sensitive to the way I was experiencing the surrounding world of nature and culture and wanted to acquire the skill of using words expressively . During those early days, I started following the writers whose language attracted me. I started loving the rhythm of words and acquired a taste for poetry I had encountered through the learning process of school textbooks as well as through those I discovered in libraries or bookstalls where I was delightfully attracted to the rows of books displayed. I started playing with words and found that I could also write.

In later years, I discovered, my childhood memories were evocatively strong and a rich source of thematic contents as well as metaphors. The childhood was the formative age that lay the foundation of my attitude and sensitivity to the world, and the experiences of later years were only additions to this foundation with alterations and adjustments necessitated by mature experiences of adult life. There is no break between the child and the man and it can be compared to a tree whose trunks and branches are the continuation of the roots.

S.B.: Did you ever nurture any hidden ambition of being a writer and if so how much you drew from your surroundings?

HKD: Yes, I wanted to be a writer as soon as I started reading various writings of different authors. I was fascinated by the world of words from the very beginning of my discovery of that world in various texts. The world of words is fictional but it has to draw its images and metaphors from experiences of our reality to which we are exposed through our senses and understanding. The surroundings filled with people, society, nature and its environment and cultural interactions with them in space-time is the source from which I have drawn most of my building materials for my imaginative world.

S.B.: Did you struggle as a writer during the initial stage? Were you inspired by any idol?

HKD: It has always been a struggle between realization and expression. What comes as comprehension of thought and feeling has to find a structured expression in language. The inadequacy of language has to be overcome by inventive metaphors and in attractive style free from clichés. I had many favourite authors but consciously tried to avoid influences.

S.B.: When you started writing Assamese literature was quite vibrant and fertile. How do you remember those days?

HKD: We got exposed to a very new trend which later came to be known as modernist literature. There were altogether new experiments, particularly in short story and poetry. It was exciting as well as confusing to begin with. Romantic outlook was replaced by a sharp awareness of the changes brought about by the nation's post-Independence expectations and excitement as well as conscious understanding of the progress-prospect of modernity with its attendant vulnerability. Literature tried to reflect all these through a kind of experimental literature. In our literature, modernism did not fully break from romanticism. In the Assamese mind the lyrical impulse was quite strong and modernism was a reorientation of axis with romantic fervor flowing as undercurrent.

S.B. : You are basically a poet. You have always striven towards producing fresh images, metaphors and symbols. Did you need to be inventive for that?

HKD: To begin with, my preferred vehicle in younger days was poetry but a story writer lurked behind the poet. You can notice, against the lyrical-experimental trend of the then poetry, I fused narrative elements with lyricism. I was inventive and always looked for fresh metaphors. I avoided the moulds shaped by my predecessors.

S.B.: Your identity of being a poet has overshadowed your other achievements. How do you view yourself as a poet?

HKD: My poetry and my prose fiction are complementary, though I ventured into prose fiction much later. When I felt that certain experiences needed an overtly narrative structure and poetry would not be a suitable vehicle for their expression despite my bringing narrative elements into some of my poetry, I started writing short stories and novel much later. Imagination plays a strong role in my poetry but most of my inspirations are drawn from the reality I have experienced in the social surrounding. Nature comes as a backdrop, and a source of symbols and metaphors. You will find a lot of irony and satire in my poetry but I have written many tender love poems as well.

S.B: You have written a number of important short stories which exhibit your mastery of western literature. How do you view yourself as a writer of short stories?

HKD: I am well-acquainted with western literature but I don't call it a mastery. I have made many experiments in fiction, both in structure and language as well as in subject-matter. I take my fiction writing as seriously as my poetry.

S.B.: You have penned a novel called 'Agantuk' and that was a sort of journey as a novelist. Looking back, how do you feel about it? What triggered that maiden step?

HKD: Though I was asked by many people to venture into novel writing for a few decades, I was quite hesitant to write a novel mainly because I got a lot of satisfaction in writing short stories. But Diganta Ozha, a young intellectual who is also an acclaimed writer of socio-historical criticism and was also associated with the editing of a magazine pressed me to write a novel for a special issue with which he was involved. He was so persistent that I had to give in, since I was fond of him. I was thinking of a short story on a theme of an alien's view of the civilization we are in. As a short story I conceived it differently but for writing a novel, I had to change the canvas and my orientation. I was surprised that it was received well and even an unknown person wrote a critical article on it. This encouraged me and I was inspired to write my second novel, with an innovative approach. Nothing like my second novel 'Yatra' has been attempted in Assamese literature. My third novel is likely to be a detective novel , but with some difference.

S.B.: Recently you have written an experimental novel 'Yatra' which is unique in the realm of Assamese literature. You have also experimented with form and structure of story telling in this novel. Tell us something about such refreshing experiment.

HKD: Yes, 'Yatra' is unlike any other novel in Assamese literature. It begins with a prelude which is a short story written by a writer and it is not his own plot. He was goaded by an explorer whom he never met and their encounter was through correspondence. The explorer , who provided the materials, was not satisfied with the outcome of the story and criticized the writer for his alleged failure to realize the 'truth' that literature should aim through imagination to enhance the knowledge of reality. The writer decides to write the story afresh filling up the gaps in the materials he received from the explorer by using his imagination. This forms the core in the middle of the novel and it deals with a hypothetical tribe completely unknown to the civilized world. The writer imagined that this invented tribe developed a vibrant culture of their own and yet this culture remained frozen in time. The core portion of the novel tests how far a writer's imagination can visualize a future if he is given some ethnographic material. This runs parallel to another story developed around the 'core-periphery' question debated often in a nation like India. Both stories converge at a point where the actual journey taken by the writer to an area of his nation (considered a part of the heartland) comes to an end with a number of adventurous and painful experiences. At this level, the writer himself is one of the two protagonists of the core-periphery story, the second protagonist, being an escort of the writer, himself involved in an agitation on the conflict over a people's sense of human security and a development plan of the country that does not meet the security expectations of those people. The second protagonist at this level seeks his own answer to the core-periphery relations of a State and it is he who meets a tragic end. Both the protagonists on their journey try to resolve their doubts dialogically but fail to find a common answer. On their journey, they meet a third character, a young woman, socially committed and intellectually alive, who joins their dialogue and provides many inputs shedding fresh light on the core-periphery dialogue. The writer contrives an end for the sake of his core story but the unseen omniscient narrator finds it a contrived ending with questions unanswered. Hence, he calls it an unfinished novel. The writer finally finds a way of finishing the novel by inventing some clues that leads to a love story. Structurally, the novel is sandwiched between two stories with different orientations, both of which have different styles of narration and tonality, distinctive from the core novel. The colonial question has been explored by juxtaposing a modern situation and a hypothetical situation that hints at the disturbing consequences of the civilizing colonial missions of the western civilization.

 Delving Into Different Literary Terrains

India, Assam and an imagined Amazon-like location form the background of the parallel narratives joined at different points.

S.B.: You are also writing a serialized memoir in a reputed Assamese magazine. How have you conceptualized it and how is it different from your autobiography which you could have written?

HKD: I did not want to write my autobiography serially narrating my life story from the beginning to the present day. An autobiography often becomes exhibitionist and the life's story always remains unfinished. It is very subjective. I do not want to write such an autobiography. Instead, I have started writing my memoirs of some significant experiences of the past life by drawing out metaphors from those significant moments. These metaphors are made to evoke memories going back to my childhood and returning to the present, often linking my creative self to those metaphors and their significance in my mental growth.

S.B.: You were an administrative officer who reached the higher echelon of power. You have seen and gathered many experiences about those years. Do you think your writings got some boost from those experiences?

HKD: Immensely. My experiences in my field and administrative career immensely helped me to understand and empathize with human situations and gave me raw materials for my poetry and my fiction. I could not have written a highly praised story 'Bandiyar' without my first-hand experience of the insurgency situation in Assam. Many of my poems are responses to situations I witnessed as an officer. Many of my satirical poems and short stories are based on the prevailing politico-social situations observed from a vantage point.

S.B.: You have received the prestigious Sahitya Akademi award and a number of other awards. How do you feel about it.

HKD: I took them as recognitions of my writings but never hankered after any award. I consider the acceptance of one's writing by a class of discerning readers as the bigger award and I like to shun populism.

SB: You are a voracious reader of world literature that is reflected in your writings. Who are your favourite writers and why?

HKD: My favourite writers are too many. I read a lot from the world literature through English and I also read Bengali literature. I do not want to name any particular writer. I keep my taste open and any good writing from the past and the present attracts me. I do not have the modernist inhibition against romantic literature and rather consider some literatures of the romantic age as of enduring value.

SB: In the contemporary scenario of globalization how do you feel about the future of vernacular or regional literature? Please tell us something about this with special emphasis on Assamese literature.

HKD: I find a bigger threat coming from market forces taking over the field of literature in order to create taste for mediocre literature rather than the effect of globalization. The space is expanding for populist literature due to very clever propaganda by market forces that variously use media and online sites. They sell low taste as high taste through hype. Globalization has enormously increased the space for international languages but vernacular readership has always been small and these literatures have survived in their own space. One threat is there from another angle. Economic dreams have led the middle class to seek education for their children through English and they neglect their mother tongue. But since there is a language and cultural identity for every individual, loss of this identity will eventually have a disturbing impact with consequent effect on vernacular literature. It is the same thing with Assamese literature. My observation is based on the phenomenon I have witnessed in the vernacular scene of Assamese language and literature.

S.B.: What is your future plan as a writer?

HKD: I do not go by any plan for my writing. I will go on writing as long as I feel inspired to write and as long as language does not desert me.

Interview With Sunil Ganguly

Question 1: Sunil Gangopadhyaya is an iconic name in the realm of modern Bengali literature that inspire both respect and admiration from readers and critics alike. But there is also an interesting story behind the emergence of today's Sunil Gangopadhyaya. Very few writers can say that they have spent their childhood in both rural and urban background like you. And both these locales have been important in your works. How much do you think your childhood shaped you both as a person and a writer?

Ans: It is generally accepted and believed that the initial twelve years of life shapes a human individual for the rest of his/her life. In the creation of literature these formative years become important later on. During childhood, child burns his hand, drowns himself in water and thereby he learns lots of things. I spent my early childhood in what is now called Bangladesh. In my writings, I often revisit this place through memory. Then I studied in Calcutta. I experienced the intricacies of urban life in Calcutta. That is why both urban and rural life have been reflected in my writings.

Question 2: Many important historical and political events ran almost parallel to your growth. You have yourself said that your father became a victim to the evil effects of the World War II. There was great famine in the 1940s which shattered human values in Calcutta. You have said, "The decade of the 1940s was the decade of death." You witnessed these and survived through all these upheavals. In your writing we often find an international concern. Do you think all these events had any relevance to your writerly life later on and if so how much and why?

Ans: Every experience is important in building life. Artists or film makers also utilize experience from their lives. We had been witness to many turning points in history. I was born when our country India was under the British rule. India got independence when I was just thirteen-years-old. There used to be many anti-British processions carried on the road. I have said many times that my body carried the marks of British torture. In one such procession organized by people in North Calcutta,

I was spotted by a white policeman. There were a few Indian policemen who used to behave like the Englishmen. They used lathi and tear gas to dissipate the crowd. I was pushed away by a white complexioned policeman and I fell down on the road. I felt extremely proud. We thought that our problems would be solved overnight once we attained independence. We expected that education would be guaranteed to all. Jawaharlal Nehru promised that all black marketeers would be hanged on the lamp-posts. But after independence we discovered to our utter chagrin that it was the black marketeers who dominated everywhere. We felt betrayed, disappointed and we protested. We launched student agitation movement towards the end of our school days and our slogan was, "This independence is a lie. Don't forget this." As a consequence, Left Orientation Movement was born. I became a member of Student Federation. I used to take part in processions. During the college days, Soumitra Chatterjee, the famous film actor and I were regular participants in many such processions. But gradually we saw that the Left party dictated many members. One leader once warned me, "Don't write love poems." I asked him, "Who are you to dictate me?" Gradually, I became disillusioned and quit the party.

Question 3: You have said in one of your books, "The country got independence. But we lost our country." This ambivalent statement brings out your sadness, anger and hatred that the partition of the country resulted in. Do you think Sunil Gangopadhyaya lived with a divided and fractured sense of psychic and emotional leaning towards two countries and do not you think Bengali literature has been more or less silent on the immediate and aftereffects of the partition?

Ans: It is a sad fact that the day of India's Independence is also the day of partition. On that day I saw great celebration – balloon, graffitis everywhere. But at home, I saw tears in my father's eyes. All were sad in our family. Our real country was East Pakistan. We lost our homeland forever and memories of sprawling gardens, ponds and trees tormented us. My mother used to ask, "Shall I never again see the tree that I planted ?" This sentiment can only be grasped by the real sufferers. However, we were better than other refugees. We didn't cross borders like many, nor did we live in camps set up for refugees. We did not experience the horrors of diseases and hunger. Sealdah station was crowded with refugees. It was really unbearable and pathetic to see with one's own eyes their sufferings. In those days there used to be many outhouses of rich people in Calcutta. The refugees took hold of those houses. Police could do nothing. A rich friend of mine too lost his outhouse because the refugees took possession by force. I felt sorry for my friend's family but I was also elated as I was sympathetic towards the refugees. Thus there is a dichotomy here and I used this experience in my novel 'Arjun'. I always identified with the refugees as I could also have been one of them without the grace of destiny.

Yes, it is a fact that there have not been many works in Bengali literature regarding partition. My own novel 'Arjun', Atin Bondopadhyaya's 'Neelkantha Pakhir Khoje', and Prafulla Roy's 'Keyapatar Nouko' are a few exceptions. It is true that as compared to Punjab, Bengali literature has been quite silent on partition. I think that there is a sociological factor behind this. The population exchange was uneven. In Lahore, non- Muslim Punjabis were butchered. In India, Muslims were murdered. There were trains full of dead bodies going towards Pakistan and coming towards India. In spite of population exchange, a large number of Hindus and Muslims stayed in our country. Similarly, many also came here. Pakistan accommodated eleven percent (11%) Hindus and India provided shelter to twenty percent (20%) Muslims. Our Bengali writers were aware of this sensitive issue and real presentation of this horrible reality could have triggered further riots. That is why, many of our writers avoided the issue of partition. And the writers whom I mentioned wrote from nostalgia, not from real point of view.

Question 4: When your family shifted to Calcutta permanently you attained some sort of subjective freedom. You started frequenting cinema and theatre that moulded your cultural taste to a large extent. The hardship of a refugee life and the trauma of shouldering financial burden were also major factors in your early life. You embarked upon a career of tuition that started from 1949 and lasted till 1963. In the midst of all these hardships when and under what circumstances the writer in you emerged?

Ans: During our school vacation, my father used to give me the task of translating a few poems of the English poet, Tennyson. During the afternoon, my father compelled me to sit with this work as he wanted me to be confined to home. I had to translate two poems each afternoon and father thought such exercise would also improve my English. I felt suffocated as it turned out to be very difficult and painful for me. But I could not disobey my father. Suddenly, I discovered a way out. When I realized that father was not correcting the poems line by line then I composed my own poems only keeping the title intact. I found no difficulty in writing poetry. Father could not detect that I was deceiving him. I memorized lots of poems by Rabindranath Tagore and gradually I became conscious of rhyme and metre. I sent a poem to the celebrated Bengali magazine 'Desh' and the poem was published. I was extremely surprised and I thought that the people who selected my poem were probably incompetent. When I was 15 to 16-years-old, I developed weakness for my friend's sister. During those days, free-mixing between boys and girls was not permitted. Even written letters were censored. My first poem titled 'Ekti Chithi' was actually sent to that girl. She read the poem out and could not believe that I wrote it. That was the beginning. In college there were many budding poets and so I also started writing poems.

Question 5: The publication of the poetry magazine 'Krittibash' in 1953 was a landmark event in the history of Bengali literature. Your editorial for the first issue set the tone of the magazine and in that editorial you also expressed your regret for not being able to include poets from East Pakistan. In the subsequent years, 'Krittibash' created a new poetic sensibility and also gave birth to many a novel poetic talents. How do you assess the contribution of 'Krittibash' towards creating a new poetic aesthetics and how do you differentiate the poets associated with 'Krittibash' from their predecessors and how do you relate them to their contemporary context?

Ans: The assessment of 'Krittibash' will be done by others, not by me. When we started the magazine, we were very uncertain. We did not have adequate funds. I earned a meagre amount from tuition. But there was a rebellious spirit in me. I decided that I would only accommodate young poets in 'Krittibash'. We politely refused to publish many senior poets. We did the exact opposite of other mainstream magazines which published poems of established poets only. I was 29 then and interestingly, Shakti Chattopadhaya never wrote before publishing in 'Krittibash'. Shankha Ghosh was also there and gradually we built a young and vibrant poetic group. But one radical change that the poets of 'Krittibash' did was that they pioneered the mode of confessional poetry in Bengali literature. Earlier Bengali poets had to hide themselves behind their creations. But we openly expressed our own secrets of life without any inhibition. We experimented with language by discarding the chaste expression of Rabindranath Tagore.

Question 6: You started your literary career as a poet and later on switched over to other literary genres as well. Your poems are marked by a pervading romantic strain, dexterity in creating visual imageries through apt selection of words, art of embellishment avoiding verbosity and boldness of diction. How do you assess yourself as a poet and do you consider poetry as a special vocation and which poets inspire you as ideals and why?

Ans: When someone asks me about my own favourite poem, I reply that it is yet to be written. I like T. S. Eliot's poems whom I met during the 1960s. Majority of my writing these days is dominated by prose but still today, whenever I write a small poem I get extreme satisfaction. Yes, I believe that poetry is a special vocation and Allen Ginsberg once told that, "poetry is a 24 hours business. Once you get in, you can never get out of it."

Question 7: In the domain of modern love poetry you achieved unparalleled admiration from your readers and the identity of your poetic muse and beloved 'Neera' has puzzled critics and readers over the years because of your stubborn refusal to reveal her identity. The intensity of emotion expressed in your 'Neera' poems remind me of Pablo Neruda's love poems. When and under what circumstances you felt the urge to write these memorable love poems and do you think pure love poems can also achieve dazzling intellectual heights?

Ans: 'Neera' has many shapes in my poetry and when I started writing my 'Neera' poems, I did not have an advanced chalked out plan. **Neera – Naari -- Rani** – I could play with many connotations of the title. Whenever I am asked to explain 'Neera's' identity, I reply, "read the poems. I cannot explain in prose."Every poet wrote love poems.

Yes, love poems can also attain great intellectual heights. My favourite poet Louis Aragon wrote love poems as well as Neruda. Even Jibanananda Das wrote love poems regarding Banalata Sen.

Question 8: Rabindranath Tagore has been a constant source of reference in your literary oeuvre and it is an interesting fact that at one point of time you wanted to repudiate his achievements. How do you view this contradiction and do you think every writer lives with and lives through such contradictions?

Ans: Yes, every writer has contradictions. A writer changes all the time because his experiences cannot afford to be static at one specific point. Though I expressed an anti-Tagore stance in my youth, I was not against the great poet. But I disliked the blind flatterers of Tagore who used to address him as 'Gurudev'. The word 'Gurudev' invokes religious connotation. But even if one wants to deny the importance of Tagore, one must read his works first. Though my friend and fellow writer Sandipan Chattopadhaya used to say that there was no need to read Rabindranath Tagore.

Question 9: The discussion at Coffee House, 'Horbola Club', Signet Press – there was a community feeling among Bengali writers when you started your writing career. You were a part of that milieu which is now missing from the domain of Bengali literary circle. Do you think you gained both as a writer and a human being from such discussions with senior and fellow writers? If so how?

Ans: I admit that the literary atmosphere and climate have changed now. Age is also a factor in this context. When we used to gather in such assemblies, we had more attraction for friends rather than for girls. But later on we drifted apart. But still the young writers get together on a few occasions.

Question 10: You were invited by the Iowa University to participate in its Writers' Workshop Programme in the 1960s. America was undergoing a turbulent socio-political phase at that time which you witnessed with your own eyes. Major American poet, Allen Ginsberg became your friend. But you suddenly decided to come back to Calcutta in spite of getting lucrative opportunities abroad. Do you think such decision marked a decisive phase in your life and how much do you think your stay in the United States enriched your literary and cultural vision?

Ans: Actually, it did wonders to me. I got exposure to the outside world in a big way. I had no way or resource to go to the United States on my own. So, the scholarship money paved my journey. I got the opportunity to meet many contemporary young poets from France, Spain, Italy and other countries. I then realized that Bengali poetry was lagging behind in terms of linguistic experiment and newer trends of world literature. The language of Bengali poetry could not accommodate the harshness of day-to-day life.

Staying back was quite easy for me as Paul Engle arranged a decent job for me in a library. I also got adequate time to write. But then I asked myself – what would I do in life? No doubt I liked writing. I had my girlfriend Margaret there and I also had easy access to food and wine. But when I decided that I would only write in my mother tongue then I realized that I must go back amongst my own people where the living rhythm of the language would be available. The famous Bengali poet Amiya Chakravarty who lived in West found it very difficult to write poetry later on. His poems were full of lexical words as he was away from his root. The living touch was missing from his poems. That is why I decided to come back to West Bengal. Though I knew that it was a great risk as I had to face great financial crisis after coming back.

Question 11: From poetry to novel – it was a paradigm shift in your literary career and with this significant switch over, modern Bengali novel gained one of its greatest practitioners. Was your decision triggered by economic necessity or you yourself felt drawn towards the more sprawling genre? When and under what circumstances you wrote your first novel?

Ans: Apparently it might appear that economic necessity drove me towards writing novels, but looked at from a deeper level, it was not the real reason. There was an urge in me for self-expression and that is why my first published novel was titled "Atmaprakash." When the editor of the reputed Bengali magazine, 'Desh' Sagarmoy Ghosh asked me to write a novel, I was a bit puzzled. I was very nervous regarding the structure of my first novel. Then I remembered Jack Kerouac who once told me, "Writing a novel is no difficult task. Pick up any day from your life. For instance, it may be 23rd March. Then try to remember what happened on that particular day. You were perhaps at a bus stop waiting for a bus. Then the bus came, you boarded the bus. The bus moves ahead. And then your novel also moves ahead." One morning, the younger brother of my friend and poet Shakti Chattopadhaya came to meet me and asked, "Do you know where is Shaktida? He has not gone home since yesterday night." And it was precisely this which inspired the first lines of 'Atmaprakash'. In all my early novels, the bohemian lifestyle of myself and my friends were reflected to a great extent.

Question 12: In each of your novels, you have tried to explore new subject matters and narrative style. Your significant novel in two parts 'Purba Paschim' (East West) covered a huge historical time span that includes many a major events. It has been viewed as an epic saga in prose about Bengali life. When did you conceive the idea of writing this novel and how did you execute your plan?

Ans: My first few novels like 'Atmaprakash', 'Jubok Jubotira', 'Aranyor Dinratri' and 'Pratdwandii' were fictionalized accounts of my own life to a great extent. Then I suddenly realized that I was getting monotonous. So I decided to shift gears. I was always inclined towards history though academically I studied science and economics. History as a discipline always fascinated me. I decided to question a few historical facts. As was mentioned earlier, there was not much literature regarding either partition or the birth of Bangladesh. I realized that though I could question the authenticity of a few historical facts, I could not afford to distort history. I did a thorough research before writing the novel – I read lots of autobiographical, historical accounts and of course, many reminiscences. I went to the India Office Library in London where I got the desired material. After the partition, when both India and Pakistan quarreled over the rights for many rare historical documents, the Britishers decided to take these with them.

Question 13: Bengal Renaissance has been a major area of research and scholarship for a long time. Your novel 'Sei Samay' (translated into English as 'Those Days') is an important socio-cultural domain of a particular period in Bengal. How did you balance your scholarship with the demand of a novelist and why were you drawn towards such a subject?

Ans: Through this novel, I actually wanted to question the authenticity of the Bengal Renaissance and Bengal's consistent claim for such an achievement. Through my engagement with books and archival materials, I could realize that Bengal Renaissance was not a comprehensive achievement like the Italian Renaissance. Bengal Renaissance saw some developments in literature and religion only. There was not any achievement in art and music during Bengal Renaissance. Bengal did not have any classical music or dance forms like Assam and Orissa. But there was an attempt to achieve religious reform by the brahmans that initially appeared to be a welcome movement. But it was confined only within the upper class people and it failed miserably to bring the Hindus to a common platform. A person belonging to servant class or a prostitute's son could never become a Brahmo. Unlike Christianity or Islam, it was not accommodating enough. Thus, ultimately it died down.

Question 14: You have shown extraordinary interest in novelistic life writing and your novel 'Prothom Alo' ('First Light') is a glaring example of that where you portrayed characters like Ramakrishna Paramhansa, Swami Vivekananda, Rabindranath Tagore and others. In more recent times, you have written novels on the lives of a theatre artist Sisir Kumar Bhaduri and the wandering minstrel, Lalon Fakir. Why have you been repeatedly drawn towards this genre and how do you balance fact and fiction in these cases?

Ans: For this sort of genre, I always chose historical characters who brought significant changes. The canvas of 'Pratham Alo' was much larger than anything else. Sisir Kumar Bhaduri brought radical changes in the domain of Bengali theatre and I always consider him as a great modern person. That is why, I wrote 'Nishshanga Samrat' based on his life. Lalon Fakir thought ahead of his time by defying orthodox religious boundaries and he tried to bring harmony between Hindus and Muslims. But the life of this great wandering minstrel has been shrouded in mystery and through my novel on his life I have tried to balance between fact and fiction. In 1905, when Bengal was partitioned for the first time by Robert Clive, it was reunited. But when it was partitioned in 1947, it was different. I have feelings and memories of that period and I knew it would be never reunited again. I wanted to depict a time in this novel when Bengalis through their courage and integrity forced the Britishers to change their decision. I again blended fact and fiction . While writing about history, you cannot deviate from accuracy. But I was not interested in writing history, I was indeed writing a novel and so I created fictional characters that granted me liberty. I cannot afford to change the lives of Ramakrishna Paramhansa, Swami Vivekananda or Rabindranath Tagore. So, I adopted the persona of Bharat that helped me to do that balancing.

Question 15: You have written with equal interest fictions for children. Your detective protagonist, **Kakababu** has enthralled many over the years and **Kakababu** marks a conspicuous departure from the conventional stereotype detectives encountered in many fictions. When and how did you conceive the idea of creating such a character and do you think Bengali writers have payed relatively less attention towards this genre?

Ans: I once met a person in Kashmir who was climbing a hill with the help of a crutch. It was very difficult to do so. When I asked him how he could bear so much pain and difficulty, he replied with a gentle smile, "No, I do not feel any pain. I am not physically climbing. I am doing it mentally. You know there is a saying in Sanskrit that means even a lame person can climb a mountain with the help of God's blessing. But I am doing it with my mental strength, not with God's blessings." I got inspired by that man and in **Kakababu**, I created a prototype of that man. **Kakababu** solves natural mysteries more than solving murder mysteries. I realized the fact that children cannot bear harsh realities. So, in my **Kakababu** tales nobody dies.

Question 16: You have written under the pen-names of Nillohit and Sanatan Pathak and your writings under these names have been hugely popular. Please shed some light regarding writings using these two pen names.

Ans: When I returned from America, I could not manage a job for six long years. But I had to meet the demands of life. So I started writing newspaper features and I wrote a lot of these. But people would have felt tired and disgusted if one man wrote so many different things. That is why I adopted different names. I had another name apart from the names you mentioned – Neel Upadhaya. My Nillohit tales were basically centred around the life of a 27 years-old vagabond who liked to travel, who did not have interest in any job even if he got one and who had a girl friend. Under the name of Sanatan Pathak, I wrote literary pieces and through the name of Neel Upadhaya, I wrote national and international political features.

Question 17: Your artistry in the realm of short story is well known because of their novelty of subject matter and subtlety of expression. I am reminded of your story 'Tajmohole Ek Cup Cha' ('A Cup of Tea at Taj Mahal') in this connection. Do you view short story as a totally different genre that requires a different conception of art and what have been your individual concerns as a short story writer?

Ans: In Bengali literature, there have been many great short stories. Compared to novel, Bengali literature is very rich in short story. Rabindranath Tagore set a very high standard in this domain. So when I started writing short stories, I took the challenge on my own terms.

Question 18: Bengali writers have more or less neglected travelogue as a distinct literary genre. Your books like 'Chabir Deshe Kabitar Deshe' ('In the Land of Paintings and Poems') and 'Itihasher Shopnobhango' ('The Shattering Dreams of History') were notable travelogues because of their perceptiveness and critical viewpoint. What is your assessment regarding this genre and how do view yourself as a practitioner of such mode of writing?

Ans: I like to read travelogues. In order to write good travelogue, one must be well read in the history, culture and literature of that country. I was always fascinated by the poetry and paintings of France. Mere geographical or physical details do not make a sound travelogue. When the socialist world collapsed like an Empire without any bloodshed I was amazed and I had the great fortune to witness that momentous historical event – the fall of the Berlin Wall with my own eyes. I always think that there must be an in-depth analysis in a good travelogue.

Question 19: From a great writer to the President of the country's most prestigious literary organization Sahitya Academy - it has been a fascinating journey. Does Sunil Gangopadhyaya the man still nurture any unfulfilled wish in his heart and what is your future plan as the President of Sahitya Academy and as a creative writer?

Ans: As a creative writer, I still have the urge to write new things. I want to write some more poems, at least two or three more novels. But since the day

I became the president of the Sahitya Academy, my time has been stolen away because of the obvious responsibility. As the President of Sahitya Academy, I want to introduce a few things. I would ensure fellowships to some writers who want to go out by taking leave to concentrate on their creative urges. I also want to encourage the body of children's literature that is much neglected in India. I am introducing an award for children's literature. I would also emphasize on the need for more meaningful interaction between regional Indian authors.

Question 20: Who have been and are your favourite writers and what message would you like to impart to the aspiring writers? How do you view the prospects of our bhasha writers in the immediate future?

Ans: The budding writers should read the best writings of their literature and they must familiarize themselves with their own literary history to write something new and meaningful. These days English is emphasized at the cost of regional languages. Children must know their mother tongue. Even scientists are telling that learning two or three languages makes the brain sharper. The British Government has a notice that announces that every child must learn and speak his/her own language at home. In our country, the parents must be trained thus. Parents should be first taught their own language. Then the children would naturally follow. Even a third language can be learnt. There would be better prospects then. As far as our regional languages are concerned, these will never die as such a large number of people speak these languages.

Interviewer: Subhajit Bhadra

Kabiganga

Translated by Subhajit Bhadra

Originally written by -
Manikuntala Bhattacharjee

Kabiganga! I can faintly remember 'that' when I heard the name for the first time in my life, I was merely a learner of lower primary standard. My father was an administrative officer. He earned a good reputation by his ability to solve the problems of the citizens and also by his honesty and sincerity. As a result, some people propelled by their sense of gratitude to his services felt great to offer some gifts to him. On that day also a man carrying two long pipes entered into our backyards through our backdoor. At a corner of our backyard, I was enjoying a swing which was nicely tied with a bamboo frame. I could not apprehend whether the cause of my father's anger towards him was due to his presence or the long pipes dangling from his hands. He left the verandah and came inside the house. The man with the pipes was keen to say that he did not want to bribe my father and that he brought those things out of love and gratitude, but his speech was still unfinished, he went back towards the same direction of his arrival with difficult steps.

I came across the same person in the afternoon on a public square of the town just two to three hours after the earlier incident. I was just trying to get used to the art of riding on a bicycle then. Cycling became my favourite pastime in my leisure hours. I would manage to ride on the cycle somehow and a boy who was my next-door neighbour would follow me wherever I went.

I would recognize the fellow even from a distance. It seemed that he also was also in search of me. He put his hands on the handle of my bicycle stopping it to move any further. He bought a handful of friend grams from a vendor sitting under a tree and gave all those stuff to me. I said to him straightway, "what did you fill those pipes with?"

   DELVING INTO DIFFERENT LITERARY TERRAINS

"Curd my dear. Its quality was damn good. I wanted to give them to you. But as your father declined to have, I gave them to one of my friends in the name of Kabiganga."

"Who's Kabiganga?"

"I've got a favourite poet. He is as solemn and sacred as the mighty Ganga itself. The kind of high thoughts he expresses through his poems are excellent and if we can manage to put a little of his thoughts into practice, then our life will be worth-living indeed – as good as taking a dip in the holy waters of the Ganga. I keep telling those to all my students when I teach my pupils lessons at the school. I teach them to become as cultural-mined as that of Kabiganga."

"Where does he live? What is he?"

"You'll get to know all these later, my dear."

He smiled affectionately and looking at the setting sun, said to me, "Go home, little lady. Then wash your hands and feet and sit down with something to read."

Coming home, I opened the books but my mind was filled with the haunting thoughts of Kabiganga. I went down memory lane. I found no resemblance whatsoever of the name of the poet that I had seen or heard, not even in my textbooks.

At that period, a little baby also existed in our house. She was none other than my younger sister. Mother kept herself always busy with her. Even in those chilly nights, she could not manage to come to me to keep the blanket on my body in proper order. In a large two-bedded room, I lay with my father while on the other bed lay my younger sister and my mother. I chose to lie with my father. Mother kept the baby pinned to her bosom as if it were a huge fortune or wealth to her. She took utmost care to handle the baby. I heard the light sound emanating from its act of sucking its mother's breast milk which reverberated in all directions. I noticed that act through the dimly, dully and bluishly lit room even though I could hardly keep my sleepy eyes open. Oh! Once my mother certainly had held my tight in her bosom. I took, sucked the nectar of life to my heart's content. The same kind of sounds must have echoed all throughout the room. Just like this, I hope so. My heart became heavy at such a thought. Warm drops of tears rolled down my checks in spite of my best efforts to control them. Perhaps because of the heavy load of grief that my heart had already been burned with, deep sounds of sighs were coming out every time I exhaled. Perhaps,

I could feel my pulse. May be he could understand my feelings as he said instantly the moment I slept on the bedstead, "Move this. Mother and the baby have long slept. Move towards me, darling. I'll tell you nice stories."

Instantly all the loads that my heart seemed to be filled with, evaporated in the air like steam. Truly, he started telling me stories. Most of those were related to either space or under sea-water stories.

Although he sometimes told me stories of ancient mythology, Arabian Nights and to top them all, some wonderful excerpts of the life of Rabindranath Tagore, which were really a feast for my ears, were told to me by him in tandem. Rabidranath was his idol. One day he translated one of Tagore's poems to me. The poem was about the clouds which produce thunder and lightning in the sky. That night, too, was a thunderous one. I was a silent listener of all he said. I put one of my hand on his neck and put one of my legs on his body I listened to those stories in delight and slept. But one night, breaking the poetic subtleties of my father, I enquired to him all of a sudden.

"Who's Kabiganga, papa?"

"Which Kabiganga are you talking about, dear?"

"One who writes poems. He is a man of a great mind."

"Writes poems, huh? Who told you about him?"

I remained silent. I could then remember the man with two long bamboo pipes who went away walking with difficulty in the morning. I also remembered the irritated visage of my father at this sight. I, therefore, debarred myself from telling his name. I preferred to remain silent.

After a while he started uttering something like a soliloquy, "No dear, I don't know a single poet in this name. it may be another name of a new poet. But I know almost all the famous new poets! Whatever it may be, I think he is one of those new poets whose hobby is to write poems. Listen my dear, I prefer the poems full of the description of spring to this poem of Rabindranath. Grow up. You can read them all."

He told a lot of things which I didn't understand as I turned a deaf ear to all his wise deliberations. That man, I thought, which school does he teach in? Where can I meet him once more? Once I meet him. I shall try to get all the requisite information about Kabiganga. Kabiganga! As sacred as the Ganga river, I really became curious about the man in a peculiar way.

Two weeks after this, I came across that teacher once more. My mother knew how to knit sweaters by wool. It required four sticks to knit the neck region of a sweater. She sent a boy of the next door to know if such a stick could be found in a definite shop in that locality. He loved me very much. He told – "Come, let's go together."

I went. Again I met the same fellow under a tree by the public square. I said, "Uncle, can you remember me?"

"Why not ? I can. But you need not call me uncle. Just call me 'Sir'. I have got many students like you. I teach each of them to be honest men and women. How we can make our lives sacred by high thinking ...."

"Like Kabiganga ?"

He seemed to jump up in joy hearing the name of Kabiganga from my mouth. He held my hands and said, "Let's go onto the bridge and there I shall give you lessons about a river. Do you know that this river has not become as sacred as the Ganga ? Doesn't it sound amazing ? "

My next door boy told me somewhat harshly, "Come, let's go back home soon."

The man felt awkward a little. I, too, became a little annoyed with that boy. On that occasion, he turned a deaf ear to all my protests and dragged me home almost forcefully. All the way back home he murmured, "The market is full of all such nuisance these days. You must not come this way on your bicycle."

This boy with filial gratitude thought himself to be gentle and honest. The persons that his parents abhorred, were considered no better than insects by him. I particularly disliked such an attitude of him.

I dragged my hands from him. Being astonished he asked, "What's wrong? Why are you so angry?"

"I had something to discuss with that teacher, but I couldn't."

"Teacher ? Who's the teacher ? Oh, you mean that fellow ? Don't you ? But let me tell you that he is a bit angry by nature. He always abuses the river standing on the bridge in the morning. He takes pleasure in ruling the groves of the Amara field."

"But he is a teacher."

"Where does he teach ?"

"In a school."

"Can't say for sure. May be he is. But you shouldn't go near such persons. Who knows what he is. He may be a child lifter, you know !"

I, however, did not like this remark. I was least scared about this class of people called child lifters. Perhaps this was the result of the effect of an adventurous story which my father once told me.

Again, I became unmindful at my studies. Oh Sir! Why do you abuse the river ? And the grooves ? Why are you bent upon showing your physical prowess. I was really shocked, very shocked at heart. The undercurrent of curiosity suddenly and quietly moved towards the teacher!

Many days later, I came across the teacher once more. This time I felt extremely excited the moment I saw the person. One of my teeth was about to fall off. My father took me up to a dentist to get the tooth uprooted. Seeing him, I cried out to my father, "There is he, my teacher, there ...."

"Teacher ?"

"Oh Sir, should I move towards the teacher quickly and get back ?"

Father did not say anything. I had many teachers at that time besides the academic teacher. Yes, I frequented the music and art classes regularly.

I rushed to him in a jiffy. Seeing me, he asked affectionately – "Alakananda, where have you been so long?"

"Yes!"

I was extremely surprised. This wasn't my name. had he not recognized who I was?

Before I could say anything, he again asked, "Are you alright ? Are you studying well ? You got to come first in the scholarship examination! But, who have you come here with ? With Sir ?"

I was restless, "Oh God ! How can I ask what I want to know ?"

Thoughtlessly I cried out, "Sir, tell me something about Kabiganga."

"He is my favourite poet."

"Where does he live ?"

"By the river in my village."

"What does he do there?"

"We have much paddy fields. There is a watch-tower like house on the middle of the paddy field. He climbs up and lives on that. If you wish, I can take you there."

Immediately, I moved my face towards my father. He was busy in talking with a gentleman.

Again, I moved towards the teacher. And I started thinking seriously how to pay a visit to that river bank. Because, my father, by any means, wouldn't allow me to go there, for sure.

With hope and excitement, I whispered, "I'll go."

"Will you, really ?"

I nodded my head. He said, Then you should keep waiting outside your house. I shall bring a jutkaful of vegetables to sell in the market. While going back, I'll take you with, will that please you, little lady ?"

"Tomorrow, but when?"

Without having a word, he looked at my face and smiled affectionately and moved off to meet my father. He said something politely with folded hands. I noticed my father reciprocating him with gentleness.

The following day my sister's 'annaprasana' was being celebrated with pomp and splendour. Lots of our acquaintances gathered inside and outside of our house. They were enjoying the luncheon with rice. They ate with smile and jokes. It was only I who couldn't eat. Indeed, it was I. I was having furtive glances towards the entrance door.

All at once, I came across the teacher. Having seen him, I slipped my feet into a pair of slippers. He said, "sit on my jutka. My daughter loves to side on too. She keeps riding on my jutka."

He wrapped a traditional napkin or 'Gamocha' across his head and came here like a jutka driver. He wore a soiled and worn-out shirt on his body.

Looking at all possible directions, I took the initiative to ride on the jutka. To ride on a jutka was not as easy as riding on a rickshaw. But, somehow I managed to sit on it and he pushed along. My heart was beating fast and breath of air was coming out of my mouth. Then, I was on my way to the river bank with my teacher where Kabiganga lived on a watchtower like hut. He was as sacred as the river Ganga. What kind of high-thinking he might undergo ? What was really called high-thinking ?

But I asked some different questions to him.

"You don't like this river. Do you ?"

"You are right, I get crossed. I call it names. But, it is always deaf to my words."

"How can a river hear ? Has it an ear ?"

He looked as if he wanted to halt the jutka and retorted. "What do you say ? A river has hands and feet, nose and ears as we have. It has a living soul. A river has a life. Otherwise how can it flow continuously. Else it would have been fixed as that mass or rock."

"Why do you abuse the river ?"

"It carries garbage, but that I do not take into account. But when it rains, it submerges the villages near its banks and causes innumerable pains to us and our paddy fields. I keep telling it so much – Oh river, be gentle and calm. But no, it does not listen to my appeals at all."

His speeches were becoming increasingly unintelligible to me. I did not pay heed to the latter part of his speech. Again I said, "Why do you punish the groves in the Amara field ?" He burst into laughter. I looked at his face. He looked at one or two pedestrians walking along on the road in a lovely afternoon.

"What do you think ? Don't you know ? They are my students. I teach them to be as humble as a grassland in a forest. No boy or a girl could show discourtesy in Amara field in their presence. Just once you need to go there and see for yourself the wears and tears you may find on your clothes."

Meanwhile, I started thinking about the next door boy of my house while the teacher was talking in tandem. He called this man crazy.

I swallowed something and asked slowly –

"Sir, where is your school ?"

"I have got many schools. Even in the paddy field. Its Headmaster is, of course, Kabiganga. There was a light ripple in my chest. Does the teacher have all the pupils like the grove in the forest ? "

Looking at his face, I started moving. That road was inclined on one side. The teacher said, "road was inclined on one side." The teacher said, "Hold the jutka tightly using both of your hands. We shall move rapidly now." We really slided down the road. I was thrilled to experience the gust of wind lashing against my mouth and cheeks. I asked, "How far is the paddy field from here?"

"Here we are, little lady. Come, get down. We'll keep the jutka over here. You'll have to follow me all the way, okay ?"

The paddy field was full of cereals. He dragged the 'dhoti' he wore with one hand and counted one, two, three. Then he started running with long strides. I was about to laugh. I, too, started running. Finding it difficult to run on a broken road, I got my slippers at hand, and started running. My little laughs of pleasure echoed all round the field and it looked as if the cereals were in a festive mood.

Running on the field, we reached the spot where the watch-tower like house stood. There was a ladder to climb up.

Having controlled his breathing, the teacher said, "This was the house I was talking about."

I raised my neck and looked up. The teacher said, "Follow me as I go up. You won't fall down. Come this way." I somehow managed to climb up the ladder.

Oh, this was another world! I felt out of the world when I sat on top of that house. The smiles of cereals all across the field, a free flowing river at a short distance, the blue open sky and I was in the midst of everything. There was none to watch my every movement and none to rule me even. I was free. I was really free here.

I took a deep breath. The teacher gave me a bamboo pipe and said, "Take it to your lips and blow it. I looked at his face. Taking the .pipe on my hand, I asked, "But Kabiganga ? Where's he?"

"Okay, you blow it in his name."

I became a bit uneasy. How could I call someone by his name who was elder than I. I asked again, "And your school ? Kabiganga may be there !"

He burst into a peel of laughter. He said, "This is the school. All the cereals that you can see are my students. Kabiganga is the Headmaster here. Look, if there is a cloud in the sky !"

"Looking at the sky, blow the pipe. He'll answer you."

Tears were about to roll down from my eyes. Did the teacher go crazy ? He stood up. Spreading his hands apart he looked up at the sky and said, "Oh mighty Kabiganga, make me as free and noble as you are. So that I can laugh under the open sky. So that I can think well about all living on this earth. So that I can as clear as you are. Oh Kabiganga, bless me with one or two rhyming couplets from your great poem. Bless me. Look, a new person has come to meet you. She is as sacred as you are. Alakananda."

I was amazed at this and looked at the teacher's face. The teacher told me in gentle tone, "Take the pipe to your lips and blow as I said. He'll surely answer."

I blew the pipe. To my utter surprise, I found the echoes of the sound I generated and I thought I got my reply.

The teacher said, "Oh! that's great. Now speak your heart out. If you have anger or sadness, speak it out now."

Touching the pipe at my lips, I told in a shaky tone, "My mom is great. But after the birth of my younger sister, she is no longer showing me love and affection as before. This makes me really unhappy."

"Tell something about your anger too."

"Yes, I have anger. I feel angry at the boy living next door. He cares little of the people who are not rolling in money. Even he neglects the poor students that I study with. If some of them come to see me, he drives them away."

"Now, tell what do you want to become."

"I want to be grown up. I want to do whatever I like. I would like to keep everybody happy."

"Say more, say more."

"I want to be as great as you are. I would like to remain in that top-house like my teacher."

"Now blow it thrice."

I blew it. So did he. Then we climbed down the top house. I chewed some seeds of peas and sat on the jutka to go back home. It was entirely a different situation at home. I saw from a distance that a large crowd gathered near our entrance door. I thought about the invited guests. But when I drew myself near the house I found it was not so as I thought. My father was talking to policeman wearing 'Khaki' uniform. Before I could reach the entrance door, the 'Khaki-clad' policemen surrounded me from all sides. Someone of them pulled me from the jutka and started asking me critical questions which put me to a great discomfort. Father rushed in there and said, "Take this fellow away". He looked at me and said, "You come this way."

I was trembling in utter terror. I could not feel, whether I was dead or alive. Looking downwards, I had replied to all the questions asked by my father and the police station in-charge. Father said, "Go, rush to your mom."

I grasped my mother and cried loudly. I cried although I had no feeling of any fault or crime or repentance. I was shocked to see people feeling so much anxious at this trifle. I also felt troubled and anxious about the condition that my teacher was in. The person who got displeased to see a man coming with two bamboo pipe-full of curd, would he like the same person taking his daughter away on his jutka to a unknown place ? Will he take it easy ?

I moved my face from my mother's chest and looked at the road. The person who filled up my life with new words, gave me the taste of a freedom that would be taken away by some 'Khaki-clad', rough and tough guys who would literally drag him all the way to the police station. My loving teacher was silently walking with them as if nothing had happened to him. His hands were tied with the cruel handcuffs. I cried twice as loudly as I cried earlier. And I started weeping then.

On that night, my father who was lying next to me was awake and I said to him, "You need not tell me a story today. Answer me, papa."

"What ?"

"Is my teacher a strong man ? So affectionate, he can make so much fun. We climbed up the top house and taking pipes, we blew towards the sky, we told everything to God. We ran and played on the field. The cereals on the field were his students. The field was his school. Kabiganga was their Headmaster. Like God, he hid himself inside the clouds.

"Sleep now."

"I won't. You'll have to tell. Tell me now."

"Yeah, he is stout. You saw his school and his students. Didn't you ?"

"Huh, that is not done. Your Rabindranath, too, taught the railings on the verandah as his students. Taking a cane in his hand, he beat his students !"

Father grasped me close to his chest. I kept asking those questions while I was weeping for a long time. Father was silent. He was caressing me with his hands on my back and on my head. He released deep breaths. But he spoke nothing. Truly, he had no answer.

I was not allowed to go to school on the next day. I was being guarded at home and remained confined there. The person behind the clouds might have felt my anguish. Mother started showing me as much affection as she had shown to my younger sister. She took me to her laps. She took care of my body. And on bedtime during the day she took the opportunity to ask me a few questions quietly. Mother's quiet questions were – "Did your teacher take you to his laps ?"

"No, he didn't."

"You've put on such a nice frock. How about your pantie. Let me see. Did he say such words ?"

"No, he didn't say so. Why will he say so ? Do the teachers at the school ever say so ?"

Mother kept quiet. In the afternoon, the boy next door called me to sit on a swing. He sat on a stool next to me and was filing his nails. Feeling the situation, I said to him, "Is the teacher at the police station ?"

"No, he is not there. I heard that he would be sent to Tezpur the following morning."

"Why to Tezpur ?"

"Don't you know ? There is a lunatic asylum there."

******

Many years passed by since that incident took place, but when I closed my eyes, I found my memories were as fresh as that day. Thinking about my teacher and Kabiganga, I noticed many times that tears rolled down my cheeks. Placing my feet on a stool, I climbed up a guava tree lying on our backyard and making a pipe with a piece of paper I blew it many times. While taking bath, I spread my hands upwards and taking the name of Kabiganga. I cried towards the water falling from the bath shower. I covered my face with my face and said weepingly, "Sir …. Sir … I not forget you, Sir !"

******

Having stayed in this fashion for days, my father took all of us to his younger brother's house to stay there. There we managed to stay for ten days. Then all of us prepared to move towards a new place and to experience a new environment. Yes, my father was transferred to another town by virtue of his job.

Since then I started looking for the table of education so that I could take a dip in the great Ganga of my life.

Radiance Of The Setting Sun

Madan Sarma

A languid afternoon. The sun was going down. Bidyut Choudhury was sitting outside on a cane chair. A lone crow flew over his head and sat on the tin roof of Mr. Bhuyan's newly built house. The lonesome cawing of the crow made the afternoon more lonesome.

Mr. Bhuyan's son Abhinab was getting married. The new bride would come home after a few days. The responsibility of painting the newly built house fell on Naren Barman, the painter who lived in the neighbourhood. Work was going on in full swing for a fortnight. After giving his helpers some instructions, Barman came downstairs for a smoke.

Bidyut Choudhury lived in a rented house just behind Mr. Bhuyan's newly built house. Choudhury's face lit up the moment he saw Barman at a distance. He left his chair and advanced towards the iron fence that stood between the two houses. He took a 'bidi' from Barman and lit it.

Sometimes the two men would stand like this on either side of the fence and felt nostalgic for the two shops of the two villages that they had left behind. The smoke of 'Banar Boy' bidis, entwined with translucent fog in the murky light of the two hurricane lamps hanging in front of the shops, would draw them into the warm inside of the shops filled with familiar smells. Since they were of the same age and had passed through similar experiences of life, it was natural for them to grow quite close.

Bidyut Choudhury said, coughing and lowering his voice a little, "My wife will create a scene if she finds out that I'm smoking. She says, why do you smoke, why such outdated bad habits? And how can anyone smoke a bidi?"

Barman laughed. Choudhury joined him and took a long and satisfying puff at his bidi. Smiling, they exchanged glances to indicate that it was useless to try to make women understand these things.

Choudhury was not in any regular employment anymore. Two years had gone by since his retirement from a company job. There was neither any pension nor post-retirement benefits; these were not meant to be there. It was not a government job. Now he took care of the accounts in a shop. He had spent his whole life in a rented house. The two of them - he and his wife -would manage somehow. Sometimes he wondered -should he go back to his house in the village. He just thought, but did nothing concrete about it. Naren Barman seemed to be more active in such worldly matters. He had built a house of his own but had not painted the walls yet. Bidyut Choudhury often told him, "You go on painting other people's houses and the walls of your house are yet to be painted." Naren Barman just twirld his moustache, and smiled.

A lone wagtail, lively and loving, flew in, danced for a while in the reddish sunlight in the open space near Choudhury's house, and flew away.

"She comes here sometimes. It makes me happy," Choudhury said.

"Who? There is no one nearby. Who are you talking about?"

"I am talking about the wagtail."

"Wagtail?"

Barman didn't show much interest in birds and animals. Letting a whiff of smoke out, he twirled his moustache and was about to say something funny, when suddenly a door at the back of Barua's house opened.

Both of them tried not to look towards it as it was the door of the room where the newly wed couple of the Barua family lived. The room was built exclusively for the couple who got married nearly a month ago.

The first person to come out of the door was Barua's eldest son, Akan. He was well-dressed. He was followed by his wife, the new bride, who was even more beautifully attired. Choudhury thought her name was Ranjana and Barman said she was Anjana. Both of them had not tried to ascertain who was correct.

Barman said, lowering his voice, "Isn't she very beautiful?"

Choudhury agreed, "Yes, but after marriage all girls look more beautiful."

Both of them smiled, as if both began to remember something pleasant. Choudhury looked towards his left and Barman looked towards his right at the same time. Instantly the sweet smell of a perfume filled their nostrils and lingered in the blank space between the two. Both of them took a deep breath and started to move away from each other....

*****

As soon as one opened the door, along with the familiar smell of the mangoes, or rather sliding over the smell of the mangoes, a lively and captivating fragrance wafted in.

As the afternoon shadow enveloped the mango tree and the breeze passed through its leaves and glided by the vermillion-coloured mangoes, the shy youth Bidyut moved hesitantly towards his wife Jonali who was standing under the mango tree. Jonali began to look more beautiful, lovelier and more endearing than ever. Her full body was filled with the anxiety and pleasant feelings of her forthcoming motherhood. She placed her head shyly on Choudhury's chest and looked at the descending darkness.

A vermillion-coloured mango fell from the tree. Choudhury's mother called out from the house, "Jonali, it's almost dark. Why don't you come in?" The old lady grumbled, "This time of the evening ghosts and goblins move about..."

Bidyut's mother believed that ghosts, spirits and goblins moved about freely in the bamboo groves and thickets near this riverside village at this hour. These spirits possessed the young women and pregnant women.

Hearing his mother's voice, Bidyut hurried towards the road. He came back home only after spending two hours in a friend's place. In those days, any husband who spent a little more time with his wife or who showed some affection or love for his wife openly was regarded as a henpecked husband. And now?

A few weeks later as the season of the mangoes came to an end, Jonali stumbled on a mango root and fell. Oh, how she lay in a pool of blood – Oh! It was as if it happened yesterday. That pain of losing their child still tormented their souls. After that she suffered miscarriage twice. Jonali broke down after these incidents and then they left everything to settle down here.

******

The familiar smell of chemical paints wafted across to him. No, not the smell of paints, Naren guessed, it was the smell of the colour powder people used to sprinkle around during the Holi festival. He was about to smear colour powder on Rumi's cheeks, but stopped abruptly. She was trying to push him away. There was a naughty smile playing on her lips. He whispered in fake anger or with real affection, "let Bihu come, and then- ---.

Many years ago, Naren Barman's great-grandfather came to Upper Assam in search of livelihood or in an attempt to put an end to the incessant quarrel in the family . They might have heard of the place from the people of their village who came to live here before. After spending a few years here and there, they started living permanently in this place which remained cut off from the outside world for almost six months of the year. They might have decided to stay permanently in this flood ravaged area because of the availability of arable land. While carrying on farming, his parents continued the hereditary trade or profession of making earthenware utensils. These utensils were loaded onto a boat and were taken to far off villages to sell. In one of such journeys Naren quarreled with his father and left home. After wandering here and there, he reached this city. Here he learned to paint houses with some Bihari or Bengali painters. A season of Bihu passed, but Naren could do nothing. Rumi lost her patience waiting for him. In the next Bihu, one day at dusk Naren just lifted Rumi from the river landing, put her in his boat and brought her to the city. They settled here. Many years had passed. Then the news came that his father had died. He went home only to find that his brothers had already divided the land and property among themselves, treating him to be dead.

Naren's elder brother Khagen said, "You live in the city now. I'm sure, you are not going to cultivate or make earthenware utensils anymore."

Naren was trying to make a pot on the wheel then. He angrily hurled it at his brother's face and returned to the city. He came back and reached home in the evening when people usually lighted earthen lamps under the basil plant. Rumi was lighting an incense stick when Naren quietly approached her and embraced her from behind. A fragrance mixed with the fragrance of the incense sticks enveloped him, and------.

******

Choudhury and Barman looked at each other's eyes and without any intention of doing so they noticed that Barua's son Akan alias Kalyan was saying something to Ranjana or Anjana and then he almost embraced her. The couple might have been oblivious of the world outside. Smearing the light of the reddish setting sun on their faces and bodies, they advanced towards the gate in front.

Two long sighs came out from either sides of the iron fence.

******

    Delving Into Different Literary Terrains

Suddenly, hearing the muffled sound of crying from Choudhury's house, Barman looked at his friend's face. The severe stomach pain that Choudhury's wife often suffered might have started again. Whenever Choudhury advised to take her to a good doctor, he just replied, "Yes, I'll have to take her outside the state." Barman knew it would never happen. Choudhury might not have the means to do that. Choudhury hurried towards his home without saying anything.

After some time Barman started to climb the stairs of the new house. He took out the mobile phone from the pocket of his dirty shirt and made a call to his wife to remind her to take the medicine. The phone rang, but no one responded from the other end. What if she was lying senseless? There was no one else at home.

As if darkness fell all of a sudden. The weather turned chilly. The helpers were in a hurry to go home. The lights were switched on in the new room of the Bhuyan's. He thought of working for some more time. Rumi knew that he would be late. But she would wait for Barman for dinner. Their neighbors slept early. But in Barman's house lights were still on till late. He called once more. No reply. He started worrying. He didn't wait.

As he was getting ready to leave, Abhinab, the bridegroom, said, "You've finished early today?"

"I'll come early tomorrow morning. My wife is not well. Choudhury's wife has taken ill. He doesn't take her to a good doctor, only gives her good for nothing homeopathic medicines."

Abhinab said, "Have some tea."

"I will have more tomorrow."

Abhinab smiled. His father was working in the garden. Abhinab said, "Why do you need to do these things? Just sit somewhere quietly for a while."

Bhuyan stood up. Looking at Barman he said, "They are bent upon making an old man out of me."

Barman smiled. Opening the gate Barman stepped onto the half dark half-lit road. All of a sudden he felt very lonely and old. Yes, he was getting old but he couldn't think of spending time idly. He was very worried about his wife Rumi. Sometimes he said to Choudhury, "It's good that we don't have children, you know. There will be no sorrow of leaving anyone alone."

"Anyone?" Choudhury asked smiling, "And what about the sadness of leaving this beautiful world?"

"What are you saying? Barman is not as educated as Choudhury. He doesn't understand many things. He understands that it's not safe to be alone at this age."

******

Choudhury was gazing at his wife with love and anxiety. Jonali was closing her eyes hard as if trying to keep off the pain. Choudhury took the bamboo stool near the bed and sat there. He arranged the quilt over her body, put away the locks of hair from her face and looked at her face. The house was still. Almost fifteen years had gone by since they had taken the house on rent. They had not faced any problem only because the landlord was a good person. One day Mr. Kakati, the landlord said to him, "Why you don't buy the house?" Choudhury couldn't guess whether he was joking or he was serious. Mr. Kakati had many big rented houses, much bigger than this one.

After his retirement the number of Choudhury's friends quickly dwindled. He became lonely. Jonali was lonelier than him. She could not forget the pain of losing their children before they were born. He too couldn't. The families of Choudhury's two brothers expanded and with it increased problems too. The house built during their father's time seemed to be smaller. Quarrel never stopped in the house. At that time he left home with Jonali after getting a job in a steel factory. He never returned to that house, neither could he build a new one. If someone asked, he said, "I have my father's house. But he knows, he is just a guest in that house, not anything else."

Jonali opened her eyes and looked at him. Then she cried out in pain. He couldn't understand what to do. The pain might have stopped after sometime. Jonali said in her weak voice, "Let's go home."

"Home?" Choudhury was astonished, Isn't this place home where they had spent fifteen years?

"Let's go to our home in the village, will you? If something happens to me, who'll look after you here?"

Choudhury looked at Jonali's face speechlessly. She never said these things. What had happened to her? He said, "don't say such things now."

Jonali cried out in pain once more.

Choudhury felt very helpless. His eyes turned moist.

******

Coming to the front yard, Naren Barman stopped, as if frozen. Sounds of laughter came from the front room. He failed to guess what's happening and just went into the room. He heard the melodious voice of his wife Rumi:

"The forest catches fire, everyone can see

Ashes fly in the sky

My body catches fire, no one can see

It burns the heart to ashes…"

Some girls began to sing after her.

Pushing the curtain aside, Barman looked around. It's really surprising. Pushing all the neatly arranged furniture of the room to the wall, a group of girls were sitting on the floor.

"What's this?" Barman asked.

"We're practising Bihu," a girl said. "Aunt is teaching us to dance."

"Aunt?"

Rumi looked at him with a smile, "I have grown old, haven't I?"

"No, no, no one is too old to sing or dance Bihu," Barman said. "But you said you are ill."

"Now, I am fine," Rumi said shyly.

"How can you not be fine with these girls by the side?"

The girls started laughing. Barman felt relieved. Youth was amazing. It could sweep away all sadness in the blink of an eye.

Someone knocked at the door of the drawing room. Choudhury went out controlling himself. It was Bhuyan's son, Abhinab at the door.

"Is aunt all right?"

"Yes, these things happen often."

Abhinab went into the house without heeding him, as if he was a frequent visitor there . Before Choudhury could reach Jonali's room, Abhinab came out of it, saying, "I am calling in a doctor, you stay with aunt. She has to be hospitalized if necessary."

Abhinab went out without giving him a chance to say anything. His marriage was drawing near. He had got so many things to do. Yet, he had come out to help another person. He was really a good man. He didn't give him the chance to say that he had no capacity to admit her in a hospital and bear the expenses. He came back and sat down near Jonali. She whispered, "I'll go home."

******

The weather was getting warmer. The days looked brighter. Jonali's pain too decreased after her return from a week's stay in the hospital.

That day Choudhury and Jonali were sitting outside on the cane chairs. The radiance of the setting sun was warming their bodies. Seeing Barman coming towards them, Jonali went into the house to bring another chair.

Barman sat in the chair left by Jonali and asked directly, "Are you thinking of leaving the place for good?"

"Who told you?"

"I heard when I came to Bhuyan's house the other day."

"Yes, that thought crossed my mind," Choudhury said. Jonali often fell ill. "What will happen if something happens to me?"

"We too are in the same state. Who knows what the future holds for us? At times I too think like you. And sometimes I think – there are so many people like us everywhere," Barman said. After a pause, he asked again, "Are you really going to leave us?"

Jonali came out with a bamboo stool in her hand. Barua's new daughter-in-law Ranjana also came to the backyard to hang the clothes to dry. Nowadays, Ranjana talked to Jonali for hours, standing near the fence. Sometimes she came to Choudhury's house too.

Ranjana smiled at Jonali. "How are you, aunt?"

Jonali went near the fence. Both of them started talking busily in a hushed voice.

Sounds of laughter came out of Bhuyan's house, now filled with so many people. Choudhury lifted his head and looked in that direction. In the balcony of Bhuyan's house Abhinab and his wife burst into laughter, then stopped as they saw them and then waved their hands at them.

Barman was looking at Choudhury's face anxiously. Choudhury smiled and looked all around through the radiance of the setting sun. All around him he found the restlessness and bustle of life, surrounding him there was the companionship of the people whom he had known for ages. Leaving all these where would he and Jonali go? Well, one day they all must go, still –

Barman won't understand all those. Looking at the familiar, happy wagtail dance in the open space near the fence, Choudhury said as if to himself, "I haven't thought about leaving for good –."

******

Translation of the original story in Assamese **"Henguli Belir Pohar"** included in the collection of short story **Athaba Prem (Love),**2nd edition,2013, pp 139-148. Astha Publications, Guwahati.

Translated by Subhajit Bhadra

Review Of Shera Panchashti Golpo (50 best short stories) By Nilanjan Chattopadhyay

Published by Days Publishing in 2012.
Price: Rs 400

Reviewed by : Subhajit Bhadra

In the realm of contemporary Bengali literature Nilanjan Chattopadhyay has carved a niche for himself by dint of his short stories which are examples of the rich literature of the said culture. Apart from being an accomplished short story writer, Nilanjan is also a very good and original novelist. His variety of themes and novelty of expression adds to the stories an aura of their own. Nilanjan experiments with subject matter, theme and technique and each of his stories is unique because of the writer's deft touch. He chooses his character basically from middle class background and provides a scrutiny of their behavior, psychology and life style. Nilanjan successfully blends reality and imagination in his stories and this fact becomes his strength. He uses metaphors, images and symbols in his stories and his language is chaste and urbane. The book under review highlights Nilanjan's variety which is his major strength. Nilanjan's stories and novel should be translated into English and other Indian languages to make it widely available.

In Gandha (Smell) the protagonist, Jeeten hails from a middle class background and he does not feel any moral qualms to do corrupt practice. The story starts with a peculiar incident of a mad dog which suddenly starts to frequent the residential complex of Jeeten and everybody seems to be nauseated by the vomiting smell of the liquid that comes out of the mouth of the dog. Jeeten lives two simultaneous lives - one that of a nice middle class gentleman who has earned the respect of the people around him and the other of a corrupt lusty individual who has an extra-marital relation with a lady called Bashanti who, however, wants to suck money from Jeeten. The smell seems to be symbolic in this story in the sense that

Jeeten can both literally and metaphorically understand towards the end that the vicious dog resides inside him and he also prepares him to kill the dog with a stick but he has to stand up in darkness being at a loss.

In **"Do Nomboor Ashami" (Convict Number 2)** a simple innocent man is compelled to commit suicide as he is pressurized to become the scapegoat for a rape case. All the pretentious behavior of the people of the village including the behavior of the corrupt police officer is brought to light by Nilanjan and the story becomes a testimony of suffering of innocent people who often have to sacrifice their lives in order to save the people in power. In such a sad predicament a writer can only show the suffering but cannot offer solution. Nilanjan builds this story brick by brick and is ultimately able to bring out the pathos.

Shahaber Dukkho (The Grief of the Officer) explores the loneliness of an aged government officer who has never allowed any one near him any space to breathe freely. He has always shown his rude manner and patriarchal attitude both in office and at home and thereby distanced himself from his near and dear ones. The story takes a dramatic turn when his son rebels against him by first choosing English literature as his subject instead of Computer Science as desired by the father and also by becoming a professor. The rebellion reaches its zenith when the son informs the proud and self-controlled officer that he is going to marry a girl who was once his classmate and the son also announces that his mother would also move away from the officer's home along with the son in his new house. One day the proud officer goes on a long drive and ruminates over his life and it is exactly at this point he realizes that how essential in life it is to love and to be loved. The author Nilanjan here seems to speak here on behalf of lonely individuals who make their lives miserable by empty pride and vanity. Nilanjan sings the song of love and creates an elegy of boredom and lovelessness in the officer's life.

In Bhar (Heaviness), Nilanjan again chooses a character called Shubhendu, a typical middle class character who is corrupt in the truest sense of the term as he books a flat for himself in a posh area by paying a handsome amount of 2 lakhs and he arranges this money through a corrupt deal in his office. When his wife congratulates him that he has been able to book the flat through his hard earned money he feels a peculiar weight and guilt and this fact is aggravated by the murder of his honest brother-in-law. Nilanjan shows the contrast and almost slaps the central character Shubhendu who cannot resist his greed and that is where the success of the storyteller lies. There is both "telling" and " showing" in the story as suggested by Wayne C. Booth in his monumental book titled **'Rhetoric of Fiction'**.

Durer Akash (The Far Away Sky) brings to life the pathos of life and the frustration left behind by the relation that could not flower fully. Sunita, the protagonist is married into the family where she has to take care of everything and her husband does not care about her emotions and sentiments. The sudden visit of Sunita along with her husband to Chandipur brings back a flood of memory when she visited the same spot along with her family members and lover Shaurav ten years ago. During that visit Shaurav confessed to Sunita that he was a revolutionary and was even a brutal murderer but he also talked about his repentance and the futile dream of a new revolutionary society. Shaurav could realize the blatant truth that revolution could not be achieved through bloodshed and this realization provided him with a new opportunity to recognize his life. But one day he was shot dead by the police and Sunita could only nurture the sad memory and their momentarily love-life. After ten years when Sunita visits Chandipur again along with her busy husband she searches and finds out the carved letter on the stone of a mountain which was done by Shaurav and tears roll down from her eye which she desperately tries to hide from her husband. It is a deeply moving human story where the twin qualities of sensitivity and compassion are evoked. The language of the story is also at par with the theme and the readers come across a beautiful sentence like "the sea is lying like an indifferent monk."

In **Dushon (Pollution),** the central protagonist Kumaresh works as a clerk in a government office and one day he earns the wrath of the union leader who wants a favor from Kumaresh. The union leader wants the transfer of his girlfriend and then one day Kumaresh sees both of them in a cinema hall and he also marks the movement of the hands of the union leader around the girl's upper part of the body. Kumaresh cannot tolerate this tainted relation and he refuses to sign on the office file of the transfer of the girl. As a result of this unpleasant incident this simple and honest man gets transferred to another department where there is hardly any work and where Kumaresh has to work under filthy conditions and circumstances without the assistance of anyone.

He gradually finds him into a cocooned existence and whatever he does goes wrong, a fact which earns the wrath of his boss. But Kumaresh charges his officer one day in a sudden burst of anger and immediately after that he goes back to his home where he discovers his wife indulging in an illicit relation with a man whom Kumaresh also knows and a person who pretends to be their family friend. In a sudden burst of anger and frustration Kumaresh strangulates his wife and in a crazy manner he rushes to a nearby police station and confesses his guilt and also expresses his desire to sleep for sometime which astonishes the police officer. Nilanjan has been able to chart out Kumaresh's downfall almost in a crude naturalistic style which reminds one of Zola's work and the writer's masterstroke elevates an ordinary narrative into an extraordinary height.

In **Jelkhanar Jangla (The Window of the Prison House)** is a wonderful tale of the freedom and confinement of an artist who has been taken as a prisoner because he supposedly wrote anti-national articles and involved himself with anti-state elements. When he is given the sentence for lifelong imprisonment he only appeals to the judge that he would require his artistic equipment so that he can paint and survive. He surprisingly paints a window on the wall of the prison which brings forth fresh and vibrant light to his cell and this act earns the wrath of the jailor who accuses the artist of creating nuisance. To the jailor this drawn window appears to be artificial but to the artist it appears to be real because he has painted it with the quest for freedom. Ultimately the artist flies out of the window into an open space where the jailor sheds tears by realizing for the first time in his life how imprisoned he is in his own world. Nilanjan shows the duality of reality and illusion and champions the victory of art over everything else.

Gotanugolik Premer Golpo Othoba Pikashor Chobi (A usual Love Story or Picaso's Painting) is a post-modern tale where Nilanjan experiments with both texture and structure of the narrative. It speaks of the confinement and ultimately liberation of a girl called **Tilottoma** who became the reason for the dual between two men who yearn to earn the love of their beloved. There is a character like **Borof Shaheb** who is a criminal and whose anti-social elements and activities cast a gloom over the story. He is a ruthless criminal and cunningly arranges for the duel which could earn him lots of money as it would become a major event which would be highlighted by the media. There is inter-textual reference to T.S Eliot's poem and Pablo Picaso's painting which makes it a wonderful narrative structured around a set of different mini-narratives within the grand narrative.

This story is at par with the very best stories of world literature and Nilanjan has been able to create a polyphonic text in this story in the

Bakhtinian sense of the term. Art can elevate life to a higher realm and this story bears testimony to this truth. Nilanjan's conception of the story is novel and his execution of the narrative is unique and the story ends in the surreal or magic-realistic manner. The story also demands active intellectual participation on part of the readers.

In **Tan (Attraction)** Nilanjan weaves a wonderful account of conflict between reality and fiction as he depicts the history of a murder through the perspective of a human rights commission officer, who also happens to be interested in creating a story. Nilanjan does not specify the crime that has happened but he has been able to show how a child finds it difficult to recognize his father. The story is divided into many different parts and all the seemingly undeleted incidents forms a cohesive whole which adds a different aura to the tale. Again, Nilanjan has experimented with form and technique of narrative in the story and the ending of the story is heart-rending. The human appeal that is found in the story is able to clinch compassion and sympathy from the readers. A child is supposed to be the witness of an incident of murder and which is supposedly committed by his own father and the victim happens to be his mother. The father returns from custody after six years of imprisonment and visits his son twice in a child-home. On each occasion there is hardly any talk between the father and the son but towards the end when the story reaches its climax there is a hint given by the narrator that the son probably recognized his own father.

In **Kamanapukur (The Pond of Desire)** Nilanjan depicts with aplomb the difficult and complex relation between a husband and wife, who do not have any child of their own. The wife wants to go to a pond where there is a scope for wish-fulfillment but it is very superstitious and unscientific. The husband is rational and calm and quiet but the wife remains obsessed with her desire to bathe in the pond where she believes she will be able to fulfill her desire. Even though the husband does not believe in such irrational belief yet he is compelled to take her to that place in order to maintain the emotional and psychic balance of his wife. The pain of remaining deprived of motherhood torments the wife and the husband also suffers equally. The husband tries his level best to support his wife who can never become a mother according to the report of the gynecologist. Nilanjan has exhibited his knowledge of medical science in this story which hints at his devotion towards his chosen vocation – A good writer has to have knowledge of every aspect of life and Nilanjan has proved in this story the truth of this argument. The ending of this story is quite dramatic as the husband finds it difficult to trace his wife in a mammoth gathering of people and it ends in an uncertain note.

The story **Ashukh (Disease)** starts with a dramatic incident as a small child suddenly disappears from a multi-storied complex and her parents find no trace of her. The father searches every nook and corner but his effort goes in vain as he becomes unsuccessful in tracing his daughter. But to the utter chagrin of everyone the girl returns and tells a scintillating story of being kidnapped.

She tells that she was lifted by a few unknown persons in a car and when the criminal found that this was not the girl whom they wanted to pick up, they immediately dropped her on the road from the car. The next section of the story becomes very interesting and meaningful in the sense that the girl's habit of telling lies and forgery becomes evident to the father which is reported to him by the headmistress of the school where the girl studies. The father surprisingly learns that the girl has earned the habit of fabricating fictitious tales and it becomes apparent that she is not in her proper senses. All these incidents create misunderstandings between the parents of the girl and the corrupt middle class mentality of the father comes out to the fore. The word 'disease' becomes symbolic in the story as both the father and the daughter seem to find themselves in a mire of corrupt practices.

Nilanjan is a voracious reader of world literature and that is reflected in his stories.

The Poetics Of Polyphonic Discourses:
A Critical Reading Of J.M Coetzee's, Disgrace

Subhajit Bhadra

Asst. Professor, Department of English,

Bongaigaon College, Bongaigaon, Assam

Subhajit.bhadra@gmail.com

The aim of this paper is to provide a critical reading of J.M. Coetzee's Booker winning novel, **Disgrace** and to show how a variety of discourses merge within its textual universe that in term points towards its intrinsic strength. However, for the sake of critical convenience and also for a sustained focus, I have basically attempted to discuss four discourses contesting within the textual domain of **Disgrace**. These are: (a) Post-colonial discourse (b) Patriarchal discourse (c) Moral and ethical discourse and (d) Aesthetic discourse.

In order to add strength to my arguments, I have made an attempt in this paper to balance theoretical standpoints with adequate textual reference. Though the central argument of the paper borrows its contours from the Russian thinker ,Mikhail Bakhtin's idea of the novel as a contesting site of multiple voices, yet there has also been an attempt here to incorporate and critically analyze other theoretical standpoints in context of the text. However, it is not a theoretical paper as there has been a conscious attempt to critically examine every theoretical perspective in light of the text.

J.M. Coetzee's, **Disgrace** was published in the last decade of the twentieth century when a number of critics as well as thinkers were deliberating upon the possible and probable demise of the novel as a literary genre. In fact, V.S. Naipaul, one of the most celebrated and distinguished writer who is also a Nobel Laureate went to the extent of declaring the death of the novel but the irony lies in the fact that Naipaul himself subsequently wrote two novels titled, **Half a Life** and **Magic Seeds. Disgrace** was published in 1999 which fetched the prestigious Booker Prize to J.M. Coetzee for the second time and it was basically because of the international popularity and worldwide acclaim generated by the novel which ultimately witnessed Coetzee claiming the much deserved Nobel Prize in 2003. The harsh criticism that followed in South Africa after the publication of **Disgrace** compelled its author to leave for Australia and subsequently settle there. **Disgrace** is not only a powerful novel that provides a political critique of contemporary South Africa, but it is also an extremely rich novel of ideas and that is why it would not be an exaggeration to state that the novel is both Coetzee's masterpiece and swansong. Within the textual universe of the novel, a variety of discourses contest with each other, without canceling out each other and this in turn tempts one to view the novel as a poetics of polyphonic discourses that generates a number of relevant debates and concerns.

The Russian critical thinker, Mikhail Bakhtin was the first to consider the novel as a serious literary genre and he was also one of the foremost earlier thinkers who proved that the novel form was capable of engaging the attention and concentration of serious academicians. Bakhtin formulated his view on polyphony and carnivalesque in his celebrated book, **Problems of Dostoevsky's Art (1929)**, the ideas of which were subsequently revised and expanded in **Problems in Dostoevsky's Poetics (1963) and Rabelais and his World (1966).** Bakhtin, as Rene Wellek argues in one of his essays, combines "...acumen, analytical power and historical eradication..." Bakhtin points out that Dostoevsky created a radically unique kind of novel he calls "polyphonic" i.e, it consists of independent voices which are fully equal, become subjects of their own right and do not serve the ideological position of the author. Bakhtin asserts – "In this actively polyglot world, completely new relationships are established between language and its object (that is, the real world) – and this is fraught with enormous consequences for all the already completed genres that had been formed during eras of closed and deaf monoglossia. In contrast to other major genres, the novel emerged and matured precisely when intense activization of external and internal polyglossia was at the peak of its activity; this is its native element. The novel could, therefore, assume leadership in the process of developing and renewing literature in its linguistic and stylistic dimension". **(Epic and Novel, 12)** The assertion brings to light Bakhtin's preference of the novel as a unique literary genre that is capable of doing justice to the variety of linguistic and stylistic registers embedded within the texture and the structure of the narrative. The novel, for Bakhtin, turned out to be a form that could incorporate within its fabric, a number of different competing discourses, that he calls "polyphonic", which has, in turn, lent a valuable critical and analytical perspective to subsequent academicians and critics. As Michael Holquist points out – "The simultaneity of these dialogues is merely a particular instance of the larger polyphony of social and discursive forces which Bakhtin calls " heteroglossia." Heteroglossia is a situation, the situation of a subject surrounded by the myriad responses he or she might make within a particular point, but anyone of which must be framed in a specific discourse selected from the terming thousands available. Heteroglossia is a way of conceiving the world as made up of rolling mass of languages, each of which has its own distinct markers. These features are never purely formal, for each has association with it a set of distinctive values and presuppositions " **(Dialogism: Bakhtin and his World, 63)**

As argued by Bakhtin and pointed out by Holquist the polyphonic voices in the novel contain various discourses, and each discourse has its own point of view, register, nuance and of course, a site of power. Since the history of human civilization down the ages, various discourses have established themselves as potent forces during different periods and each discourse carries with it a distinctive set of values and site of power. It should always be kept in mind that discourse is inextricably related to power – politics and in fact, it can be asserted without any reluctance that each discourse uses a particular language to exercise power and thereby dominate and subjugate other discourses as ideologies and as groups. In the recent years, discourse has gained importance through at least two different, simultaneous developments in the general theorizing of knowledge and a broadening of perspective in linguistics. Michael Foucault, the celebrated French intellectual historian signaled a seminal shift in epistemology through his unique theorizing of knowledge. As pointed out by Brown and Yule – "The analysis of discourse is, necessarily, the analysis of language in use. As such it cannot be restricted to the description of linguistic forms independent of purpose on functions which these forms are designed to serve in human affairs." **(Brown and Yule 1983:1)** Adam Jaworski and Nikolas Coupland also point out the pertinent perspective that Bakhtin brought to light.

"For Mikhail Bakhtin, all discourse is multi voiced, as all words and utterances echo other words and utterances derived from the historical, cultural and genetic heritage of the speaker and from the ways these words and utterances have been previously interpreted. In a broader sense then, 'voices' can be interpreted as discourses – positions, ideologies or stances that speakers and listeners take in particular instances of co–constructed interaction." **(Jaworski and Coupland 1999:9)**

Thus it is seen from the above arguments how the novel as a literary genre becomes a site for contesting discourses and it becomes a hugely enriching experience when one applies Bakhtin's formulation of polyphonic discourse in context of a densely textured novel like Disgrace which problematizes our understanding of every given value.

II

Looked at critically, **Disgrace** is a treasure trove for the post-colonial critics but it should be borne in mind that a hackneyed or a unilayered post- colonial perspective can cause massive injustice to the richness of the text that questions and often subverts many of the received assumptions associated with this specific theoretical discipline. Every text has a context of its own, a trajectory of its own and also a uniquely designed intention of its own. J.M. Coetzee and Nadine Gordimer have a unique place in the canon of literature of the African continent as they have to write within and from a context where the blacks have been at the receiving end through a larger historical span. Both Coetzee and Gordimer because of their white identity already and always exhibit a tendency in their work to appear neutral, not to take sides. This however, contributes both to their strength and weakness as creative writers as they suffer from the anxiety of representation because more often than not they are unsure of their politics. While it is an accepted fact that J.M. Coetzee has been less overtly political in his writings in comparison to Nadine Gordimer, it is this very political tentativeness that has defined and also in a way formulated and determined Coetzee's creative universe. He has always been more than eager to depict the bleak reality of his country beginning from his debut work **Dusklands** to the most recent of his publications **Summertime.** Coetzee has ruthlessly and almost clinically depicted the darker and malicious designs of white racism during the apartheid in novels like **Life and Times of Michael K** and **Waiting for the Barbarians** where the blacks were brutally dominated and tortured by the oppressed machinery of the whites. It should be kept in mind that South Africa never underwent formal colonization like the other African countries where oppression was the legal right of the white westerns. But South Africa had a long history of apartheid – a form of racial segregation that witnessed the utter deprivation and dehumanization of the blacks by the whites. **Disgrace** marks a conspicuous departure from the stereotyped and received post-colonial contours as it reverses the colonizer/ colonized equation within the changed historical context of South Africa and the novel also interrogates certain set assumptions associated with post-colonialism.

David Lurie, the central protagonist of the novel around whose fate the entire plot revolves behaves like a typical representative of the white western who has constructed a stereotyped image of the "Other" in his mind. Lurie teaches communications in a Technical University in Cape Town, has an impulsive sexual affair with a black student Melanie Isaac and when the affair becomes publicly known, Lurie is asked to seek unconditional apology to save his job which he eventually refuses to do, loses his job, retreats into the rural where his daughter from the first marriage Lucy supposedly runs an autonomous farm, is subsequently beaten by a group of black rogues, sees his own daughter being gang-raped and ultimately lives an animal existence in utter disgrace. David Lurie epitomizes the typical traits of the white colonial master both in his behaviour and action – such as seeing and framing the "Other" (in this context the blacks) in a derogatory manner, using abusive and offensive language while describing the "Other", an insistence on reinforcing the white western ethos wherever he goes, a stubborn refusal to understand the importance of dialogue with the "Other", a ruthless urge to dominate and subjugate the "Other" and an almost pathological disdain for everything related to and associated with the "Other". The post-colonial discourse in **Disgrace** become interesting as a result of the consistent clash between David Lurie's painful discovery of the fact that he has turned out to be the very "Other" that he always disdains in the changed political scenario of contemporary South Africa and his stubbornly foolish refusal to understand and accept this fact. When David Lurie withdraws to the rural location where his daughter Lucy ruins a farm he surprisingly discovers that a change in location also changes his identity. As Ruth Frankenberg and Lata Mani argue in their essay, **"Crosscurrents, Crosstalk; Race, 'Post-coloniality and the politics of Location"** "....We would argue that the nation of the 'post- colonial' is last understood in context of a rigorous politics of location, of a rigorous conjuncturalism. There are, then, moments and spaces in which subjects are 'driven to grasp' their positioning and subjecthood as 'post-colonial' ; yet there are other contexts in which, to use the term as the organizing principle of one's analysis, is precisely to 'fail to grasp the specificity' of the location or the moment."

 Delving Into Different Literary Terrains

Because of a twist in history, David Lurie suddenly finds himself in a state from where he can only "look back in anger" as all his colonial pride and ego become meaningless. Petrus, a black farmer who helps Lurie's daughter Lucy to manage her firm suddenly threatens to become the master that first dismays and then enrages David Lurie. When Lucy asks her father to help Petrus, he immediately retorts, "Give Petrus a hand. I like that. I like the historical piquancy. Will he pay me a wage for my labour, do you think?"(77). It is nothing but the anguish and disdain of the white master who is historically trained and privileged to dominate, to subjugate, to extract labour from the black without giving him the proper and due wage, who must degrade and dehumanize the black as the "Other" for the glorification of the self. Lurie here voices the collective anguish of the entire white population who find themselves at the receiving end because of the inevitable change in power equation in South Africa brought about by the April 1994 election. When David Lurie is singed by the black rouges he finds the very marker of his colonial identity under threat." He looks at himself in a mirror. brown ash, all that is left of his hair, coats his scalp and forehead." (97) Even when his own daughter has been raped in front of his eyes, he realizes that he still has been lucky to have escaped with a little, but this is only a momentary realization as the white colonizes is ingrained in his whole being. There is a German name Ettinger in the country who is one of the last sentinels of the white colonial pride as he held a licenced gun in his hand which is ineffective anyway. The readers are informed the " Ettinger is a surely old man who speaks English with a marked German accent. His wife is dead, his children have gone back to Germany, he is the only left in Africa". (100) David Lurie's psyche is so enmeshed in the white colonial vision that his every discourse is replete with a stubborn refusal to reach to the "Other". When Bill Show, a black neighbour offers help to Lurie after the shattering violence unleashed upon him and his daughter by a group of black rogues, David Lurie behaves like a typical white westerner who always views the black man with disgust, and dismay. Lurie says, "Not one of them you can trust." (109)

In contrast to David Lurie's typical gesture of a white colonial master, his daughter Lucy provides a counter-discourse to white colonial ethos in **Disgrace** as she refuses to lodge an official complain against the wrongdoers. It is not that Lucy is foolish in her behaviour, in fact, she is wiser than David Lurie as she understands and acknowledges that the days of the white colonial master ruling over their slaves are over. When Lurie keeps on pestering her to lodge an official complaint, she replies, "In another time, in another place it might be held to be a public matter. But in this place at this time, it is not. It is my business, mine alone." (112). In answer to Lurie's further interrogation, "This place being what?" (112), Lucy replies "This place being South Africa." (112). Lucy not only seems to contradict and counteract Lurie's typical colonial discourse, she also challenges the white man's stupidity arrogance devoid of any sting. The equation between the master and the slave is reversed by Lucy when she articulates the simple but horrifying fact (horrifying to the white western represented by David Lurie in **Disgrace**) to Lurie, "I can't order Petrus about. He is his own master." (114) David Lurie also gradually realizes that history has turned towards a different direction when he thinks –

"In the old days one could have had it out with Petrus. In the old days one could have had it out to the extent of losing one's temper and sending him packing and hiring someone in his place. But though Petrus is paid a wage, Petrus is no longer, strictly speaking, a hired help. It is hard to say what Petrus, strictly speaking... he sells his labour under contract, unwritten contract, and that contract makes no provision for dismissal on grounds of suspicion. It is a new world they live in, he and Lucy and Petrus. Petrus knows it, and he knows it and Petrus knows it." (116-117)

Language plays a pivotal role in the post-colonial theoretical domain as it becomes both a marker and a preserver of identity. As Dennis Walder points out in his book, **Post-Colonial Literatures in English,** "In the history of colonialism and decolonization , the literary dimension is apparent not only in the themes and preoccupations of literary producers, but also and mere profoundly in their chosen medium." (42) David Lurie at least moves towards a road to realization when he thinks, "He would not mind hearing Petrus's story one day. But preferably not reduced to English. More and more he is convinced that English is an unfit medium for the truth of South Africa." (117) David Lurie's paranoia regarding the future plight of his race is articulated when he thinks, "Petrus has a vision of the future in which people like Lucy have no place."(118) There is an important feature in the standard post-colonial discourse which brings to light how the white colonizer imagines and constructs territories through stereotypical preordained nations about the imagined space. Ania Loomba effectively and succinctly argues in her book **Colonialism/Post-colonialism –**

"The construction of racial differences had to do both with the nature of the societies which Europeans visited, the class of people who were being observed, as well as whether trade or settlement was the objective of the visitors. The crucial point is that such constructions were based on certain observed features, the imperatives of the colonists, and preconceptions about the natives." (109-110)

David Lurie reinforces the same colonial discourse when the readers come across the sentence, "To Rosalind in darkest Africa." (121) Lurie envisions a future when his race will again dominate the so-called inferior races but as he indulges in such an imagined utopia, he also laments the collapse of the colonial "grand narrative" – "By the time the big words come back reconstructed, purified, fit to be trusted once more, he will be long dead." (129) When Lucy accepts Petrus as her protector and subsequently declares her intention of atoning of the crimes of her race by marrying Petrus, David Lurie is reduced to the stature of a mute spectator. It is a historical irony when a black man becomes a white woman's protector and Lucy articulates a spine-chilling truth to her father when she says, "It was history speaking through them ... A history of wrong. Think of it that way, if it helps. It may have seemed personal, but it wasn't. it came down from the ancestors." (156) David Lurie turns out to be the slave and he colonized as he gradually loses all the markers of his typical colonial identity. Lurie says, "yes, agree, it is humiliating. But perhaps that is a good point to start from again. Perhaps that is what I must learn to accept. To start at ground level. With nothing. No cards, no weapons, no property, no rights, no dignity."(205)

Lucy, however, behaves more maturely as she not only accepts and acknowledges the defeat of her race, but also exhibits a positive sign of reconciliation when she decides to give birth to the child born out of a forced liaison with a black person or a group of black persons. Thus J.M. Coetzee does not facilitate a stereotyped or straightforward understanding of post-colonial concerns in **Disgrace,** rather his credit lies in problematizing the contours of post-colonialism and as Lucy moves towards an unknown future, the novel also points towards a post-apartheid South Africa that has no place for any display of white colonial aggression.

III

The second most important discourse that finds a prominent place in the novel is the patriarchal discourse which is inextricably related to the feminist and the lesbian discourse as well. David Lurie voices a typical patriarchal discourse when he tells Melanie, "I don't collect pictures. I don't collect women" (29) That Lurie thinks of objects and women as parts of the same category is a case in point of his patriarchal attitude and in fact, he really does not collect women, he simply uses and abuses them, a statement that can be substantiated by the proof of his two failed marriages and countless sexual liaisons. David Lurie again behaves like a typical patriarchal figure who only subjugates women and partakes in gross physical pleasure of the female body when he unashamedly declares, "I was not myself. I was no longer a fifty-year old divorce at a base end. I become a servant of eras." (52) During the course of his trial regarding his affair with Melanie, Lurie consistently keeps on validating male desire as a given license and thereby he reinforces the patriarchal discourse. Patriarchy has always been interested in constructing women from its own point of view and it is patriarchy that has been responsible for the suppression, oppression and marginalization of women down the ages. The body of the woman has always been an object of male gaze and it is seen in **Disgrace** that David Lurie's male gaze devours the body of his own daughter Lucy –

"A year has passed, and she has put on weight. Her hips and breasts are now (he searches for the best word) ample. comfortably barefoot, she comes to greet him, holding her arms wide, embracing him, kissing him on the check." (59) In fact, Lucy seems to titillate Lurie without she being aware of this fact. David feels an irresistible desire surging within him when he sees Lucy approaching him –   "A long time since he last lived with a woman. He will have to mind his manner, he will have to be neat. Ample is a kind word for Lucy. Soon she will be positively heavy. Letting herself go, as happens when one withdraws from the field of love." (Page 65)

Thus the body of the woman consistently occupies in David Lurie's male gaze as well as in his fantasy – because he seems to renew his existence only through bodily encounters with women. Lurie equates a woman's beauty with the shape of the body she possesses and he says, "because a woman's beauty does not belong to her alone. It is part of the bounty she brings into the world. She has a duty to share it."(16)

Londa Schiebinger rightly points out in the introduction to her book, **Feminism and the Body,**

"A central principle of feminist theory has been to recognize that gender differences are not fixed in the character of the species but arise from specific histories and from specific division of labour and power between the sexes. By the same token, it is important to look at the specific history forming feminist body studies and accounting for its theoretical structure. (1)

Lurie is a typical representative of patriarchal ethos who keeps on constructing conditioning and even configuring the body of the woman to subjugate and colonize them. David Lurie gives vent to typical male anxiety which can also be interpreted from the Freudian psychoanalytical perspective when he says, "The truth is, they wanted me castrated."(66)

Allied to the patriarchal discourse embedded within the texture of the novel, there runs the parallel discourse on lesbianism and feminism in **Disgrace** which both problematize and enrich our understanding of Coetzee poetics. Since the inception of human civilization same sex loves and same sex relations have been viewed with suspicion, intolerance, arrogance, insensibility and in fact, disdain. Same sex love has always existed within the margins, in the so-called "sub-altern" zone, outside the domain of normal everyday lives where heterosexuality prevails. Patriarchy has always tried to strangulate, stifle the voice of same sex love which poses threat to the very ethos and normative yardsticks upon which the structure of patriarchal edifice rests. However, in the last two decades, writers, thinkers and activists all over the world have exhibited an increasing awareness and concern that has in turn, resulted in a major shift in the social perception regarding same sex love.

Noami Holoch and Joan Nestle convincingly argues in the introduction to their book, **The Vintage Book of International Lesbian Fiction –**

"While the word lesbian is not global in its use and significance, it is clear, as these stories show, that emotional and sexual intimacies between woman do indeed exist throughout the world. Although most of the authors included here write out a constant connection to a lesbian sense of self, few extremely powerful works in this volume, deep-rooted in specific cultures and embodying lesbian themes, were written by authors who do not define themselves as lesbian."(xiii)

The lesbian discourse in **Disgrace** becomes significant from three perspectives –

a) The authorial perspective of J.M. Coetzee whose gender rules out any direct identification with lesbianism.

b) The non-western perspective of a white writer in terms of location who is deeply steeped in the western cultural and aesthetic tradition.

c) The patriarchal perspective of David Lurie who finds it difficult to come to terms with his daughter's sexual orientation.

However, Lucy's relation with Helen also brings to light another crucial dimension of lesbianism which is generally brushed aside by the accepted patriarchal hegemony that seeks to validate only heterosexual relations as normal. David Lurie's hypersensitive mind finds it quite difficult to analyze the nature of Helen-Lucy relationship.

"...Is his presence here keeping the two of them apart? Would they dare to share a bed while he was in the house? If the bed creaked in the night, would they be embarrassed? Embarrassed enough to stop? But what does he know about what women do together? May be women do not need to make beds creak. And what does he know about these two in particular, Lucy and Helen? Perhaps they sleep together merely as children do, cuddling, touching, giggling, reliving girlhood – sisters more than lovers. Sharing a bed, sharing a bathtub, baking gingerbed cookies, trying on each others' clothes. Sapphie love.: an excuse for putting on weight."

As Lucy's body gradually turns out to be a typical male destination, she becomes a mere apology to her earlier self and it is precisely the way patriarchal structure dwarfs and erases the identity of a woman. As Lucy decides to move under the wings of Petrus for protection who grants her the status of his third wife, her subjugation becomes complete. In this specific context, **Disgrace** exhibits how a woman also turns out to be an accomplice who both authenticates and vindicates patriarchal discourse. Lucy's own words lend credibility to this observation –

"Objectively I am a woman alone. I have no brothers. I have a father, but his is far away and anyhow powerless in the terms that matter here. To whom can I turn for protection, for patronage ...Petrus may not be a big man but he is big enough for someone small like me?"

However, a feminist reading of **Disgrace** would reveal not only the pattern of patriarchal discourse reinforced through the text, but also the subversive design that the author might or might not have intended. Coetzee is not a self-avowed politically conscious writer like Nadina Gordimer, but it would provide an innocent reading of **Disgrace** from the point of view of a woman. As Lynne Pearce convincingly agrees in her book, **Feminism and the Politics of Reading** –

"To reflect upon the constraints, conditions and expectations imposed upon each and every one of us when we undertake to read a text as a woman / as a feminist is in itself a profoundly political act, and however much were forced to laugh at our efforts to protect our ethical integrity it is, in my opinion, a useful form of intellectual narcissism." (Pearce, 41)

The strength of **Disgrace** emanates from the fact that as it seeks to validate the patriarchal discourse through the character of David Lurie, it also provides a counter – narrative through Lucy even though she ultimately conforms and confirms the same.

IV

J.M. Coetzee's **Disgrace** subtly juxtaposes the moral and ethical discourse that are reflected and refracted through David Lurie's liaison with his student Melanie, his defiant attitude towards the trial and his lackadaisical attitude towards his responsibilities as a teacher. When David Lurie first brings to bed his student Melanie, he is pricked in his conscience as he becomes conscious of his ethical responsibility as a teacher – "No matter what passes between them now, they will have to meet again as teacher and pupil. Is he prepared for that" (12) Melanie remains absent form the number of academic classes conducted by David Lurie on the pretext of drama rehearsal, but Lurie, in spite of knowing his moral and ethical obligations as a teacher keeps on marking her present in the register book and Lurie is again pricked in his conscience for his act.

"She is behaving badly, getting away with too much; she is learning to exploit him and will probably exploit him further. But if she has got away with much, he has got away with more; if she is behaving badly, he has behaved worse. To the extent that they are together, if they are together, he is the one who leads, she the one who follows. Let him not forget that." (28)

When Melanie attends David Lurie's class long with one of her boyfriends he not only finds it objectionable like any other teacher under such circumstances would find, he also becomes assertive about his own ethical duty that his profession demands. He tells Melanie –

"I have obligations to my students, all of them. What your friend does off campus is his own business. But I can't have him disrupting my classes. Tell him that, from me." (34)

David Lurie's ironic moral/ethical standpoint stems from the face he is implicated in the same irresponsible and ethically intolerable action for which he scolds Melanie as he has maligned the generally accepted sacrosanct relation between a teacher and a student. In fact, he pleads guilty before the trial committee and he does not display any tinge of remorse or self-pity as he tells "There are more important things in life than being prudent." (49)

The moral and ethical discourse in **Disgrace** remains inclusive as David Lurie shows a reverse gesture when he visits Melanie's home to seek forgiveness from her parents and sister which he eventually does and Coetzee's credit lies in the fact that has not passed any moral judgement anywhere in the novel.

V

David Lurie is not only an academician who takes delight in the domain of arts and letters, his life is also inextricably related to art and at times he confuses art as reality and reality as art. Looked at from such a perspective, Lurie behaves like a typical aesthete for whom everything can be subordinated to the alter of art. He plans writing an opera on Bryon whose bohemian and promiscuous lifestyle somehow mirrors Luire's life. Lurie revels in the delight of books and he equates the joy of love with the joy of reading poetry – "But in my experience poetry speaks to you either at first sight or not at all. A flash of revelation and a flash of response. Like lightning. Like falling in love."(13)

Lurie provides a brilliant aesthetic discourse on his favorite poet William Wordsworth in context of the poet's **The Prelude,** to which his students react with only utter silence, not in applause or admiration, but in boredom and lack of interest.

However, David Lurie's intended project of writing an opera on Bryon comes to a halt as his life moves through darker trajectories that almost pulls him out of the comfortably complacent aesthetic realm which he mentally inhabits in David Lurie's aesthetic discourse which is also enmeshed in his patriarchal discourse when he decides to critically examine Byron's relation with his mistress. Teresa. As Lurie contemplates upon the possibility of writing a chamber opera based on Byron's relation with Teresa, he thinks,

"Can he find it in his heart to love this plain, ordinary woman? Can he love her enough to write a music for her? If he cannot, what is left for him?"

Lurie arrives at the following conclusion regarding Teresa which bring to light his patriarchal bias –

"Bryon's love is all that sets her apart: without him she is nothing: a woman past her prime, , without prospect, living out her days in a dull provincial town, exchanging visits with women – friends, massaging her father's leg when they give him pain, sleeping alone." (182)

By the time David Lurie becomes aware of his limitations as a human being after the brutal rape of his daughter, an incident that subsequently triggers a lot of major shifts in his life, his dream of writing the opera remains a mirage. The aesthete in David Lurie is subdued, submerged if not dead because of the grim reality around him and the aesthetic discourse in **Disgrace** remains myriad that in turn radiates a glow of its own.

VI

In conclusion, it can be argued that the novelistic strength of **Disgrace** stems from J.M Coetzee's remarkable success in blending a variety of discourses within the texture and structure of the novel that is significant not only from a generic point of view, but also from historical point of view. Milan Kundera makes a remarkable observation in his book, **The Art of the Novel (1986)** –

"The sole raison d'être of a novel is to discover what only the novel can discover. A novel that does not discover a hitherto unknown segment of existence is immoral." (Kundera, 5-6)

Disgrace does "...discover a hitherto unknown segment of existence..." as J.M. Coetzee creates an unforgettable poetics of polyphonic discourses which problematize our understanding of many received nations about identity, post-coloniality, patriarchy, lesbianism, ethics, morality, art and above all life, that itself is the biggest and most complex polyphonic discourse.

Works Cited

Mongia Padmini, 'Contemporary Post-colonial Theory - A Reader', Oxford:OUP,1997.

Jaworski, Adam and Nikolas Coupland (ed.), 'The Discourse Reader', London: Routledge,1999.

Schieninger, Londa, (ed.), 'Feminism and the Body', Oxford, New York, OUP, 2000.

Holoch, Naomi and Joan Nestle, (ed.), 'The Vintage Book of International Lesbian Fiction', United States, Vintage Books, 1999.

Kundera, Milan, 'The Art of the Novel', New York, Faber & Faber, 1990.

Bakhtin, Mikhail, 'The Dialogic Imagination: Four Essays', trans. Michael Holquist and Caryl Emerson, United States of America, University of Texas Press, 2004.

Holquist, Michael, 'Bakhtin: Dialogism and his World', London, Routledge, 1990.

Coetzee, J.M, 'Disgrace', Vintage, 2000.

The Window Of The Prison

*(Originally written in Bengali by NILANJAN CHATTOPADHYAY,
Translated by SUBHAJIT BHADRA)*

One artist was arrested on the charges of supporting those people who had proclaimed revolt against the state and delivered lectures openly about it.

The artist was arrested without much hype and publicity. He went far away from the city to enjoy a few days by the sea-side. But he was not alone. His girlfriend also accompanied him whose beautiful face could be observed in many of the portraits and sculptures of the renowned artists.

A lonely house was there by the sea-side. It seemed as if a huge bird furled close its big wings and was thinking whether to fly away or not. The artist was sitting with his girlfriend in the first floor of that house. A thin candle was the only source of light there. There were electric lights as there should have been. There were vapour lights at a pre-planned and at regular intervals by the sea-side whose spectrum mystified the sea-beach. The hotels lying at certain intervals by the sea-side were also adequately decorated with lights. On that night, the sky was surprisingly silent. There was no absolute hegemony of either the moon or the stars in the sky. The sky was overcast with clouds. There were some signs of flashes of light at times. But there was no sound of thunder.

The artist was lying in wait for a downpour or at least a shower. He put out all the electric lights of the house. Instead he lit a narrow and thin candlestick. The paragon of beauty was lying on a bed - the one and only friend of the artist. She was lying entirely without a trace of a piece of cloth on her body. Having used two pillows to increase the height, she placed her milky white shoulders on it and she was lying in half-sleeping posture which resembled the graceful legendary, Queen Cleopatra. Two surprising butterflies seemed to perch on her nipples of the breasts. One of her hands was placed low. Another hand of hers was kept at the back of her head. As such the grayish hair of the armpits lying close to her shoulders was visible.

Such tuft of hair is habitually kept hidden by women. Men are attracted to them as they are kept hidden. It was not that the artist was busy in sketching out the half-slept lady. The artist was looking at the nude lady by means of the light of the candle. He was focusing on her spread out white legs where the lines of the pillar and tomb cast a shadow. A cat of black and white texture was sitting quietly at a corner of the house. The dull light of the candlestick made the cat look like a mummy. There was a small table lying close to the wall by which the artist was sitting. A swollen bellied bottle of Vodka, a half-eaten apple and white wine in a red glass was lying on that table.

Looking at the nude and silent woman

And the mummy of a cat.

The fat bellied bottle of Vodka lying on the table and

Watching the fraction of the apple

The artist is preparing

To enter into cave of his own heart in the mysterious candle light.

Immediately, the creaking sound of shoes could be heard on the stairs. The sound was not coming out of the single pair of shoes, but of many pairs together. It was like the sound of some people on the drill. Many people were coming upstairs. Who were they after all?

The door of the room was kept ajar. Knocking sound could be heard twice. Knock, knock. The door was flung open even before the artist could say 'come in'. Two to four tall persons entered with their army uniforms on. The women in half-sleeping posture covered her nude body with a shawl immediately. Before the artist could say anything, the officer commanded him - you will have to accompany us......

"Do you have arrest warrant with you? the artist enquired.

"Of course, I have....Let's go now. Please hurry up."

The artist smiled looking once at the face of his girlfriend, thereafter he went away with the officer and his attendants. The black police van started carrying him. Suddenly the cat started weeping.

A conspiracy hatched against a state is a serious offence. Therefore, a prolonged court procedure is carried out. The artist was kept confined in a faintly lit room for many days. Even the artist could not remember the duration of his confinement exactly. But the hair on his head gradually turned grey. He never grew beard on his face. Of late he looked like a crazy worshipper with his beard and moustache on. The artist would have to go to the court. He would again come back to his cell. The hearing would sometimes last for a prolonged period. Many witnesses provided evidences against the artist standing within the witness box. Many of such persons were unknown to the artist. The judge would sit on a heightened seat. The artist would think him to be a lonely lighthouse. The artist assumed that the judge would feel helpless on a heightened seat when the witnesses provided evidences one by one, when the public prosecutor and the artist's lawyer would engage themselves in verbal battles quite dramatically. Mainly he experienced a mental fatigue. The judge would look at the eyes of a dead fish. The artist could not feel which way he would look at. Once during a hearing day, the artist found him dozing which remained unnoticed by others. He felt very compassionate for the judge. Oh God, the man did not sleep peacefully at night for a long time. He would remain obsessed with many thoughts. He would think about the court cases also. This particular case was too complex to solve. There were so many arguments and counter-arguments. What kind of judgement could be given! The judge would have to think whether he would give death sentence, lifelong imprisonment or allow the person to get away scot-free till late night hours. As such his sleep would remain disturbed.

The verdict of the judge was, however, clear in this case. Having received the witnesses of three hundred eleven odd persons, the judge pointed the artist as the chief conspirator against the state. The conspirator was awarded lifelong imprisonment.

The artist heard the verdict of the judge with an expressionless face. Normally before the announcement of the verdict, the judges would ask the convict - "Have you anything to say? We have known the general replies of the convict since long."

But the present judge was slightly different. Having announced the verdict, he asked the artist - "Do you have anything from me to ask for?"

The artist said smilingly - "You have already announced the verdict, Sir. Is there any justification of such question now?"

"But still... you still need to survive for a long period of time. Literally speaking, lifelong imprisonment implies imprisonment for the whole life till death. But the matter is not so in reality. You will be imprisoned for fourteen years only. This is our law."

"If someone dies before fourteen years then…."

-Yes, that will be a separate issue. Therefore, I was saying that a period of fourteen years is a long period of time in a man's life. It is also very difficult to survive in a jail for so long. I know you in a special way. I somewhat know about your class as an artist. In fact, I have a few water colour portraits at my home drawn by you. My wife is a fan of your art works."

"It turns out to be so," the artist laughed again. His laugh was a little curved.

"Means? I could not understand," the judge asked him.

The artist said with a smile, "I have observed from my experience that the wives of the successful big bureaucrats, ministers, judges are the connoisseurs of art, readers of literary texts." This has come to be really true in your case also. Perhaps the arrow of words pinched the judge. But the person he had recently given judgement was lying on the edge of a gorge. What more was left for him to get hurt? So the judge tried to digest the critical remark and change the topic of discussion.

He said, "Please tell me if you have anything to ask for."

"Shall I have to ask for anything?"

"Speak out. Hurry up."

"See, I am an artist. I'll have no peace of mind if I can't draw portraits daily. I can't even have a sound sleep if I can't draw anything. So….."

"Speak out now."

"If you permit me to do…."

"What permission?"

"I want you to ensure regular supply of colours, paintbrushes, easel so that I can draw the portrait. If I can draw portraits then I'll become oblivious of my situation. The term of fourteen years will also pass with ease."

"Such a prayer of yours is hereby granted. I shall send necessary directions to the jailor of the jail where you will be kept. All the necessary art-tools will be provided to you within the jail. You'll be able to draw portraits regularly. "

Coming out of the court, the artist saw that there was a large gathering of people there. Especially the people related to the print and electronic media were trying their best to come near him. They were arguing with the policemen present there. One microphone came near the face of the artist. The question was put - "What is your reaction to find that a great artist like you have been sentenced to lifelong imprisonment? The artist replied, "I am thinking about painting portraits in a different format...."

Normally the convicts are kept together in a prison. But this is for those convicts whose cases have not been resolved by the court. On certain occasions they are kept in separate 'cells'. The person sentenced to lifelong imprisonment was kept in one of such separate 'cell'. It was lonely and full of pitch darkness. Having pushed him into it, the guard went away. There was a big sound. The artist felt that he had suddenly turned blind. Everything was dark in front of his eyes. He stood there like a fool. High up in the walls of the cell on two sides, there were two ventilators. It was afternoon. It was not exactly afternoon also. The sunset was imminent. Some grayish and sorrowful lines of light were creeping inside through the ventilators. The artist was gradually becoming used to darkness. Even through the thin lines of faint light, he could feel that the lonely and quiet cell was not very big. It was not big in length. In breadth also it was short. To be exact, two persons could not sleep together. They would be irritated when they would push each other while moving about. Would he have to live in such a cell for fourteen years? It would have been better to die than to live in such a condition. He would not be able to see the sky according to his wishes. The scenic beauty of nature which inspired him many times to paint pictures, would not be visible before his eyes. Only the four walls of the geometric sizes would be lying before him. Today was the first day of imprisonment. But he felt as if the walls would come near him and they would crush him to death. Suddenly he shouted out of fear. The own screaming voice of the artist echoed back strongly to his ears in the lonely and quiet cell. Having felt some pain, the artist pulled his hair, he pulled his own beard.

He was behaving in an unnatural way out of pain and fear. Feeling everything as useless, he covered his face with the palms of his hands and cried. He could remember the guerilla warriors. Those were the persons who hid themselves for days together in forests and hills leaving their families and relatives. They had dreams in their eyes. They had countless dreams. They dreamt of saving the country from an autocratic ruler. Their dream was to ensure the fact that every person could get enough to eat and to wear, to ensure their survival with dignity. The artist could find similarities with their dreams. As such he spoke in favour of the guerilla warriors in open meetings or at public places. He wrote articles in their favour in different newspapers. So he became an eye-sore to the ruling class. He was imprisoned under their rules. He was bound to live within the jail for fourteen long years. Can anyone survive while staying away from one's society, family, friends, lover and books? Perhaps he would die much ahead of the completion of fourteen years.

The artist could not sleep for the whole night lying on a torn mat on the stone floor. He was repeatedly thinking that there should have been a window to allow the light, air and the cry of life. Would the jail authorities pay heed to his words? Would they make provision for a window breaking the wall of the prison cell? That was impossible. There would be anarchy within the jail if the jail authorizes would become so compassionate to the criminals, their criminals would express their endless desires one by one.

What could be done then?

There was a need of a window in that cell. Otherwise an artist would not be able to be confined there for long. He might have to choose the option of suicide. Therefore.....

Therefore he spent a sleepless night. Thinking in this way, the artist chalked out a plan.

He would paint a window on the wall of the cell.

He did exactly as he had thought. An artist possessed colours, paintbrushes and other painting tools. The artist was permitted by the judge to keep all the necessary art tools with him even during his imprisonment. In the early morning, when the early sunlight had not even spread out to its fullest form, when the darkness was not still over, the artist got on with the task of painting a big window on one of the stone walls of the cell. He could not get sufficient light. He did not also have a source of light that he could light it as per his necessity. There was no scope of doing so. But the artist did not get discouraged at this. The source of light lay within himself. He had endless light of imagination. With that ray of light he could see everything clearly. The artist did not have any difficulty to draw a window on a stone wall.

A window, a window

On the lifeless stone wall

With the unending light of imagination

The artist drew out a window.

The dawn had already set in with fullness. Putting his face on his self-drawn window, the artist saw the outer world. It was very nice to look outside from a great height. It was really high. The cell in which the artist was kept was on the top floor of the jail. The artist had no idea how high the cell was. But it must be four-storied. Or it might be even more. It might have five or even six-storied building. It was because the street below, the houses of people and even people there looked smaller in size. The artist felt good to think that the window would help him to survive his imprisoned life. Through this window –

He would see the sky
The floating clouds
The birds in the air
The power of the sun
The disappointment of the clouds
The smartness of the road
The efficiency of the moving cars
The hare, the children
And look at the maidens
With love-laden eyes.

The captives of the jail were entitled to get tea in an earthen pot and a dampened piece of biscuit. There was an opening of the door of the prison cell. The staff of the jail entered with tea and a biscuit. Having entered, his eyes were struck with the puzzle of light. At first, he closed his eyes. Having controlled himself after a while, he found that light was coming inside through the window. What a surprise it was! Where did the window come from? Was it an illusion for him? No, why should it be an illusion? It was clearly a window. And the sufficient amount of light was coming through it.

"Where did the window come from?" the employee asked.

"I drew the window," the artist said with a smile.

"You drew it, did you? Do you know how big a crime you have committed? There should be no window in the cells of the captives who had been sentenced to lifelong imprisonment."

"I drew it," the artist announced it again.

"For so long..do you know for how long? I have been working in the jail for 28 years. I have never witnessed such a strange incident in my career. I am going to report the matter to the jailor right now."

The staff forgot to deliver the tea and a biscuit to the artist. Those items lay in his hands as they were. He rushed to report the matter to the jailor. Having received such an amazing news, the jailor somehow reached the cell of the prisoner in a jiffy. His eyes were also struck to see the most unexpected bright light from outside. At first, he could not believe himself. When he saw that a window was really lying there, then a wave of anger was thrust upon the artist.

Having burst with extreme anger, the jailor said," What have you done?"

"I have drawn only a window," the artist replied quietly.

"That I can see," the jailor told with a squeezed mouth," but the window has been painted on the wall. How can so much light come into the room then?"

"It's true that I have drawn a window." "But it is a real window. The window is open and so, there is so much light inside," the artist replied. Stretching his hand towards the jailor, he said," Would you offer me cigarette, Sir? I could not smoke even for once since last night. It will be nice to have a cigarette." Looking at the face of the artist, the jailor developed a kind of compassion. Drawing out a cigarette from the packet which was kept in his pocket, he offered it to the artist. He also lit a cigarette. There came out a nice melody when the lighter was lit. Both lit their respective cigarettes from the same stroke of fire.

Releasing some smoke in the air, the jailor said," What kind of magic have you started? This is a solitary cell. How can so much light enter here from outside?"

The artist said once more," The window I drew is a real window. Both the parts of the window are open. So there is so much light in the room."

"Again you are speaking nonsense, aren't you? That is simply a painting of a window on the wall. It's a simple drawing only. Can a painted window be real? Just see I am putting my hands on the wall. This is a painted window. But it looks like a real one indeed. You have an expert hand in painting, I must admit it..."

"You can take that drawn window to be a real one if you have some imagination."

     Delving Into Different Literary Terrains

"Imagination? Do you really mean it ?"

"Yes, it is imagination. As imagination is needed to create an art, so the same thing is needed to understand it." The cigarette came to an end due to frequent puffs to it. The artist threw the burnt end of the cigarette in a corner of the cell. The cigarette was put out.

"Leave aside those ideologies," the jailor said with a squeezed mouth. "There is no problem with the ordinary prisoners. The problem lies with the intellectuals, litterateurs and the artists like you. Your behaviour is really unpredictable."

"Did I do something illegal?"

"You painted a window over there. I wonder how the judge is. I may be charged with contempt of court if I say so...how could he give such a judgement that you might be allowed to stay inside with your art equipment? Having received those facilities immediately after your arrival, you have started creating nuisance."

"I have been sentenced to lifelong imprisonment...it means that I need to stay in this small cell for fourteen long years. How shall I be able to pass my time without being able to enjoy the sight outside through a window? How shall I survive? "

"It is up to you how you will survive....don't they survive? All the captives, I mean, all the lifers pass away their time in this manner...don't you know that men are slaves to their habits? I have seen some captives who don't like to go back home after the end of term of their imprisonment, they don't like to go back to their own societies. They tell that they have been used to the loneliness and quietness of the jail. What shall we do getting back to human society after such a long period of time? We shall not be able to adjust any more....I have seen such captives with my own eyes."

"Yes, this may happen," the artist said very thoughtfully, "therefore I made a window for myself feeling that the same thing may happen to me..."

"That's a great thing you have done. Now wipe off the window hurriedly... simply wash it off."

"How can I wash off a window which is a real one?"

"You have become crazy once more, I see...please stop this bullshit...you draw whatever you like, draw a mango, a blackberry, a hare, a man, a nude woman, rhombus, triangle, pyramid or any other shape or thing you like. But you can't draw a window. "

"Why can't a window be drawn, sir?"

"It's because the light from outside will enter the moment it will be drawn. The source of light from outside is prohibited inside the cells of the jail...."

"Say what you like, Mr. Jailor. That window can't be washed off. This is because it is a real window."

"Can you prove that it is a real window?"

"What kind of proof do you need?"

"There is no bar to the window you have drawn. Can you jump outside through that window?"

"Would you see if I can?"

"Just see."

The artist immediately sat on the window. Poking his head out of it, he once saw what was lying outside. Then he jumped. The jailor rushed to the window. Thrusting his head out, he noticed that the artist was floating in the atmosphere. He was looking just like a bird. Or like an aircraft. Or like a trapeze artist in a circus.

He was floating and floating...our artist was floating in the air.

That act of floating was without any burden. That act was being done without a single word.

That happy moment of floating was directed towards the endless universe.

The artist was laughing. It looked as if white pearls were being dropped from his laughter.

It was like a star flower. The artist was singing a song in a full-throated ease.

It was a song of liberty, a song of disinterestedness, a song of absolute freedom. The artist waved his hand towards the jailor from a distance. It meant - you, too, come with me. You also float with me....

But the jailor would not be able to fly in the sky of freedom like that of the artist. How could he get such a power of imagination? Flying in this

DELVING INTO DIFFERENT LITERARY TERRAINS

manner, the artist was moving far, far away. He then looked like a small point. Tears were rolling down the cheeks of the jailor - having thought of his chained life. After a long time, the jailor was weeping......

****

UMBRELLA

There was only an umbrella at home, and it had at least fifty holes in it! The sunshine made its way through them, and gave a glittering shine on the hair and the face! The pearl droplets would ooze out during the rain! It was, therefore, quite natural that there would be anxiety and sadness in the mind when the only umbrella at home got lost! It was, however, not known how the umbrella had been lost. But it was being assumed that it had flown away.

It had obviously flown away. Because when Bhaktibabu, Indu's father searched for the umbrella on such a thoughtless rainy day, then Indu spoke, "Wait a second, father, I have covered the cat with the umbrella. Otherwise, the way it is sleeping near the water-tank, I am sure it will get drenched fully. Poor cat! It does not have much strength left to move a bit! I am bringing it right now."

Bhaktibabu expressed his grief for the cat with a broken waist. He said, "You've done the right thing, dear. But I do need to go out, it will be better if you can push it inside or else arrange for its bed at the staircase."

Gosh! Where was the umbrella? Reaching the roof with a few long hops and jumps Indu became extremely surprised. Umbrella? The cat was there. The water-tank was lying in its place. But the umbrella had vanished!

The sky was overcast, and heavy drops of rain had been falling since morning. There was a terrible storm a little while ago! As if it would not stop. Now, it stopped raining a bit. A mild breeze was blowing now. Both the mind and the weather were gloomy. Indu became philosophical for a moment. She thought that something that had been a part of her mind, had just flown away! It did not know where it was leading to. It was just gliding in the air by cutting through the current of the air. But she had the feeling that it had flown away. Indu was nineteen-years-old now. She had kept her eyes fixed towards the sky. Her sight got blocked at a green forest. She began to hum a song— the crazy wind on cloudy day.. Bhaktibabu called her from downstairs, " Indu darling, Indu! Umbrella?" Indu searched every nook and corner of the roof. But it was found nowhere. It was indeed a strange incident. Indu rapidly moved downstairs. Looking at his sordid face , Bhaktibabu asked,"Is the cat okay ?" **matter missing**

said,"Why are you suspecting the domestic helper? Everything would have been difficult for you, if she had not been there for your help!" It did not seem that Sudha paid any attention to his words. She sat down to think deeper with a frowning look. Then Bhaktibabu said,"Well Indu. Is it not the revenge of the umbrella against the exploitation that we have done to it ?" Indu had full faith upon the creative imagination of her father. Because she also liked to imagine. Recently her imaginative faculties spread their wings with joy. Just a few days ago, a kite hung itself on the roof; and when she picked up the kite with joy, she noticed that there was a name written on it—Tirthesh Sen ! Her heart beat with an unspeakable feeling. Such feelings were common to her any time during the day, but she failed to understand why such feelings were generated these days. She became upset at the slightest or no excuse, sometimes she became excessively happy, sometimes she liked to sing or dance without any rhyme or reason. Mother looked at her with suspicious eyes when she would observe some difference in her behaviour. She asked,"What's wrong with you?"

"Nothing special," but the mother still suspected her. She felt the prick. Her mind became somewhat different when she saw the kite on that day. A little while ago she was witnessing a battle of kites. One of the kites got torn away and flew down to their roof in front of her eyes! The kite had a very long thread attached to it . While she was rolling the heavy red-coloured thread on her finger, an imagination started brewing in her head. Then the same kind of thought started revolving round her all throughout the day and night. She kept a constant vigil on the piece of the red thread. She could see before her eyes

"What do you mean by that?"

" Not there means not there, father. It was nowhere on the roof. I really opened it over the cat. Sudha's mother Indu rushed from inside the house. Some of the conversations between the father and the daughter reached her ears. Being surprised, Sudha said, " Are both the father and the daughter under the influence of the hemp in the broad daylight? How can you say no so easily? Let me see."

Bhaktibabu quickly remarked, "Give a missed call."

"Oh dad!" Indu had almost screeched. She said,"You too, dad"...saying so, she wore a smile. Bhaktibabau scratched his head and looked at Sudha with fear. He said, "It has become a habit now."

Sudha had already been angry, and the joke from Bhaktibabu had not been palatable. Thinking so, Indu sent the growing smile back to her belly. Sudha had already come back from the roof quickly. There was a shadow of anxiety in her face. She said, "It's true, the umbrella is not there!" There began a hue and cry at home immediately. Many disconnected thoughts regarding the expected destination of the umbrella crossed everyone's mind. Sudha said, "I can't understand the head or tail of it. Where can the umbrella go from the roof! The main door is locked, there is no possibility that an outsider will come and take away the umbrella from the roof, it can't be so. When Andha's mother went back after finishing her household chores, I stood there and locked the door myself." **Bhaktibabu became angry. He said,"Why are you suspecting the domestic helper ? Everything would have been difficult for you, if she had not been there for your help !" It did not seem that Sudha paid any attention to his words. She sat down to think deeper with a frowning look. Then Bhaktibabu said,"Well Indu. Is it not the revenge of the umbrella against the exploitation that we have done to it ?" Indu had full faith upon the creative imagination of her father. Because she also liked to imagine. Recently her imaginative faculties spread their wings with joy. Just a few days ago, a kite hung itself on the roof; and when she picked up the kite with joy, she noticed that there was a name written on it—Tirthesh Sen! Her heart beat with an unspeakable feeling. Such feelings were common to her any time during the day,but she failed to understand why such feelings were generated these days. She became upset at the slightest or no excuse, sometimes she became excessively happy, sometimes she liked to sing or dance without any rhyme or reason. Mother looked at her with suspicious eyes when she would observe some difference in her behaviour. She asked,"What's wrong with you?"**

"Nothing special," but the mother still suspected her. She felt the prick. Her mind became somewhat different when she saw the kite on that day. A while ago she was witnessing a battle of kites. One of the kites got torn away and flew down to their roof in front of her eyes! The kite had a very long thread attached to it . While she was rolling the heavy red-coloured thread on her finger, an imagination started brewing in her head. Then the same kind of thought started revolving round her all throughout the day and night. She kept a constant vigil on the piece of the red thread. She could see before her eyes the sago was being boiled, the glass powder and barley were also being mixed with it. Then the red colour was there on the top! One was attaching glue made of powdered glass, etc. to the piece of thread spread between two lamp-posts. Who was he ? She could not see him. But still his figure came in her imagination. The night passed and the dawn set in—but at some point of time, she closed the door of imagination and slept. The glue –attached thread and the kite settled in her memories. And the figure of the person went with them ! **matter repeated**

Today, Indu became worried at Bhaktibabu's words. She said,"You're quite right, father. There is only a single umbrella with a thousand holes! We've never thought of repairing the cloth of the umbrella even once. One of the metal sticks came out of it, I managed to drag and stitch it somehow. It was running with that stitch. Haven't we pulled and dragged it too much

Sudha was listening to the conversation between the father and the daughter so long. When Indu stopped, she started, "What will you prove with that? Has the umbrella got upset with us and walked away to an unknown destination? Sudha once looked to her husband's face and also to her daughter. She said , " Oh, how strange your thoughts are ! Crazy! Crazy! I run my family with two insane persons! Oh God! How unlucky I am!"

Indu had already discovered a destination of the umbrella from father's words. But she liked to think that the umbrella had flown away with an air of egotism. Truly speaking, nowadays she would also like to go far away whenever her self-respect got hurt. Though the matter of the departure of the umbrella was painful but she derived pleasure out of it in other ways. But just at that point of time she was uncomfortable with the words of her mother. Because, in reality, it was impossible for an umbrella to go anywhere on foot, just like her abrupt departure from her house. So she said, "Mom, What do you think?"

Sudha said, " Think seriously for once if you have picked up the umbrella before that. Perhaps due to the forgetfulness of mind—it never comes back once you keep it somewhere . Then one can nicely recall it once you worship Haran Thakur (a folk god of losses) with some salt.

"Then let me offer a worship. Nothing costlier than salt is required. Isn't it? I am offering right now"

Bhaktibabu laughed after a long while. He said, "Where will you get the idol of Haran Dada? How will you worship without an idol?" Sudha threw an angry look at her husband. She said, " Let me tell you clearly enough that do not cut a joke with God." Then she looked at Indu and said, "Go

  DELVING INTO DIFFERENT LITERARY TERRAINS

Indu, Put off your salwar-kameez and wear a fresh apparel. I am keeping some salt in a bowl. Keep a glassful of water and a bowlful of salt in a corner of the house and chant this in your mind—Haran Thakur, have salt and water and give back the lost ones. You should say it thrice—got it?" Bhaktibabu could not help smiling at this. He said, "Does Haran Dada have low-pressure? Salt is restricted for the persons with high-pressure. He may die straightaway."

Sudha could feel the heat of fire inside her head—a fire with inexhaustible flames! Sensing danger to see the fiery face of her mother, she said, "Let's make a move. We shouldn't delay more. Dad, you'll go out, won't you? Go out this time. The rain has been controlled. Let's try to find out the umbrella."

Bhaktibabu went out with the drizzle falling on his head. After a long time, a debtor had assured him over the telephone that he would give back his money. Therefore, he had to go. Sudha was still blabbering, "Cutting jokes with God. Will there ever be any good to this house ? He is saying that Haran Thakur will die ! Phew ! Go Indu go, pray attentively. The Gods also test who is praying with devotion and who is not.Where will the umbrella go? God is testing us. God can make someone blind even though one has a sight. You'll worship God and close the door, okay?" She said,"Okay mother!" But she could not help asking, "I have never seen an idol of Haran Thakur, then how shall I pray to Him?" Soon afterwards she thought something over and said, "Better you close your eyes and pray silently in your mind so that he would take salt and water, and give back the lost items. Pray, this will do. We got back so many things in our childhood! Go, I say."

It was not, however, known whether Haran Thakur drank water or not. It was also not known if he had taken salt or not. Sudha became perturbed. She knew it really well that Bhaktibabu was not going to spare if the lost things were not found.

The whole day was spent. Sudha and Indu searched for the umbrella vigorously, but did not find it. Bhaktibabu came back before evening. Coming back, he enquired about the umbrella. Indu made a gesture towards her father to inform that he should not cut a joke. Because Sudha had been already mentally upset.

Having felt that Sudha was disturbed, Bhaktibabu changed the way of his amusement. He said, "Actually you know Indu, we have got a bad habit. We take anything for an inanimate object except a human being."

Being a little insipid, Sudha sat hesitatingly close to the father and the daughter. She said, "What's that?"

"It's nothing. I wish I knew that the umbrella is a living being! Now, I can remember that how much damage we have done to the umbrella due to overuse! What colour was it of ?"

"Dad, its colour was maroon. Although that could not be understood of late. It was discoloured. Then there were holes on it! Indu felt really bad about it. She said, "Dad, you gave me the umbrella when I was in class five!"

Bhaktibabu was surprised.He said, "It has been rendering its service for so long! From class five to first year!

"You're right, dad."

"Was it not repaired even once?"

"No."

"Then it had to go. There is a limit of endurance for everything. Isn't it?"

Sudha was sitting downcast. She was really looking exhausted. It had been four months since the hundred watt bulb was being used after the tubelight had gone off. The reddish light of the house made the atmosphere gloomy. It was raining heavily outside. There were frequent sounds of thunders. Sudha raised her head and said, "It has been a useless gossip between the father and the daughter since then. How funny! Has the umbrella suddenly developed a pair of wings or a pair of legs that it could fly away whenever it wished to?"

Bhaktibabu smiled his trademark laughter. He said, "Does Sudha go away whenever she wishes as she has two legs? Perhaps not. Otherwise you would have gone much earlier!"

Sudha seemed to be utterly surprised. She said, "What kind of a talk is this? You are uttering some meaningless words in the evening hours ! Where the hell shall I go?"

Sudha was indeed in a hell. "Where will such wives like me in the lower-class families go?" "Your lifestyle would have been different had you been a wife of a rich man. Then you could have the courage to leave the family, and could have found places of shelter. You could have many candidates readily waiting for your accord!"

Sudha looked very uncomfortable initially. Her expressions revealed that many reactions had taken place immediately within herself. Being extremely crossed, Sudha said, "As I am not one of those, then your words do not make any sense here. I have told Andha's mother to arrange for an umbrella for the time being. She said several vendors would visit their slums daily. They would sell umbrellas also. An umbrella will be available at fifty rupees. She will bring one if she is given money.

"I'll give that. Let's have tea before that." Having said so , Bhaktibabu got down from the bed. He said, "Today, I'll prepare tea for you. The real Punjabi tea! Thereafter he looked towards her daughter and said, "You'll then say, who's a good cook—your dad or mom."

"Oh,stop it. You need not burn your hands in making tea after having reached home drenched in the rain." When Sudha was advancing, Bhaktibabu dragged her hands and forced her to sit on the bed. He said to her daughter, "See to it that your mother should not be anxious. Don't allow her to move, okay?" Indu felt great at this remark. The rain arranged such a situation that the three members could gossip together after a long time.

Sudha felt really uncomfortable. She did not like the idea that men should go to the kitchen. She was very sure that Bhaktibabu would put everything at sixes and sevens while preparing two cups of tea. She continued, "Heaven knows what's wrong with your father today! Do that carry any meaning? Just see what he will make of my kitchen! I'll have to work double for that!"

Indu abused her mother, "Mom, why don't you shut up? Don't you take this as a special case as he is preparing the tea merrily at his own accord? I'll clean the kitchen room, okay? Now, sing a song for the rainy season and let me listen."

Sudha got shocked, "A song—g ! Me! Have both of you gone mad owing to the loss of the umbrella?"

Indu smiled at the words of her mother. She said. "Do we appear mad?"

"What else? That song got boiled up with the rice and vanished in the air much ago! Have I sung a song in the last twenty one years?"

"You do sing alone. We've heard. Dad appreciates your song."

Bhaktibabu came with three cupfuls of tea. The aroma of the tea spread everywhere in the small room. He said, "Just have it. And Indu, you and me will prepare the hotch-potch dish tonight. Today is the rainy day for your mother."

"Wow, that will be fantastic." Indu almost jumped at the proposal. "We will prepare **khichdi** with brinjal fry..Dad, we'll surely prepare brinjal fry."

"Do you know what to fry **khichdi** with?"

"Don't worry, dad. We need dried red chillies, cumin and bay leaves."

Sudha was listening to their discussions with wonder. She laughed this time to hear about the items of **khichdi** fry. She said, "Are you throwing a party with the sense of the loss of the umbrella?"

"Ha-ha-ha" Bhaktibabu burst into a hilarious peel of laughter. He said, " Indu,see what your mom is saying. Am I throwing a party? Ha-ha-ha... yes,I am."

"What will you say about that matter?"

"Have tea."

Sudha felt that she was offering a sip into the heavenly nectar. Bhaktibabu felt really satisfied to see the expression in her eyes had a shadow of her mind. He continued to look towards his wife. Then he became absorbed in himself for a moment. Within a short while he got back to his usual senses. Looking at his daughter, he said, "Indu, just think. The umbrella had been upset for a long time." Indu joined herself with her father in the realm of imagination. It was then clear before her eyes that the feelings of sorrow had accumulated in the mind of the umbrella. Indeed, the umbrella sometimes looked very depressed and gloomy. It had already been discoloured, but even then the umbrella looked pale or insipid! And sometimes yet it looked like a new one. Indu was mentally surprised, "Why upon earth she did not think about all these earlier? If she had given much attention to that, then this unexpected incident would not perhaps have happened. Bhaktibabu continued, "You kept the umbrella under the big sky above, the poor umbrella perhaps got the first opportunity to stand alone under a big sky! Even we would like to fly away having seen such a cloudy sky. Don't you desire, Indu?" Indu nodded her shoulder, "Right, dad. But I feel differently to see a cloudy sky. I feel like sitting quiet. I remember my old friends...I feel some kind of sorrow at my heart. And again I feel nice. And Dad, I feel like flying immediately when the pieces of clouds move freely in the blue sky spread across the horizon with an air of freedom to move anywhere they like! I feel like going far-far away!"

"You also like to go away, Sudha, don't you. Tell me."

Sudha was feeling somewhat unusual that day. Bhaktibabu had never talked to her in this way all these years! It seemed that the day began to put everything in disorder. She nodded her head, "No' I don't. A caged bird never wishes to fly away."

"Perhaps they do. Due to non-movement of the wings, they become inactive like our appendix, which they fail to understand ! The wings then become heavy, and therefore they can't fly even though they desire very much! And we think that they do not wish to fly away. As if we thought so much about them! Phew!" Then he addressed Indu, "Think, when the umbrella saw that it was lying alone....and a big sky overhead..then it remembered all its sorrowful thoughts and the air told it to run away, the tiny yellow bird showed it how to fly by flapping its wings , signaled it, and then the small bodied umbrella flew in the air !" Bhaktibabu's eyes were about to shut while he was talking. He continued, "What fun for it after this! The moment it went up in the air leaving the ground , it occurred to its mind—Freedom! Freedom! Independence! Oh ! It heaved a deep sigh of relief...it flew and flew....and flew across the sky."

Indu was awe-struck. Sudha was extremely surprised. Indu spoke, "Will we not feel sorry for the umbrella? It grew up with me from the fifth to the eleventh standard! We feel sorry for it, dad. Will it not desire to come back ?"

"Pain for it? That is for sure! But it is difficult to say if it would like to get back! Actually it got such an unbridled freedom for the first time in its life! Right now it is difficult to say where it will fall—whether in the jungle or at the mountain peak as it has become extremely happy to get a freedom after a long time of bondage! It may be broken to pieces! And if it is found by anyone—who knows?"

"Dad, it is not going to fall in anybody's hands." It appeared that Bhaktibabu smiled a bit. There were signs of gloominess, signs of regret, and a faint sign of happiness in that smile! He said, "Well said,dear. It went with so much of experience! Sudha had never become so much surprised in all her life. Forgetting her tea, she had so long been looking at the father and the daughter. She found it really difficult to believe that the umbrella had flown away. Losing her composure this time, she said, "Heaven knows what has driven both of you crazy! They are flying with the umbrella attaching the wings on their backs! Phew! It is, after all, an umbrella only. To feel sorry for that! To feel the pains for that! Oh God! Let me go now—won't you have **khichdi?**"

Bhaktibabu burst into laughter, "Are you not Sudhamayee, the goddess… today we'll prepare and you'll enjoy it comfortably."

"Dad, have you called mom as Sudhamayee?" Indu was laughing with surprise.

"Say how beautiful the name of your mother is! And I have shortened it to only Sudha! Do you know the difference in meaning between Sudha and Sudhamayee? Sudha means 'Heaven's nectar' and Sudhamayee means 'full of nectar.' Ahoy! While using a name, we forget that a name is a life.. it has a name, a character, a feeling of desire and that of rejection. Oh no! I am going to call you Sudhamayee from today. I'll listen to nothing. Let's go, let the father and the daughter show today that they are not inferior to anyone. Get a move on."

The cooking programme was started amidst lots of noises, as if it were a place of worship. Sudha stood close to the kitchen door and laughed. She was prohibited to cross the threshold of the door that day. While Indu was about to pour a spoonful of turmeric powder after having used one tablespoon already, she shouted, "Hello, don't pour more of that…not any more."

Bhaktibabu threw an angry look at her, "Poking your nose yet again! It has become your habit. Haven't I told to sit quietly on the bed, darling. You will give orders from there and we'll carry them out. Just g—o."

"Mom, do move away from here." Indu begged her this time. Sudha's feet did not want to move away from the threshold of the kitchen door. She looked back while going away. The wall of the kitchen was a thatched one with yellow paint on it. The sixty-watt electric bulb looked insipid with a cover of soot on it. The plastered wall came off at many places. But this was the most favourite place for Sudha. She looked back again and again. The mixed scent of rice and pulse were spread in the air. Sudha felt a connection between the continuous rainfall outside and the smell of the **khichdi** inside. She felt that she did not get the smell while cooking. But on that day she got a strong smell from a short distance, Sudha was feeling really great. She sat on the bed. Opening one window,she desired to watch the rainfall. And she was surprised at this. She never had such a desire earlier. What a surprise! What would the daughter think if she opened the window to see the rainfall? And her husband? He will not spare her. But she was developing a strong desire. But she was defeated in the hands of her desire the next moment. She opened the parts of the window and stood there. The raindrops were coming in. Sudha's face, eyes and neck were getting wet. And the cold wind accompanied the rain. What a heavenly feeling! There was a constant flow of happiness in every vein and artery within her mind and body...it continued to flow! Someone seemed to sing from within Sudha—on a cloudy day with the flow of crazy wind...it was raining. Nothing located far was then visible. The lights in the lamp-post were being drenched in the rain. The street was devoid of people. Sudha started to sing. Someone inside Sudha started to sing.

Sudha did not notice when Bhaktibabu stood at her back. When the song which was being sung from within so long stopped with a note of depression, Bhaktibabu kept one of his hands on her shoulder. What a shame! What a shame! Sudha seemed to be reduced in shame. While she tried to close the window hurriedly, Bhaktibabu said, "Let it be open. Today you are really looking very beautiful with the rainfall on you, Sudhamayee. You sang after a long time. Did you want to fly away? Eh? We were careless about the umbrella." There was short deep breaths after the end of Bhaktibabu's words. The drops were coming inside. Then the raindrops falling in the direction of the windflow drenched both Sudha and Bhaktibabu and even the floor of the house. Bhaktibabu was looking at some distance. He said, "The umbrella took the revenge! How far can it go with its broken body? It must have fallen somewhere. I feel extremely sorrowful, Sudha. It has given us shelter during sunshine, rain and the storm alike without any trouble and we have used and kept it carelessly. Perhaps Sudha caught cold. She started coughing at regular intervals. Bhaktibabu closed the window. He rebuked her mildly. He said, "Wipe off your face and neck immediately. See, you've caught cold. Pay a visit to Dr. Nagen tomorrow." Bhaktibabu shouted, "Indu, Indu! Accompany your mother once to the doctor tomorrow." Having said so, he ran towards the kitchen. Bhaktibabu and Indu came back in a short while, carrying a dishful of **khichdi** in her hands. The hot smoke was coming out of that. Neither on the floor nor on the termite-ridden broken wooden table, the eating arrangement was made by spreading newspaper on the bed on that day.

Sudha was using her finger to remove the smoke and then to eat. Her facial expression was superb.She failed to remember when she had a palatable dish like that in all her life. The amount of saltiness, sweetness and the hotness seemed to be proportionate. Bhaktibabu looked at Sudha with his heart's content. He could not remember when he had the last opportunity to watch the nose, eyes and mole on the neck of Sudha. Indu said, "Is mother not very beautiful to look at? I wish I were a bit like her! Oh!"

Bhaktibabu nodded his head. He said, "We did not care for the umbrella properly. I wish I got another opportunity." Then he told in an annoyed way. "You could have told , my dear. Can I always be so careful ?"

Sudha could not still believe the episode of the disappearance of the umbrella. She was eating but the thought was moving in her memory. The matters of pride and vanity of the umbrella was meaningless to her. The umbrella flying away with its wings was also a wild imagination for her. She interrupted during the conversation between the father and the daughter, "Will you ever stop? Stories are being told in turns here!

That day seemed entirely different from any other day. Bhaktibabu had kept on speaking meaningless things before he could go to sleep at night after a long time! He said, "Could you remember the day when I went to see you, Sudhamayee?"

"Why not? You looked as if you would swallow me up!" Sudha shrinked in shame while saying so. She said, "Just shut up. The useless stuff!"

"I neglected you very much. What more can an ordinary teacher do? But I know that attention may be paid even against all the odds. Do you never get angry with me or at the family, Sudha ?"

"Why don't you keep quiet!" Sudha felt that her heart was getting spongy soft. She said, "It is raining heavily.Isn't it?"

"I feel really bad for the umbrella! I would not have felt so bad if it had been lost in the trams and in the buses."

"I, too, can't understand. Where can it go? A cat was covered with it, and then it was nowhere-- !"

"Finding an opportunity, it flew away!"

"Heaven knows!" Sudha did not like to think more . On the other hand, she needed to have a peaceful sleep, so she shut her eyes.

The morning started again with the sunshine. The leaves of the trees got sparkling smooth having taken bath in the rain. Indu was first to wake up that day. Having washed her face, she went upstairs on the roof to see the beautiful morning. Then she squeezed her eyes for sometime. She saw. She saw it again. The umbrella was quietly standing at one corner of the roof! It seemed as if it were standing like a criminal with its folded hands and feet and with bowed head! There was the glitter of sunshine in its rain-athed body. Indu could not believe. Was it her umbrella? Did it elope from any other household? Who knows! There was nobody on the roof yesterday! She became somewhat afraid. Holding her breath, she rushed downstairs and almost shouted , "Mom, Dad. The umbrella! Get up quickly..." This shout of Indu was enough for Sudha and Bhaktibabu to wake up.

"Dad! The umbrella! On the roof!"

"What!" Whatever the trace of sleep was there in the eyelid, was gone immediately. The eyes of Bhaktibabu were big with surprise, he said, "Whose umbrella is this?"

Meanwhile, Sudha also went upstairs. She began shouting from the roof, "Hello, Come here and see. Our umbrella has come back!"

The maroon-coloured pale umbrella was standing in a corner by the wall! Bhaktibabu, Sudha and Indu looked at one another; that look was inexplicable. That look only said, "How is it possible!!!"

Sudha said, "I searched it thoroughly." Indu said, "Me too, mother." Then........?

Bhaktibabu advanced towards the pale and withered umbrella with slow steps.

Unveiling Patterns Of Patriarchal Politics
In Valmiki's Ramayana

The aim of the chapter is to examine the various patterns of patriarchal politics in **Valmiki's Ramayana** with special reference to the changing trajectories of Sita's fate. **Valmiki's Ramayana** brings to light how women were oppressed, subjugated, harassed and even objectified in India since long past and this chapter specifically makes an attempt to portray the plight of Sita whose life was a long tale of suffering, disgrace and trauma. This chapter makes an attempt to read various incidents of **Valmiki's Ramayana** in the light of contemporary feminist theoretical paradigm that always advocates for the need of subverting patriarchal power structure. However, it should be borne in mind that to apply any contemporary critical/theoretical hindsight in context of a traditional epic like **Valmiki's Ramayana** would naturally demand a rigorous textual engagement and that is why there is an obvious attempt in this chapter to strike a balance between theoretical insight and textual evidence. But it should be stated in the very beginning that this chapter examines many incidents of **Valmiki's Ramayana** from a subjective viewpoint though the principal aim is to bring out both the explicit and the implicit layers of patriarchal politics.

Patriarchy has always been responsible for the oppression, subjugation, humiliation, marginalization and even construction of women from a particular perspective. Patriarchy does not, necessarily, imply a huge assemblage of men; it rather refers to an oppressive system/structure based on power and hierarchy. Traditionally women have always been viewed as weak, vulnerable, unstable, emotional, stupid and even inferior and men have always dominated women on the basis of these arguments. However, one must keep in mind that these adjectives assigned to women are definitely not their ingrained characteristic traits, rather these adjectives are deliberately assigned to them to strengthen patriarchal power structure. This exactly draws one's attention to the aspect of social conditioning and reveals how a particular point of view turns out to be

     DELVING INTO DIFFERENT LITERARY TERRAINS

a powerful discourse through a process of incessant repetition and the French sociologist and cultural historian of the twentieth century, Michel Foucault brought to light the hidden dimensions of discourse. During the second half of the last century there was a great upsurge of feminist literary theory in the West, particularly in France and later on the entire European and American continent absorbed the revolutionary rhetoric of feminist writers and thinkers. However in the West, there was already a tradition of feminist thoughts and cross-currents though earlier it was known as the 'women's movement' and books like **Mary Wollstonecraft', A Vindication of the Rights of Women (1792), Olive Schreiner's, Women and Labor (1911); Virginia Woolf's, A Room of One's Own (1929) , John Stuart Mill's, The Subjection of Women (1869) and Fredrick Engels,' The Origin of the Family (1884)** exemplify the validity of this statement. Peter Barry rightly points out the efficacy of such a statement -

> **"The 'Women's Movement' of the 1960's was not, of course, the start of feminism. Rather, it was a renewal of an old tradition of thought and action already possessing its classic books which had diagnosed the problem of women's inequality in society, and (in some cases) proposed solutions." (Barry 2002:121)**

The most important book from which feminists derived a lot and which changed the outlook of a generation of thinkers, intellectuals, students and readers was **Simone De Beauvoir's, The Second Sex (1949)**. While 'sex' is a biologically given entity 'gender' is actually a constructed category by patriarchy which always regards woman as the "other". De Beauvoir powerfully asserts in her seminal book –

> **"When man makes of woman the Other, he may, then, expect her to manifest deep seated tendencies toward complicity. Thus woman may fail to lay claim to the states of subject because she lacks definite resources, because she feels the necessary bond that ties her to man regardless of reciprocity, and because she is very often well pleased with her role as the Other." (De Beauvoir 1949:108)**

Thus patriarchy not only subjugates woman and strangulates the voice of woman, it also de-humanizes and objectifies woman. Women were made to feel helpless, inferior, useless and worthless since time immemorial and that is why patriarchy consolidated its power structure within every sphere of socio-cultural and economic realm.

A traditional epic like **Valmiki's Ramayana** provides a convenient scope to the diligent researcher to untangle the layers of patriarchal politics and show how women were viewed in traditional Indian societies and what position they occupied in a socio-cultural, political and economic sphere where patriarchy defined the norms of life. It must also be borne in mind that **Valmiki's Ramayana** depicts a Hindu society or nation (there also are exceptions) and in traditional Hindu societies male violence has more or less been a norm. In this context P.K. Vijayan writes –

"Besides permitting the Brahminization of Hindu personal laws – the most significant feature of which was the uniform relegation of women to the private realm and the family, with significant curtailment of rights and claims in relation to male members of the social order and the family ...." (Vijayan 2002:89)

Valmiki's Ramayana is replete with incidents, discourses, instances and episodes which glaringly exhibit the plight of women in traditional Indian societies and the various patterns of patriarchal politics are sought to be highlighted in the first chapter.

Women in **Valmiki's Ramayana** have been portrayed in a derogatory light and some of the women have been depicted as lustful creatures existing for the sake of fulfilling male desire. Rishyasringa , an ascetic, was only interested in the single-minded pursuit of deep meditation. Sumantra, Dasarath's humble servant narrates to the king how the ascetic Rishyasringa can become Ramapada's son-in- law in order to facilitate the birth of a son to the great king. Rishyasringa always avoided earthly pleasures and he was very devoted to the austerities and finding no other alternative to wake him from his meditation it was decided to lure him with 'sensuous' women. Sumantra tells Dasarath –

"We will bring him to the city by luring him here with pleasures that agitate men's minds! Let the most beautiful courtesans adorned in all their finery go to him." (The Ramanyana, 22)

The above comment shows how women were viewed in traditional societies and it also brings to light the position of a woman as mere commodity, her existence depending upon the dictate and wish of a male, in this case subtly exemplified by the use of expressions such as "luring", "pleasures", "agitate", "beautiful" and "finery".

Traditionally women have been viewed as seducers and Indian society has witnessed the towering presence of courtesans like Amprapali and Umrao Jan Ada, to cite only a few legendary examples.

In a particular episode in **Valmiki's Ramayana** the great sage who turned out to be a Brahmin because of the tremendous power of his meditation incites Rama to kill a woman. Jataka is addressed as a "wicked yakshi" by Visvamitra and the sage provokes Rama to kill her without any delay. Nilanjana Gupta rightly points out in this context –

"We have all grown up with stories of supernatural beings – the rakhsasas , demons, witches, churails and the myriad bhuts that constitute some of the earliest stories that children heard ... Traditionally, stories have served the purpose of providing moral frameworks for the societies that have produced these stories and obviously the stories serve to reinforce existing systems of value."
(Gupta 2002:40)

Visvamitra tells Rama exactly a "story" about Jataka and this is done to "reinforce existing systems of value" – in this case patriarchy. Rama listens to Viswamitra's story and he is spellbound by the sage's narrative skill. In spite of being an incarnation of Lord Vishnu, he lacks the power to judge on his own what Jataka exactly is. It is the very nature of a discourse to be ideologically supported and Visvamitra creates a convenient ideological ground to kill a woman. Visvamitra tells Rama,

"Have no hesitation about killing a woman, for you must do what is best for the four castes. A king must do what will benefit his subjects, even if it is unrighteous, for such is his duty." (The Ramayana , 46)

Rama succumbs to Viswamitra's inflammatory discourse and inflicts severe violence upon the body of Jataka and ultimately kills her with joy and enthusiasm. Ram partakes almost a perverse joy when he proclaims –

"Watch how I cut off the nose and ears of this creature who has mastered the art of illusion and who is practically invincible!"
(The Ramayana, 47)

What is most striking is how Rama is not only influenced by Viswamitra's angry rhetoric but how Rama diminishes his own stature as a gigantic epic hero by killing a woman. This incident also reveals how the woman's body has always been used as a site of male violence, a typical concern of the radical feminists who argue the need to subvert and even demolish all existing patriarchal structures.

A woman always fulfils herself by being a mother and it is the deepest urge and craving of any woman to attain motherhood. To deprive a woman her right to motherhood is one of the most heinous crimes one can commit. Due to the sexual intercourse between Lord Siva and Uma, she became pregnant. When Siva was releasing his semen, the other gods became frightened and contemplated the destruction of the world. They approached Siva and urged him to abstain from sexual pleasures and to direct his attention towards austerities. They succeeded in convincing Siva to do so and Uma, a woman, was deprived of her due right to motherhood. This is a manifestation of patriarchal power structure that seeks to control and regulate the sexuality of a woman. But Valmiki has also given voice to the anguish of a woman who is deprived of her due right and in this context one is reminded of Chaucer's unforgettable character of Wife of Bath in **The Canterbury Tales.**

Uma voices her anguish as she says,

"Since my desire for a son ended in this sterile union, the same thing shall happen to all your wives. From this day onwards, your wives shall be barren!" (The Ramayana, 57)

Patriarchy often conditions and controls the life of a woman and patriarchy asserts that the value of a woman's life lies in her ability to show patience. There is a particular incident in **Valmiki's Ramayana** where Ganga's free movement and flow were regulated by Lord Siva. A woman cannot exercise her will. She has to always listen to the dictates of a male and bow down before the command of patriarchal power.

"Ganga fell onto Siva's head and got entangled in his matted locks which seemed like the Himalayas. She could not find her way out and reach the ground." (The Ramayana, 67)

Patriarchy has always conditioned women in a certain way and qualities such as submissiveness, timidity, humility, etc. are highly appreciated in a

 DELVING INTO DIFFERENT LITERARY TERRAINS

woman. The 'apsarases' were always highly appreciated for their physical beauty but they had to cater to the gratification of all without having the good fortune to be recognized as someone's wife and this fact again brings to light another pattern of patriarchal politics which makes the life of a woman deplorable.

"The resplendent apsarases, the very essence of womanhood ... But none of the gods or the gandharvas would take them as wives and so they are known as sadharanas, 'common to all'."(The Ramayana, 71)

Patriarchy has always attempted to control the sexuality of a woman and this fact is brilliantly demonstrated by Valmiki in a particular episode in **The Ramayana.** Ahalya was the wife of the ascetic Gautama who always concentrated his energy on austerities and meditation. Though there is no direct evidence in the text to argue that she was dissatisfied sexually with her husband, yet this manifests itself when she succumbs to the temptation of Indra who fulfils her urge and completely satisfies her. A woman is a flesh and blood creature and it is quite unethical to expect from a young woman to tame her passions as it would be unnatural. Ahalya does not commit any crime, she acts as a human being and pays a severe price for that as her husband Gautama curses her to become a stone, another example of sheer patriarchal arrogance. Gautama curses Ahalya most severely –

"You shall live on air, without food, and you shall sleep on ashes. You shall be invisible to all creatures as you do penance in this hermitage ... Wicked woman, when you offer hospitality to Rama, you shall be freed of your lust and passion." (The Ramayana, 74)

What is interesting here is that a man is projected as both the tormentor and liberator of a woman, in this specific instance Ahalya is tormented by her own husband, Gautama and sought to be liberated by another man, Rama.

Women have been projected as seducers and tantalizing figures in **The Ramayana** evoking desire and lust in the heart of the male. Women have been projected as active hunters and men have been portrayed as passive victims and this aspect unveils another strong device of patriarchal politics. Dasaratha is enthralled by the charm of Kaikeyi and when she forces her husband to banish Rama to the forest he cannot act against her wish. In reality, Dasaratha is ethically bound to fulfill his own promise as he promised to give Kaikeyi a boon long ago. However, the patriarchal power structure transfers all the blames on the shoulders of Kaikeyi and holds her responsible for leading the rightful King astray. Apparently Dasaratha seems to be captivated by Kaikeyi's charm and beauty –

"You know that there is no one except Rama who is dearer to me than you. You know how much I love you. Ask me for anything and lift my heart from the depths of despair. I swear by all the merit I have earned for my good deeds that I shall do whatever you ask."
(The Ramayana 118)

It is none but Dasaratha who has created the condition and consequence of Rama's destiny, but he does not suffer from any moral qualms to attack Kaikeyi verbally. Dasaratha uses very strong and abusive words against Kaikeyi, another sign of patriarchal arrogance and holds her responsible for his won misdeeds.

"Destroyer of my clan! Vile woman ! … I had no idea that you were a poisonous snake, determined to destroy me.
(The Ramayana, 119)

Patriarchy constructs women in a particular way in order to uphold certain values in the society and as a result of that a few qualities in women are highly rewarded while exhibition of a few other characteristic and behavioral traits invoke severe punishment. Kaushalya's "devout" nature is highly appreciated while Kaikeyi's rightful demand is treated with disdain and arrogance because it challenges patriarchal power structure. Kaushalya is admired because she never transgresses the limit set up by patriarchal norms and she strictly conforms to the typical stereotype of an ideal woman. The following lines authenticate the validity of such statement.

"This devout woman, who always kept the prescribed fasts, was dressed in pure white and was pouring oblations into the fire as she recited the auspicious mantras... Overflowing with love, she spoke sweetly to her resolute son." (The Ramayana, 128)

Kaushalya has been compared to a "delicate banana plant" and this stereotypical representation helps in objectifying a woman, devoid of her won strength as a human being.

When Dasaratha decides to send Rama to exile for a period of fourteen years in order to fulfill the promise he made to Kaikeyi, Kaushalya suffers from intense trauma as she is distressed beyond measure to contemplate the anguish of the impending separation from her own son. It is natural for a mother to wish to accompany her son whenever he faces any trouble or crisis and looked at from this perspective Kaushalya's reaction is only natural. As Kaushalya desperately wants to accompany Rama and Lakhsmana , Rama utterly fails to understand her trauma and he speaks like a typical patriarch as his discourse is couched in a commanding male rhetoric. Rama tells his mother –

"A woman cannot abandon her husband. It would be a cruel thing to do and is, therefore, impossible. Put that thought out of your mind. As long as my father, the ruler of the earth, is alive, so long shall you attend and care for him. That is the eternal drama." (The Ramayana, 135-136)

Rama takes recourse to the same discursive tone when his wife Sita expresses her wish to accompany her husband to the forest. It should be specifically borne in mind that Sita is newly married to Rama and it is quite natural for her to express her desire to stay with Rama. But Rama metes out the same treatment to his mother and wife because he always speaks to them as a male patriarch and they always listen to him as passive objects. Rama tells Sita –

"Dearest wife, I am going to the forest. But you, my queen, must stay here and live in such a way that no one can criticize you. This is what I want you to do… A woman must be like the shadow of her husband's feet…" (The Ramayana, 139)

A woman, according to patriarchal ethos, must regulate her desire and adhere to the norms set for her and any attempt to do otherwise would invite social ostracization. But Sita behaves like a contemporary angry feminist when she voices her dissent – a daring gesture that provides an opportunity to compare her to Ibsen's character Nora in **A Doll's House.** She (Sita) utterly ignores the dictates of her husband and articulates a counter discourse that seeks to challenge patriarchal status quo and ultimately when she succeeds in pursuing her husband to take her along with him she also ironically reinforces the same patriarchal norm which she seems to defy because by accompanying her husband to the forest, she literally behaves "like the shadow of her husband's feet".

Sita articulates her wish to Rama quite clearly and forcefully as she says –

"I need no advice on what I should do now. I shall live in the forest as happily as I lived in my father's house, with not a care in the world, concerned only with my loyalty to my husband." (The Ramayana, 139)

Sita further claims that she would certainly die if she is separated from her husband and thus we find that the dissent is just momentary and ultimately the patriarchal *status quo* is maintained.

Just before embarking on an exile for a period of fourteen long years Rama and Sita have to make elaborate preparations and they meet King Dasaratha who suffers from intense grief for his conduct. Rama and Sita get rid of their royal garments and wear the robe of ascetics, a fact which saddens both Kaushalya and Dasaratha beyond measure. Patriarchy has historically constructed women as weak, vulnerable and incapable of doing certain works which are not based on any verifiable logic. As Sandra M. Gilbert and Susan Guber quite convincingly argue in their provocative way –

"It is debilitating to be any woman in a society where women are warned that if they do not behave like angels they must be monster." (Gilbert and Guber 2007:53)

Sita is admired by all because she ultimately behaves the way patriarchy wants her to behave and her "vulnerability" and "helplessness" is appreciated by the agents of patriarchy. The following sentence vindicates this fact –

"All the people who had gathered there were incensed when they saw how helpless and vulnerable Sita was and they murmured against the King. (The Ramayana, 150)

The above sentence brings to light how the ordinary people of the kingdom sympathize with Sita's plight but they are also voiceless like women in that particular society and that is why they can only "murmur", but cannot articulate their protest. Looked at from such a perspective both women and common people become "sub-altern" entities who cannot speak. Kaikeyi cannot proclaim anything as Rama's banishment also seals her fate of a tongue-tied woman who bears the agony of abusive expressions directed at her like "wretched women" and "vile" creature. Kaushalya is also repeatedly projected as "vulnerable" that can be protected by men.

 DELVING INTO DIFFERENT LITERARY TERRAINS

Unable to bear her anguish Kaushalya voices dissent against the dictate of Dasaratha only to be snubbed and silenced by him.

"You also know that to a wife, a husband is like a god, whether he is good or bad." (The Ramayana, 175)

In Valmiki's The Ramayana, there are numerous instances when men not only treat women disrespectfully, but also time and again rebuke those using abusive expressions which testify to the fact that such a society treated women as mere commodities, not as human beings. Bharata voices his anguish as soon as he comes to know the severe consequences of Rama's banishment and he does not display any sign of respect to his own mother against whom he uses the most objectionable words.

"You entered this family like death! And my poor father unknowingly embraced glowing embers." (The Ramayana, 188)

The above sentence unveils another pattern of patriarchal politics that seeks to transfer the male guilt on to the body of a woman and the use of expressions like "poor father" and "glowing ember" glaringly exhibit the diametrically opposite viewpoints regarding man and woman. Shatrughna, the youngest brother goes to the extent of making him ready to beat Manthara, another so called "cunning" woman who has supposedly incited Kaikeyi to bring doom to the family of Dasaratha. However, Bharata resists Shatrughna, not out of any respect or compassion for woman, but because of pity and this fact unveils another dimension of patriarchal politics which teaches and preaches to look at women as helpless and deplorable creatures in traditional Indian societies. Bharata tells Shatrughna –

"Women should be protected from assault from all creatures ... If Rama hears that we have killed this miserable hunchback, he will never speak to us again." (The Ramayana, 191)

Kaikeyi is time and again referred to as "deceitful", "greedy" and "cruel" and she receives these disgraceful adjectives from her own son, who is basically a strong patriarch.

As stated in the beginning of this chapter, patriarchy does not merely mean a huge troop of men fighting against the liberty of women or subjugating women, a woman can also act and behave like an agent of patriarchal power system and in **Valmiki's TheRamayana**, Anusua does play exactly the role when she praises Sita for accompanying her husband Rama to the forest.

"You are truly virtuous, Sita, … you have given up your family and friends, splendor, wealth and adoration, to follow your husband into the forest. Women who love their husbands no matter whether they live in the city or the forest, whether they be wicked or virtuous, are the ones that go to heaven." (The Ramayana, 225)

During their stay in the forest, Rama and Lakshmana encounter many supernatural characters and one of them is Viradha. Viradha sees Sita and is immediately possessed by lust. Traditionally, the body of a woman has always been a male destination but with the onslaught of feminist concerns, the body of a woman became her own destination. However, Viradha cannot restrain his lust and he shamelessly displays his male prowess when he urges Rama to leave Sita with him in order to facilitate the fulfillment of his male desire for the relish of a female body.

Valmiki's The Ramayana vividly brings to light the existence of a society where women are not respected at all; they are looked down upon and portrayed in a very derogatory manner. Women are not thought to be worthy of partaking in any debate and within such a society it is considered below dignity of a man to enter into argument with women. Rama displays typical patriarchal concerns when he attacks Sita thus –

"I cannot argue with you because you are like a goddess to me. But I am not surprised to hear such words from a woman, Sita! Women are like this everywhere in the world. They are unrighteous and fickle and they breed mischief." (The Ramayana, 274)

This uniform construction of women as "unrighteous" and "fickle" brings to light another matrix of patriarchal politics to subdue women. A woman in such a society is not considered as an individual human being, a woman is just part of a mass and thus she loses her individual identity which is again another patriarchal device to objectify a woman. Ravana possessed many women to mitigate his lust and except Mandodari we do not know the names of his umpteenth number of wives.

"With Ravana peacefully asleep, it seemed as if the golden lamps watched over those splendid women with fixed, unblinking eyes." (The Ramayana, 420)

In **Valmiki's The Ramayana** women are treated as commodities who can be lured by earthly pleasures and when Ravana urges Sita to give up her "delusions" and become his wife, he simply reinforces the patriarchal norms. As Ravana tells Sita

"You can be my chief queen, ruling over all the women I have gathered from all over the place," he just reduces her to a commodity. The most significant evidence of patriarchal violence in the text is found when Lakshmana "pulled out his dagger and cut off Surpanakha's ears and nose." (The Ramayana, 245)

Surpanakha is Ravana's sister and a woman who expresses her love for Rama and the violence inflicted upon her body is an unpardonable offence that also diminishes the magical aura of Rama and Lakshmana. Indrajit, the valorous son of Ravana is guilty of the same crime when he brings Sita, a helpless woman to the battlefield and assaults her.

"Indrajit was in a rage when he saw the monkey forces. He unsheathed his word and grabbed Sita by the hair. In front of everyone he slapped her hard…" (The Ramayana, 592)

However in a rare gesture, Rama justifies the right of a woman to come out of the closet and step in the public domain, but he categorically states that it is only on exceptional situation that a woman can be granted such freedom.

"A woman's behavior is what protects her modesty – not a home, nor fine clothes, nor high walls or honors such as these ! Women can be seen in public in times of calamities and emergencies, in times of war, at their own weddings and at religious rituals." (The Ramayana, 632)

However, Rama clearly states that he has protected Sita out of love and concern for her, but in order to vindicate his honor and to display his manly strength to the rest of the world. Rama demonstrates a typical patriarchal trait when he tells Sita.

"I have terrible suspicions about your character and conduct. The sight of you is painful to me as a lamp to a man with diseased eyes." (The Ramayana, 633)

Sita seeks to prove her chastity by walking into the fire and later on Rama banishes her to the forest where sage Valmiki looks after her well-being.

Rama displays typical patriarchal aggression when he urges Lakshmana to exile Sita and Rama does not show any sign of love, mercy or compassion for his beautiful and lovable wife. Rama urges Lakshmana –

"Take Sita and leave her just outside the borders of the kingdom! ... Leave her in that desolate place and come back quickly." (The Ramayana, 664)

Ultimately Sita is given refuge by the goddess of earth and we see how Sita's life and fate are sacrificed at the service of patriarchy.

Thus we find how **Valmiki's The Ramayana** priorities the subtle interplay of various patriarchal discourses and this chapter has made an attempt to unveil the various layers of patriarchal politics embedded within the narrative of the text.

Bibliography

Barry, Peter, Beginning Theory: An Introduction to Literary and Cultural Theory, Second Edition, Manchester and New York : Manchester University Press, 2002

De Beauvoir, Simone : The Second Sex, trans –H.M Parshley, New York: Vintage Books, 1989.

Gilbert, Sandra and Guber, Susan, The Madwoman in the Attic: The Woman Writer and the Nineteenth Century Literary Imagination, First Indian Edition, Delhi: Worldview Publications, 2007.

Gupta, Nilanjana, 'Fears and Fantasies: Controlling and Creating Desires; or, Why Women are Witches,' in Brinda Bose (ed.), Translating Desire: The Politics of Gender and Culture in India, New Delhi: Katha 2002.

Valmiki, The Ramayana, trans. Arshia Sattar, New Delhi: Penguin Book India, 2009.

Vijayan, P.K. 'Outline for an Exploration of Hindutva Masculinities, in Brinda Bose (ed.), Translating Desire: The Politics of Gender and Culture in Indian, New Delhi : Katha, 2002.

The Aesthetics Of Dialogized Discourse:
A Critical Reading Of Anita Desai's:
Baumgartner's Bombay

Subhajit Bhadra
Stuti Goswami

The aim of this paper is to provide a critical reading of **Anita Desai's novel, Baumgartner's Bombay** and to show how the novel facilitates the interplay of a double-voiced or dialogized discourse within its textual universe; which in turn points towards the novel's intrinsic strength. However, for the sake of critical convenience and also for a sustained critical focus, we have sought to confine ourselves to discussion of the interplay of dialogized discourse in terms of thematic contours. These discourses are -

a.   The Jewish discourse

b.   The Post-colonial discourse

To add strength to our argument, we have attempted in this paper to balance theoretical standpoints with textual references. Though the central argument of this paper borrows its contour from the Russian thinker Mikhail Bakhtin's idea of the novel as a contesting site of multiple voices, yet there has also been an attempt to incorporate and critically analyze other theoretical standpoints in the context of the text. However, it is not a theoretical paper as there has been a conscious attempt to critically examine every theoretical perspective in the light of the text.

Published in 1988 **Anita Desai's: Baumgartner's Bombay** was hailed as a major achievement. The novel and the novelist managed to cover newer trajectories as it prioritized the trials and tribulations of a wandering Jew, Hugo Baumgartner in the new land - a land that both accepted and rejected him. The novel provides the perceptive reader with a scope to go beyond the familiar critical paradigm within the creative oeuvre of Desai's fiction. The textual richness in the novel is corroborated by a comment by Dr. RK Gupta in his book, **The Novel of Anita Desai: A Feminist Perspective** -

**This novel is applauded as a masterpiece and it is rich, powerful
and piercing study of human solitariness. This novel portrays an
authentic picture of intense mental torture. Once again we have
tension between the individual and the social forces or pervaded
social values. The novel covers both India and Europe.**
(Gupta 134-135)

As a novel **Baumgartner's Bombay** is exceptional for it addresses
a number of important issues generally neglected and or overlooked by
Indian writers writing in English – in this particular instance the Jewish
issue, which in turn raises a number of other important concerns. Within
the textual universe of the novel, a variety of discourses context with each
other, without canceling each other and this tempts one to view the novel
as an aesthetic of dialogized discourse that generated a flurry of (relevant
debate and concerns.

The Russian thinker, Mikhail Bakhtin was the first to consider the novel
as a serious literary genre. He was at the same time one of the foremost of
earlier thinkers who proved that the novel form was capable of engaging
the attention and concentration of serious academicians. In his essay
'Discourse in the Novel'; Bakhtin writes –

**Double-voiced discourse is always internally dialogized. Example
of this would be comic, ironic or parodic discourses, the refracting
discourses of a narrator, refreshing discourses in the language
of a character and finally the discourses of a whole incorporated
genre - all these discourses are double-voiced and internally
dialogized. (Bakhtin 324)**

This assertion brings to light Bakhtin's preference for the novel as
a unique literary genre that is capable of doing justice to the variety of
linguistic and stylistic registers embedded within the texture and the
structure of the narrative. The novel, for Bakhtin, turned out to be a
form that could incorporate within its fabric, a number of different and
competing discourses, what he termed 'polyphonic' or ' dialogic' which have
in turn, lent a valuable critical and analytical perspective to subsequent
academician and critics.

In recent years, discourse has gained importance through at least
two different simultaneous developments - in the general theorizing
of knowledge and in a broadening of perspective in linguistics. Adam

Jaworski and Nikolas Coupland point out the pertinent perspective that Bakhtin had brought to light.

> **For Mikhail Bakhtin, all discourse is multi-voiced, as all words and utterances echo other words and utterances derived from the historical, cultural and genetic heritage of the speaker and from the ways these words and utterances have been previously interpreted. In the broader sense then, 'voices' can be interpreted as discourses... ideologies or stances that speakers and listeners take in particular instances of co-constructed interaction.**
> **(Jaworski and Coupland 9)**

Thus from the above argument we see how the novel as a literary genre becomes a site for contesting discourses. It is indeed a rewarding experience when one applies Bakhtin's formulation of dialogized discourse in the context of densely textured novel like **Baumgartner's Bombay** that widen the horizons of Indian writing in English.

Baumgartner's Bombay turns out to a unique novel as the prioritization of Jewish discourse both widen the horizons of Indian English writing and makes an attempt to vindicate the presence of such marginalized protagonist within and out the text. The central character of the novel, Hugo Baumgartner is an embodiment of the classic displaced figure as larger historical incidents compel him to become a perpetual wanderer, an anguished vagabond, a drifting individual and a restless human being devoid of any specific location. Baumgartner leaves his native country Germany during the Second World War owing to Hitler's systematic persecution of the Jews; and in a desperate move to save himself comes to India leaving behind his ailing mother in the throes of death. Baumgartner's drifting and eve wavering life gains a different dimension because of his Jewish identity as the Jews have always been imagined and constructed as homeless people, devoid of any specific root or place. It is also ironical that history has more often than not validated such constructions as the truth. Baumgartner behaves like a masked protagonist who attempts to hide himself in different ways because of the burden of his race that also accentuated his personal crisis. However, in this specific context we have been able to identify three different tropes - (I) The self hiding from the society at large (II) The self hiding from its own real self (III) The self playing/ performing roles in order to project a different image in front of others. Baumgartner is perennially aware of his non- belongingness in an alien land. (Consequently) he exhibits a tendency to hide, a characteristics traits of Jewish protagonist in the classic novel by Saul Bellow, Bernard Malamud and Philip Roth.

He was very aware of his lack of business; if he were ashamed of it, he was relieved too, relieved not to join the crowd, the traffic, but to amble along into the lanes and alleys that made off from the main road, and shuffle past the old dingy houses that no one bothered to paint, that stood perpetually in the shadows, and where life washed up in drifts, like debris.
(Baumgartner's Bombay 16)

Baumgartner feels at ease only in the company of Farrokh, a Parsi businessman who understands the former's pain and anguish because of the common status of minorities in India. And yet while Farrokh is a more acceptable minority figure, Baumgartner is a non-acceptable one. Baumgartner cannot remain at ease anywhere as he is compulsively drawn towards hiding, both internally and externally, a fact that can be evidenced during his visit at Farrokh's place -

"He stepped long enough to place some coins beside his glass, glanced into the murky corner at the pile of flesh and fur still carelessly spread in a crumpled heap - a furred carcass before it disintegrated- and then made his escape." (Baumgartner's Bombay 26-27)

The word "escape" succinctly captures Baumgartner's plight; throughout the novel he exhibits this specific anxiety to camouflage himself, wear a mask - albeit in the figurative sense.

Maeera Y. Shreiber writes in her essay, 'Jewish American Poetry'-

The objection is predicated on an essentializing link between Christianity and the poetic, based upon a mutual investment in the "Universal" which necessarily precludes Jewishness, a category of being which Bloom sees as bound up with historicity and specificity. Furthermore, Bloom provocatively suggests that the poetic alliance between a Jewish poet and a "Gentile Precursor" (such as Milton), a Jewish self mixing with a foreign other, is in some way transgressive - a violation perhaps of a culture deeply committed to keeping its borders intact. (Wirth-Nesher and Kramer 149)

     Delving Into Different Literary Terrains

Indeed there has always been a historical problem with the Jew because of their alleged inability to assimilate with, and into the 'mainstream'. Baumgartner had lived in India for almost half a century and yet he does not feel at home. Of course it is another thing that Baumgartner's assimilation has been doubly difficult because of the prejudiced outlook of Indians.

He had lived in this land for fifty years - or if not fifty then so nearly as to make no difference - and it no longer seemed fantastic and exotic; it was more utterly familiar new that any other landscape on earth. Yet the eyes of the people who passed by glanced at him who was still strange and unfamiliar to them, and all said; Firanghi, foreigner. (BB.28)

The trait that makes out Baumgartner is that he carried a nagging sense of non-belongingness everywhere he goes (such that) he turns out to be the proverbial marginal figure, the ' ex-centric' in Linda Hutcheon's words. "Was it just that he sensed he did not belong to the radiant, the triumphant of the world?" (BB47)

Baumgartner has never been able to recover from the fear and paranoia which he witnessed during the persecution of the Jews by the Nazis; scare that had tainted a panicked childhood. The Jews learnt only to hide, to escape, to die. And Baumgartner internalized this compulsive need to hide as a potent defensive strategy that often appears to him as shameful. His mother used to tell him "Hide, we must hide. Sigfried." (BB 54) Baumgartner eventually learnt to do so, but not without damaging effect it entailed." Hugo found himself shamefully willing to do so; even the broom cupboard seems a heaven on that night." (BB 54) The Jews have always been historically accused of living in ghettos, in cloistered or secluded places, away from the mainstream or the majority, eking out their own lives but the accusers often forgot their historical compulsions. Baumgartner and his mother live also in the ghetto because of the fear of Hitler's persecution. "Their lives fell into a groove and remained there; they might have been an old married couple, Hugo and his mother, seldom leaving the apartment, looking after each other with stricken concern." (BB 64)

In many instances of world literature one encounters the individual being pitted against forces beyond his/her control. Likewise Baumgartner too turns out to be victim of history. Very often history dwarfs, crushes or erases the individual but there are occasions when the individual overcomes the historical obstacle by will-power or great fighting spirit and vigorous efforts.

In the history of the twentieth century, Hitler's genocide remains a bleak phase. The holocaust claimed thousands and lakhs of innocent lives; it wiped out at one swipe uncountable lives that were unable to fathom the frenzy of a ruthless dictator. Till today the holocaust continues to haunt the collective psyche of the Jewish race; the magnitude of atrocity continues to torment the survivors. Baumgartner had been able to luckily find a place away from the centre of atrocity, but he had internalized the fear and a compulsive urge to hide.

> **Although a part of him greedily, hungrily took in every morel of information that came his way of the situation of the Jews in Germany, of their disappearance, of the labour camps, of Nazi propaganda, another part frantically built a defensive bridge against it. It was as if his mind was trying to construct a wall against history, wall behind which he could not crouch and hide... (BB 142)**

The cited passage brings to light Baumgartner's desperate attempt to shut out any trace of history that might disrupt his new life, far away from bleak historical reality, but ironically caught up in the vortex of a rather bleak phase of history, in this context the Partition of India.

The figure of the Jew has always been imagined as an escapist, an introvert who does not socialize much, an obsessively morbid being who resists assimilation. But the Jew does not always create such conditions; that historical forces become both the condition and consequence of his/her life. Susannah Aeshel writes in her essay 'Imagining Judaism in America"-

> **The religious thought that emerged in the last decade of the twentieth century sought a recovery or precisely those aspects of Judaism that has been vociferously rejected by the preceding generation of the modern period...one outcome of the recovery was also in turn away from assimilation toward more traditional religious observance, which brought with it a new valorization of physical expressions of Jewishness and concomitantly, of Jewish body.**

> **(Wirth-Nesher and Kramer 40-41)**

      Delving Into Different Literary Terrains

Owing to this the Jew develops a withdrawal syndrome or symptom as an attempt to assimilation might usher in newer complications. Baumgartner wants to go back to the oppressively safe but 'enclosed' space that provides him the illusion of liberation, in an ironical way -

" In a panic, he wished he could flee, return to that enclosed world, the near barracks, the vegetable fields, the fixed hour for baths, meals, lecturers, drill, the release from the pressures of outer world."

(BB 193)

Baumgartner had been able to build only an illusion of safety and security - he knows that the defense he has thus built around him is fragile; and yet "He stayed in more and more now, he stayed in." (BB 207)

Baumgartner's fear psychosis is not only related to the trauma of holocaust; the extraordinary pressure of his boredom and loneliness had forced him to develop a withdrawal syndrome or symptom. He desperately searches for a spot where he can hide himself. But as he realizes there probably is no such place... as yet. Baumgartner feels the necessity to keep his secret to himself. He realizes the need to tighten his defense mechanism. He has almost retreated into a cocoon as his Jewish identity keeps him at tenterhooks all the time. His problem intensifies as he; a Jew feels constantly a pressure that is both historical and metaphysical. Though he has lived in Bombay for almost half a century, yet he is always drawn towards hiding -

"The migrants seemed neither to hear nor to speak but Baumgartner, for one shuffled part with his head bowed and his eyes averted - not to avoid contamination as the others died, but to hide his shame at being alive, sheltered, and privileged."(BB 247)

Baumgartner has never even honestly attempted to assimilate, he begins and ends his life as a typical minority figure; hiding becomes both origin and destination of his existence.

"If he became aware, from time to time, that the world beyond the curtain was growing steadily more crowded, more clamorous and the lives of others more hectic, more chaotic, then he felt only relief that he had never been a part of the mainstream. Always somehow, he had escaped the mainstream." (BB 252)

The Jew has to behave like an actor because of historical necessity. She/
he is always aware of the fact that he/she is, in fact, acting our already
given role in the world. This adds to the comic aspect of his/her character
and Anita Desai provides a number of instances in Baumgartner's Bombay
to strengthen the point where the Jew behaved like a trickster performing
a continuous comic role According to Calude Levi Strauss, the French
anthropologist -

**"The trickster is a mediator. Since his mediating function occupies
a position halfway between two polar terms, he must retain
something of that duality namely an ambiguous and equivocal
character."**

(Levi Strauss 226)

Baumgartner consistently meditates between the "Two polar terms" his
bleak personal life and his compulsive need to hide the dark reality that
creates a tragic-comic dimension of its own. Andrew Stott writes in his
book Comedy-

**"The comic mobility of the trickster therefore is a means to
bringing about reconciliation through the interpenetration of
apparently irreconcilable realms of existence. By having a foot
both in the sub and super-binary worlds and embodying a moral
ambiguity, he acts as a signifier in which opposites can come
together; through the mediation of the trickster, life and death
are reconciled." (Stott 55)**

Both Hugo Baumgartner and his father attempt to reconcile their
"apparently irreconcilable realms of existence" through laughter - that
both mitigates and accentuate their pain. Henry Bergson writes in his
seminal book, **Laughter: An essay on the meaning of the comic -**

**"Laughter, then, does not belong to the province of esthetic alone,
since unconsciously (and even immorally in many particular
instances) it pursues a utilitarian aim of general improvement.
And yet there is something esthetic about it, since the comic
comes into being just when society and the individual freed from
the worry of self preservation begins to regard themselves as
works of art." (Bergson 17)**

Hugo's father continued with his normal day-to-day life even in the midst of great historical turmoil. He refused to be subdued either by the fear or the threat of persecution of the Jews as he used laughter as a defense mechanism.

"Seemed to need to come away in order to laugh out loud - coarsely, perhaps - to push his hat back from his forehead and turn terracotta with laughter." (BB 33)

Hugo Baumgartner also does the same as the following passage brings to light -

Hugo was awed by so much of ridiculous, hurrying almost running towards the music and the dance, burst again and again to look at the comic pair. (BB 34)

There is almost an esthetic dimension, as noted by Bergson, in Hugo Baumgartner's tentative gesture towards laughter that can act as a corrective device against the towering personal odds.

Baumgartner found himself standing with his hands dangling, his knees buckling, while they looked him over and joked; he found himself trying to join in the laughter, uncertain whether to do so would help or worsen matters. (BB 130-131)

Baumgartner suffers because of his racial burden, as the Jew is a perpetually misunderstood figure. For the Indians there is no difference between a German and a Nazi German.

They don't even know there are German Jews and there are Nazi Germans and they are not exactly the same. All you can do is hope to get a chance to speak to someone who does know - some Englishman. (BB 128)

The figure of the Jew has been historically constructed as deplorable. At the same time there has always been a conscious attempt to erase the identity of Jews, the classic example being Shylock in Shakespeare's **The Merchant of Venice.** One does not look at the Jew because Jew and Baumgartner experiences similar fate. "They watched him fearlessly - to them he was nobody, an old man with an empty bag. Finishing with the pots, the women spat into the gutter, than to pick them up. (BB 15)

Unable to bear the burden of his race, making desperate attempt to protest his own self from the invasion of others, playing roles to survive, wearing a comic mask to conceal his sorrows and anguish, Baumgartner gradually loses articulation, not literally, rather in the figurative sense, as "… silence was his natural condition."
(BB 140)

The post-colonial discourse in **Baumgartner's Bombay** turns out to be interesting because of a reversal of the standard paradigm between the oppressor and the oppressed. Though Baumgartner represents the ethos of the White Western World, he turns out to be an oppressed figure in India. Baumgartner is and remains a Jew throughout the novel. The post-colonial discourse gains momentum in the text as the protagonist frames the 'other' and is framed by 'the other'. The white Europeans have constructed a particular image of the orient as timeless, strange, dark, degenerate, diseased and feminine. The inhabitants of the orient turns out to be 'the other' which in turn has propagated and nurtured prejudice in the mind of the white westerners. While assessing Said's contribution to post-colonial studies in **Orientalism (1978), John Mcleod writes in his book Beginning Post-colonialism -**

Crucial to orientalism was the stereotype of the orient's peculiarity. The orient is not just difficult it is oddly different, unusual, fantastic, and bizarre. Westerners could meet all manner of spectacle there, wonders that would beggar belief and make them doubt their Western eyes… If the occident was rational, sensible and familiar, the orient was irrational, extraordinary, and abnormal. (McLeod 44)

The occident nurtures not only geographical prejudice about the orient, but also cultural prejudice that seeks to demean, belittle, and even erase the rich cultural heritage of the latter. Hugo Baumgartner's mother exhibits such a prejudice when she articulates to her son - "Ach Hugo, don't be ridiculous. Why should your mother read a bangalische poet when I can read beautiful verses of our dear Friendmanns?" (BB70) This is precisely the kind of articulation that reminds one of Macaulay's' infamous proclamation in the minute. Baumgartner's lifelong companion Lotte, who provides him solace in a moment of crisis also reinforces the familiar occidental prejudice against the orient when she exclaims before

Hugo - "I had forgotten, I was living in India.. India, the land of sari - of veiled women - what did they know about hats? Such an idiot I was, I really thought they would wear my hats."(BB93)

The white westerner feels a nagging sense of unease as a result of his encounter with the orient and Baumgartner's reaction reveal such anxiety typical of the occident figure.

"Somewhere beyond that veranda was the street, the traffic, the noise, and beyond that sea, the ships, the rose-red arc of the Gateway of India. Baumgartner felt his world not merely opening up but torn open, hacked open, to the Eastern light." (BB 107)

The orient as a location remains a threat to the white European as it is full of death, disease and dirt. The white European always exhibits an anxiety that he/she might be contaminated or infected because of his/her encounter with the orient. This concern finds expression in the following passage -

"The passengers. A Jesuit father on his way to the seminary in Chandernagore. Returning after sick-leave. Dressed in black. His face haggard and green with many seasons of malaria and dysentery. Reading the Bible, also in black. His lips moving eating the words. Then eating a banana. Looking across at Baumgartner and saying "The only thing you can eat on a journey in this country. It is not touched by their hand, you see, it is protected by its skin" (BB108)

The orient has also been imagined as a king of vacuum - a space devoid of history. The following passage from the novel exemplifies how the white westerner absolutely denigrates the orient.

"When he overcame and left behind his initial horror at the sight of women carrying excreta on their heads. And digging their hands into it as they might into wet dough or laundry, and her initial bewilderment at lives so primitive, so basic and unchanging; he began to envy them that simplicity, the absence of choice and history." (BB 133-134)

The impression conveyed there is that Indians as a people, as a nation has no history behind them. Post-colonial critics and writers have expressed consistent concern with language as it remains a potent marker of identity.

Many indigenous communities lost their respective language... (if not cultures) as a direct consequence of colonization and it also signified the loss of this very identity. Danish Walder rightly points out in his book, Post-Colonial Literature in English -

In the history of colonialism and decolonization, the literary dimension is apparent not only in the themes and preoccupation of literary procedures, but also and more profoundly in their chosen medium. (Walder 42)

Baumgartner also suffers from the anxiety of losing his language that would mean the loss of his identity. The anxiety manifest itself in the following passage which also brings to light the white westerner's perpetual fear of being contaminated by the orient -

He found he had to build a new language to suit these new conditions - German no longer sufficed, and English was elusive. Language sprouted around him like tropical foliage and he picked words from it without knowing if they were English or Hindi or Bengali - they were simply words he needed... (BB 111-112)

Thus we find that the post-colonial discourse in **Baumgartner's Bombay** belies out standard conception of particular theoretical paradigm as there is dual-edged irony in the protagonist's encounter with the orient. However, it must also be borne in mind that the novel reinforces some of the major but familiar trajectories of post-colonial theory and literature.

In conclusion we may convincingly argue that **Baumgartner's Bombay** facilitates a critical reading in the light of Mikhail Bakhtin's formulation of the genre of the novel as a sire of dialogized discourse and an alert perusal of novel bring out the rich and subtle interplay of both the Jewish and the post-colonial discourse that adds to the destiny of Desai's marvelous creation. However, the aesthetic of dialogized discourse in **Baumgartner's Bombay** may not be conclusive as great creative writers also believe in non-conclusive of life itself.

Endnotes and References

Desai, Anita Baumgartner's Bombay - New Delhi: Random House India 2002

Gupta, RK The Novels of Anita Desai - A Feminist Perspective. New Delhi: Atlantic Publishers and Distributors, 2002

Bakhtin, M. "Discourse in the Novel". The Dialogic Imagination: Four Essay by M.M. Bakhtim ed. M Gologuist, tras. Caryl Emerson and M. Holquist Austin, Texas: University of Texas Press, 1981

Jawrorski, Adam and Coupland, Nikolas. "Introduction" The Discourse Reader. London: Routledge, 1999

Levi-Strauss, Claude Structural Anthropology trans. Clari Jacobson and Brooke Grandfest Schoe. New York and London, 1963

Stott Andrew. Comedy. New York: Routledge, 1969

Bergson, Henry. Laughter: An essay on the meaning of the Comic. USA: Book Jungle, 2007

McLeod, John. Beginning Post-colonialism. Manchester and New York: Manchester University Press, 2007

Walder, Dennis. Post-Colonial Literature in English: History of Language Theory. Oxford: Blackwell 1998 Wirth-Nesher and Kramer Michael P. eds. Cambridge Companion of Jewish American Literature. UK, USA: Cambridge University Press 2003

The Journey Of A Writer

Indira Goswami in Conversation with Subhajit Bhadra

An exceptional novelist who has extended the geography of Assamese fiction, a brilliant short story writer who has mesmerized readers with each of her tales, an evocative poet with original and refreshing expression, a relentless crusader for peace in her turbulent state, a philanthropist in her ideals and actions, a successful academic who taught in the Modern Indian Language and Department of Delhi University for over thirty years, Indira Goswami who is also known as Mamoni Raisom Goswami in her region, endearingly addressed as Baideo by many has carved a nitche for herself in the literary and cultural horizon of her state and country. She has earned almost every prestigious literary award of India including the **Sahitya Akademi Award** and the **Bhartiya Janan Pith Award**. Most recently the Government of Netherland conferred on her one of the country's most prestigious literary awards, **The Prince Claus Foundation Award** in recognition of her outstanding literary output.

It was a hot summer evening in Guwahati when I reached her local residence at Gandhi Basti 7 p.m. A soothing tranquility and peace of mind descended on me as soon as I entered into her drawing room that radiated a rare intellectual energy. Photographs taken over the years with different dignitaries and literary stalwart of the country and abroad, numerous prizes and different accolades, the books scattered here and there - the room excluded a unique charm. And above all, the gentle presence of Indira Goswami herself, always smiling and obliging others, assured a meaningful conversation. What follows is the result of a conversation conducted in two different sessions which was characterized by candidness and honesty that has been the hallmark of her life and literary output.

Subhajit Bhadra: It is generally believed that every child is a perspective adult and every adult nurtures within him/her lost child. Childhood as a formative phase of life is always important in case of any individual human being and it becomes significantly special in the life of a writer. The most important thing about you is that you have still retained a childlike simplicity in your appearance and behavior - looking back how much you think your childhood has shaped you both as a human being and as a writer.

Indira Goswami: I think my childhood is very important in shaping me both as a human being and as a writer. I have always drawn inspiration from my childhood. My family happened to be economically solvent as the family members happened to be 'adhikars' of Amragna Suttra situated in South Kamrup of Assam. We possessed lots of elephant and as the roads were in an atrocious condition, elephants were used to pull our cars in our village home. Whatever I have achieved in life and what I am now is because of my childhood. My father was a scholar in his own right and he was also the Director of Public Instruction in undivided Assam. He had great love and affection for me and I used to imagine being a writer. Father used to tell me that without knowing the Bible and the Koran. I would never become a good writer. I wrote a few poems and drew some portraits of Christ. I also wanted to be a painter. I wanted to attend scripture class but was told that Hindus and Muslims were exempted from such classes, but I took that class voluntarily. I first learnt about Christ when I was 9 or 10 years of age. My teacher used to speak about the bloodstained clothes and Jesus. And gradually my mind was inclined towards Christ. My father used to console me. Though we were financially sound, our lifestyle was simple and reflected our down to earth attitude. Even my birthday celebration was not allowed by my father. I did not posses many good clothes. This austerity was imposed by my father who wanted us to learn through hardship the lesson that life demands everyone to understand.

These things taught me to write about the poor and the oppressed later on. When I went to T. C Girls School for matriculation, I did not initially get admission into the Assamese class because I had learnt little Assamese at Latashil Primary School. But the great daughter of Ambikagiri Roychoudhury, Suchibrata Roychoudhury, who was teaching English in T. C Girl's School, convinced the authority to give me admission. And then I learnt Assamese thoroughly. And I am not nostalgic about my childhood as it was harsh. I suffered from a great depression because I lost my father and dearest uncle. So, I don't want to remember that difficult phase. Though depression was always in me it intensified after the death of my father.

S B: You belong to one of the most prestigious families of West Assam that has been well-known for its love for learning, respect for tradition and veneration for values that sustain and nurture a healthy life. The numerous references to Sattras in your works and a specific socio-cultural ambiance add to it a unique touch. How much do you think it was an advantage to you as a writer to be born into a family and ambiance that would contribute to creativity?

IG: Yes, I consider myself fortunate to be born into such a family. My mother was a great human being. She was not even a matriculate but her manner, conduct and personality greatly moulded me. She offered me the desired freedom and because of that many eyebrows were raised. She was extremely beautiful and everybody praised her beauty. I did what I liked and my mother always supported me. My mother's family had to sell a tea garden for just 300 rupees out of necessity. During the time of my mother's marriage, a Muslim friend helped with finances. I attracted the attention of many boys and their character sketches could produce a voluminous book. My love also increased with the passing of time. During my childhood, the then editor of prestigious **Daily** who used to reside in front of our house taught me Assamese and encouraged me to write a short story in order to test my creativity. I wrote about an elephant which was given as a plaything to me and my elder brother, Satyabrata. The mahout had a great affection for me and showed how to prepare opium. Once I tasted it and I also developed a fascination for drinking. Thus the entire colorful ambiance, apart from the family background significantly contributed towards my creativity.

SB: You have experienced life in all its diversity and from each experience you have been able to squeeze out something vital for your creativity. That you underwent tremendous trauma, depression and suffering during the earlier phase of life is well-known to those people who have read **An Unfinished Autobiography (Adhiskha Dotavej in Assamese).** But the tragic and unfortunate period made Indira Goswami the person and the writer tougher, more resolute, stronger and more humane. Your creativity also bloomed subsequently to reach enviable heights. Please tell us in detail about the difficult period when you married the person whom you loved most and lost him.

IG : Much to the chagrin of many, I married a construction engineer from South India, Madhvan Raisom. Ours was a love marriage and we loved each other from the core of our hearts. So, there was no problem regarding adjustment in spite of different socio-cultural background. The short period after marriage with Madhu was one of the most blissful periods of my life. But cruel destiny intruded in my happiness as Madhu was killed in

     DELVING INTO DIFFERENT LITERARY TERRAINS

a road accident near Udhampur in Kashmir. After his death, I underwent tremendous depression and mental trauma. I found it extremely difficult to regather the broken pieces of life again. For a long time, I could not look above towards the sky. I lost all interest in life and was constantly brooding over the tragic incidents that had taken away from me the dearest person in my life. I started chasing his shadow everywhere and I realized that nothing remains after death. At that time, my bag was full of sleeping pills instead of sweet perfumes as I developed suicidal tendency. But gradually I recovered from the trauma and resolved to cry any more. It was really a battle for me to come out of that dark phase. It was a battle with tears and the blood gushing out of the heart. I decided to devote myself to writing and my pen never ceased.

SB : During the troubled phase of your life you found great solace in the **Ramayana** and since then you have been consistently engaged in an endeavor to spread its message among the people. When, how and under what circumstances were you first drawn toward the **Ramayana?**

IG : The **Ramayana** was not my favourite text first because I had some doubt regarding it. A few aspects of this great epic bothers me such as Rama killing Bali from behind, the disfigurement of Surpnakha, the killing of Shambuk because he, a shudra, dread to tapas and the banishment of Sita. I got the PHD scholarship from the government of Assam after the death of my dear husband. I registered with Guwahati University for PHD on literature. But my mother insisted on my switching over to the **Ramayana** which is regarded as a sacred text by the Hindus. My guru, the great teacher Upendrachandra Lekharu also wanted that. I still had my doubts regarding those puzzling aspects of the **Ramayana**. This time my guru asked me to write to Father Kamil Bulke who happened to be a Jesuit priest (Jesuits were more conservative then the Catholics). He was an engineer by profession and had come all the way from Belgium to India to learn Hindi. Subsequently he did his PHD in the **Ramayana.** This celebrated book **Ramakatha** happens to be a great scholarly work on the Ramayana tradition. It is written in Hindi. In it he discusses diverse Ramayana in India and abroad. Intially, I doubtful whether he would meet me or not. But to my utter surprise he replied within one week after receiving my letter. And I still have that letter with me. I decided to meet him in St. Xavier's College, Ranchi where he taught. I journeyed to Ranchi with my lifelong friend and companion, Kaikua Burjor Satarawala who looked after me for thirty long years till he died in 2003. He was a Parsi engineer. I was twenty four years then and travelling with Kaikuas was a relief. It was a big and beautiful garden where we located father Kamil Bulke reading something. When I stood near him he was surprised to see me and said, 'You are like an angel, come inside my quarter.' While he was preparing coffee, I raised my doubt regarding the **Ramayana** and he told me, "My child, these are only interpolations." Then he pointed towards a flying aeroplane outside and told me, "I have written in detail about these interpolations in **Ramakatha.** In only one version of Ramayana - (I) Dakshinatya version (2) Paschim Uttariya version and (3) the Gouriya version. The North-east follows the Gouriya Version. The Shambik Vadh is only in the Dakshinatya edition. Go, and immediately switch over to Ramayana" Thus it was the turning point of my life. I switched over from Mantra literature to Ramayana. Mathura Mohan Goswami - the then Vice-Chancellor of Guwahati helped me to switch over because he knew my background and was also a good friend of my father.

SB : The **Ramayana** is not merely a sacred text to be simply read and venerated, you emphasise its socio-cultural values. It is not an exaggeration to argue that you have been largely responsible for propagating its value outside India in numerous international seminars and conferences. Please tell us about your experience aboard with regard to **Ramayana** and also something about the various foreign scholars who have contributed towards Ramayana studies.

IG : Ramayana really helped me to see the world outside India. I went several times to Mauritius. I came to know about and saw the plight of indentured labourers of Suriname, British Guyana, Fiji, Trinidad, etc. These labourers were so poor that they had nothing with them but they carried a copy of **Ramcharitmanas** wherever they went. In the evening after a day's hard work they gathered under the shadow of a tree and recited verses from the **Ramcharitmanas** which provided them great solace and inspiration. They compared their plight with that of Rama who had likewise been exiled and wanted to go back to their homeland. But in reality that never happened. Now these indentured labourers have been ruler in some of those countries. In the 1980s there were regular sessions of discussion on the **Ramayana**. Even today **Ramayana** is sold in a large number in Mauritius. **Ramkatha** is also largely popular there. I met many international scholars on **Ramayana** like Jing Jinjhan who had translated **Ramayana** into Chinese and who used to meet me in Delhi. I met AP Barannikov who came to my Delhi residence. He told me about his great scholar - father.

S B : Barannikov has translated **Ramcharitmanas** into Russian. It was a general belief in the West at that time that India today is only a caricature of its earlier self and creative ability had declined after the Mughal conquest. Scholar like Max Muller also argued that there were not many significant works to be translated from Indian languages. Barannikov took the challenge and translated **Ramcharitmanas** into Russian with 2000 footnotes that explained many things about India. This effect opened a great door and Russian people became interested in India. It must be emphasized here that this door was opened by **Ramcharitmanas**, not by politicians. When Barannikov died, a couplet from Ramcharitmanas was engraved on his tomb following his great wish. The couplet was "**Good people do good and evil do evil, it can be compared with nectar and poison. Nectar gives eternal life and poison brings death.**" I also met Mura - great, Mexican scholar. I met Ston Suranga Potphipia, a great devotee of Rama and a scholar of **Thai Ramayana** who became my intimate friend. Apart from Indian scholar of Ramayana like Satyavrat Shastri and Lalan Prasad, a devotee and scholar of Ramayana, I also met Tora and Japanese scholar on Ramayana.

SB : You believe that some of the most important work in the field of Ramayana research had been done by Christian and Mohamadan scholar beside the Hindus. You have also established a Ramayana research centre at your home in Guwahati. What do you think of this secular aspect of Ramayana and what are your future plans regarding the institution you have built?

IG : Yes, I believe that **Ramayana** is a secular text as it had established its appeal over people belonging to different religious communities over the ages. Sir George Grierson said that, "The influence of Ramayana in Bengal, Punjab, Himalaya, Vindhya and Madhya Pradesh is most great than that of the Bible in the world of England." Yes, it is true that I have opened the South Asian Ramayana Research Center at Guwahati. It has a library exclusively devoted to Ramayana. There would be lecture session throughout the years where different scholars will be lectured on various aspects of Ramayana and every year at least two books will be brought out by this center. A scholar will also do PHD on Ramayana affiliated to Guwahati University.

SB : From Vrindavan you made a journey to the threshold of prestigious Delhi University and your life also significantly shifted after that. Do you think that going to Delhi was a decisive phase of your life and how do you assess your academic life apart from your creative life? Do you think they have complemented each other?

IG : Yes, they have complemented each other. I taught in the Modern Indian Language Department of Delhi University for over 30 years. Going to Delhi was definitely a decisive phase of my life. I would not have become what I am today staying in Assam. My academic life has helped me in my writings. I have written a novel based on the experience of my academic life titled **Dasorathir Khoj** which is coming out from Cambridge Guwahati under the title, **The Quest for the Divine.**

SB : When you started your literary career, Assamese literature was vibrant with the presence of many literary stalwarts. When and where was your first significant works published? Was it really difficult to carve out a niche for yourself because your happened to be women writer?

IG : My significant published work was the novel **Chenabor Srot (Current of Chenab** in English translation) based on the lives of the labourers of Chenab in Kashmir.

I never found any special difficulty as a woman writer and I personally do not believe in any such distinction. I am however not denying that woman cannot face any constraints. But basically I think only creativity matters in the end.

SB : You have been engaged in creative writing for over four decades and you witnessed many trends in Assamese writing. You have widened the horizons of Assamese fiction as you have ventured outside to different geographical location to focus on different communities and their problems - as it evident in work like **Ahiron, Chenabor Srot** and **Neelkanthi Braj**. Do you think that venturing out has helped your creativity? Don't you think that most of your contemporary Assamese writers have been too cocooned?

IG : I consider myself extremely lucky as I have the privilege of venturing out, Basically, I am a humanist. So, geographically borders do not matter to me. When I portrayed the agony of Bengali windows in **Neelkanthi Braj,** I was 25 years of age. Then I wrote novels such as **Mamore Dhora Torowal, Chenabor Srot** and **Ahiror** based on the wretched lives of the labourers. I have the opportunity to stay with the labourers in their barracks. My husband was at Chenab and later Kaikaus was at Ahiron. They had allowed me to stay with the labourers. Yes, I do think that some of my contemporary could have enlarged their experience though they have produced many good works. Even within the Assamese tribal communities there was great material for fiction. But, nobody was interested in this sort of endeavors.

SB : You have always been concerned with the plight of the oppressed in your work and also championed their cause. This genuine concern for women has manifested itself in works like **Neelkanthi Braj** where you depict the miserable, suffocating and deplorable lives of widows in Kashi. You have also depicted the lives of the opium- addicted Gossainees of various Sattras in **Dental Hathir Uie Khowa Howda (The Moth Eaten Howdah of a Tuskar, A Saga of South Kamrup in English translation)**. How were you repeatedly drawn towards the plight of women? Do you think being a woman you could portray their psyche better?

IG : Well, this is true, but I have also portrayed male character with Compassion and sensitivity. And it is true that being a woman myself, I could comprehend women's psyche better.

SB : The Moth Eaten Howdah of Tusker. A Saga of Kamrup is not merely authentic socio-cultural document of a period spanning over hundred years. Amitav Ghosh in his most recent novel **Sea of Poppies** had shown extraordinary scholarship in digging out material regarding opium trade that significantly contributed towards English economy and you had dealt with this theme long back in the **Moth-Eaten Howdah of a Tusker** where you depicted how opium addiction plagued Assamese society. Please tell us how did you feel the urge to write on a theme like this and how did you do the required research?

IG : The protagonists were drawn from my own family acquaintances. The village is the novel where I spent my childhood in Sattra, the poor people there poured their affection on me. I always believe that distance purifies one's feelings. So when I wrote that novel in Delhi, I could portray everything with objectivity. I remembered the love of the people; I could not forget my elephant. I also suffered immensely when that elephant supposedly become mad, ran amock, destroyed everything and ultimately was shot dead by the order of the government. I knew how the communists started agitation. But because of misunderstanding innocent people like Indranath were killed.

At that point of time many villagers in Assam were under the evil grip of opium. It was openly sold. My father and others tried their best to free people from the grip of opium. Many people sold their land and property coming under the evil influence. Later on, camps were set up for the addicted people. However, the British did not play a positive role in this regard. They rather gave license for opium-selling. But later on they helped in the setting up of camps.

SB : You have always written novels specially marked by thorough research, fascinating subject-matter and a stubborn determination to expose the truth that in turn often brought much controversy. Your stunningly magnificent novel **Chinnamaster Manhutu (The Man from Chinnamasta)** infuriated many. Please tell us how you planned the framework in the novel and also about its after-effects.

IG : From my early childhood, I was an animal lover. Our family used to observe the ritual of animal slaughter which pained me. That pain was always growing inside. Rabindranath Tagore's play **Visarjan** also inspired me. I was also inspired by the ideal of Mahatma Gandhi. So I had to bring out what I felt. I drew my materials from real life. The character in the novel **Dorothy Brown** was modeled on the wife of Arthur Brown,- the then principal of Cotton College who had a Khasi deep. My father was a student of Arthur Brown. My father also became the Principal of Cotton College later on. I contemplated what trauma Arthur's wife underwent because of her husband's involvement within the Khasi women. It was not clear whether Arthur married the Khasi women or not. But the issue of marriage became important; the turmoil of Dorothy became most important. I got a idea about Arthur's character of Jatadhari was modeled on those educated people who came to Kamakhya becoming priest. I also stayed in Kamakhya for many days and gathered an insider's knowledge about what really happened there. I talked to various sadhus. This novel was first serialized in the Assamese magazine **Garioshi**. The novel created lots of unwanted controversy and some complained that I had become an animal lover losing my human concern. Some complained that I have been selective as I did not criticize the Muslims for animal slaugher. Anuradha Sharma Pujari, the editor of the weekly newspaper **Saadin** brought out a letter for and against the novel. The sanyasis became agitated and told that animal slaughter should not be stopped as it was an integral part of Hindu ritualistic religion. Kalikapuraoa supports animal slaughter but it also says that Baikuntha could be obtained by offering a garland of flower also. There were also street protests demanding a ban on the novel. But 75% of the young generation supported me and they demanded that animal slaughter should be banned in Kamakhya. It was a spectacular success for me. Some young people were mentally affected and unable to withstand contributed toward insurgency. An enlightened publisher came to my house and kept 50 thousand rupees on my table demanding the copyright of the novel. But after sometime he retracted because he supposedly saw a dream. He did not want the money back but wanted another book. My family people were afraid to allow me to go outside. After sometime, I left for Delhi again.

SB : You were an eyewitness to the 1984 Sikh carnage in Delhi that is notorious for massive man slaughter and looting. Your book on Delhi, **Pages Stained with Blood** gives an insider's view of this fabulous city much like Khuswant Singh's account of Delhi in his novel of the same name. Now that you are away from this great city that has given you a lot, don't you feel an yearning to go back to the city if not physically, but at least mentally?

IG : It is true that I witnessed the terrible riot after Prime Minister Indira Gandhi's assassination. I went to the affected areas, Houses were burnt and there was lots of looting. I took two Assamese students from St. Stephen's College along with me. One of them is Pawan Barthakur who later on became an IAS officer, another one works in a bank. We went to Jahangirpuri and other affected areas. That was a terrible sight. Some Sikhs took away turbans that showed blood - clothes were also stained with blood and houses were reduced to dust. Everywhere there was blood. The morgue at Roshanara Bagh was full of scattered bodies. Hindus set up rescue camps at Sabji Mandi. I saw many parentless children there and it was tragic. I did a thorough study before writing this novel. I saw how objects from looting were amassed in the slum areas. I had the desire to see Indira Gandhi's dead body but 144 was already clamped on various parts of the city. Yes, I do feel an yearning to go back to the city often. At the same time I had a duty towards my native land. I donated the 60 lakh rupees I got from the **Prince Claus Foundation Award** from Netherlands. I donated the money for the hospital which is situated at Amranga near Mirza in south Kamrup. I also established the **South Asian Ramayana Research Center** since **Ramayana** has been a big text in Assam from the 7th century onwards.

SB : Apart from being a distinguished novelist, you have also been an accomplished short story writer and flamboyant poet. You have published a book of poems **Pain and Flesh** in English that has exhibited your poetic sensibilities with deft and urbane touch. How did you strike the balance between different genres and manage to leave a distinct stamp on each of them?

IG : Many people had asked me this question before when I published my books of poems after I received the **Jnanpith Award**. I consider my poetry a footnote to my prose. I always wanted to publish the poems before my death in order to make people aware of my identity as a poet. One or two of my poems were published much earlier in **Ramdhenue** which was edited by late Birendrakumar Bhattacharya. Our family friends and the great painter Jatin Hazarika did the illustration for **Pain and Flesh.** I started my career with a short story at class 7 . From that time, I have written hundred of short stories. It is quite strange that I never faced any difficulty switching between different genres. I also wrote a few radio plays. I always followed the style about existentialism, surrealism and other artistic and literary movement but I always followed my own instincts regarding writing and developed an individual style with the passage of time. This style was followed later on by many writers in my native place.

SB : Awards and accolades have poured forth from all quarters. You have achieved honour and distinction that have made your state and country proud. Do you have any regret over something which you could not achieve?

IG : Never, I do not regret anything. I am always proud about the love which ordinary people have bestowed on me. I am proud of the love which the government of Netherlands showed to me by giving the prestigious award.

SB : You have recently started a novel that provides a short alternative history of Assam and bring into focus the life of a Bodo woman. How do you intend to go ahead with this work and what future plans do you have regarding your creative life?

IG : There are many fictional materials within the tribal community of Assam. But no writer has used those materials. During my childhood, I spent some time in Bijni in lower Assam, interestingly the Ahoms never ruled there. The royal family of Bijni had friendship with our own family. We roamed Bijni on elephant's back. At that time, I used to read her ballads about **Theng Fakhri** who became the first women revenue collector in British India. I used to imagine her character mentally and later on thought seriously about writing a novel based on her life. But there was great paucity of material. After coming back to Guwahati from Delhi I started gathering material from various sources. I did research about the marginalized position of women in Theng Fakhri's time. There was hardly any written history about lower Assam. Only heresy prevailed. The Bodos helped me immensely. They also showed me the places where **Theng Fakhri** stayed.

     Delving Into Different Literary Terrains

Then I met Batiram Bodo, a veteran of more than hundred years, I talked to him. He supposedly saw Theng Fakhri. I went to the specific village with a host of local people. I also started reading history books to have a grip over chronology. Now, I want to finish this novel.

SB : Who are your favorite author and what are your favorite books.

IG: From my student days, I have been a great admirer of Hemingway whose **For Whom the Bell Tolls** and **A Farewell to Arms** have always inspired me. I also read Dostoyesky's books in English translation. The Japanese writer Yukio Mishima's **The Golden Pavilion** has been a great book to me. Among the Indian writers, I liked Phnishwar Nath Reny's, **Mail Achal,** Shohan Shital's, **Jug Badal Gaya** and U. R Ananthrmurthy's, **Samskara.**

SB : What was the happiest moment in your life and what message or advice would you like to give to the upcoming writers of today to hone their creative prowess?

IG : Of course, I always wanted to share my happiest moment with my mother. When I received the two great awards in the form of **Jnanpith Award** and **Prince Claus Foundation Award**, my mother was not there. My happiest moment was when my husband proposed me by telling that I was the most beautiful woman he had ever seen. At that time, I was young. I always believed in humanity. I am not a feminist, I am a humanist. Humanity should be the priority of young writers of today. Sincerity and spirituality should proceed hand-in- hand and only then we can avoid all catastrophes.

The Evolution Of Modern Assamese Poetry Since The 1980s To The Present

Subhajit Bhadra

If any intrepid scholar makes an attempt to chart out the trajectory of Assamese poetry between 1980s to the present time, he or she will be awestruck with its variety and different hues. If we want to talk about post 1980 Assamese poetry then it becomes essential to make an attempt to understand the contemporary socio-political environment. During 1979 to 1984 there was a conscious movement (Known as Assam Agitation Movement) to drive away the non- Assamese people from Assam who, according to the native Assamese people, were eating up the economic framework of the State .During the poetry of that period we find a typical Assamese community consciousness. During that period some of the poets became progressive in their attitude of course, according to some critics, that kind of consciousness was integrally related to the formation of Assamese community as a whole. The Assam accord which was signed as a result of the Assam agitation Movement brought about a new sense of being in the mindset of middle class people who thought with enthusiasm that change would come. One also finds a sense of new dawn and the rise of regional politics which gave birth to a narrow sense of provincialism. This sense of enthusiasm felt by the middle class did spread among the contemporary Assamese poets. Parallel to that the rise of ULFA and their activities of terrorism brought about a huge change and that period also witnessed the rise of small communities who were striving to form their own identity. Some there was a feeling of disenchantment and the sense of shattered dream affected the poets of the contemporary period.

Some of the tribal communities were also demanding sovereignty which found reflection in the contemporary poetry. The dream which was visualized by the contemporary middle class people during the Assam Agitation Movement was shattered by the happening and incidents of terrorism that took place during the 1990s because of full fledged arm struggle spearheaded by the ULFA. Assam was shattered due to the failure of Assam accord, fundamental or communal hatred, conflict, murder and continually increasing violence.

Against the background of such a scenario contemporary Assamese poetry advanced in a fragmented way. There was the rise of a huge number of poets, they continued to practice poetry, some could not leave the field of poetry but some other poets totally disappeared after writing a few poems. The poetry starting from the 1980s saw a departure from the poetry of the 1960s as it became less complex in tone and reader-oriented in tenor. Even though the sense of urbanity witnessed in the poetry of Nabakanta Baruah had not totally vanished yet the present Assamese poetry has become more and more anti-urban in nature. Assamese poetry has enriched itself because of the participation of a few tribal writers who are writing their poems in Assamese. Regarding the aesthetics of Assamese poetry the contemporary poets are quite influenced by the western poetry of symbolism and imagism. Newer techniques have been applied by the Assamese poets and one can even witnessed the influenced of movement like magic realism. A sense of uncertainty, an attempt to visualized readers as merely consumers, a distrust of universalism, and belief in the sense of plurality an anguish against everything pre-determined, rejection of a sense of cohesion , accepting poetry as a commodity, a sense of spiritual emptiness , socialists thought, disbelief in any sort of ideology, distrust of any unified movement regarding the change of society, to regard men as playthings in the hands of destiny- all these can be seen in the contemporary Assamese poetry in fragmented way.

Sameer Tanti (born in 1956), started writing his major poems since the 1980s and his poetic voice has been recognized as unique. He has penned several poetry collections – some of those are Poems of Battlefield, The text books of Torture, Green Festival, Context of Famine, Companion of Melancholy, and the Boat of Blood and Darkness. He has also exposed in his poems political ideology, has offered his own criticism of politics and thus he has also expressed anguish, desolation and these have given birth to a voice of protest. According to the Sahitya Akademi award winning poet Harekrishana Deka, 'Sameer Tanti is not an ordinary poet . The way he has expressed the political restlessness of contemporary period in his poetry has not been seen in the poems of any other poet.' He has presented to us a blending of so called socialist poetry and modernist poetry. If we look at the tenor and life blood of his poems then we would find the so- called progressive trend but if we look at his language and its expression then we can find the experimentative streak of modernism. He has expressed the turbulence of the 1980s in his poetry which cannot go unnoticed. His poetry becomes a witnessed of the contemporary political unrest, loss of communal harmony brought about by a strong sense of provincialism, the ruthlessness of state machinery and death, murder and violence of society. But yet he has expressed a sense of protest and optimism in many of his poems. There is also a sense of universalism in his poetry. His poetry is not bereft of the concept of love-though that love is directed towards his native land, his compatriots, the tortured and subjugated simply human being, the vulnerable and fragile people or sometimes an unknown beloved. His poetry basically expresses political plight of the State but there has been witnessed a sense of lyricism in his later poetry very strongly.

At certain times, his poetry has assumed a sense of individuality and subjectivity. His poetry portrays nature, love, emptiness and a consciousness of death. In many of his poems he has depicted the life of tea-tribes. We find a smell of soil, the sound of drums, the tribal dialect along with polished Assamese language in some of his poems.

Anupama Basumatary (born in 1960) has registered an individual voice in the domain of contemporary modern Assamese poetry. She deserves credit for popularizing contemporary modern Assamese poetry and it has become possible because she has successfully bridged the distance or gap between common people and poetry through a unique linguistic touch.

Though she has been born into Bodo familiy who have their own language (Both oral and written) yet she has found her true poetic expression in Assamese language. She is also one of those women Assamese poet who has got a distinctive poetic style. She believes that poetry is the mirror of heart and soul and yet her poetry is not devoid of intellect and the depiction of freedom of women. Her poetry brings us closer to sensibility which has the audacity to discard traditional rigid social values and who can tolerate the ups and down of life, who can distinguish between moral and immoral and create a path of her own and who can candidly express every incidents or secret of individual life. She had given expression to the loneliness of women and their pain and sorrows. She has experienced a lot in her life and she transparently expresses those experiences in her poetry. She has taken life as a scientific laboratory and dissected the complex relation between males and females. One of the major themes of her poetry is love and this has been pinpointed by readers and critics alike and she does not disagree with them totally. Love has come to her life at many times and she has given expression to those poems in her poetry. But she does not agree with those critics who have said that she has wasted her poetic talent by writing simple love poems. She has written two unique poems taking snail as a symbol where she depicts the poignant experience of life. The tribes to which Anupama belongs eat snails. In her poems we find solitude in the midst of company and strong sense of feminine sensibility.

Nilim Kumar (born 1961) has given a new lease of life to modern Assamese poetry through new experiments and he is not only widely recognized but also hugely popular. He has made a departure from traditional subject matter and form. His poetic sense has evolved through paradoxical intellectual crosscurrents. On the one hand we find in his poetry a sense of melancholy and desolation while on the other hand we find a sense of raw enthusiasm and a sense of revolution. He becomes nostalgic in some of his poems as he departs from traditional cultural rituals. He rages a battle against the traditional Assamese poetry and he has been compared with the Beats poets of the 1960s and 1970s. He has shown that he can blend emotion and intellect, a tendency to experiment, a mixture of symbol and images, a keenness to observe life from different viewpoints etc. One of his most famous poems Narakasur shows or exhibits these tendencies. He laces his poetry with narrative story, and he uses a strong sense of intellect to give a sense of dramatic turn to serious and unsolved mysteries of life. In Nilim Kumar's poetry we find anecdotes regarding women, their sensibility. In this context Nilim himself says,- 'My poetry has taken its shape through the contemplation of women body and its transcendent existence. I want only the Midas touch to love to impart me the much cherished pain.

According to Dr. Madan Sarma Nilim Kumar's poetry has a rare charm and an unusual freshness. Though always aware of and alive to the contemporary reality, he tries to negotiate with it in his own way, always exploring the self. Love, sexuality, spontaneous, exuberance of joy at richness and variety of life, indefinable sadness and gloom at times from the thematic concern of his poetry. Insecurity and uncertainty of the present after take him to the past, to the childhood memories and even to the womb, to a pre-lapsarian state. A remarkably unsentimental, even a little playful poem on childhood memory and disappearance of simple, familiar and uncomplicated rural ways of living is "Chor" (thief). His poetry has a variety of moods and a resonance of multiple voices.

Anuvab Tulsi (Born 1959) has been writing since the mid 1980s and he has exhibited a unique poetic sensibility in the realm of contemporary modern Assamese poetry. Dr. Hiran Gohain aptly pointed out in the preface to Tulsi's maiden poetry collection 'Nazma'. 'Nazma is a new experiment in Tulsi's poetry. Thought his economy of words of sense pain found in Japanese poetry, inner beauty etc... The lucid picture of Assamese folk culture is expressed in his poetry through beautiful imageries, symbolic hue and a strong sense of lyricism.' He has not neglected social reality. Because of his intricate symbolic tune the readers have to go through intellectual exercise to understand his poetry. The colorful portrayals of his birth place, intermingled with his existence in Guwahati, reading of English Literature and his knowledge of western cinema has added a modernist touch to Tulsi's poetry. Depiction of nature and rural life have given a unique touch to his urban experience. Love is a central matrix of his poetry and it is found in his poetry in different dimensions.

Among the poets who could avoid NabaKanta Baruah's poetic style is Rajib Barua and he has discovered a new linguistic medium of poetry of conscious effort and hard labour. He has also shown a Wordsworthian streak to democratize poetry through the simplification of language. He penned a poem titled 'Football' where he has used a comment by Miroslav Holub "Poetry should aspire to the condition of newspaper and the experience of watching a football match..." Rajib Barua has exhibited an intimate poetic touch through the observation of common human life. He has used both satire and narrative style in his poetry and these have turned out to be his strength. Some of his poetry show a spirit of French symbolic pattern but it would be an exaggeration to comment that Baruah is an exponent of Symbolism. In the context of post Laxminath Bezbaruah Assamese poetry Rajib Baruah has exhibited a style of satire which was practiced by Jaigeshwar Sharma.

Bipuljyoti Saikia (born 1966) started writing poetry since middle of 1980s and his poetic oeuvre is colorful. His poetic universe consists of a quest to understand the meaning of existence and the bitter and sweeter experiences of life. His poetry bears witness to the Assam agitation movement of the 1980s and the communal strife which gives a historical framework to his works. He has never tried to be apolitical in his poetry and his poetry acts as the sentinel of contemporary society. Some of his poetry can be called protest poetry but he never degenerated to slogan or clichés. Many of his poems bring forth the theme of war and it is known by everyone that war is harmful and that is why his poems talk about peace.

Nilima Thakuria Haq (born 1961) is a familiar name in the domain of Assamese poetry. Her poems bring out fresh images and she tries to deal with contemporary society in her poetry. She also talks about the evil tendencies of human beings but she is thoroughly grounded in her root. She has painted the picture of death, dread and violence in her poems but she has also tried to transcend those. She had satirized the evil trends of consumerism and its bad effects.

The basic tone of **Lutfa Hanum Selima Begum** (Born 1962) is romantic. She is not conscious of the harsh realities of life and she speaks about the bitterness and happiness of human life. Her language is lucid and one can find a picture of rural life combined with a romantic spirit on her poetry.

Among the post 'Ramdhenu' poets of second phase **Ajit Gogoi** (born 1968) is remarkable for his simplicity of style. But he seems to be serious against the lighter tendencies of some of his contemporary Assamese poets. He has satirized the artificial culture of contemporary society. He has also given voice to the sense of pain, anguish and desolation felt by people. He has portrayed a picture of the loneliness and broken dreams of modern life. Even though Gogoi basically talks about the melancholy of human life yet he is optimistic about man's future on earth. He can be called a painter of the darker realities of rural life and he has been able to exhibit a strong sense of realized experiences of life.

Gangamohan Mili (born 1968) has exhibit a sensitive style, a lucid language and expression of folk culture in his poetry. He has himself said about his poetry, 'I feel it unethical to betray people by portraying the false realities of life.' He depicts the rural realities of life and brings alive river, forest, trees and parallel to this he talks about the sorrows and broken dreams of people.

He has expressed the lived realities of rural people who basically live on the basis of agriculture and that is why a tone of regionalism can be found in many of his poems. There is a touch of sensitivity to fellow human being in his poetry and he basically sympathizes with the oppressed class of society. He belongs to the Miching Tribe and their culture customs are revealed in his poems. He had given expression to the lived realities of his own tribe which has added a unique charm to his poetry.

Jeeban Naraha (born 1970) has expostulated a fresh idiom and subjects matter in his poetry. He also depicts rural life and that is why his poetry is devoid of artificiality. The folk life portrayed in his poetry is his strength and his poems appear to be natural. He has advanced towards a sense of modernism through the use of contemporary images and symbols. Even though there are regional portrayals in his poetry yet he is free from provincialism. His poems are universal in nature and some of his poetry brings out a sense of desolation. His poetry also shows social awareness.

Rajib Borah (born 1970) has portrayed in his poetry the human response to life and the world. He avoids complexity but uses the experience derived from the knowledge of nature and human life. His poems have a smell of the soil and he feels unique attraction to common man. He has used tradition in a modern way and his poetry can be a mirror of contemporary Assamese rural life. It would not be an exaggeration to call it Assamese life-scape. Some of his poem emanate from a strong sense of history.

Kushal Dutta (born 1975) is a significant name in the realm of contemporary Assamese poetry. His poetic sense has evolved from a combination of emotion and intellect. He has discarded complexity and experimented with new subject matter and technical innovation. He has consciously attempted to break tradition and he had tried to weigh certain philosophical ideals in his poetry. He tries to move closer to the spoken language of common people. He does not give place to unnecessary images and symbols.

Biman Kumar Doley (born 1971) is another significant name in this context. He has given expression to childhood experience based on the rural life. Even though he lives in urban location yet he has taken recourse to the imaginative life. His poetic universe consists of folk life and its various nuances. He has also dealt with Miching life and its various rituals in his poetry.

Mridual Haloi has adopted a different trait in his poetry. Harkrishna Deka says about Haloi's poetry that, 'His poetry has created faith in my being and he is a strong contender to take a major place in the domain of Assamese poetry.' His poetic expression, his language and his sensitivity appealed to the seasoned readers of poetry.

Kabita Karmakar (1987) has expressed the confluence of life and youth in her poetry. The most significant point to that she has expressed the lives of common man and she can be considered as the daughter of the soil. She has also expressed the terrible picture of violence and dread, exploitation and subjugation.

Pratim Baruah is serious poet who has been quite consistent regarding the quality of his poetry. He has been writing in various magazines for quite some time now and he has a unique style which has been inculcated through his reading of various kind of poetry. In one of his poems titled 'Time' he began with a line by the Maxican poet Actavio Paz which reveals his grasp of western poetry. He has also written a few experimental poems and we can say that his poems will be more mature over the years.

Bivarani Talukdar is a strong voice in the realm of recent Assamese poetry and she seems to combine both tradition and modernity in her poems. A strong feminine sensibility dominates her poetry but she cannot be called a feminist. There is a balance between subject matter and style in her poetry and one has to wait for the complete flowering of her poetic talent.

Apart from the poet discussed above some other poets are also writing good poetry since middle of the 1980s to the present time. Some of the names of those poets are Arup Kumar Nath, Anupama Das, Alokesh Kalita, Ajit Bharali, Ajit Kumar Bordoloi, Ankur Rajen Changmai, Abedul Rehman, Amrita Basumatary, Archana Baruah, Uday Kumar Sharma, Uajjal Paogam, Utpola Bora, Kaustav Mani Saikia, Prem Narayan Nath, Cheniram Gogoi, Junmoni Das, Mira Thakur, Prajal Sarma Basistha, Bijoy Shankar Barman and others.

Kamal kumar Tanti also hails from a tea tribe community and in his poem we find materials drawn from folk life. There is also reference to history injustice and he looks at this from a post- colonial perspective. He also reacts in his poems to the immediate socio-political incidents. He has at the same time, experimented with theme and technique.

Ranjit Gogoi's poem present before readers a sense of despondency and through such melancholy he indulges in self- introspection to find out the difficult answers of life. The familiar folk-life of Assam in reflected in his poetry and the smell of soil emerges thoroughly. He has given a Mobile dimension to his poetry which he derives from a deep sense of rootedness. A Sense of inquisitiveness dominates the texture of his poems. It has given him a sense of realization regarding the gains and losses of life. His imageries are drawn from the rural life of Assam and he can intricately design the form of poetry. His poems are also popular because he is deeply rooted in a particular secio cultural milieu.

Debaprasad Talukdar is remarkably original poet who has exhibited his reaction to the changing pattern of society and he graphically chronicles his heart-felt realizations. He has not written cheap poetry for the sake of popularity and he has written stronger poems based on his own experiences. In some of his poems he has offered a pan- Indian panoramic view and his poems offers a sense of freshness. He has been able to cement his place in the realm of contemporary poetry through his grasp over both traditional and modernity. He also laments the loss of something vital from the life of Assamese people and their culture.

Jyotsna Kalita writes intellectual poems which have cerebral appeal. She never writes poetry for the sake of writing it or for the sake of mass consumption. Her poetry shows the contemporary urban landscape and her total output can be judged on the basis of quality, not of the basis of quantity as she writes only when she feels the urge to write. She is well read poet and that reflect in her poetry. She has never drifted apart from the particular standard of poetry.

Ajit Bharali is another addition to the list of the contemporary Assamese poetry. He does not write sensational poems but his poetry reveals a deep realization of life's varied experiences. He does not commodify poetry; rather he tries to present contemporary life as it is. Some of his poems are full of sensitivity and compassion as he writes from the core of his heart. In some of his poems the nostalgic streak manifests itself.

We can also identify some of the major trends in contemporary Assamese poetry. Globalization has made the world a global village but it has also given rise to a new sort of opening up of economic structure and these things are reflected in Assamese poetry of the recent time. The rise of consumerism is a major factor in this context.

The cultural invasion of English has also affected contemporary modern Assamese poetry. Some of the words found in present Assamese poetry reflect this development. Poets are unhesitatingly using English words in their poems.

The Proliferation of knowledge ushered in by the internet is also a major factor in this context and this has affected recent Assamese poetry. Even small children are playing complex games through internet and recent Assamese poetry is not altogether silent about this. More and more people are driving their children to study in English medium and internet is used to a large extent by these small kids. Recent Assamese poetry is highlighting these issues.

The rise of Ambedkarism during the 1990s affected Assamese poetry of the time. The exploitation of the so called lower caste and communities gave birth to an awareness of Dalit paradigm. The poets wiring during that period gave full expression to those sensibilities in their poems.

Some of the other trend which have been observed in recent Assamese poetry are as follows;

1. The number of poet writing in newspaper and magazine has increased though there is a lack of quality. Emotion has become the predominant motif and it seems as if the recent poets are cut off from the tradition.

2. After the 1990 there is a sense of stagnation in Assamese poetry. There is very little experimentation regarding form and technique. But it does not mean that contemporary Assamese poetry is bereft of substance.

3. Some of the contemporary Assamese poets are not well read. That is why some of the poems are ordinary.

4. Recent Assamese poetry has become more and more attuned toward societal issue which is a good sign.

In the conclusion we can say that Assamese poetry since the mid 1980s to the present has presented to us a wide spectrum of poetry which is both original and thought provoking.

The effect and impact of globalization can be evident in recent Assamese poetry. The economic liberalization which gave a different hue to Assamese poetry in the post 1990 scenario is to be considered cautiously. Popular culture brought about by the cross- current of post modernism becomes evident in recent Assamese poetry. Recent Assamese poetry of the contemporary period displays a wide hue and the prospect seems to be optimistic. However, one has to be on guard to make any generalization about recent Assamese poetry. This entire survey is a humble attempt to make the non-Assamese reader aware of the cross-current to Assamese poetry from the mid-1980 to the present. There may be many short-comings as it is not a definitive survey, nor it claims to be one.

GP Sharma

A remarkable academician of Assam who graced the chair of Dean, Arts Faculty and Head of the Department of English, Gauhati University, an outstanding critic with original and insightful views, a novelist, a philanthropist from the core of his heart, Gobinda Prasad Sarma has also rendered a valuable service to the domain of Assamese creative literature – a fact that can be authenticated by his remarkably significant collections of short stories such as Chitra Bithika, He Aranya He Mahanagar, and Soali Hostelot Agoraki Lesbian. Sarma has created a significant oeuvre of critical and creative works for a period spanning almost four decades that is capable of consolidating a secured position for him in the literary and cultural horizon of Assam. His book Nationalism in Indo – Anglian Fiction remains a canonical work in the academic world and it has been cited as a major reference book by a generation of researchers and students pursuing Indian Writing in English.

However, Sarma has exhibited remarkable prowess in the genre of short story and his stories are notably different from his contemporary counterparts because of the novelty of theme and lucid narrative style. In the west, short story as a specific and independent literary genre originated in the 19th and flourished in the 20th. But in India it established itself as a prominent genre only in the post – independence period though there had been instances of notable practitioners of short story during the pre-independence period also. Gobinda Prasad Sarma deserves credit as he has both extended and challenged the familiar frontier of Assamese short story by concentrating his attention on the exploration of animal life and human concern, natural world with its flora and fauna and above all, stories based on individual human characters endowed with unique eccentricities and additions. Sarma writes without any burden of consciously adopted experimental constraints; in fact, he writes so lucidly and spontaneously that the readers are touched by the simplicity of diction and its effect lingers long after the perusal.

Sarma's unique collection of 12 evocative short stories make an attempt to both extend and challenge the accepted boundary of the genre in context of Assamese literature as each story in the collection concentrates on the life of one particular protagonist who most often lives in an ideal world and does not perform their day to day practical obligations Sarma himself mentions in the preface to the collection that "whether these are pen – portraits or biographical essays or stories, I do not know . Even if these are not flawless post modern stories, I have still attempted here to transgress that border line ." Sarma concentrates on the exposition and exploration of twelve different "eccentric" characters in the collection who somehow threaten the existing value – system and status – quo of the contemporary society and in this connection the author reminds us how eccentricity is viewed with suspicion and intolerance in our society whereas in the West eccentricity is not only respected, but also often rewarded. Sarma juxtaposes both pre – Independence and post – independence Assamese rural society in Chitra Bithika and though he writes with a subjective and retrospective stance about characters and places encountered long ago, yet there is an attempt to achieve an objective aesthetic gaze. Sarma's style of narration is full of humor and bantering irony without any tinge of malice and his portrait of a fading society together with lost ethos is a gentle reminder to the contemporary readers about the necessity to remain true to roots and be humane in attitude. Most of the stories are open-ended narratives, and though the form is traditional, the content is often postmodern and that is precisely where his credit lies.

He Aranya, He Mahanagar is another unique collection where animals occupy centre stage along with the exploration of natural world, compassion for domestic animals, tolerance towards creatures other than human beings, the need to preserve ecological balance and above all, the discipline to tame material greed. The title story portrayas the plight of an elephant who suddenly finds its place/ space usurped by human beings and the author obliquely lashes out at the contemporary evils of industrial and technological civilization. The authors makes it clear that both men and animals are unique creatures of God and each should provide space for the habitation of the other and the responsibility lies more on the human beings because of their rationality and civilization . Sarma also juxtaposes the worlds of forest and city in the story as the two elephants fall victims to the designs of human beings oblivious of any concern for animals. Laikaloi Manat Pore is both an evocative and poignant story based on the life and death of a domestic dog and Sarma shows the severe consequences of the dangerous attempt of human beings to domesticate animals that have a natural territory of their own. Sarma highlights how both humans and animals crave and care for the company of each other and the references to Fifth George, Queen Victoria and Emily Bronte authenticate such arguments within the text. Sarma's story thus turns out to be not merely homage to a dog – but a nostalgic and sympathetic tribute to animal world as a whole. Gach Aru Manuh highlights Sarma's concern for nature, environment, the need to strike a balance between human greed and autonomy of natural territory and a plea to curb human cruelty. Apart from these, Sarma also concentrates on animals such as cows and monkeys in the collection, a fact which makes one ponder over the many beautiful natural and animal contacts we are losing day by day or have lost permanently. Saoli Hostelot Egoraki Lesbian is a unique story in the realm of Assamese literature because of the boldness of the subject and the author's daring attitude to sympathetically deal with them of lesbianism within the context of Assamese society. Through the seemingly dispassionate but sympathetic gaze of a female narrator, Sarma brings to light the joy, pain and struggle of two lesbians within a predominant heterosexual society that looks at their "Others" first with suspicion and then with hatred. As the two protagonists intensify their struggle to build a female utopia, the narrative shifts the attention back to the impact of such attempt on the mind of the objective narrator who gradually starts identifying with the cause. Sarma's stories are capable of evoking compassion and sensitivity from the readers and he writes so naturally and vividly that reminds one of the saying "Tree Art lies in concealing art".

Translated Poems Of Subhajit Bhadra

The following Bengali poems of Sri Subhajit Bhadra, Assistant Professor, PG Dept of English, Bongaigaon College have been originally published in the book called "Maya Paki" authored by Sri Bhadra and published by Booksway Publishers, Kolkata, India. Sri Bhadra has many other reputed books of literary criticism to his credit.

The poems have been translated into English by Dr Kusumita Mukherjee, faculty, Department of English, Kalyani Mahavidyalaya. Dr Mukherjee is teacher, poet and author. Her stories have been published in The Times of India and the e-journal Muse India.

1. Complaint ("Avijog"----original title)

-----Subhajit Bhadra
Translated by Dr Kusumita Mukherjee

The lost years assemble in a crowd
Stand and stare, without blinking
Point questions at me----
Who gave you the right
To dillydally with us?
You have only breathed, you are
Still Breathing today, you were never
Alive on this earth as a human being; I too
Gaze at them with unblinking eyes
My heart feels heavy with tears, I say
Have you ever given me anything?
You have only made false complaints; today
What use is it at life's twilight zone

to bicker amongst ourselves?

Next year on such a day you might lament

My lost friends----for a lost friend.

2. Life incense ("Jibonghran"----original title)

-----Subhajit Bhadra

Translated by Dr Kusumita Mukherjee

Every tree is my myrmidon, ally

Is every star alight the night sky,

In your evergreen peace abode I

Simply perch----thirsting of life

Speechless, yet boshek 1 arrives

Over again impregnated with articulate earth's

Beguiling syllabary, in my life

This time a novel insemination----dynamic furtive heart,

In the scorching aubade just the alluring warmth of love.

Finally each breath wafts in

The sterling incense of our lived lives.

Boshek- the word in rural dialect for the Bengali month of Boishak, the month in spring in which the Bengali New Year is celebrated.

3. Life Rhythm/ Life Cadence/ Rhythm of life ("Jibonchanda"----original title)

-----Subhajit Bhadra

Translated by Dr Kusumita Mukherjee

Your perpetually outstretched penumbra finally

Caresses my heart's chin, when Nilachal's

Scorching effulgence tires in Dhanshiri

Sneaks in the shadow of its hedging in, within

That penumbra the ethereal oscillates, oscillates our
Life story, thereafter in the evening's tidied
Courtyard some mysterious entities sketch alluring intricate patterns,
Green bird proliferates the entire assemblage of our imagination.
Let your fragrance be infused in the sweet aurora,
Thereafter dejection's manuscript extinguishes life's rhythm.
Nilachal and Dhanshiri are both names of Hostels.

4. Pen Peroration ("Kalamkatha"----original title)

-----*Subhajit Bhadra*

Translated by Dr Kusumita Mukherjee

Home and hearth there are none, just a few desultory
Illusions, at eve the thought bird
Stalks, aquatic life floats on mystic river,
The smell of autumn spreads over the blithe lake,
Beaming water eyes are tinged even today, lusting for life,
Words emerge from deconstructed words, words engender mystical beatitude
The crooked smile of the heart vessel is initiated by dejection sperm;
Pen peroration writes up in verdant branches 'I am restored'.

5. Shadow Poet ("Chayakabi"----original title)

-----*Subhajit Bhadra*

Translated by Dr Kusumita Mukherjee

The depressed morning of the fallen leaves of spring
Prudently integrates hued consciousness;
Every hue metamorphoses to light, every illumination
Fades away, forlorn breeze momentarily respires
In the golden hair of a whimsical girl;
All those that were pitch black have now transpired to

Alien light; thereafter through mystic churning
Evolves tattered life's fragmented reflection;
The self overrides its very own
Self portrait in deep affection holds on to simulacrum.

6. Green World ("Sabuj Sansar"----original title)

-----Subhajit Bhadra
Translated by Dr Kusumita Mukherjee

Afterwards there are nothing called words,
Only silence persists,
Our cosmic love, our
Comprehensive soul discourse, on the rock of words
Words echo, only silence
Is quiet, in your eyes emerge
Undistorted world view, one by one
The melancholy boy, brings home each spec,
Thereafter it is just your life rhythm
That sustains our unwithered green world.

7. Assassin ("Atotayi"----original title)

-----Subhajit Bhadra
Translated by Dr Kusumita Mukherjee

Last night in a dream
I am startled by a dead corpse.
Unfamiliar visage, yet it awakens
In the heart an unaccustomed yearning,
With forlorn eyes I gaze in dismay----
Dead eyes as rigid as stones,
Wan face, ashen complexion
All of a sudden it sits up,

It moves in even closer,

At once I sense the lighting up of

Hundred lights, now I clearly

See, this is no corpse,

This is my very own reflection, I wake

And ponder----it may be so that I am

Dead, and someone else who is just like me is my assassin.

8. At your Funeral ("Apnar Shokshabhay"----original title)

-----Subhajit Bhadra

Translated by Dr Kusumita Mukherjee

I missed your funeral.

Do forgive me. Who were you

To me? I don't even know this. May be

You knew. Even then not once

Did you speak about it. I too

Never demanded to know anything.

May be I knew it at heart. Was familiar.

Quite intimate with you. Possibly.

Can't say it for sure. We were never able to

Supersede the intricate mesh of unfamiliarity.

Yet within both our hearts ebbed and flowed

Many words. Each desired to embrace the

Other. Yet were never successful.

This is why I never made it to your funeral.

Even at the time of the final adieu incessant tear drops flowed unstoppably. Abrupt.

Is it so that I loved you? That is why I could never make it to the phony funeral.

Do forgive me.

Encountering Variety

Apart from being a successful novelist and short story writer, Anuradha Sarma Pujari has shown her prowess in essays and articles also. The book under review is a collection of miscellaneous editorials written for the weekly newspaper 'Hadin' and Pujari has been able to show variety in these pieces. The book is titled 'Homoyor Prishtha' (Pages of Time) and it is appropriate as it incorporates within its framework essays and articles on various periods of time as mentioned in the preface. The articles cover different subjects from philosophy to history, literature to politics, contemporary socio-economic reality, music to painting and there is also a marked interdisciplinary approach as Pujari switches from one topic to another.

She writes about the brutal and often shocking reality of contemporary journalism and blames contemporary journalists for lack of proper homework. Being herself a journalist, she is able to gasp the crux of the matter and she never misses the point. She writes about Indira Miri, the great social activist based on whose life she has written a critically acclaimed novel titled 'Mereng' which was initially serialized in the monthly Satsori before being published as a book. She writes about the illegal immigrants from Bangladesh who sell their cheap labor in exchange of reasonable amount of money but who are quite gentle and devoted to their work. She writes about corruption which has turned out to be a day to day affair in India and in our state in particular and she candidly lashes out at the corrupt politicians. She writes about her brief meeting with the great Indian expressionist paint Maqbul Fida Hussain and his continuous effort to be on the limelight as he represented himself as a jovial person even when he was above eighty. She writes about Dr. Bhupen Hazarika, the great cultural icon and singer......... of Assam who had to deal with so much pain and humiliation in his life but who never broke down. She writes how he deserved and deserves to be crowned with the Bharat Ratna and her arguments are sensible enough to accumulate the approval of readers. She writes about Mamoni raison Goswami and her great significance in the cultural context of Assam.

The editorials contain weight; they are crisp, pithy and pointed. They are argumentative and written in urbane language. But there is one mistake as the dates and years are not mentioned at the end of the essays which poses problem for the serious readers. Otherwise, Pujari deserves credit and the book deserves to be widely read.

The title of the book – Homoyor Prishtha

Publisher – Banalata

Price – 200/-

An Engaging Intellectual Endeavour

By: Subhajit Bhadra.

Postcolonial Indian English playwrights have basically attempted to write back to the empire through historical revisionism and an inner urge to examine the legacy of colonial cultural gifts. In contrast to their stance the vernacular

dramatists of India have attempted to directly explore socio-political themes and it is precisely in this context that one has

to look at the plays of Badal Sircar. Manujendra Kundu in his book titled "So near, yet so far – Badal Sircar's Third Theatre attempts to chronicle the growth, genesis and culmination of one of Indian literature's first rank theatre workers- in fact, Kundu both reconstructs and deconstructs the dramatic legacy of Sircar from postmodern critical and theoretical perspectives. The resonance of the title is very evocative in the sense that in spite of the effort of Badal Sircar to stay near to the audience through his exploration of the third theatre Sircar ultimately found himself so far from his aim because of peculiar experimentation that Kundu highlights. Kundu shows how Sircar heavily borrowed from various western playwrights and plays and one such example is Pirandello's Six character is search of an author which influenced Sircar so much that he ultimately ended with a play called Natyakaren Shadhne Tinti Chartre (Roughly translated as three character is search of a dramatist) Kundu uses poststructural paradigm of Roland Barthes and even makes use of Michael Foucault's power knowledge discourse to analyse the play of Indian literature's

one of the most enigmatic playwrights and theatre workers (
which Sircar liked to call himself). Though Kundu satirizes
Sircar for borrowing extensively from Western drama yet he
himself uses lots of Western theoretical framework to evaluate
and analyse Sircar's plays which is quite ironical.

The book is divided in seven chapters and each chapter reveals
a particular agenda of Kundu- that of charting out the dramatic
trajectory of Sircar vast body of work. In his initial period
Sircar dealt with the proscenium arch and some of his attempts
become legendary- one can cite the example of Ebang Indrajit
in this context which Kundu analyses with ease and precision.
Kundu points out how this play by Sircar can be called a true
absurdist drama in the mode of Backett, Eunesco and Pinter but
the crux is that Sircar has been able to make it a typical Indian
play in spite of western influence. Sircar's initial plays
appealed to the urban middle class people but his views
changed later as he confidently created a new brand of play
popularly known as the third theatre and Kundu directs our
attention to both the success and failure of Sircar in this context.
The legendary group of "Satabdi" is a forgotten name now but
nobody can deny its crucial role in postmodern Indian theatre.
Kundu points out how the folk element is vital in Sircar's plays
in spite of western orientation and he also draws on the legacy
of Sircar's print plays. Kundu deals with Sircar's plays in their
historical evolution and he draws heavily on personal
interviews of prominent theatre personalities, Sircar's own
writings (particularly) his autobiography and memoirs) and
other critics of repute to add authenticity to his analysis. Kundu

is very informative in his book as he reveals many hitherto
unknown facts about his works and life in general. We came to
know Sircar has a Christian background and Kundu points out
his bitterness and orthodox Christian rituals which often remind
of V. S Naipaul in a different context. Kundu also explores in

detail Sircar's stay in London which determined the later plays of the genius. Kundu is occasionally very critical of Sircar's experimentation as it created a sort of bafflement in the mind of many theatre personalities and critics.

Sircar was self- avowedly critical of accepting money from the viewer even through in his own life he accepted donations and Kundu lashes out at Sircar for his double standard. Each of the seven chapters in Kundu's book explicates a central focus in this context of Sircar's plays. Some of Sircar's plays contest power structure and become plays of protest and in this connection Kundu points out how Michil is a subversive play of protest that reminds an alert reader of Harlem Renaissance which carved an aesthetic of resistance. Kundu does not ignore the greater political events like the rise of the Naxalite Movment in Bengal and the clamping of Emergency by the then prime minister Indira Gandhi in 1975, events which produced in Sircar a strong response and he dealt with these themes in his plays.
Kundu's attitude to Sircar's dramatic evolution is not couched in fake sentimentalism or shabby bitterness. He reads Sircar according to his own finding and uses various archival documents and other personal sources. There is deep

engagement with Sircar's work throughout the book and Kundu's wide reading manifests itself from beginning to the end. Kundu's language is urbane and lucid and throughout his admiration does not abstain him from being critical. The book is full of revelation and insightful and it would spark further interest in the minds of readers to explore deeper. Ultimately it can be said that Manujendra Kundu's book on Sircar third theatre is an enjoyable reading experience.

A Disappointing Critical Appraisal

To write a review of a book which itself is a review of someone else's work is a daunting task. Purbanchal Prakash is an emerging publishing house in Assam which basically publishes average and below average novels and non-fiction in Assamese language has recently come up with a project which is interestingly titled "Studies on Modern Assamese Writes" must be examined with care. The same project sees the publication of a critical work by Tapati Baruah Kashyap which is actually the book under review. Long back the prestigious Sahitya Academy launched a series of books under the nomenclature makers of Indian literature which is still continuing and Purbanchal Prakash's book on the aforementioned project seems to be an imitation of that. The selection of writers who are deemed by the owner of the publication house as modern Assamese writer is always based on arbitrariness. However the book under review is Tapati Baruah Kashyap's sum up of Nirmalprabha Bordoloi's creative and critical works and the book is written in stunted English with lots of semantic and idiomatic hiccups. The writer seems to be overpowered by the awe inspiring stature of Nirmalprabha Bordoloi and her analysis is actually an emotional ode to the writer's work and the book is also replete with overt emotional outbursts which cripples the writer's (oe rather reviewers) critical stance. The main intention of the book seems to make non-Assamese readers aware of the treasures of Assamese writer's achievement and output. The writer minces no word to assert or highlight her personal relation with Nirmalprabha Bordoloi and it is precisely this lack of "disinterested endeavor" (Mathew Arnold) which reduces the worth of the book to the level of simple panegyric.

However the book under review is an assortment of strong regional sensibilities and poor critical acumen. Such books can never play the role of harbingers of a strong critical stand point. Nirmalprabah was one of the most gifted writers of Assam who contributed both as a teacher also as a creative writer. She had curved a niche for herself in the domain of modern Assamese literature and culture and her works carried the smell of the soil. She tried her hand almost in every genre of Assamese literature and she gained recognition even as early as 1980s. Her voice was significant poetic voice she created beautiful poems out of the tussle with her soul. She wrote many a song which were sung only by the greatest singers of the time but those very songs enhanced her popularity in the poetic domain a strong and determined personality, she faced many hardships in her life but she never surrendered to the odd factors which sometimes threatened demolish her stature as a creative and critical writer. Her father's influence was very strong in her life and she was inspired by her father at many crucial junctures of her life. All those facts are highlighted by Kashyap in this book. However kashyap does not have the rigorous critical alertness to do justice to Nirmalprabah's work she (kashyap) merely chronicles the details of her life and work, does not interpret the facts. Nirmalprabha's strong influence as a writer sometimes colored her own poetic rhetoric which kashyap fails to understand. Kashyap also fails to understand that a critical book should look a critical estimation of the subject's works, not a formal praise.

Kashyap divides Nirmsalprabha's creative and critical life into many segments. She attempts to chronicle Nirmalprabha Bordoloi's achievements as a poet, as a research scholar, as a lyricist, as a children writer, as a humanist, as a novelist, as a biographer, as a critic, as a translator, as a playwright and also as a writer of autobiography. An introductory note on the life and achievements of Nirmalprabha accompanied by a epilogue also finds place within the gamut of Kashyap's book. Nirmalprabah Bordoloi's achievements as a writer should have been judged more critically but kashyap repeats the same points again and again which makes the book drab. The rigorous critical balance is lacking and the translation of Nirmalprabha's poems and prose are not up to the mark. Kashyap tries to be lucid but often the many strenuous demands of the genre mar the effort. The footnotes are missing on many occasions and non-Assamese readers would find it very difficult to understand the nuances of many cultural terms. However the book has one saving grace and that is Kshyap's admiration for the subject. In conclusion we can say that Tapati Baruah Kashyap's critical work on Nirmalprabha Bordoloi fails to add to the existing literature of the latter's creative and critical output.

Texts In Contexts : Reflections On Literature

Enjoyment always comes before understanding. What we learn with joy and happiness we remember that forever. No Literature can be produced in a vacuum . Every literary text is a product of a particular context. What is literature? Literature , as the noted Hindi poet cum intellectual told in a personal interview is nothing but an alternative reality. Literature makes available what is missing from our day to day daily life which is nothing but humdrum and monotonous. The concept of reality takes us back to the Ancient Greek thinkers like Socrates , Plato and Aristottle . Modern theorists like George Steiner, Edward W. said to Slavor zizek have debated over such concepts. Literature primarily appeals to our sensitivity and compassion . But in order to see this in reality one must have sensibility and sense. Literature provides us enjoyment as well as it sometimes teaches us morality . But here an important question arises – what is the primary function of literature : to give pleasure or to prescribe moral rules . While George Bernard Shaw , the Fabian Socialist and a vocal modern Irish dramatist was in support of literature as a moral tool, his fellow country man from Ireland Oscar Wilde said that "all art is useless". While the slogan "Art for Arts Sake" became important for the precursors of modernism, to some literature also became a pragmatic moral tool. No one can deny how literature has played a vital role in human civilization and the progress of human culture , right from the liberal humanists to the social anthropologists cannot deny or forgo the influence of literature. Art and culture can not be borrowed , but it can be imbibed through passion and hard – labour, as T.S Eliotmight have said .In the twentieth century when the dark clouds of the First World War hovered over the sky of the western world and civilization and T.S Eliot was mentioning the danger of London bridge falling down ,he also wrote in a different poem- "Where is the life we have lost in living ? Where is the wisdom we have lost in knowledge ? Where is the knowledge we have lost in information?The cycle of Heaven in the twentieth century Bring us further from God and nearer to dust"Literature was often used by the dictators as propaganda but it has also been noticed that propagandist literature has not survived the test of time. The most glaring example of this is the undivided Soviet Russia . When Stelin was rulling over Russia he made life hell for the creative writers where writings were giving support to crises of the country. Whether it was Alexander Solzhenytsis being restricted not to accept The Nobel Prize for Literature , or Ivan klima and Milan Kundera leaving their homeland , or Salman Rashdie being given the Fatwa by the Iranian Mullah Ayatullah Khoemani , or the Bangladeshi woman writer Taslima Nasrin being chased away from her own native land, or more recently the banning of the book The Hindus by Wendy Doniger in India- all of these are nothing but the inherent superlative power of literature as a whole. What is the nature of literature? Is it abstract or concrete . Whatever may it be, in this domain one must encounter organicity . No one can deny the dynamic and organic power of literature because it is always moving , never stagnant. The congruity between form and content is an important component. In the Twentieth century the New critics in Southern part of America said that literature is an autonomous and autotelic entity. In order to read literature, a person should not study the biography of the author or poet, or the socio-political-historical and cultural economic background of the social context, rather one should only study the impact of language upon that text. John Crowe Ransom, I.A Richards , William Empson , Cleanth Brooks, Allan Tate and others tried to facilitate the divorce of texts from their contexts. This also has a political history behind it. There was the civil War in America regarding the issue of slavery between the North and the South. In that war the North triumphed over the South. The South became diffident and withdrew into a cocoon. This narcissistic tendency later on impinged upon their willingness to withdraw into a shell and thus they propagated the autonomy of the text. Important books like Seven Types of Ambiguity and The Principals of Literary Criticism became Bible for the New critics. During the 1930s the Marxist group of poets started a new phase in English literature. Poets like W.H Auden , Luice Mekneice and Stephen Spender tried to contextualize literary products. But this was also the time when critics like Walter Benjamin , Theodor Adorno and Hokheimar were trying to look at literature from a new angle and they established a new school called The Frankfort School . Herbert Mercuse was also with them. But gradually Mussolini and Hitler came to power in Italy and Germany respectively . They started using art and culture from needs emanating out of their opportunistic goals. Even the world famous Kabiguru Rabindranath Tagore was misled and misinterpreted by the Italian media quite intentionally . Mussolini killed his opponents and Hitler killed Lakhs of Jews in concentration camps. Gandhiji said out of frustration that their (the Jewish Peoples) destiny was to collectively commit suicide. The genocide of Hitler was so traumatic that the survivers like Paul Celan either committed suicide or novelists like Imre Kartes showed the meaninglessness of life in his fictions like The Liquidation or Kaddish for a Child Not Born ("Kaddish" is the jewish word for prayer for a death of a person). But the history of torture and persecution of literary artists (particularly Writers) was happening since a long time back . But it reached its pinnacle in the twentieth century when Anna Akhmatova's husband and son were killed due to stalin's dictatorial stratagems . Akhmatova's long narrative poem Requiem bears witness to this fact. But it is also true that literacy writers like Hemingway and Lorca joined wars and fought in battles . The wound and trauma of war created the great novel A Farewell to Arms which came out of the pen of Hemingway . Again it was Pablo Neruda who expressed the sense of happiness and rebellion of the Spanish people in his poems. Like the characters of Waiting for Godot we can only wait and only with hope, not with hopelessness . The Existentialists like Camus and Jean Paul Sartre hoped for the best but prepared for the worst. 'No one can ever forget Camus' character Mersault's famous words at the beginning of the novel The Stranger –"Mother died today. May be yesterday. I do not know". And who can forget Sartre's unforgettable words-"The blinding sun of torture is at its zenith. It lights up the whole country .Under that merciless glare there is not a single laugh that does not ring false, there is not a single face that is not painted to hide fear or anger and there is not a single action that does not betray our disgust and complicity". (Jean Paul Sartre, from the Preface to the Wretched of the Earth by Franz Fanon). Coming back to the concept of alternative reality as espoused by literature one must proceed with caution. Literature is also a sort of wish- fulfillment and that is precisely where the concept of "willing suspension of disbelief" (Coleridge) comes. Literature enables us to see dreams, hope a new, see life amidst death, mirth in gloom and freshness in farewell. If literature is a reflection of society, then society also reflects literature. Literature does not make one weak, it rather makes one strong. Literature, after all, is a mode of defamiliarization as the Russian Formalists advocated or what Bertolt Brecht told "Alienation effect". Literature, if it is true, then it must speak for humanity as a character says in Saul Bellow's The Dean's December "For God's sake, let's open the universe a little". Literature teaches one to be humble, benevolent and humane. It also teaches one to be vocal against injustice, oppression and dictatorship. Literature never limits one's existence, rather it opens up a broad horizon, it shows us to accept our strengths and foibles equally. Literature expands our mental horizon, it teaches us to be submissive and benevolent. The grace that one often showers on others comes from the core of the heart and that is where human beings' mystery of compassion lies. We do not know when death will knock us down but we do know that as long as we live we should do good deeds. Literature awakens and strengthens our moral sensibility. The concept of ideology in literature is as old as antiquity. Every author colours his/her literary work with a certain kind of ideology. But having said that it must be noted that no writer should be ideologically so biased that the human aspect is missing from the work. In Marxist paradigm literature has often been looked as a testament to a particular type of ideology- i.e; that of class struggle. According to the Marxists the "base" is the economic aspect and "the superstructure" is art work and both of these are integrally related. Nobody will say no to literature showing a glaring path to a blinding person but that blind person must have the desire to confront truth. We can triumph over our innermost fear, paranoia and unease through the perusal of literature. Henrik Ibsen, the famous playwright of Norway once said "Living means fighting within you the ghosts of dark power; writing means putting on trial your inmost self". Literature, according to the modern psychological exponents like Sigmund Freud is a product of neurosis. He believes that all art is a product of sickness. But if we reflect upon this comment that literature is nothing but a product of sick mind then a question immediately comes to our mind- are all writers mentally disturbed? The statement however appears to be authentic if we look into the examples like Virginia Woolf, Sylvia Plath, Hemingway, Charles Dickens, Jean Jenet and many others. Harold Bloom said that every writer tries to evade and be enriched by his/her previous writers in his book the Anxiety Of Influence. All art need not necessarily be product of sick mind but in all art the life of all mind becomes important. It is only through the exploration of the "life of the mind" that one can catch the essence of literature. All Literature must strive towards producing a particular ideology – i.e, the ideology of humanity. We all are human beings and we are all mortals and that is why we should not be like Icarus or Doctor Faustus. During the time of the Renaissance the philosopher Erasmus said that "Man is the measure of all things". From the dawn of the Western Renaissance onwards man's gradual journey towards an anthropocentric universe began. In the twentieth century there was mass killing, then two world wars and as George Steiner said that the same age was the age of transcendental homelessness. With the arrival and appropriation of many critical theories from the second half of the twentieth century our approach to literature changed. Structuralism, post- structuralism, deconstruction, psychoanalytical criticism, myth criticism, Marxist criticism, New Historicism, Gynocriticism Post-positivism, Reader Response theory and other criticial Schools totally shattered our conventional view of literature. Again literature became associated with context. The literary texts were interlinked with their contexts. All these critical schools came from France or rather Paris. No one can forget Roland Barthes' jump from structuralism to post structuralism, no one can forget Derrida's concept of "Differance" or "Aporia" or "Deconstruction". Theories became new windows for us to look at traditional and conventional literature from a new angle. When Gayetri Chakravarty Spivak translated Derrida's seminal French book Of Grammatology into English , it shattered every arm-chair intellectual's critical view on literature. Who can forget the historical debate between Derrida and Emanuel Levinas? Thus literature and theory became integrally related. With the coming up of postcolonial critical theory our conception of traditional texts like Shakespeare's The Tempest and Jane Austen's Emma totally changed. When Edward W. said published his culturally seminal book Orientalism in 1978 the new network between colonial venture and scholasticism came to be exposed. Thus we find from all our above discussion that every piece of literary work (rather text) is a product of a particular context. The sub-altern critics brought to light the condition of the marginalized voice or what Gayetri Chakravarty Spivak asked in her important essay "Can the sub-altern speak"? Our answer to it can be framed like this if the sub-altern cannot speak, then the sub-altern can at least listen and spit.The responses of critics to literature have always been biased by their own ideologies. But it must be asserted that a critic should look at literature from a dispassionate viewpoint. And that is what our contributors have tried to do in this book. Literature can hardly be ignored in our contemporary period as it is the sentinel of our conscience. We live in a world shattered by different perverse ideologies, dangerous thinkings, off-beat views, global warming, mass-killing and terrorism. Everyday we wake up with the fear of loss, anxiety and cataclysmic feelings. And it is precisely in this context we can say that literature can give us some consolation and mental food for thought. Literature again is nothing but an alternative reality but that alternative reality is much more beautiful than the world we live in.

Short Story The Dream Of A House
Madan Sarma

Ruma held onto the slender branch of the Krishnachura tree and went on gazing at the house. Her grandfather had built it with so much hard work and such loving care. Once the outer walls were painted, the house looked so beautiful that passersby could hardly help themselves stopping for a while to look at admiringly. When asked who had designed such a lovely house, the grandfather would smile and proudly declare that it was none other than him. However, he didn't forget to mention that the son of one of his friends had made the drawing under his direction.

Ruma let her gaze slide between two coconut saplings and linger on the verandah of the house. Her grandparents were sitting in cane chairs, placed on both sides of the three-foot wide passage leading to the interiors. The nearly seven feet long passage right from the gate to the verandah looked like a strip of a soft green carpet. The old couple's eyes were fixed on the night jasmine flowers that had been strewn by the wind on the passage. The sweet fragrance of the night jasmine wafted towards them. The cool autumnal breeze touched their bodies. Their hearts were filled with contentment.

The old man had started the construction two years before his retirement. He had to sell the ancestral property in his native village and spend a big chunk of his retirement benefit to build the two-storied house. At the initial stage he had to take some loan too. During the hectic period of construction he lost much weight and grew weaker. His savings were almost gone. Ruma knew that her father and uncle helped the old man to complete the house.

The old couple lived in the left half of the ground floor. Ruma and her parents lived in the right half. The construction of the upper storey is yet to be completed. However, there was enough space there for the younger son, his wife and their two kids. The old lady thought that the house should have been more spacious. Their younger son would face much difficulty if they had guests planning to stay with them for a few days.

The old man would curtly say that he had done whatever he could. Let the two brothers do the rest. However, the two brothers had bought two plots of land in two different places and both wanted their parents to live with them.

Her uncle Amiya's new car stopped near the gate. Her aunt and two cousins, Sonma and Bubu started walking towards the house. The kids picked up the night jasmine flowers as they kept briskly moving towards the verandah. Their mother followed them.

The kids went bustling in past their grandparents and started climbing the stairs leading to the first floor. Meanwhile, Ruma's mother came out of the house, carrying two cups of tea on a tray and seeing her sister- in- law, smiled. In a moment the house was filled with pleasant noises. Songs could be heard from the upper story. Somewhere a TV set was on. The old couple held the cups of tea in their hands, exchanged glances and broke into broad smile, the smile of contentment brought about by their loving house. They had all along been dreaming about such a house.

The scene, accompanied by the sounds and the sights, could have been imagined just this way. But the reality was not like this. Ruma rubbed her eyes with her hands. The picture of her imagination vanished. Once more she looked towards the verandah. Her grandparents were sitting in the cane chairs. They were looking at the road with a vacant expression. The traffic was rather light. Only a few cars, one or two motorbikes and a few passersby passed by the road. The atmosphere of the place was just like that of a village although it was situated at the edge of the city, and villages were two kilometers away from this place. There was a thinly wooded patch a little ahead, beyond which the entire stretch was vacant at one time. Now houses were coming up there.

The house was strangely quiet. Her uncle's new car stopped at the gate without making any sound. Her uncle and aunt were about to enter the house without saying anything to the old couple. Her grandmother said to her aunt, "So, you are back."

Ruma could not hear what her aunt said in reply.

Ruma felt really sorry for her grandparents but she could not make anyone understand how she felt. She also felt very sad when she looked at her mother. She used to be such a cheerful person, but how morose she had become now! As if she had grown old all of a sudden. Not only her mother, her grandparents had also grown older, and even she had suddenly grown older as if time had nothing to do with age. The things which she had read about in stories published in books and magazines, the stories that were visually represented on TV, had now unbelievably crept into their lives. Now and then her father came home. She felt uncomfortable when she looked at him. Her mother did not talk to him. Her brother asked, "Where's father gone, why doesn't he stay at home?"

In the last six or seven months her father had turned into a man whom she did not recognize any more. He stayed away from home for a week or even for a longer period than that. Most of the time he returned home very late. She heard her parents argue. After that she often found her mother weep at midnight. She asked her what was wrong. Her mother just went on weeping. One day she was waiting for her friends near the teachers' common room when she overheard two of her teachers who lived in their locality say something about her father. She was shocked by what she had heard. She clearly heard one of them say, " He shouldn't have done that ." She hurriedly left the place. And later she came to know that her father had married again. He lived with the other woman in a rented house. So that's why he did not come home on so many occasions. Even when he came home, he would talk with her grandmother and then leave.

Her father had left a little while ago. He bought something for her and her brother Roon. But she did not feel like unpacking the gift to see what it was. As he was leaving, she heard grandfather say to him, " Don't come to this house anymore." She saw her grandmother quietly wipe her tears.

She remembered those days when her brother was hardly two years old and she was just five. They had gone to Darjeeling, and they were so happy then, travelling by the toy train, climbing hills and looking up towards the snow-covered mountain tops. Her father bought her a lovely little coat. Ten two years back they went to Puri. Their family and her uncle's family stayed in a hotel facing the sea. She was so happy, so excited, trying to ride the rushing waves, gazing at the blue expanse of the sea, and listening to the incessant roar of the sea. In the evening, while walking towards the Lord Jagannath temple she and her cousin Sonma lost their way and stood in a dark corner, weeping. Her father found them after a long search. After that he again took them to the beach. How beautiful were those days! How loving was her father! He brought something for her on every birthday. Her mother scolded him for buying such expensive gifts. Last year when she stood first in the class her father bought her that beautiful green bicycle. Sonma too wanted one or she would not go to school. Her father,

Ruma's uncle bought her a red bicycle. Now Ruma did not want to ride her bicycle anymore. For the last few days she had been walking to school. That day when she saw her father standing silently near her grandparents with a grim face, she felt pity for him. Why did her father ditch her mother and marry another woman? Sonma said she had seen that woman. She said, "My aunt is more beautiful than the new aunt."

Why were men like this? Last night she told her mother that she would never marry. Her mother hugged her. She said nothing. Just a few drops of tear fell on her arms. And her heart was bleeding. She could not concentrate on her studies. Her teachers scolded her for that. A week before Jaya had asked her loudly if her new mother was really beautiful to look at. She did not pay heed to her. Her classmates scolded Jaya. They were so loving, so understanding. Why didn't the grownups try to understand anything at all?

A car stopped near the gate. The old lady looked through the window of the sitting room. Her elder daughter-in-law Chitra's brother Binanda and his mother got down from the car. She had not moved from her place. Her daughter in law's mother came up to her and sat near her. Nobody spoke. Then she said, "I have come to take them with me."

"Why are you so worried?" The old man said, "We are still there. Why should Chitra leave her home?'

"I know you love Chitra like your own daughter. But if they stay here, Ruma's studies will be affected. She has to take the school final exams next year. And Chitra will not be able to live in peace in this house. Your son will be here now and then."

"I have asked Hemen not to come here anymore," the old man said.

"Still it is his home. It will be good for her if she stayed away for a few days. She needs a break. This change may help her to remain normal."

Both of them knew that their daughter- in- law would leave sooner or later, may be forever.

The daughter in law, Ruma's mother Chitra came to say goodbye. The old lady's heart ached as she looked at the haggard face of her daughter- in-law. She hugged her and said, "Come to us whenever you feel like coming here." Ruma and her little brother Roon were crying . The grandmother hugged them and said, "This is your home, don't ever forget." And then she added in a faltering voice, "And don't forget us."

The house looked empty. In the evening the old lady switched on the lights of the rooms vacated by her daughter-in-law and the grand children. She stood there in the middle of the large living room and looked at the furniture. Suddenly the door of the wardrobe fell open. It was empty. She entered Ruma's study room. Ruma forgot to take with her the image of goddess Saraswati that she had bought at some fair. She lighted some incense sticks. In verandah there stood Ruma's green biycle. Had she forgotten it, or had she not taken it because her father bought it? I have to send it to her somehow, she said to herself.

A week after Ruma and her mother had left, the old lady saw her younger son discussing something with his father. She heard the tired voice of the old man, "You must have considered everything before taking this decision." Their younger son Amiya said "We are not going stay far away from here. It's just fifteen minutes' drive from here. But it will be very inconvenient if I do not stay near the factory now,"

It had been months since he opened the factory. Till now he had been working from home. The old lady wanted to ask if he did not face any problem all these months, but she didn't. She understood that they also wanted to leave their parents. Since Ruma left, Sonma had been saying that she did not want to live in this house anymore.

Amiya said, "I want to move out simply because it will help me in my business. I had hired such a big house and spent so much money on rent all for nothing, it seems."

The old woman came away without saying anything. Suddenly she felt weak and sat down on the last step of the staircase. Her younger daughter- in- law Nirmala held her and led her into her room. She did not notice her tears.

Amiya and his family too left.

In the evening the old lady stood near the gate and looked at their house. The first floor was dark. Lights were on in the ground floor

The house was quiet. Her husband was sitting in the verandah amidst darkness. She went and sat beside him.

After some time her husband said, smiling, "You always complained that the house is rather small, it should have been bigger. Now who will stay here? It will be a house of ghosts."

"What? What did you say?" the wife said. Both of them remained quiet for some time.

"The kids will grow up. And then they will come back home again," said the old lady.

"Shall we be alive till then?"

The wife said nothing. She just pulled her chair closer to his. And they went on looking at the thickening darkness in silence.

Translation of the original Assamese story "Eta Gharar Sapon" from Madan Sarma's collection of short stories Athaba Prem ,Guwahati:Astha Publication , 2nd enalarged edition 2013, pp 17-22.

Translated by Subhajit Bhadra

1. Every child nurtures within him a prospective adult and every adult nurtures within him/her a lost childhood. Kindly tell us something about your childhood.

Though I was born in a town, I grew up in a village. Now I realise that the richly varied experience of growing up in a village and the intimate knowledge of the rural reality that I was fortunate enough to acquire have helped me to write about rural life with greater confidence. I still cherish the memory of the sights, the sounds and the silence that pleased my senses when I was young. I grew up, marvelling at the pristine beauty of nature around the villages, the largely uncomplicated nature of the villagers and all the production –oriented activities that took place in the family that had stretches of rice fields, bamboo groves, so many fruit trees, trees that we used to climb, more than one fresh water pond (where we learned to swim), bullocks and a bullock cart, cows, goats, ducks and pigeons. In those days we had plenty of time for leisure and a hundred different ways to spend our time, playing and indulging in childlike adventures. We went to school at the age of six. I had a happy childhood during which I was exposed to traditional songs and naams sung by grandmas. I think I unknowingly benefitted from the story telling sessions conducted by our grandmas as we sat on a large mat (dhari),spread in the courtyard that was bathed in silver moonlight.

2. You are basically a creative writer. How far do you think that your surroundings impacted upon your writing?

I think my surroundings, the society, the people and the diversity of life around me have had a great impact on my writing (whatever be its worth!).

Even while dealing with the complexity of the inner life of the characters/ individuals that throng my stories, I am very much conscious about and alive to what is happening around me. In my humble way I have been trying to look critically and imaginatively at the complexity of the inner world and the world outside. I cannot remain indifferent to what is happening in the society, in the world at large. The conflicts and contradictions in the society (especially noticed in Assam between the 1970s and 1990s) and the vicissitudes of life in a world that is getting more and more complicated naturally find their resonance in my writings.

3. Critics often say that creative impulse comes suddenly to a writer. When did the first creative impulse come to your life? Tell us about the formative phase of your writing.

At this moment I cannot recall exactly when I felt a sudden impulse to write something creative. I think like any other child I just started writing poems when I was at school. Like many of my contemporaries I began with poetry, publishing a number of poems first in children's sections of a few newspapers and then in one or two magazines. However, I started writing poetry seriously in my late teens. In fact, my first book was a collection of poems (Atabor Taraphul—So many star-flowers)published in 1987. I started writing short stories in early 1970s. In those days my stories were regularly published in the Sunday editions of a few newspapers.

4. When you started writing in Assamese, then there were many stalwarts were present in the literary domain of Assam. How did you negotiate your space as a creative writer under such circumstances?

I started writing short stories at a time when we had a number of accomplished short story writers (Syed Abdul Malik, Jogesh Das, Saurabh Kumar Chaliha, Mahim Bora,   Bhabendranath Saikia and others)who continued to produce works of very high quality. I used to read some of their stories (especially those by Saurabh Kumar Chaliha) again and again. We had a desire to emulate them (we were young!). And then we came across stories from the great fiction writers from Europe (and   much later, from Latin America).We were inspired, but not overawed by our distinguished predecessors. We kept on writing regularly in the leading magazines (and in   newspapers, too) in those early years, making an effort to write somewhat differently. Sometimes we succeeded, most often we failed.

5. You have written many short stories and your creative writing basically is dependent upon this genre. How do you view the genre of short story as a complex area within the context of your own writing?

I often think that it might be easier to write a reasonably 'good' novel than a really 'good' short story. A short story demands concentration, compactness and precision. One has to say something significant or really meaningful in the space of a few pages (not in hundreds of pages). The process of reading and discovery of what is narrated and suggested (because a short may not always 'tell') in a short story must be interesting and engrossing for the reader. How much and what aspects of the reality or imagined reality can or should be chosen for a story, how to make an apparently ordinary experience, thought or idea significant for the reader and what narrative strategy is likely to be suitable for a theme or topic of a short story, how much of what the writer has gathered or imagined should be included in a short story---these and other questions often make a short story writer reflect on his/her craft (or art). But the very process of 'making up' and writing a reasonably good, technically compact short story is indeed creative and therefore enjoyable.

6. You have written many novellas and a few novels. How do you keep the balance between these different genres? How is writing novellas and novels different from the act of writing short stories?

I think constraints of space in literary magazines and also in the special issues brought out by some newspapers induce writers to write novellas which usually tend to have lesser number of characters and fewer or less complicated sub-plots. A novel is much larger in scope than a novella. I believe one enjoys greater freedom in the process of fashioning and writing a novel or novella than while writing a short story. Writing a short novella (yes, a novella can be very short too) can be more challenging as one has to be very conscious about inclusion of characters, situations and events or series of events. A story teller obviously enjoys the freedom given by the novel. A short writer does not enjoy that freedom. A good short story demands greater concentration.

7. You have written many critical essays and published a few books of literary criticism. How do you view the act of literary criticism and the position of a critic in the context of contemporary Assamese literature?

I believe literary critics not only explicate a literary text but also (and more importantly) help readers to read, understand and appreciate any work of literature. In our context (where literature is not often taught as something significant and enjoyable), a literary critic should emphasize the joy of reading even in the days of technological innovation. A discerning literary critic may draw the prospective readers' attention to a good book or a book worth-reading. Very often a good book that does not receive any publicity or sponsorship for some reason remains unknown, unnoticed and unappreciated, which is rather sad. A critic may encourage the readers to buy and read such a book. I think we need more perceptive, considerate and patient critics who may try to prepare and motivate Assamese readers to read good and readable books written in Assamese. The critics can serve as a bridge between the author and the reader.

8. You are also a translator and have translated some works of English literature as well as world literature into Assamese. How far do you think that translation is important? Kindly tell us about your experience as a translator.

I have been translating mostly from English into Assamese. In one of the columns that I have been writing for an Assamese daily Dainik Asam,I write about important or leading writers of different countries and also about such works of world literature that are worth reading. And very often I am required to translate samples of such works to convince my readers that these, indeed, are significant creations.

I enjoyed translating Navakanta Barua's children's classic Siyali PalegoiRatanpur (Ms Fox Arrives at Ratanpur) into English. I also enjoyed editing a collection of short stories (Biswar Baraniya Galpa, 2018, Asam Sahitya Sabha)written in different languages of the world.

I think translation of important books (not only works of literature) into Assamese is very important as such translations can enrich the language and expose the readers to good or great literature and more importantly to great thoughts.

9. Apart from your writing you also have an identity as a serious academician. You taught for so many years in Tezpur University. Kindly tell us about your identity as an

academician and your experiences in Tezpur University.

I have always enjoyed teaching and writing about literature and language. I have guided research, leading to PhD, in literature, English Language Teaching and Linguistics.

I think I was enriched by my experience of teaching and interacting with thousands of young people during my long stint (twenty-four years!) at Tezpur University.

10. You had written many stories about the erosion of moral values, the mundane lives of workers in the village, the loneliness of urban couples, the troubled phase of Assam when Ulfa was active, the effect of globalization in small places of Assam. Kindly tell us about all these concerns in your writing.

The immense diversity of life around me excites me and offers the materials for my short stories. I try to respond to what is happening—both disturbing and pleasant—around me and write about the challenges and joys of living in our troubled times. Apart from the erosion of values in the society, I try to understand and write about the hopes, frustrations and aspirations of the common people, of the young people. And I think I share an optimistic vision of life with many of my young readers.

11. You are a voracious reader of world literature. So please let us know about your favourite authors across the world.

Literary works produced in different languages in different parts of the world have always excited and attracted me. I try to read, understand and write about some of the great or good works of world literature---especially those written by the leading writers of our time. Among the modern writers (outside India)I like reading most are –novelists Alejo Carpentier, Yasunari Kawabata , Gunter Grass, Gabriel Garcia Marquez, Italo Calvino, Umberto Echo, Mo Yan, Ngugi wa T'iongo, Mario Vargas Llosa , Saramago and Javier Marias; short fiction writers Jorge Luis Borges, Guimaeres Rosa and Runyosake Akutagawa; poets Pablo Neruda, Adonis (Syrian poet), Tomas Transtromer and Seamus Heaney; and playwrights Samuel Beckett, Harold Pinter and Dario FO.

12. What do you think about the future of Assamese literature in the context of globalization and the growing aggression of English as a language? Kindly also let us know about you future projects as a creative and critical author and also as a translator.

Literature written in Assamese and some of the Indian languages is adversely affected by dwindling readership. One important reason is that a large section of the students do not or are not required to study their mother tongue at all. The habit of reading is ignored in our schools and colleges. Teaching is often exam-oriented. In my opinion literature is often taught in a very unimaginative manner, in a mechanical manner. Young people are not exposed to the joy of reading.

At the moment I am readying two books for publication—one, a collection of novellas and the other short and compact essays on world literature (authors and works). I hope to complete a novel in the next few months and start writing a book on laughter—humour and satire--. And of course I'll go on writing more short stories.

Interview of Rheea Mukharjee

An Artist traversing untrodden territory Rheea Mukherjee has registered her presence strongly in the realm of Indian English fiction with her novel The Body Myth which might remind a voracious reader of the classic American non-fictional work with the same title. The author has explored a hitherto unexplored territory in her novel and her fiction The Body Myth is different from run off the mill Indian English novel where either migration or immigration are the motifs. Rhea has shown extreme, rather superlative control over her subject matter and her controlled analysis of both physical and mental disease has been graphically accurate. The novel basically revolves around three characters- Mira, Sara, and Rahil who share a peculiar love-hate relation which is resolved only at the end. Rhea Mukherjee has not embellished her characters with artificial or redundant metaphor but the author's superb erudition is scattered throughout the pages of the book. The novel is extremely philosophical and unconventional but that does not make I boring. In fact, the novel is so strong throughout that readers would feel like both crying and shouting at times because of the pathos generated by the texture and structure of the novel. This novel, indeed, will be remembered for a long time by any sensitive reader. The author has done lots of research in medical science before writing this novel and it is evident that she is a hard working author. Rhea's graceful style and punctuated narrative is simply unputdownable. Her language is vivid, lucid, and almost soft to the extent of cotton. The fictional town of Suriyam is the locale of the novel and interesting words like "Chamomile" and "Rasagura" make it far more absorbing. What makes the novel unforgettable is its unpretentious integrity and superb craftsmanship. What follows is an exclusive interview between the author of The Body Myth Rhea Mukherjee and the reviewer Subhajit Bhadra.

1. Rheea first of all congratulations for writing such a brilliant work of fiction. How did you conceive the idea?

Thank you so very much. The Body Myth comes from two failed attempts of writing a novel. Those old manuscripts had nothing to do with this novel, but they were critical in my own journey of understanding what kind of writer I wanted to be. I have lived my life between the U.S and India for the most part (although I've moved back to India now for the past 8 years). This influence had me trying to examine the stories I wanted to tell, and they definitely were not immigrant fiction. We're living in times that are acutely globalised and capitalistic in aspiration. Urban loneliness, anxiety, and mental health are issues we are confronted with in very new ways, I think I was exploring a lot of that in the book. I have always been captivated by our minds and how the medical world tries to label every part of our illnesses while still admitting that each body and mind work uniquely. I think that discussion is part of the novel in a subtle way.

2. There is a famous American non-fictional work with the same title the body myth. Is there any similarity or is it merely a coincidence.

The only reason I know about the other Body Myth, is because when we came up with the title, my publishers checked to see if there were any major fiction titles with the same name. The only title that matched was a non-fiction book, so we decided to go with it since my version had no fiction counterparts. But no, there is no link to my novel and the non-fiction book.

3. kindly let us know something about Suryam, chamomile and Rasgura which add to the novel a special dimension.

When I was writing the novel, I very quickly realized that the book was insular, intimate, and quite frankly, fragile. The fictional city became a very natural choice for me, it was everything a real Indian city was in present day, but the name and the fruit that grew there allowed me to play with a slight mythical dynamic. Chamomile to me, is a very quiet word, it sits in the backdrop of memories, soothing the perpetual confusion and trauma Mira works with throughout the book. Some people have come back to me and said they didn't like that Suryam was a fictional city, but it's the one thing I was very sure of when I wrote the book. As for the other metaphors one can make of the city and the Rasagura that is very much the readers' prerogative.

4. How did you arrive at a synthesis among the three characters-Mira, Sara and Rahil. They seem not only to complement each other but also to contradict each other often. Please share your view.

They definitely are contradictory characters. Again, readers can have their own interpretations, but I see Mira as a woman who is using intellectualism to protect herself from the world and make sense of it at the same time. And yet she needs validation of her thoughts and ideas about the world. Sara is the challenge here, she is almost dismissive of intellectualism and has spiritual answers to everything. And there lies the attraction, two women trying to validate and seek attention from one another by thrusting their contradictory worldviews against each other. Rahil, to me is a man who sees his purpose in providing. He would not know what to do with himself unless he was providing: care, support, middle-class infrastructure. He doesn't question the notions both women have about the world, he accepts them, sometimes very passively, but without him, everything else would combust.

5. You have extensively used the comments of the French Existentialists in your novel. Is it because the author has a special leaning towards them or the character of Mira is enriched or even consoled by their views.

I actually had to spend months researching basic philosophy and history to get into the mind of Mira. I am naturally attracted to the subjects of philosophy, spirituality, psychiatry and especially like to view them from the lens of oppressors and voices that were margliansed because of them. That said, I am not as well read as Mira. I even wrote an article on writing a character that is smarter than the writer, at least in a bookish sense. A lot of it is research, and then letting go of a lot of that same research to see what comes out naturally from the mind of Mira. It was tricky at first, but then it just flowed. Ultimately, I think all 3 characters, despite their sets of knowledge, are figuring out who they are. Adulthood is this arbitrary age cut off where we're told we should know the basics and get on with life, but the truth is, most of us don't get to know who we are. We live under constructs of fear, biases, culture, a parochial traditions, and this is further complicated by social location, education, race, and economics. So in its essence, all three are philosophically engaged whether they know it or not.

6. What is your view about the complicated disease that Sara has. Does Mira contribute to the healing?

To me, Sara represents the world we're living in. How parental paranoia, ambition, and social expectations start to twist, turn and manifest as repercussions of childhood trauma. I do believe traumatised minds can manifest physical illness, and while the world of science is starting to bring nuance to the table in that regard, we're still living in a culture that tells us to suck it up and get on with life. At one level, it makes sense, we should be motivated to work the scars of our past and make new beginnings, but to do that you have to be able to know and trust yourself without a doubt. I don't think most of this world gets an opportunity to do that. Is Sara sick because she likes the attention? Is it her body's way of asking her to change her environment? Is it just physical illness? Or does she live with delusion? I think depending on the perspective you ascribe to, these are all valid answers. This is precisely why I didn't answer it with clarity. When it comes to the mind and its complexities (ones even the medical world is not sure of), perspective is the strongest voice. To that effect, I think Mira and Sara both heal each other, but in very different ways.

7. You have shown lesbian relation in your novel but your handling of it is classic. Kindly say something about it.

Mira and Sara come together romantically and sexually without overthinking what those labels meant to them. When they are together, a lot of their dynamic are based on the silent questions they ask to each each other. To me, their attraction was so natural I didn't think to steer it with any label and this is why I didn't take a voyeuristic approach to their relationship. I think, when people come together, however untraditionally, people see it as a part of their lives, a certain inevitably that led them there. I was just capturing Mira's grief and her existential curiosity as best I could.

8. Education, family and society- three important pillars of society are questioned in the novel. What would you say?

I think we are always evolving what these pillars mean to us. Right now, I am most frightened about education. Today education is gridlocked between the ambition of hyper capitalistic goals and its subsequent understandings of productivity. Propaganda is easy to infiltrate into our books, and we're definitely suffering from a system that's taught us to follow instead of lead or question.

I think family and society are very important to all of us, it holds us down to a certain rhythm. But we have to be open to what it means to us. We can't use one heteronormative and patriarchal idea of what family is for everybody. We have to be open and curious about people coming from very different perspectives of what love, sex, family, and joy mean. An optimistic society is one that is open to a multitude of experiences and ideas of communities with an equal regard. In India we are too quick to give this god-like stature to family and marriage, as if no bad can come out of it. The truth is, a lot of trauma, abuse, confusion, and utter despair comes from family as well. When that happens, we find our chosen family. We rethink the values we were taught and find places to recreate our lives in ways that might not be accepted by the families we were brought up in. In general, traditional families and traditional societal expectations form the dominant culture, so anyone living otherwise will always suffer in some way. That's what we have to change.

9. Please unveil the mystery of the title of your novel and let us know about your favourite contemporary writers.

The title actually comes from a process of renaming my novel. The title was originally Malaise which my first publishers in the U.S didn't think was dynamic enough. My publishers and I brainstormed for a couple of weeks.. I had put forth a quote by Simon De Beauvoir that said 'the body is not a thing it is a situation'. We played with that until we arrived at The Body Myth. I think it captures the arguments of what our bodies ultimately are: constructs based on how we're told to be and respond to things. And there is the notion of the spiritual soul and our lives as humans a mere physical manifestation of it. But once again, it's interpretation it's up to you.

10. Do you think that in the present context of globalisation literature still holds a unique significance?

I do. Though, I think we are a different kind of reader today. We live in a constantly updated world- and that means being updated on the personal front and on the global front. We don't have the mental bandwidth to sit with a book undisturbed the way we used to in the 90s. That said, there are still old-school readers out there, but I am more interested in seeing how literature evolves in the next few decades. I believe it will still be a sacred space where the individual can reckon with themselves in isolation. Where we can find quiet moments of imagination and realisation. Reading can be an act of rebellion, a space you demand from the world.

11. Kindly tell us something about the future of Indian writing in English.

I am excited for Indian writing in English. For far too long it was relegated to being something exotic, something that the West could feed their curiosity with. Today we are writing for ourselves and that is liberating. Although, fiction in regional languages have always led with imagination, the English language was a double edged sword for Indian writers. The language demanded you speak for the world and satisfy a specific aesthetic. But now we can write thrillers, science-fiction, and blend genres however we want, because there is no one Indian story. There never has been.

12. Kindly tell us something regarding the role of a creative writer in the contemporary context of socio political unrest.

I think writing is always a political act. Even if you are not writing about something that's on the nose, you are writing from a certain lens that's layered by class, caste, gender, patriarchy, culture, and vernacular. I think it's important to be reasonably aware of these things as writer.

Personally, I think writing has responsibility attached to it, and in a political climate that is getting increasingly dogmatic and downright fascist, writing is the only weapon we have to heal minds and possibly change them. Writing can give refuge and moments of peace to readers, it can educate and it can lead people into collective revolutions. We won't solve everything in our lifetime, we won't come close, but we will all have personal evolutions that will lead to a paradigm shift. Writing and reading is a massive part of this. I think this is a historical truth.

 Delving Into Different Literary Terrains

Laxminandan Borah A Name To Recon With In The Assamese Literature

Laxminandan Borah, a popular name in the Assamese literature, was born in a village in Nagaon district of Assam in a farmer's family on June 15, 1932. He was born to his parents after a gap of nearly 20 years since his eldest brother was born. When he was born, his parents were elderly and his brother was already married. This created a lonely world for him and he grew up without enjoying the companionship of children his age in the family. However, he received utmost care and affection from his family members. When he was in the local L.P. School, the class mates taunted him as an old man's son.

At school, Laxminandan was a favourite chap among the teachers. He often mixed with the people in the nearby villages and liked the local cultural activities. He often participated in such activities. This had a lifelong experience on his mind that is revealed through his literary works.

When he joined Cotton College for B.Sc. with honours in physics, he was in the circle of some of the best minds who later became famous in their fields. Later he joined Presidency College of Calcutta University, where he got legendary teachers like Satyendra Nath Bose and S.C. Chatterjee. Laxminandan remembers it with pride that he was an acquaintance with Late Tarasankar Bondopadhaya and Late Budhadev Bose.

Typically being a student of science, Laxminandan had little interest in literature initially. But his association with the people and life in Kolkata attracted him to literature. When he was in the final year at Presidency College, the Assamese people organized a meet on Sankardeva, where he delivered a speech on Sankardeva. People lauded him for his speech and persuaded me to try creative writing. Finally, he composed his first ever story Bhawana in Kolkata. Since then his journey in writing began.

After completing his education, he joined Assam Agricultural University as a teacher, although with low interest. Gradually, coming across brilliant students, he became more interested in teaching as he liked to nurture new talents. He had the grace of being the first doctorate in Agricultural

Meteorology perhaps in the entire northeast India. Agricultural Meteorology was a new area of study then. He spent some time in Walt air, Visakhapatnam also where he did research on his coveted area.

Laxminandan had a rich exposure to foreign countries where he contributed on several notable research projects. He was a visiting professor of Climatology in Johannes Gutenberg University in Germany and worked as a Project Director on another research scheme the very next year. He visited several European countries on different projects and academic positions. His observation is that standard of education in European countries is very high where research is given high importance.

On the other hand, Laxminandan was miffed over the social life of those countries as he found the people there self-centred and marriage life lasted for a measurably short period. The young people hardly took care of their parents. No one cared about the others. This aspect of western life finds place in his novel "Kayakalpa".

Laxminandan chiefly wrote short stories for fifteen years. His stories generally reflect the rural life and simple people. He had a keen observation on how people talked and spent life, specifically the people of the Satriya culture. His novel 'Ganga-Chilanir Pakhi' is the perfect example of his interest and handling.

He was heavily influenced by Sankardeva and Laxminath Bezbaruah, particularly because they both contributed a lot to the literature and had immense impact on the common people. Sankardeva, however, had a special place in his heart. He wrote the novel "Gakeri Nahike Upam" eulogising these gurus, which has been a best seller since 1993 running into several editions.

Laxminandan is credited to withhold the interest of novel reading among the readers. During the 1980s, when TV became an alternative source of entertainment over reading, Laxminandan introduced several new elements to the Assamese literary cannon such as modern themes, unpredictable dramatic situations, gripping story plots, and more importantly he made opium and smuggling the main story backdrops. His novel 'Patal Bhaisnavi' revolves around such elements which not only earned him Sahitya Academy Award, but has been widely appreciated by the readers and critics alike that made the book come out in several editions till date.

His themes in novels vary a lot like the streams of life itself. He had strong belief in the philosophy of Kayakalpa that is rejuvenation – a self-

     Delving Into Different Literary Terrains

transforming power that keeps life new and fresh for ever. He practiced yoga and was an ardent admirer of Aurvedic system of medicine, although he studied the modern gerontology at the same time. His novel Kayakalpa is on such themes for which he was awarded Saraswati Samman of K.K. Birla. The Chairman of the selection committee opined that no other Indian author attempted a novel on this theme so far.

During the while he was the President of Asom Sahitya Sabha, he attended meetings throughout Assam on regular basis. This opened a wider spectrum for him to know Assam more intimately. He came in close contact with various types of people who enriched his creativity and love for the Assamese people even more. He believed that if the immigrant Muslims and tea industry workers become the part of the main stream of the Assamese life, Assam as a nation would evolve as a great land. Laxminandan had the strong belief that Asom Sahitya Sabha has the centrifugal force to achieve this one day. His autobiography Kal Balukat Khoj is a very popular composition among the people that explores such views.

His contribution to his editorial journey is immense. He advocated that new voices should be encouraged and promoted. He suggests editors must understand the pulse of the contemporary people and hence new angle of writing must be recognized and given the chance to flourish. He wrote until his last days. Literature is highly indebted to Laxminandan who breathed last on June 3, 2021.

1. Kindly tell us in detail about your childhood as it the formative stage of life.

Ans: Though my native place is Baligaon under Jorhat district, yet I have no hazitation to say that I was born in Mangaldoi, Tengabari. My father was a govt serviceman and for his service, our whole family had to stay there for many years. But when I became one and half year old, he got transferred to Nagaon and we came there.

2. Kindly tell us about your place of origin and upbringing.

Ans : As I have already said that my original place is Baljgaon, Jorhat, but my birth place is Mangaldoi; we have been in different places due to the transferable job of my father. Besides Mangandoi, We stayed in Nagaon and Dergaon in the early part of my life. Finally, we returned to our original place, Baligaon, Jorhat where my father was born and brought up.

3. When did you start your early education and how was the environment of your primary school.

Ans : I have started my early education in the last part of seventieth decade of last century. During the Primary education, upto class III, I read in Nagaon Town Prathamik Vidyaloy. Then I read in Dergaon Town Balika Prathomik Vidyaloy from which I have got Primary Scholarship. I never forget the teachers in my primary education whose guidance and affection shown me the way to be built up as a human being. High school education was started in Dergaon Indranee Devi High School. Teachers of that institution were very caring and kind hearted as well as they were very good mentors. In that institute, I read upto class VIII. Then we returned to Jorhat, and further education continued in Jorhat. I have passed H.S.L.C exam in 1989 from Jorhat Govt Multipurpose Higher Secondary School. I have passed H.S.S.L.C Exam in 1991 and B.Sc. in Physics in 1994 from Jagannath Barooah College, Jorhat.

4. Did your brahminical root affect you in any way.

Ans : No, not at all. I belonge to a very cultured and broadminded family. Born and brought up in different places of Assam, have interaction with people having different religious views, have a friendly relation with people belonging from different caste and communities. I believe that there should be only one religion in the world that is 'Humanity'.

5. Kindly tell us about your higher education.

Ans : I have completed M,Sc. In Nuclear Physics from Gauhati University and got M.Phil degree from Madurai Kamaraj University.

6. Did you always want to be a writer.

Ans: Definitely not. And also I did not believe that I am a writer. I am still a learner and reader; will always want be a learner. I am just trying to express my feelings and experiences in my writings with the colour of emotions keeping in mind the readers satisfaction. Whatever I have written, all are for readers. Readers recognition is the best award for me.

7. How do you keep the balance between your academic life and your writerly life.

Ans: I think the mainly three qualities sincerity, punctuality and honesty should be the keyword for me to keep a proper balance between academic life and writerly life.

8. Kindly tell us about your professional life and do you think that the job of professor has an impact upon society and if so then why.

Ans : In my professional life, I always try to give my best effort to my students to get the proper knowledge about the subject matter whichever is allotted to me. My effort is to make them proper human being rather than becoming a machine. I Always try to be loyal to the esteemed institution and the authority.

Job of professor has the most important impact upon society because our task is to build human resources. Students always use to observe and follow whatever we do in their presence, in the classroom and beyond the classroom. Our decency, politeness and modesty should be an extra learning for them who are going to be part and parcel of the society and which would be reflected in their behavior in future.

9. Kindly tell us about the Genesis of your novel upakul brought about by Jyoti prakashan which is multilayered.

Ans; In the ancient society, the customs and rituals of Brahmin family was very strict which somehow reflect cruelity towards widows and for those women who were unable to conceive. Story of 'Upakul' is based on such sensitive issues along which a love story which flows silently with full of sanctity and purity. I think 'Upakul' is a like a statue/deed of women psychology. I gave all my good efforts in the creation of 'Upakul' and now think that my effort has not gone in vain. Readers and mainly women accept the story with pleasure and satisfaction which I came to know from various massages and reviews published in newspapers, magazines and other social media spontaneously. I shall remain ever grateful to Sjt, Nagen Sarmah who give the proper recognition of the story by publishing it on behalf of the esteemed publishing house Jyoti Prakashan.

10. Kindly tell us about the Genesis of your novel aarohi which is crisp and vivid.

Ans : 'Arohi'-- the story of which is based on love, faith, friendship, afraid etc in family issues. This is the story of two close friends along with their family members, one of which has an uncommon past. His father had a hidden family unknown to the society. What happens in the last is full of suspense and anxiety and it ends with creating a reverberation in readers heart. At the earlier, this novel was published serially in 'Basundhara' the Sunday supplement of DainikJanambhumi and became very popular among the readers. It was then published by Rupjyoti Devnath on behalf of Jagaran Sahitya Prakashan.

11. Very soon you are coming up with another novel that will be published by nagen sarma on behalf of Jyoti prakashan. What is your view about this novel.

Ans: yes, another novel 'Sipare Jamuna' got published recently. The story of this novel is something different, uncommon. What we believe about the things, events which are happening every day, every moment in the surroundings, are they like that what they seem to be? Is there another meaning of what we frequently called 'love'? 'Sipare Jamuna' is the story of a concubine who is very brave and rigid by mind. What we called--The good and bad sides of our society, are tried to justify through her mind. 'Sipare Jamuna'—it is the resonance of mental pain of each and every common young girl. I hope the untold truth of reality—'Sipare Jamuna' will achieve popularity among the readers. Taking the opportunity, I express my sincere thanks to Sjt. Nagen Sarmah, the owner of Jyoti Prakashan.

12. You are a prolific short story writer. What is your view about this genre in context of your stories.

Ans : I believe the fact --- ' if the whole life of a person is like a huge tree, then a branch of that tree taken away by force will be a short story'. I have written more than ninty short stories which got published in renowned assamese magazines like 'Gariyoshi', 'Prantik', 'Satsory', 'Prakash','Anyayug' etc along with the popular newspapers and their relevant magazines published with special issues. It gives me immense pleasure that all the stories become popular among common readers. Through the stories I have written, I want to reveal and reflect the little but common issues in everyday life of common people. The things we see and observe in our surroundings would be the core part of my stories and very common people I have selected could be the characters of the story. I just want to say again that the readers are the capital of my writings and I have been writing only for readers satisfaction not to get analyzed by the critics and to get complements from their side. 'Without readers recognition, the literature would be meaningless'—I think and believe that reality.

13. You also write for children which is a difficult task. How do you do justice to this craft.

Ans: Actually I think that good literature for children is very important matter. Psychology of a child is very soft and full of imagination. Their brain is always ready to accept anything whichever is conveyed to them. We provide them healthy food to keep their body fit and fine; we carry them

 DELVING INTO DIFFERENT LITERARY TERRAINS

to learn music, to the playgrounds in order to keep their body and mind healthy. But for their mental enhauncement, we should provide them with good literature, such that in the near future they can grow up with proper mindsets full of good habits. In order to keep a building strong enough, the foundation should be properly built up, similarly in order to develop human resources, the children should be grown up with healthy mind; for which they should be enriched with good literature suitable for them. I use to give some time in the first week of a month only to create something especially for children. I wrote more than twenty short stories for them, lots of poems, one novel 'Beliphular rang' got published from 'Assam Book Trust' and some tales.

14. Who are your favourite assamese writers from whom you gained creative input.

Ans: there are many more esteemed assamese writers which are my favourite most. Some of them are sahityarathi Laksminath Bezbaruah, Birendra kumar Bhattachharyya, Dr. Lila Gogoi, Sayed Abdul Malik, Mamoni Raisam Goswami, Dr. Laksminandan Bora and many more. But one writer whose writing inspired me most is the one and only Dr. Bhabendra Nath Saikia. I never met him in my life, yet he is my 'Guru' whose creations trace in my heart forever. One thing more to say that I want to convey my regards to Dr Laksminandan Bora, who is just like godfather to me and without his inspiration I think I would not be in this position to create so many writings.

15. What are your future projects about a writer.

Ans : Creations of short stories, poems, drama, articles, child literature... all are going in their own way and I want to continue all these as usual. But regarding future project, I make a plan to complete two novels in the course of one year, one of which is for especially for children.

A Critical Reading Of Disgrace As
A Postcolonial Novel

By Subhajit Bhadra

Asstt professor PG Department of English, Bongaigaon College

Post Office and District: Bongaigaon 783380, Assam

Mobile No: 9957858903

J. M. Coetzee is a Novel Prize winner for literature and he sails from South Africa. Disgrace is a very powerful text (Novel in this context) which fletched the writer the prestigious Booker Prize for the second time. As a postcolonial novel Disgrace has registered its presence in the academic arena and it is humorously said that for the elites of the society which knows the English Language better than their mother tongue that not to read Disgrace is a drawing room offence.

J. M. Coetzee received both praise and condemnation after the publication of Disgrace that he had to leave his native country and settle eventually in Australia. As a writer from South Africa Coetzee can be compared with another Nobel Prize winning author Nadine Gordimar while Gordimar has exposed the brutality of the colonial power (especially the torture meted out to the black by the whites) on the other hand J. K Coetzee has depicted the psychopathology of postcolonial situation in his fictions. Disgrace can be said to belong to the postcolonial realm both periodically and temporarily and also from the point of view of his theme.

In South Africa there was never formal colonization but it; the country witnessed apartheid. It is a process of racial discrimination where the white Europeans subjugated the black natives. One can think of Nelson Mandela, the crusader for the black natives of South Africa who brought them freedom but he had to remain in colonial custody for more than two decades. One could expect that with a large number of people, the black people have to get freedom from apartheid a long time back. One can draw on interesting analogy with Mandela along with M. K. Gandhi (better known as Mahatma Gandhi), both of whom were related to South Africa

     DELVING INTO DIFFERENT LITERARY TERRAINS

who clamored and protested for equal right for all. Disgrace is a typical postcolonial test that incorporates within its fabric various themes like physical subjugation, psychological damage, marginalization of the blacks with their own cultural heritage, oppression of women, the discrimination and rift between the blacks and whites, the unease on social tension, the hostility borne out of a situation of unrest, the gradual turnaround of the black people who started torturing the whites under the post-apartheid context, the humiliation of an entire race (in the context of the novel), the utter helplessness of the once-colonizers, the issue of the subaltern, violence unpredictability of racial and political turn over, the rise of the new negro, brutality, suffering of human being who once victim of a larger political machinery, the awakening of racial bigotry the collapse of whole supremacy and above all the equal relation the colonizer and colonized.

In Disagree, Coetzee tackles the postcolonial discourse in an alert manner but with no concoction he calls a spade a spade and he does not waver an inch from his social and human commitment, which does not mean any bias. Coetzee has always depicted the bleak reality of South Africa where both the blacks and whites tortured each other under convenient political patronage. The Algerian born psychiatrist cum intellectual Franz Fanon rightly deserved in his seminal book "The Wretched of the Earth" that-

"The blinding sun of torture is at its Zenith. It lights up the whole country. Under such merciless glare, there is a single laugh that does not ring false, not a single face that is not painted to hid fear or anger and there is not a single action that does not betray out disgust and complicity." (Fanon, The Wretched of the Earth.)

Disagree was written in 1999 and this is why periodically it is a post colonial novel. Apart from this it is a postcolonial novel also because it shows the ill-effect of long tern colonization (in this case apartheid). Coetzee has also depicted very clearly the psychopathology of colonialism and the common assumption of a postcolonial approach are thwarted because in this novel it is the whites who are at the receiving end under changed political situation.

The chief protagonist of this novel is David Lurie, a professor of English in a Technical University who symbolizes all the vicious traits of a white colonizer. Lurie is a very aggressive white intellectual who does not suffer from traditional orthodox attitude; he is divorced and likes to live life on his own terms. However, like a typical white European Lurie believes that black girls exist for the conception of the so-called white superior people.

Lurie seduces or rather arranges for the seduction of a black student of his named Melenie. Moreover Lori does not merely have sex with her a number of times, the irony is that lovely tries to hush-up the matter but is exposed quite badly.Lurie wants to adore and seduce black girl and he does not suffer from any moral qualms for seducing his own student. Lori is summoned by the committee constituted by his University but he only tries to offer the arrogant point of view. He thinks and acts like a colonizer as lorry in is white but very soon he has to face the music very nicely. Melenie's boyfriend attack Lurie's house in Cape-town and destroy a lot of things. The political situation in South Africa has changed and blacks are no longer afraid of white there. Initially Lurie wants to male League schedule is black student but after being given a very harsh treatment he has to lose his job of teaching also. The colors of black is used as a metaphor in the novel which can be multiple things at the same time. Melenie is black but Lori is both fascinated and appalled by the Black figure. one example is

"Driving home from the concert then that evening she stops at the traffic light. The motorcycle throbs past a silver Dukati bearing 2 fingers in black..."

(Disgrace, Page 35)

When Lurie decides to strike a relation with Meleine he is charged up by his vigorous sexual urge but he fails to see the blacken side of the action that he plans to commit. He also fails as a teacher morally because he marks Melenie present in his classes even when she is absent. When University authorities decide to give him a last chance to defend himself Lurie remains unshaken and unnerved. When asked in a rough manner, Lurie confess his dead but the confession leads to further unrest as he says-

".. Let me confess. The story begins one evening. I forgot the date, but not long past. I was walking through the old collage gardens and so, it happened was the young women in question. Ms Issacs our paths crossed. Words passed between us and at that moment something happened which, not being a poet, I will not try to describe. Suffice it to say that Eros entered. After that I was not the same"

(Disgrace, Page 52)

After Lurie describes the process of his demonization nothing remains the same. Lurie has always colonized women, for his a woman is a commodity, who can be chewed and devoured at his will. A man is superficially and wrongly the colonizer (that means a perpetrator) and women is always mistakenly regarded as the colonized. Lurie has inherited the pride of a white European colonizer and he is always aggressive with the black people. As though Lurie does not consider a black person as a human entity and this will become more pronounced when Lurie compares the blacks along with animals. Disagree is also a postcolonial animal tale which seeks to draw several animal imageries at the same time. Seducing a black girl is a routine affair for Lurie and he does not feel hurt to cause such pain. One of the members of the investigation committee Farodea Rassool sums it up nicely-

"... he is confessing to, just an impulse he could not resist with no mention of the pain he has cause, no mention of the long history of the exploitation of which this is a part." "Disgrace, page 53)

David Lurie is an inveterate womanizer, he likes to draw himself in the pleasure of the body, he believed that a women's body is not her own possession it is a part of the bounty she brings to the world for the pleasure of a man/men. Traditionally women body is always regarded as a male destination but with the onslaught of feminism a women's body is always regarded as its own destination. Both post colonialism and feminism are concerned with one common concern- the issue of marginalization. In Disgrace, the women's body is shown as a potential site of male sexual violence and here the victimized person are both Melenie and David Lurie's own daughter- Lucy who runs a firm in the countryside along with a black person named Petrus who supposedly looks after the land. Initially in Cape town Lurie inflicts sexual violence on the body of Melenie, his own student who is also a black. Then when David Lurie retreats to the countryside farm Petrus and his black cohorts inflict sexual violence on the body of Lucy. This is a chain that continues and it is done by a typical patriarchal attitude. Patriarchy always looks at a women from the point of the view of a typical male aggression and the women's body becomes not merely as a locus of male sexual violence, but also turns out to be a repertory of all wound inflicted by women. David Lurie's act of sexual violence towards Melenie is punished in the form of Lucy's gang rape by the group of Petrus whom Lurie point as a miscreant. However Lucy thinks that instead of counter aggression passive acceptance can bring back normalcy. When David Lurie is beaten and Lucy's house is ravaged by a group of black perpetrator she accepts it without further protest and believes in counter violence. Lucy thinks that it is she who has to atone for her forefather's crimes and she eventually decides to give birth to the child who would be a product of gang rap. As opposed to Lurie's attitude Lucy decide to accept the statues of a woman in the form of a wife or harlot kept by Petrus and his associates. There is an omniscient comment in the novel Disgrace which seems to address this issue-

"It will dawn on them that over the body of the women silence is being drawn like a blanket. Too ashamed, they will say to each other, too ashamed to tell, and they will chuckle luxuriously recollecting their exploit. Is Lucy prepared to concede then the victory? (Disagree110)

Whereas on the hand the colonial pride of a white is demolished on the other hand the passive acceptance of Lucy decides to equal historical wrongs. The whites Europeans have always dominated the blacks in South Africa but in the wake of the collapse of the apartheid the blacks meted out the same treatment to the whites and this sort of the turnaround of event bring about the concept of revenge historiography which is treated by J. M Coetzee in a deft manner. In a different South Africa Lucy and Lurie are at the receiving ends and even traditional land owner like Ettinagar who also happens to be whites. Petrus does not merely want to grab the land of Lucy he also wants to become her protector. Lucy and Lurie always have shared a troubled relationship between then and the rift intensifies with the assault of Lurie and the rape of Lucy, Lucy believes that "Vengeance is like a fire" but Lurie believes that the perpetrators must be punished in the absence of which it (Such violence) will become a routine affair. It is a context where historical reality has change under such situation the white people are disgraced and become the passive watcher of black violence which is substantiated by the following comment-

"It is a new world they live in, he and Lucy and Petrus. Petrus knows it, and he knows it and Petrus knows that he knows it." (Disagree 117)

For Lucy it is a new experience as she is a lesbian who believes in the ideal of moving towards a black female utopia.

Lurie has realized the situation but his white colonial pride deters him to accept the situation as it is, but he is also unable to protest. He can only bark like a dog. But unable to bite; he realizes that Petrus is the mastermind behind such a retaliation. He realizes that Petrus and his cohort signed Lurie and raped Lucy because they are whites, the once custodian of South African administration power. He realizes at the end that political equation has changed, but having said that he is bound to be aggressive as he understand the fact that offence is the best defense.

The post colonial paradigm manifest itself also in the arena of language as we know that the colonized lot appropriate the language of the colonial master and they are capable of replaying back in the language of their master. Petrus and his associates have done exactly this and because of the political turn around the whites people find themselves mutilated and harassed in South Africa. The equation between the colonizer and the colonized is changed and Coetzee credit lies in the fact that he has problematized the postcolonial paradigm here and the result is an astonishing and heart rending novel like Disgrace A postcolonial reading of Disagree also attempts to capture the Subtle nuances or revenge historiography Petrus and his associates are figured from the margins of history but then voice becomes more pronounced in a post-apartheid South Africa. J. M Coetzee address the various historical gaps in the narrative of Disgrace and one can conclude by saying that it is a complex postcolonial text that problematizes the issue rather than simplifying it. The strength of Disgrace emanates from the fact that it is a multi-layered text which is both polyphonic and dialogue regarding its texture and structure and the post-colonial theme is central to the making of the narrative.

The postcolonial paradigm is also shown in the context of the color bias in Disagree. The black is always and already suffering from the extraordinary burden of compression with the whites.

The black is looked at with distrust and suspicion but one cannot over look the fact that the black like the white, is also a flesh and blood human being. In a post-colonial context the black is imagined as an "Other" Figure and this process of "Othering" Is done in Disagree by both David Laurie and Petrus and his associates. The postcolonial discourse in Disagree is inconclusive as Coetzee leaves the narrative open ended through various kinds of hints and there is an aura of suggestiveness. The grim ending of Disagree, however help the reader to not merely look at the text from a postcolonial perspective, but also from a human angle.

Work cited:

- Disgrace: J. M Coetzee, Vintage Publication 1999 . Print
- The Wretched of the Earth. Franz Fenon, Grove Press. 1961 Print

Unveiling Pattern Of Racial And Sexual Violence A Critical Reading Of J. M Coetzee's Disgrace

By Subhajit Bhadra
Asst Professor. PG Dept of English
Bongaigaon College, Bongaigaon, 783380 (Assam)
Cont no: +91 9957 858 903

ABSTRACT

The aim of this paper is to explore and trace the patterns of racial and sexual violence in J. M. Coetzee's novel Disgrace. The novel under discussion was awarded the Booker prize in 1999 and subsequently its author J.M Coetzee also got the novel prize for literature in 2003 When Disgrace was first published in 1999 the novel met with severe criticism from the black community in South Africa and its publication forced Coetzee to leave South Africa and settle down in his newly adopted country Australia. It must be remembered that J. M Coetzee is a white writer and his exploration of racial and sexual violence in Disgrace is very relevant to understand. The psyche of two particular classes of South Africa. Coetzee along with Nadine Gordimer (another white South African writer who was awarded the Nobel prize for literature in 1991) have always explored the various layers of racial and sexual violence in South Africa in their respective gamut of works. Disgrace is both thematically and structurally a tight novel and it adds a new feather to its writer's cap as it openly brings to light the various pattern of sexual and racial oppression or violence.

Key Words:

Racial, Sexual, Violence, discrimination, apartheid, feminism.

Full Paper:

The aim of this paper is to explore and trace the patterns of racial and sexual violence in J. M. Coetzee's novel Disgrace. The novel under discussion was awarded the Booker prize in 1999 and subsequently its author J.M Coetzee also got the novel prize for literature in 2003 When Disgrace was first published in 1999 the novel met with severe criticism from the black community in South Africa and its publication forced Coetzee to leave South Africa and settle down in his newly adopted country Australia. It must be remembered that J. M Coetzee is a white writer and his exploration of racial and sexual violence in Disgrace is very relevant to understand. The psyche of two particular classes of South Africa. Coetzee along with Nadine Gordimer (another white South African writer who was awarded the Nobel prize for literature in 1991) have always explored the various layers of racial and sexual violence in South Africa in their respective gamut of works. Disgrace is both thematically and structurally a tight novel and it adds a new feather to its writer's cap as it openly brings to light the various pattern of sexual and racial oppression or violence. Disgrace is a postcolonial novel from both temporal and thematic point of view. In order to understand it one must first pay attention to the term colonialism. Colonialism means taking away someone else's land by coercion or force and occupation of geographical territory. Considered from his angle South Africa never experienced formal colonialism like India or Nigeria or some other African countries. However Post colonialism in South African denotes the period of Apartheid colonialism has two sort of impact on the natives – one physical and another mental or psychological. Whenever the colonizers colonize a particular place they geographically occupy it and from the psychological point of view they torture the natives mentally as they forcefully denigrate the culture and language of the native people. Considering the psychological damage caused by the colonialism Franz Fanon wrote in his famous book The Wretched of the Earth (Fanon was referring to the French Colonization of Algeria and it must be remembered that he was a practicing psychiatrist.)

"The blinding sun of torture is at its zenith. It lights up the whole country. Under that merciless glare there is not a single love that does not ring false there is not a single face that is not painted to hide fear or anger and there is not a single action that does not betray our disgust and complicity." Fanon

In South Africa there was the prevailing terror of Apartheid even though there was not formal colonization there. Coetzee and Gordimer have also depicted the effects of apartheid in South Africa in their works. Coetzee's many novel Chronicle the Torture mated out by the white to the blacks.

But in Disgrace he traverses a different trajectory as he talks about black oppression to the white in post apartheid South Africa. Disgrace is a very powerful novel that compels us to rethink the patterns of racial and sexual violence in contemporary context and in this novel Coetzee's attitude towards blacks and whites is highly provocative. The psychopathology between the colonizer and colonized has been graphically portrayed and Coetzee does so in a clinical manner. During the apartheid (which means a form of racial segregation) the whites is South Africa treated the native's blacks in inhuman way. When Nelson Mandela was trying his level best to end white rule in South Africa then he was imprisoned for more than two decades. Even Mahatma Gandhi saw this terrible oppression when he was in South Africa and Gandhi also saw how the blacks were treated in that country. The Whites became the undisputed monarch of South Africa and there was supposed to be no threat to the whites. But subsequently during the early 1990s the apartheid became extinct in South Africa and subsequently the administrative power went to the hand of the blacks in that country. Coetzee has always shown in his novels that various layers of sexual and racial violence meted out to the blacks by the whites in South Africa but when the black people got power the situation drastically changed in South Africa. Coetzee shows in disgrace how the whites are at the receiving end and how the blacks people have become the imitator to their erstwhile masters, the whites. If we take into account the concept of post colonialism mimicry then we can safely suggest that the blacks became the postcolonial mimics in South Africa as they started oppressing the whites. Disgrace brilliantly highlights the layers of racial and sexual violence and my approach in this paper is both theoretical and textual.

David Laurie is a white professor of English Literature at a technical university in Cap Town. He always runs after women and it would not be exaggeration to comment that he is an innervate womanizer. He believes that beauty is not her own property; rather it is a common property to be devoured and savored by all males. He strikes up a sexual relation with one of his black female student named Melenie. Soon he discovered that pleasure of sex as he is already twice divorced but after some days he also finds to his utter chagrin that he is followed by a group of black boy appear to be menacing. The figure of the black is always and already suffering from the extraordinary burden of comparison with the figure of the white. Because of Laurie's sexual exploitation of the black female student she stops attending his classes. Laurie initially expects her but after some days he accepts the reality. Laurie even goes to the extent of tempering

     Delving Into Different Literary Terrains

with the class register in order to cajole the girl back to the class. But at all cost Melenie avoids him and this fact first irritates Laurie and then angers him. He is the meantime also contemplate an opera on local Byron. The promiscuous lover and famous bi sexual Victorian poet. However he takes notes read a lot, does research about Byron but he can not bring it to conclusion because of the mess he has created around himself. He waits for Melenie with bated breath; she eludes him as Lauries' expectations come to naught. The pattern of racial violence first finds manifestation when Laurie finds his university quarter ravaged by a group of black boy who are initially supposed to be but later on definitely turn out to be Meleine's friends. For the first time Lurie finds that racial discrimination has taken a different turn in post apartheid South Africa. Lurie is a white person and Melenie is black and previously during the apartheid period a white could easily seduce a black girl in the pretext of racial violence. But now the situation has changed. David Lurie is not longer the white colonizer and Melenie the black colonized. This changed equation shatters Lurie but he is a daredevil figure as he does not break down easily. When the university constitution as investigation committee and Lurie is asked to apologize he refuses the offer point blank. Lurie first notice Melenie's black boy friend in the class as he observes-

"After this coup de main Melenie keeps her distance. He is not surprised. If he has been shamed, she is shamed too. But on Monday she re appears on class and beside her, leaning back in his seat, hands in pocket, with an air of cockeye ease, is the boy in black, the boyfriend" (Disgrace 31)

This menacing encounter first becomes a sign of nervousness and later on it became the sign of defeat. Lurie does not seek apology and as a result of this he loses his job from the university. Lurie suffers from no repentance but later on it become ironic when he goes to the home of Melenie and seeks forgiveness from her parents. Lurie is a father himself as he has daughter named Lucy but he violates everything in the pride of racial superiority. Lurie is a white colonizer to whom the black are toys to be played with but his daughter's position later on regarding the issue of sexual violence problematize the concept of standard postcolonial paradigm. But that will be discussed later on. Initially Lurie's racial and sexual violence towards Melenie put him on a difficult and diffident situation as he has to retreat to the farm house of his daughter in rural South Africa. David Lurie behaves like typical white colonizer who can claim any black as his victim. But when he finds himself at. The receiving end he has to rethink his strategy. David

Lurie finds his privacy being evaded and he being watched and later on becoming like a dog. It must be noted that there are many animal imageries in the novel and this animal imagery represents racial discrimination. Initially David Lurie treats the blacks as animals but towards the end he finds himself reduced to the situation of a dying dog. He works in the clinch of Bev Shaw where he looks after dogs but unknowingly he himself has become like a dying dog. David Lurie's both as oppressor and and oppressed as he first attacks and is then being attacked. David Lurie's racial pride and arrogance know no bound but when he is confronted with the reality then there is no scope of hibernation for him. David Lurie behaves like an aggressor but his aggression is gradually tamed as he becomes dwarfed. When the white were ruling in South Africa and were treating the blacks in an inhuman way then the system of racial segregation in the form of the apartheid was going on. But in the post apartheid South Africa people like David Lurie have no place. The tolerance of the black for the white has reached a zero level and David Lurie is a representative of the entire white community dwarfed by the blacks. In this novel we find the psychopathological relation between the white and the black and it is not the question of who wins the game but the bleak reality of South Africa in the post apartheid situation Coetzee shows how both the once colonizers and the once colonized react to each other and one cannot escape the reality. Depending upon such a situation one question becomes significant- Is the pattern of racial violence inevitable or can it be avoided? Coetzee does not provide any definite answer to it.

When David Lurie retreats to his daughter Lucy's farm he finds that they share a troubled relation. Lucy is looked after by Petrus, a menacing black figure who does not care about the sentiment of the whites. As time passes David Lurie develops a disdain for Petrus and his other black associates. One day suddenly Lurie and Lucy's safe abode is under seign as Lurie is singed and Lucy is gangraped by a group of black boys. Lurie doubts that it is the brainchild of Petrus and his suspicion indeed becomes true later on when he discovers the identity of boy named Pollux. David Lurie tries to mentally disentangle him from his incident but cannot. His racial pride is hurt as he asks Lucy to dodge an official complaint against Petrus and his associates to which Lucy replies negatively. Lucy has nothing to do as she resigns to her fate and says that she has atoned for the crime of her forefathers. Previously the whites raped the black's girl but in a changes scenario the blacks are mating out the same treatment to the whites. Traditionally a women's body has been treated as a male destination but with the onslaught of feminism as women's body became her own destination. David Laurie fins the sexual and racial violence intolerable but there is no way to get rid of it in post apartheid South Africa. Lurie tires a hundred times but his daughter is adamant and he cannot force her to complain against Petrus. Lucy is pregnant and she accepts the option of marrying Petrus for the protection of her child. Lurie cannot tolerate this but he is a mute spectator. The pattern of the racial and sexual violence that takes in the novel is full of subtle nuances and David Lurie towards the end feels disgraced. The racial violence take place on both sides and the sexual violence also take place on both the sides. So the question is not who wins or loses the game but who is at the receiving end in post-apartheid South Africa. The patterns of racial and sexual violence that take place in the novel is bleak and calls out for a humane understanding and painstakingly security. David Lurie and his daughter Lucy are the victims of racial and sexual violence respectively. So is Meline, the black student of Lurie. Disgrace is very powerful novel that seeks to expose the various patterns racial and sexual violence and these also become the motifs of the novel.

Works Cited:

- Fanon Frantz: The Wretched of the Earth, Grove Press, 1961 Print
- Coetzee J. M: Disgrace, Vintage Press, 1999 Print

Water Hyacinth

Original Assamese: Madan Sarma
Translation: Subhajit Bhadra and the Author

As if all of a sudden there appeared , at the centre of a thin and wide patch of white cloud, a smaller and gradually widening patch of blue that looked like a deep lake, its surface undisturbed by any wave. From his seat in the moving boat, Digonto Borua was looking at the sky. For the last four or five days, the weather had been gloomy and it was rather depressing to go on looking at the same grey, cloudy sky day after day. Monsoon was coming to an end and autumn was almost there. The sight of that blue patch of the sky gladdened his heart. And then sunshine poured over the purple flowers of the water hyacinths swaying in the cool breeze blowing across the river. The flowers glistened, and sunlight slid down the dark green leaves of the plants. The whole atmosphere turned magical in a moment. Digonto began to hum softly.

Topon, who was rowing the boat, remained unconcerned about all these. As on any other day, he must have come out quite early in the morning for fishing in the bil, the shallow lake connected to the tiny river. After fishing, he guided his boat through that small stream and then down the main river. As he was about to moor the boat, his friend Digonto showed up on the other side of the rice paddy field. Topon wasn't really eager to take him on a river tour. Digonto could very well row the boat himself but Topon would never let him do so. As Digonto was to leave for Guwahati in a few days, Topon became a little considerate, "O.k, let's go. I won't be able to spend much time with you, I'm sorry."

Digonto would have liked to sail further down the river. But Topon really didn't have much time to spare. He had to collect the milk from the buffalo-herders of the river island and then deliver it to the sweetmeat shops in the town. For that he would have to hire his friend Bolen's three wheeler. He needed some extra money as he could hardly make do with what he usually earned from farming.

     Delving Into Different Literary Terrains

After quietly rowing the boat for a while, Topon asked, "How is your father now?" He knew that Digonto's father hadn't been keeping well for some time.

"He seems to be much better now. Mother also thinks so.."

"Seems like your presence has pepped him up," Topon said, "You should keep visiting him. Moving to the city makes the youngsters forget their villages."

"You think I'm one of them?" Digonto kept taking pictures with his Android phone.

"I know you aren't. The reason why I let you ride my boat."

"Look, how beautiful those blooming water hyacinths are."

"They've just started blooming. Just wait for a few days and they'll be everywhere."

A clamp of water hyacinth was slowly floating towards their boat. Digonto said, "Could you keep the boat steady for a little while?"

The boat came to a standstill. Digonto kept aside his Android phone and took out a small digital camera, "Come on, give me a smile. The sky won't fall if you smile for once."

Topon smiled. The photo should come out well since Topon's face was bathed in sunshine.

"These flowers are so lovely!" Digonto said, "The plant has a different attraction altogether, although it's of a foreign origin."

"Foreign? What are you talking about?"

"Do you think this plant, meteka, is indigenous, originally from here? It's a native plant of South America."

"What was the need to bring it all the way from America? It's found everywhere. Are you kidding?"

"No, honestly. Maybe someone was struck by its beauty and brought it here. Now people make all kinds of mats, hand bags and a variety of other items from meteka and are making money too. Such a lovely flower, isn't it?"

Topon started steering his boat towards the bank and said, "I'm really scared."

"Scared?Why?"

"Did you notice how the water has risen?"

Yes, Diganta thought, during the last two or three days, the river had swollen. It's been raining like hell. It must be pouring in the hills. If this continues , the rising water will flood the village. Every year one experiences the last rains of the season just before the Durga Puja. The entire village reels under water. And then slowly the water moves to the bil. The water goes out through the drains as well. And when the water recedes, the roads turn muddy. The flood damages most of the vegetables grown by the villagers, but it also leaves behind fertile silt in their paddy fields.

" What does meteka got to do with the rising water?" Digonto asked.

"Are you out of your mind?" Realizing that his voice was a bit harsh, Topon softened it a little, "What if the rising water pushes all the water hyacinths through the small river? This morning I faced such a huge and impenetrable clump of water hyacinth that I just couldn't push them any further. If more and more clumps of hyacinth rush towards the bil, just imagine the plight of those who earn their living by fishing in it."

Digonto had not thought about that before. He felt a bit embarrassed. He was about to say something but he stopped himself and said, "Hey, look over there, to your right. Can you see?"

A large raft made of logs and loaded with logs and planks of wood was slowly making its way through the clumps of hyacinth with great difficulty. A few men, some squatting on the logs covered by sheets of plastic, were working hard to steer it safely through the hyacinth. At night it will be disastrous to make such an attempt.

"What are those thieves up to?" Digonto said.

Topon just glanced at them once and started to row the boat faster towards the river bank.

"Aren't these stolen from the forest? Should we stop them?"

"Shut up!"

Digonto glanced at Topon and said in a low voice, "Should we inform the police, or the forest department?" He took out the mobile phone and took a picture of the loaded raft and the smugglers.

"Hide that. It's none of your business. You do your job and stay at Guwahati, don't get involved in these." Topon said with slight anger and irritation.

"What do you mean, you, topa, baldy,." Digonto said it to annoy Topon, even though Topon was actually not bald; Digonto and his village mates just distorted Topon's name to 'topa', meaning bald, to irritate him. "Then who is behind all these? Do you know?"

Topon didn't say anything.

The boat reached the bank. "Get off," he said.

Digonto leaped onto the bank. Topon got down and tied his boat. Then he carried the net and the large khaloi used to catch fish on his shoulder. Digonto was still looking at the raft with the logs. Topon said, "Let's go. Don't go on staring at them."

"Why?"

Topon didn't bother to explain right away. After walking for a little while he said, "Once in winter I brought two men to the river. While rowing around, we reached the other bank , and the men rushed into the woods with their cameras and all. I warned them but they just ignored me. The loggers chased them away. If I hadn't been there, they would have been beaten to death for sure. They might even have guns. Crores of rupees are involved in such business."

They were walking along the pebbled road when a mini truck sped past them. "Eh! Who is this now, rushing in at a break- neck speed?" Digonto said, covering his face with the handkerchief.

"It's Rupeswar. Who else could it be? The loggers will moor their raft in a deserted place ahead. They'll need to offload and hide the logs quickly."

"Has Rupeswar got a lumber yard?"

"Why does he need to have one? He'll supply these to Bihari Singh's or Doctor Boruah's son-in-law's mill. Those bastards have denuded the entire reserved forest. Now just wait and see, tigers will come out and roam around the villages."

Digonto found this last comment funny and interesting, "Oh, are tigers still around here?"

"There are still a few. Now from the denuded forest, herds of wild buffalos will come out, looking for shelter during the flood. Deer too come looking for higher ground."

"And you kill them and eat them!"

Topon glared at him and Digonto hurriedly changed the topic, "Since when has Rupeswar been doing this?"

"It's not just him, there are so many engaged in such activities," Digonto said. "Rupeswar is used by those who have connections and can't be touched by the police or forest officials. Nothing will happen to these loggers. And the poor fellows who enter the forest just to collect some firewood are beaten up. And then hundreds of monkeys descend on their villages and destroy everything. The plundered forests have nothing for them."

Digonto asked him, "Do you go fishing every day?"

"Don't talk of fishing now. What if, as it happened last year, all the hyacinths move down the river and engulf the entire bil, suffocating everything in it?"

Hemo slowly came cycling towards them. He got down from his cycle and looked at Topon, "I've heard that water hyacinth has covered everything. Could you do some fishing?"

"Yes, for a little while." Topon didn't want to elaborate, he was already late.

"Well, the situation doesn't seem to be good. Water has been rising fast " Hemo said, " Water has already entered our village. And then, these hyacinths...they seem to grow so fast!'"

"Some of these grow up to two-three meters a day." Digonto said.

"Meter? How tall exactly?"

"Say around eight of nine feet."

Hemo was shocked, "Oh, this is really dangerous! If babies grew this fast, or even trees...!"

They laughed. They found the observation rather amusing as it came from Hemo who had earned fatherhood only recently. Topon asked him, "How about your daughter? Is she growing fast?"

"No. I go on talking to her all the time, she doesn't utter a single word!"

"Everything has a time, right? It doesn't go as you wish," Topon proclaimed.

"They should grow up fast."

"It's better if they didn't ."

"Why?"

"All the problems arise once you grow up."

Hemo changed the topic, "Hey, Topon, I heard that Kripasankar, the owner of the shop you supply milk to, used to deal in timber. And now he sells sweets." He gave an amused laugh.

"So you've come to know about it now?" Topon said. "There wasn't any other option for him. It was getting risky to deal in timber. So he sold off everything and invested in that sweet meat shop. I don't know if he has any other illegal business too."

With his left foot on the pedal, Hemo said, "I heard that hyacinths have choked Dina kokai's paddy field. I'm really worried. This year I started planting rather late. What if somehow hyacinths move to engulf the field? I should go and check if everything's fine."

Both Tapan and Diganta looked at each other's face. They were shaken by Hemo's words. They were from rich farmer's families and naturally, were better off than most farmers.

They parted ways near the fields in front of the primary school.

It started raining again in the evening, though it was not heavy. Digonto had to take his father to doctor Phukan's clinic. His father had been facing problems in breathing normally since that afternoon. Bolen, who owned an auto-rickshaw. would have come readily to take his father to the doctor's chamber but the journey won't be comfortable at all for a patient. So Digonto went to Jiten Borah, the only person in the village who owned more than one motor vehicle. His sons usually took the biggest vehicle to the town. Borah was known to have some share in the illegal timber business and everyone happened to know that, although he loved to claim that he brought timbers from Arunachal Pradesh. One of his sons had a furniture house in the town. Most of the time, one of his sons would stay in the upper floor of the two-storied house he had built in the town. The shop located downstairs also stocked readymade wooden furniture so that none could accuse Jiten Borah of selling furniture made from smuggled timber.

Jiten Borah immediately sent a small car with his driver Bokul. He said, "Wait, I'm going to talk to the doctor so that you don't have to wait in his chamber."

Digonto was grateful to him.

The car carrying Diganta and his father was moving along the road that skirted the bil when a man almost stumbled across the car. Driver Bokul stopped the car and scolded him, "Are you blind?"

Digonto recognized the man. It was Okon who lived on the other side of the rivulet that dried up in winter and got filled up with water in summer.

Digonto got down from the car and before he could ask anything, the man said, " I was wondering how I could go home."

"Why? What happened?"

"The way home is blocked now. The water hyacinths pushed and broke the wooden bridge over the stream."

"When did it happen?"

"Just a while ago. It was repaired only last year."

"How do the hyacinths have so much strength?"

"You'd have known if you had only seen how they smashed everything in seconds! "

Digonto was speechless for a moment. In the falling darkness he could see only the clumps of water hyacinths. It was difficult to imagine that there used to be a bil, a lake with crystal clear water, where hundreds of birds used to feast on fishes during the day. Nobody had seen a single bird on the lake since last few days.

"So what are you going to do now?" Digonto asked

"We'll have to make a detour to reach home." Okon said, touching the heavy bag on his shoulder. "Really, hyacinths could have such strength to cause such devastation!"

Looking at the lake covered entirely by water hyacinths, Diganta slowly walked to the car. He heard his father mumble, "All the fish will die."

A small crowd had gathered near the bridge. Digonto leant towards his left and silently indicated that he would be coming back to meet them. And he did so. On their way back from the doctor's chamber, the driver dropped him near the crowd. Digonto heard someone say, "How strange! The clumps of hyacinths have gathered so thick as if someone had tightly packed the bil with them. One can even walk on them to cross the entire stretch of water. Paddy fields, bils and ponds, all have been covered by hyacinth."

Digonto silently listened to their conversation. How lovely the hyacinth flowers were in the morning,, and now....

Topon came up to him, "You were right about them. It's scary, how fast the hyacinths grow! "

While having dinner, Diganta's elder brother Hemanta said, "Hyacinths have rushed into our fields as well. And if they keep on coming like this, we won't be able to grow rice anymore. The flood water has inundated the river islands. I saw a herd of wild buffalos trying to cross the bil and then swim across the small river. I'm worried. What'll happen if the buffaloes fail to get out of the bil because of the thickly packed hyacinths? Such strong animals, yet we don't know what might happen to them. It's so sad!"

Digonto could visualize the scene---the buffaloes desperately trying to make their way through the clumps of water hyacinth even as thick clumps of the plant advanced en masse to surround and push them down, deeper. The scene shook him to the core.

His father expected Digonto to be near him. Otherwise, he would have gone out, at least, for once. Flood water had rushed across the road to enter their homestead. If the water had risen even higher what would or could he do? He looked at his sleeping father. The man who once didn't bother to move an inch even when angry male buffaloes came charging at him was now lying so weak, so helpless!

He was sitting near his father's bed. Around midnight his father woke up and was surprised to see his son still sitting beside him. Then he started mumbling, may be still a little drowsy, "We had a pair of buffaloes. You don't remember, I guess. How healthy and how beautiful they were ! For two straight years flood destroyed our crops. We were forced to sell the pair. It broke my heart. A Bihari milkman took them. He used to make them pull carts. I told him , "Don't be too harsh on them. Don't let these poor creatures suffer."

"What did he say?" Digonto asked—a little absent-minded.

"What else would he say? He laughed and said something in his Bihari language which I couldn't understand. Since then I stopped going towards his place." His father let out a long sigh and then fell silent. After a little while he said, "Now there is no need for bullock or buffalo-drawn carts. Oh, you don't need to go on sitting here. Go and get some sleep. Now I feel much better."

Digonto woke up late that morning. It was drizzling outside. He didn't feel like getting up that early but he had no other option as his mother went on calling him His elder brother Hemanta had already left for their paddy fields. Then after coming back, he would have an early lunch before leaving for the school where he worked as a teacher.

In the morning, some villagers saw two or three wild buffaloes grazing in the field. Now they disappeared. They might have entered someone's backyard, looking for higher grounds.

Digonto had the food prepared by his mother and went out. He walked fast to reach the group of people who seemed to be heading towards the bil.

He heard the shrill voice of fisherman Bubai, "You know, a raft carrying logs of wood got stuck in the thick masses of water hyacinth last evening."

"Where?"

"Near where the little river merges with the bil. And that large raft just disappeared amidst the dense masses of hyacinths as if in an instant! The thieves swam across the water and escaped. Logs worth a fortune must have got wasted."

"They wo'nt be wasted." Topon said, "The whole lot'll stay there, and once the water goes down, it will come out. But who will be the owner then? Are the forest officers aware of this?"

"What can they do even if they knew? Logs of so many expensive trees such as teak, tita chapa, and maybe khoyer were there." Bubai said.

"What? Are you drooling over it now?"

Seeing Bubai glare at him, Topon said, " I was just joking."

"Listen, yesterday in the evening I saw ten to twelve wild buffaloes. They got stuck in the masses of hyacinth. And after moving a little ahead, they just disappeared. I'm not sure whether they managed to climb up the bank and reach some villagers' backyards or paddy fields. "

Someone butted in, "Maybe they couldn't get out of the thickening masses of hyacinth. I saw two or three buffaloes from a distance while coming this way. After a while I just didn't see any of them. Perhaps they got buried under the hyacinth!"

Digonto could hear Topon's voice, "Yes, what if, pressed by water hyacinths from all sides, they just failed to breathe! O, poor creatures, what sufferings they had to go through!"

"Don't say that, let's go and see what we can do." Digonto started to walk towards the bil.

The densely packed clumps of dark green water hyacinths continued to float quietly down the water. The area surrounding the bil was calm and quiet. Only a gust of wind kept blowing from the river some distance away, carrying an odd smell from the hyacinths. Everyone was silent and still. Suddenly it started to rain heavily. Faced with the possibility of some disaster, the men stood there, speechless.

It rained intermittently during the day. By the evening It started raining heavily. Water rushed into most of the houses . And all the hyacinths that were in the ponds and tanks rushed out to enter people's homesteads.

In the wee hours of the night, whether in his sleep or in the wakeful state, Digonto heard a strange sound. Drowning myriads of sounds of the night, the sound of water reverberated, close to his ears , surrounding him and pushing him down. He desperately tried to push himself up and come to the surface, his breathing about to stop. He felt suffocated as masses of water hyacinth started to surround and choke him. To get some air, he started pushing them forcefully with his head and hands. Finally, he succeeded in making his way through them. He woke up, and lay still for quite some time.

And then came, like waves, from underneath the water hyacinths, the indistinct, insistent and primitive screams of a herd of buffaloes. He didn't know whether what he'd heard were the cries of agony or helpless rage.

The original Assamese short story 'Meteka' was published in the special AUTUMN(Durga Puja) issue of the Assamese daily Asomia Pratidin, , October ,2018

Short Story The Swim

Short story The Swim Madan Sarma The river seemed to be chasing, following him, and not only him but the entire town together with its people, homes,shops, trees and flowers. They say, much earlier the river used to flow far from this small and drowsy town. Then the river inched forward, eventually encircling the entire town. Wherever he went in and around the town, his eyes were sure to land on a smooth bend of the river, or a zigzag section of it as the river rushed in and then quickly went out of the town. After wandering around the town, he finally rented a house and that too by the riverside. The day after he joined work, he wrote a long letter to his beloved, Upama. He wrote, 'I think the river won't stop pursuing me. My mother always tried to keep me away from rivers, but they keep chasing me with a vengeance.' '...No matter wherever you go, you'll feel that the river goes on peeping at you, or that you're staring at it. You would never know, unless somebody told you, that a lovely, innocentlooking river with swift currents was flowing just a hundred or a hundred and fifty feet away from my house. It's not very wide. However, it widens a little beyond the outskirts of the town.' 'The river flows ever so silently that one might not take it to be a river at all. In the silence of the night, especially late at night, I would sometimes hear the overlapping sounds of wind and water. The river is said to be quite deep. I haven't been to the river yet.' He remembered those days in their village. There was a mirthful hilly river running through the fields in front of their house. It was rather shallow, its flat bosom covered by sand, pebbles and stones. There was no question of swimming in it. One could somehow wet one's head just by taking a hurried dip in it. When it rained heavily, the water would suddenly rise and keep rising for a few hours. The surging water would carry along a few uprooted trees and occasionally, a fawn too. He passed his childhood and teens, playing by the riverside, taking an occasional dip and frolicking in its shallow water. He never got an opportunity to swim. If he had any, his mother would surely not allow him to go to the river. The cause was his father died suddenly, untimely by drowning not in such a shallow river but in a big sea when his boat sank. Since then he and the siblings were brought up by their Bordeuta, their

     Delving Into Different Literary Terrains

father's elder brother, under a strict regimen and discipline...One fine morning they discovered a badly mutilated body of a young man on the bank of that frolicsome river. Tension mounted in the neighbouring villages. People said, it might be the handiwork of the police or the army. Should a young man, a rebel or not, be killed the way animals are slaughtered. People took out processions and held meetings on the bank of the river in protest. His uncle forced him to stay at home and not to venture out. He said, 'No need to get involved in these. Don't forget your responsibilities.' He nearly stopped going to the river. His friends taunted him, called him selfish and cowardly. The matter didn't end there. His uncle sent him to a distant city for further studies, just to prevent him from ever getting involved in what he termed as 'hassles.' His mother didn't forget to drill it into him that he should never go for a swim in any pond, tank or river. A few days later, his colleagues decided to go for a picnic on the bank of a fast-flowing hilly river. They went down to the crystal clear and icy water of the river and had great fun splashing about in it. Some of them decided to brave its strong currents and started swimming. No one could persuade him to go down to the river. He just went on sitting on a rock. He cupped a few handfuls of cold water and splashed these on his face, letting a few drops wet his head. He said, 'I promised my mother. She keeps on worrying about me. Some astrologer had told her that swimming might spell disaster for me.' Some of his colleagues laughed and mocked him, while some said, 'Might be true. Don't people talk of ill-luck and omens?' He was embarrassed. Was he really so timid? He lay on the flat top of a tall rock and looked at the cloudless sky. He kept on gazing at a broad patch of the sky that looked like a deep blue lake. The sight brought to his mind that big tank he saw when he was a little boy. Once when he was just a little kid, he accompanied Raghu who worked as a domestic help, to pick flowers from the plants and trees that grew on its banks. A huge crowd had gathered there. Raghu climbed the flowering trees and plucked flowers and he gathered them in a basket. Then he noticed some men moving about in small boats. Some of them carried long bamboo poles and continued to prod and search for something in the water. And then they lifted out of water the body of a young man and laid it carefully down on the bank. He was overcome by exhaustion as he went on swimming in the tank for quite some time. Two days after that incident he dreamt of that enormous tank. He saw the huge crowd, the flowering plants and trees dancing in the wind, and a corpse lying there. It was his corpse. When he narrated the dream to his mother, Raghu was soundly rebuked for taking him to that cursed tank.

On a late afternoon, a year after that, he was returning from a nearby village when he thought he saw an apparition gliding over the lotus leaves of an old pond near a bamboo grove. His body shook in fear. So he started wearing charms round his neck. He had no idea where those evil spirits or wandering souls had gone. His grandmother used to say that the wandering souls and spirits had lost their refuge because of the constant pursuit by humans. He laughed. But then, he felt sad too for there was no one to talk about such things, and excite the young children by narrating the stories filled with such wonder and awe. He often wondered if simple and innocent superstitions could really be less harmful than orthodox beliefs. It was already getting dark when they returned from picnic. The minibus carrying the picnickers broke down just as it was nearing the town. They had to wait for half an hour on the river bank. He took a casual walk by the river and then stopped at a spot, when his eyes were drawn to a thicket that was slowly getting enveloped by dusk and mist. He thought he had seen that mysterious-looking thicket before, but where, when could that be? A few tall trees stood still. He wondered what secrets - beautiful, frightening or unthinkable- might lurk behind them, and for whom? Could it be somehow the same thicket on the bank of that gay river he had known since his childhood, where he had almost lost himself while looking for the straying bullock? He had entered that thicket around this time. Carefully skirting the thorny grove of canes he came to a sudden halt at a clear spot between two trees. It was getting darker and yet he could see two ghosts or phantoms, one jumping onto the other. Very slowly and silently, he kept backing off and in a single leap got out of the thicket and ran to the road. Huffing and puffing, he stood under a barren mango tree when he saw the bullock with a white mark on its forehead approaching him. As he was walking behind the bullock on his way home, he met a villager, Bhadaram. 'Hey? What are you doing here this late in the evening?' Bhadaram asked. He was still trembling with fear. He said in a shaky voice, 'I saw something over there--in the thicket.' 'What did you see?' 'I think I saw two ghosts -one was pressing the other to him.' To his surprise, Bhadaram started laughing. As his laughing stopped, he said, 'Two ghosts, for real? Did you look properly? Did one of them have long hair?' 'May have, I'm not sure.' He tried to remember what he saw exactly. 'Alright, I understand. It might be a witch.' Suddenly Bhadaram seemed grave. 'Listen. Forget what you saw. Don't tell anyone at home about it. Otherwise, when you come this way again a ghost shall chase you, take hold you and possess you, making it impossible for you to live. Don't forget. And don't tell your mother.' He never told anybody. Now looking at the thicket, he felt like laughing aloud. Still, could there possibly be a spirit lurking somewhere in it as well? In his second letter to Upama, he narrated his last experience in a language aimed at making it seem funny. She gave suggestions, on the phone too, that he should not court danger by trying to unravel the mystery of any thicket. Who knows what dark forces might be active in such places? What danger? Till now, everybody has been protecting him from every possible and impossible danger. He has been used to leading an uneventful and sheltered ordinary life. His mother'ssudden but not unexpected death continued to perturb his mind for some time. After all the funeral rites and rituals got over, his brother asked the priest, 'Please advise us about the do's and don'ts.' The priest went on, 'You're not supposed to do so many things during these days. Our experts in the Shastras haven't left out anything. They took care of all eventualities. So listen carefully – do not climb trees, though you have no idea about climbing trees; do not drive any vehicle, though you can't afford one; do not cross rivers, though you don't know how to swim. Anyway, stay away from all possible dangers and sit quietly at home.' He looked at the priest's smiling face and smiled. Suddenly he felt free. Naturally, he had to cross rivers daily, not by swimming though. He had to cross many rivers to arrive at this small town and the small river that surrounded it. The rainy season began. The river water started rising. People said that many years back, when the town was flooded, a part of it was washed away by the river,. Considering the size of the river, it was hard to believe. This river was way different from the familiar cheerful river of his childhood. There was no doubt about it. This river seemed to be grave and intense, and mysterious. It might, however, be just his imagination. For a few days, the wind blew furiously and continuously. It poured incessantly. For one whole night it rained non-stop. Waking up late in the morning, he opened the front door while brushing his teeth and noticed that the river had been transformed into a sea. Water came up to the topmost step attached to his verandah. Just four or five feet away from where he stood, a snake slithered towards the corner of the veranda. He shut the door with a loud bang. The snake might have left. He was afraid to get down into the water. The veranda at the back too was in the same state. The entire town was flooded. Only the houses stood there like small islands. The sounds of people talking, arguing and shouting travelled over the water. His neighbour, Barman's young son waded through the flood water to bring him his daily newspaper as the hawker could not come to deliver it. He requested the boy to make a telephone call to his office to let them know that he would not be able to go to work that day. He was not even sure whether he could go out of his house. Hearing him, the boy bared his teeth and started laughing, 'Should I ask them to send a boat for you?' He was a smart boy , indeed! He wasn't scared of snakes, didn't worry about breaking his legs by treading on something or falling into some unseen holes And simply because he knew how to swim, he was so sure of himself. All the rivers were in spate. They had flooded vast plains, destroyed houses and property. Seated comfortably on the bed, he watched news about floods on the television. He saw helpless people everywhere-on the embankments, on high grounds, in schools and shelter homes. He looked out of the window. There was no such danger for him. Flood here was only a temporary mishap, or a minor calamity. After the calamity passed, the city came back to the normal rhythm of life. It is then that he got Upama's letter. She had complained that he had been inventing excuses to delay their marriage. She complained, 'I guess you've started considering me as a nuisance. You should be more forthright.' What could he possibly say! Let him postpone his response for some time. The days passed slowly, as if limping. The river assumed its familiar lithe form once more and got back its mystery . Every evening he began spending some time on its banks. There was no place good enough to go to in the city. It seemed as if the city had nothing of its own except the river. Though he had three days' holiday for Durga Puja, he didn't go home. After his mother had passed away, he felt so lonesome and their house seemed so deserted! He could have gone home for Upama's sake. Did he want to keep away from her? The town wore a festive look. All through the evening he would wander aimlessly and then come back to his room exhausted, as if he was just an disinterested observer. Observing everything from a distance was his duty, not getting involved in anything. However, in the end he had to get involved. He was waiting at the edge of the water. It wasn't the spot chosen for ceremonial immersion of the idol. Yet on very rare occasions one or two groups came there to immerse idols. On hearing the shouts of young men and the noise from the vehicles he turned and looked at the river bank. A motley crowd had come to submerge an idol, and within seconds the quiet and relaxing ambience of the place was destroyed. Amidst the commotion some people carried the idol of goddess Durga to a boat and pushed into the river. And then scores of men rushed down to the river. He wanted to leave that spot and climb up to the bank but just could not move at all. He was pushed by the surging crowd towards the river. He sensed that his feet could not touch the ground anymore. He felt like screaming loudly in absolute terror but his was almost choked. The boisterous young men laughed in joy and pushed him into the deeper water. He struggled to get out of the water. Several elders kept shouting from the bank, 'Help him, help him, he's going to drown.' No one bothered to help him. All the sounds – the blowing of conches , the beating of drums , the playing of cymbals, the songs from the blaring sound system somewhere on the bank, boisterous laughter of the young men—kept on moving in circles around him. A few men were swimming towards him. In utter panic, he stretched his hands and started beating the water. After some time he realized that he wasn't at the same place anymore. Was he swimming, or was the current dragging him away? Gradually, the gathering cleared, the familiar river bank moved out of sight, the noises came to a stop. Dusk had started falling. He raised his head, looked to his right, and went on looking dumbstruck. He found himself moving towards that mysterious thicket. The thicket seemed to be covered by a translucent screen of fog. A gentle breeze flew past the trees. He turned and looked to his left. He had left the light from the city and its indistinct, the incoherent sounds far behind him. So he would have to go back swimming a very long way. It was surprising. How did he come so far? He was not frightened by the fast approaching darkness that engulfed the thicket, nor did he tremble even for once, knowing that he won't find any boat or couldn't expect any help from anyone, and that he must swim, keep on swimming, all alone.

The Sky On The Other Side Of The Window Madan Sarma

How lonely, how helpless it was to see him among the apparatus of the room. That room- separated by a glass, still far away, beyond reachable, can be gazed but unable to do anything; how painful it is for not being able to do anything. Hours passed by. Days passed by too- only in waiting- only in that hope- he will open his eyes and say something as usual- I'm fine, don't need to worry about me.

He couldn't breathe himself, hung between conscious and unconsciousness, or only in unconsciousness- Ah what pain he didn't tolerate...... Did he know for him only his dearest wife, dear son and daughter-in-law were waiting. Perhaps he knew it, that's why that restlessness, sometimes impatience, anxiety to live again. After how many days he returned- from the dilemma of life and death. How short and stout his face became. He was bewildered by a fear. By touching the hands with the trembling lean fingers, he wanted to express something. He couldn't say anything; tears started flowing from the corner of his eyes.

Someone said in his ears- this is a crucial period, don't lose courage. How often he heard- it requires an intense desire to live. How easily he had expressed- Doctor, after the arrival of the daughter-in-law, that longing has increased- I feel good when she is around.

'Maa, have you fallen asleep?'

The daughter-in-law, Neena's soft voice startled her. She was sitting on the sofa of the room where people visited to see the patient.

'Let's go. She brought her to the front room.'

'How do you see him now? Say honestly'

'Honestly, I saw him better than before'

'Joon has not turned up yet'

'He'll reach. He is coming.'

He is gradually coming back from an infinite darkness to the light. All worldly words, or all the distinct-indistinct words of life, long sighs of weeping coming from a distance- sometimes, the presence of someone can be felt- the anxiety of the wife, son, daughter-in-law and all the near ones can be felt; why do you need to fear- I am still fighting, I have not given up- by seeing you all I think there is a joy in living.

A fragrance flowed near him from somewhere. As if a soft water like sound. He has opened his eyes- The father decorated the upstairs a few days before the demise of the mother- the work has not been completed yet. The father said- It is your study room. Arrange it neatly. In the window of the room beside the road, a bush of coconut was banning down. Wind flows quite well in that room. Some leafs of the coconut entered the room through the window- as if a cold touch in the body. The moonlight passed through the coconut leaves and got scattered in the room. The languid shadow of the coconut leaves and the bright moonlight. A rustling sound like new dresses. A familiar sound.

'Mo'. An indistinct word which couldn't come out of the lips.

Anxiety in the three faces and six eyes- as if a ray of hope.

'Do you want to say something?' His wife went closer to him.

'Tell me what you want'

No, no more word came out of his pale lips.

After four days, the mechanical ventilator was removed yesterday. The man is himself breathing- although with much effort. Still the eldest son Anku felt relieved about it. He comes closer. Slowly he keeps his hand in the hand of the father. He seems to open his eyes with much effort- he says something- what he says can't be understood. Seems like- Khik-khi-ki.

It can be understood that he himself wants to say something, trying to communicate something with his son, which suggests that both his mind and brain are working actively. He is still beside him.

After he was taken out of the ICU that evening, he was kept in that cabin again. From then onwards everyone has a ray of hope- since the infection is in control, there is less risk now- he would get well- though it might take some time. His wife comes and sits beside him. He seems to recognize the touch of the hand. Trying to lift his hand upward, he utters- Khik-khi-ki. As if he is trying to indicate somewhere by raising his hand.

Khiriki (Window)- his wife understood it. Oh the window- she goes to the window and raises the curtain- the window is already opened. Then he's trying to indicate to shift the bed near the window.

But there is nothing special to see on the other side of the window. And he is yet to open his eyes completely. What will he see in such a situation?

There is a familiar sound in the entrance of the house- a familiar warm fragrance. But his mother passed away 15 days ago- on the day of his last exam- was she waiting to complete the exam? He rubs the bald head through his hand where hairs are growing. The room doesn't seem like empty, someone is here and he feels the presence of someone. He also used to sit by the window on such moonlight nights- without turning on the light. The mother used to ask him from the verandah if he would sit like this for the entire evening. Won't you study? Come here and see through the window- how pleasing it is in the outside. Are you getting the wind?

He forcefully keeps his mother in the bamboo chair.

The chair is empty now. Yet with the moonlight and the shadow, it seems like someone is sitting there.

'Maa'.

Three anxious faces come closer. The faces are blended with melancholy, affection and anxiety.

He is still taking long breaths. The Oxygen mask is in readiness.

The young doctor silently comes in. He comes closer and examines everything. By turning back he says- 'It will take more time. The effect of sedative will be there'.

He moves the eyelid for a while and again becomes static.

The dark sky. By staring in the window, he sees the dark sky through the left side of the coconut tree where stars are illuminating. It seems like a piece of the star entered through the window from the sky. Some familiar stars- assembled together. Some of them are bright; some of them are only the reflection of indistinct light. He tries to remember the names, makes an attempt to connect the fictional lines. Gradually the stars are coming closer- suddenly an acquainted fragrance and a warm touch in the hand, arm and the chest. He gets frightened. She laughs loudly- 'Have you got frightened?' And she turns on the light by raising the hand.

'Will you keep on gazing the stars this way?'

'Ok, then I shall stare at your eyes'

Both of them stared at each other. Time went on. The stars on the other side of the window were going far away. The warmth of her body was entering into his body.

'Dhet'. She moves away and stands up- 'Naughty'. And she runs away from the room, he tries to call her- 'Wait'.

Daughter-in-law Neena comes closer. She can't comprehend what he says. Neena removes the hand from his chest.

A sweet fragrance touched his nose, a warm touch in his hands. He grabbed his hands. Jhan Jhan- the sound of the bracelet.

'Deuta' (Father)

He opens his eyes. A hazy face gets floated- Affectionate, sorrowful.

He says with tears in eyes- you are doing everything to save my life- you recently became one among us- How can you do so many things for me-how?

His wife comes closer.

As if he wants to say- With the person with whom I have lived a life, what does she not offer you even in the doorstep of death- Why- Is the love so complex, indistinct- Its memories get treasured in the corner of the heart- Please don't misunderstand me.

His eldest son Anku stops in the head side of the bed.

He has a lot to say to him- you returned my life- Now take me home- let me sleep near the window-open all the windows.

The doctor comes in. He says- 'now he is sleeping normally. Let him sleep. Inform me when he wakes up.'

After a long time, Anupama, Leena and Anku slept well. And another night passed by. In the morning, all of them assembled in the same room.

The doctor goes on saying- 'Still he is not completely out of danger. He has to be looked after carefully for a few days'.

Anku's mobile phone rings. His younger brother calls him. He was supposed to reach by yesterday afternoon. It can be understood from Anku what is the conversation is all about with Joon, the younger brother.

He comes after taking a long leave- it took time to manage everything-it is unsure what happens in the very next moment- for how many days-that's why.

Everything is all right. Come soon.

The conversation between the brothers. He understood. Joon has a doubtful mind- he is like that from his childhood. Do you have still doubts-Shall I be able to live without you all- do you have still doubts- I want to come back for you all, for your love.

He opens his eyes. Probably for the first time such amount of lights entered together. The sunrays enter through the window. Three faces come closer. He says- 'Let's go home'.

Translated by Subhajit Bhadra

The Naked Man

For past four days the naked man has become the point of discussion for the central market area of the city and the residential area adjacent to it. He sits near the light post at about 8 o clock every morning. With long, tangled hair; face covered with grey beard; brown well built body and opaque eyes with indifferent gaze, the naked man appears to be mad. He walks on the street or sits leaning on the light post unconcerned to this world. He eats the leftovers that the shopkeepers give him and sleeps on the ground. He could never think that his nakedness could be awkward for anyone- as if he is the ancient man, the first man to walk on this free earth.

One

A group of girls were going to college laughing happily. The Girls' College is situated one kilometers north to the town. The naked man suddenly appeared in front of them. The girls stopped laughing. They went towards the footpath ignoring him. A few young men were coming from the opposite direction. They prevented the girls from advancing. The girls stopped. The naked man stood by the road unconcerned. One of the young man commented, "See, they feel ashamed." Another said mockingly, "Have a good look, this is no offence!" Third one made a vulgar remark and they started to laugh loudly. The shopkeepers and passerby looked at them astonishingly and looked away. If they try to forbid such unruly, loose young men; no one knew what would be the consequences.

A few girl's eyes filled with tears. They hurriedly walked past the naked man with heads down cast. One of them was walking behind. She

stopped a little and told to the young men with a mellifluous voice, "You are more naked and impudent than him."

One young man rushed towards her to attack. But his companions stopped him. They immediately left the place seeing people coming towards them from the shops. The naked man crossed the road and proceeded to his definite place.

<h1 align="center">Two</h1>

Arjun Choudhury was talking to Indra Sonowal near his gate. They worked in the same school and retired a few days apart three years back. They meet in the evening and take a little walk. Sonowal came to see the house Choudhury's younger son Bapdhan was building. Whenever the discussion of the house came up Choudhury changed the topic. Everyone in the neighborhood knew that he was a student leader till two years back. It has not been even one and half year since he started small contracts. Still how could he dared to build this mansion. Choudhury starts doubting-the rumors that he hears must be true. He still remembers that boy. An army operation was going on then. The boy came in the evening with a big suitcase in his hand and hanging a canvas bag on his back. He told that he came from Guwahati. He left at next dawn. I saw him go empty handed from my window. He did not take his suitcase or bag. He got no news of the boy after that. After that when situation improved and news of huge money being recovered published in the papers, he remembered the boy again. He feared to

ask his son too. Even if he asked, he would not have got the real answer. He only asked when his wife came to show him the map of the house, "Where has he got so much money to build such a big house?" His wife replied that he had gone to head office of the tea company in Kolkata and bagged a contract to supply something to the tea garden. He has amassed a lot of money in that business. Everything she said is true. Still how could he amassed such a huge money. Choudhury was confounded as the house was nearing completion. He feels as if he has become naked to the doubtful gaze of the people.

"What are they thinking?"

Sonowal's voice brought him to the real world, "Nothing! Just thinking that the time has changed. What has happened to the people!"

"Right!" Sonowal agreed. "The daughter of Mr. Ghosh, our neighbor, became senseless that day seeing a naked man standing near their bathroom when she was bathing. The boys in the neighborhood followed and caught him. A mad young boy. His house is near Kalibari. But I am astonished to hear about the naked man of the street."

A motorcycle came and stopped near him. Bapdhan proceeded towards them from the motorcycle, "How are you uncle?"

"I am good. But what is that in your hand?"

"Oh! Its just my watch. It strap was torn while beating that rogue."

"Which rogue are you talking about?"

"I am talking about that naked man. The girls of the law college comes by that road. He was standing shamelessly under the lamp post."

Bapdhan entered the house that he was building in a heroic manner. Choudhury said to himself- Who is shameless! Indra Sonowal said regretfully, "My two sons have turned silly and immature." Choudhury mumbled, "At least they have not made you naked!"

"What have you said?"

"Lets take a walk."

Three

As the hustle and bustle of the evening subsides the naked man comes to his almost permanent place under the light post and sits there. There is still a little chill in the air outside. The weather does disturb him for sure. Probably he does not have any memory. No past, no future. He has only hunger. He greedily eats whatever leftover the shopkeepers give him.

The mason Ramcharan and his teenage helper Birender was coming from that way. Birender was dumbstruck to see the naked man urinating near the drain. When the man returned to his place he threw the gamocha that was wrapped on his head and told him in Hindi, "Put it on". The gamocha is very small to wrap on the waist. The naked man made ball of it and kept on sitting as before. Ramcharan was speechless too. He looked towards Birender and said, "You fool! How many will you save from embarrassment?"

While walking behind him Birender turned .any times to look at the man. "You fool! You are still a kid."

Four

The O.C. of the police station was very busy. A witness of a murder case has escaped. He was scolding his junior S.I and Constable for not able to find him. The hearing is after two days. And this misfortune has occurred today. The phone has rung. He enthusiastically picks it up in hope of some news related to it. A little while later his face give away the signs of displeasure.

Self styled news reporter Singh says, "What are you doing?"

Rahman becomes angry. He somehow controlled himself and said, "What do you mean?"

"It has been four days- a naked man is walking free in the market. He is walking naked in front of our ladies-"

"What I have to do with it?"

"You are asking me? Do not you have anything to do?"

"The whole country is filled with naked man, what can I do?"

"Rahman sahib, what are you saying?"

"I am telling the truth. Sorry! I am busy in some serious discussion. I shall call you later."

After hanging up Rahman has said to himself, "The court has let loose all the mad from the jail. And we have to face the consequences. He must be one of them. Family will send to jail as a mad and court will let go. We will send to jail today. But will come out the very next day. And who pays the price?"

"Who called sir?"

"Who else it be? Real reporters are nowhere to be seen. This self styles reporter cannot step out of his house in shame. This bugger brings out a news paper every six months filled with adds, gather money selling

news print. In the evening he goes searching for free liquor. You should be made naked. Just cannot control my tongue. Hey, call Saikia."

Five

Nobody saw the naked man for one whole day. He must have been sleeping behind some shop or lying in some dry drain. His body must be aching after the beating by Bapdhan and the people he instigated. Or he might have gone to other part of the city without any proper cause. The police van came twice to search for him but returned without success.

On Sunday morning he was seen in his old place. On that a market takes place in that area. The people nearby gather there for buying and selling fresh items.

Kripa Neog was coming to the Sunday market with his son Gobin. He waned to sell the last oranges that he harvested from his orchard and also wanted to do some shopping. He was astounded see a naked man standing leaning on the light post. "O my God!" He came near the man and ask3d shouting, "Hey! What's your name? Where do you live?"

The man did not reply. He looked towards Mr. Neog disinterestedly.

"Why are you naked son?"

Gobin became irritated. "Why are you disturbing that mad man? Lets go, we are late."

"Who is not mad? Oh God! See how people suffer!"

The old man looked here and there. A banner was hanging from a tree. The old man tore it. Gobin was looking at his father's action. He shouted to his father, "Father do not tear it. It's a government banner. Cannot you see what was written on it? Literacy mission-"

"Mission! This is also a Mission. " The old man was trying to open the knots.

Gobin mumbled, "The old man has also become mad."

The old man pulled the mad man aside and somehow wrapped the banner around his waist. But the mad man pulled it out instantly. The people gather around to see the happenings started laughing. The mad man started shouting, "Inquilab Jindabad."

The people started laughing again.

Kripa Neog stopped there dumbstruck. A police van came almost silently and stopped near him. A few constables tried to put him in their vehicle. The mad man sat on the spot holding the banner tightly around his chest and started crying loudly.

"Oh! He must have remembered his home. Where does he lives?" said one old man rubbing his tears by the gamocha hanging from his neck.

The police hurled the mad man into their vehicle along with the banner. The people gathered around started going to their own places. Some one commented, "Its nice, such a shameless!"

The old man mumbled, "Who is shameless? Who says whom?" His eyes filled with tears. The naked man will be in jail again. Somebody will make his wear clothes. One day he will be free. And again he will roam around namelessly the streets of another city naked ----

The First Man

I am Jhara. Jhara Basu .Strange name, isn't it? Every one is surprised in the beginning, they also ask Jha—a—a—r—aaa? Can Jhara be a name? Some of them bend their mouth and say Jhara? Oh my God! What an ugly name! Some people say there are so many good name in this world and still your parents did not find any suitable name for you?

Initially I used to be angry. Very angry. I used to be angry with my mother. I used to be angry with my father and sisters too. My two elder sisters were known as Abhishikta and Mehuli. And I am only Jhara? Like falling leaves!

Actually I used to be angry with every one. I suffered from the paralysis, an incurable disease. I suffered from anger. I suffered from pangraf sorrow. Age also has a mind of its own. And this mind acquires beautiness with the time. I am not an exception. But as I became aged, my mind also changed. And I realize it in every moment, every second. My mother used to tell me when I was a child ,"Jhara, look at the sky. How beautiful it is! " I used to look at the sky, but do you know what happened? I could not find anything special there. I did not express that. But I used to think ,what beauty does the sky possess? What does mother looked at? What is to be seen there? There is the blue sky or the ash-coloured sky, or during the sunset a reddish aky.

But my mother used to look at the sky during the sunset. I used to look at mother and then the sky sitting on the wheel chair. I could understand nothing.

Time flows very rapidly. Like the tide of river. No, I have never sen a river. I watched everything in television. River, its dense water, black colour, and the tides making a unique sound. It tumbles on the bank of the river. When I was a child I used to think how the river tumbles on the bank. Now the looking eyes have changed. Do you know what it seems to be now? It seems that the river kisses. It comes with full tide, kisses and then it returns on the other banks. She loves both the banks equally. That is why she returns to the other banks quickly. Because it would kiss. Otherwise that bank would be angry. Is the river "Swairini"? Profligate woman? Bullshit! Can it

     Delving Into Different Literary Terrains

be so? When there is no male gender of Swoirini then that word does not carry any meaning. At least it has seemed to me that the word should not have any meaning. So far instance, illicit love. What is illicit? Who will tell what is valid and what is illicit? Love is love. There is nothing related to sin there. That is why love can never be illicit. Similarly it is not also "swoirini" a profligate woman. It should not be.

Yes, time flows like air. Our ages also do so. Along with the passing of age,the mind of age also runs quickly. Now when I look at the ordinary sky of my childhood,I encounter many a thing that are not definable. Now looking at the sky is a sort of intoxication for me. Not morning, it is a mistake, now a days I wake up from bed before dawn and sit. I see the rising sun slipping on the lap of the night. What a wonderful scene that is! How beautiful! How beautiful! The sky during the sun set is my favourite. There is a golden hue throughout the sky then. So many sceneries grafted on the body of the cloud. Now I understood why mother used to look at the sky with awe-struck gaze. The mind of my mother at that point of time can touch my mind now. Or my own mind at this point of time can touch my mother's mind at that time now. Now my mother is quite transparent to me. To me my mother is no longer a married woman with red vermillion only. Now all vagueness had disappeared when I completed eighteen years. That subject which was a mystery to me at one point of time that same mystery has caught me now at the age of twenty two. There is youth largely written all over my body now. The youth of the girl whose two legs are paralyzed form the waist surprises many. Who will convince these people that there is nothing to be surprised in this? I am liking the river whose both sides are full of tides. My mind is also like that. I have two elder sisters. They are also beautiful. But the neighbors and the relatives tell that they do not look like me. Many people say that my beauty is coquettish. Now understand! One of my distant grand mother told that "even though she is lame her beauty knows no bound". Even though that girl is lame, her beauty is mesmerizing. The grown up male could be naturally attracted to her. Don't you understand why they come to take bath in the pond? There is no dearth of pretexts for them. And that Jhara, she sits near the window, like a "Kamini",a charming woman!

I saw through behind the curtain that elder sister's face hardened. There was vengeance in the eyes. The way a cat sharpens its nails before capturing a pray, elders sister is also sharpening her tooth. Grand mother said, tell her cover her boobs by the "dupatta" of the "salwar". Oh, my God! What a fulfilling body! Saying this grand mother winked her eyes and laughed a heartful laughter. She told, beware. There is no work. An empty brain is devil's workshop. Any grown up boy would be attracted towards her seeing her blooming body.

Grand mother was not quite wrong. My body is coming into its full. The lover's of my elder sisters also secretly look at me. They look at me, but they are not interested in marriage. They are interested in my body only. On the pretext of joking with sister-in-law, both Binoy da and Korok da have touched me . They touched those parts of my body which gave me satisfaction and made me shiver. I did not withdraw. Rather I desired In the mind that their touch should be deeper. Because I have known that I would not be married. Though the faces and breasts of my elder sisters can not match mine on the basis of merit, yet they have moving legs. That is why they would get married. But the eyes of their prospective husbands would be attracted towards me like magnet because of the aura of my body. And that is why now a days a sense of vengeance grows within me. Let there be no marriage for me. But let there be some thing alike to marriage. Sometimes, looking at the sky I think what is marriage? I think that am I like my mother? Does the gene of my mother dance throughout my blood? Is marriage a great ritual to acquire the right to body only? I marriage is nothing but the right to body then my brother- in-law are getting that and still they desire me without sanction of marriage. The subject is bothersome. Complex. Otherwise why did my mother fly one day looking at the sky?

Still we did not settle in this house of Ranikuthi. At that time, we used to reside in Kutighat and Sukanto mama used to visited over the house. He happened to be the friend of my small maternal uncle. Mother told us, :don't call him mama. Address him as uncle" But I argued that mama's friend would naturally be mama. Mother did not answer. We three sisters used to address him as Sukanto kaku. One day that Sukanto kaku went towards the sky along with my mother.

My father who always used to wear dhoti and kurta became depressed for few days. I was thirteen then. Elder sisters were fifteen and seventeen then. And father was forty-eight.

Time flow. Our house made became the ruling queen at home. She has been promoted. She had became a full fledged queen the house now. She looked after us like my mother. She used to cook and waited for my father at night. Two of them ate together. As time passed father's face again became sunny. At that time I failed to understand why father's face became brightened. Everything was a mystery. Now each mystery has unfolded itself.

Our mother is dead at the house of Ranikuthi. From the portrayed of mother grafted on the wall, a string of beads. But I know that mother is alive. She is alive within me. Mother had given all her seeds of desire in my blood. These desires sometimes desperately rise within me.

I passed matriculation as a private candidate. I did not wish to study further. And the Satan sometimes utilized the maximum benefit given by the mind's laziness. Satan or witch who knows? Always looking at the sky and flying through the air.

Elder sisters got married yesterday. So many rituals! Chanting of complex mantras! What is the requirement of these mantras? What a striking arrangement for the union of two bodies! Does it mean anything? But the warmth of the marriage-home and the necessary decoration seemed nice to me. I also did wear a red Banarasi saree. For the first time I clad in a saree. My sister-in-law was surprised as she dressed me in a saree. She ended up saying, "Jhara, how beautiful you are! If I happened to be a boy....! Ummm! What would have I done! Having said this , she uttered a few poisonous wards. I almost died out of shame, a feeling of ease and pride. I only thought that due to a Hindu rituals they would sleep in a flower-strewn beds after two days. I transparently see these which are not to be seen. Look would not have I been married too? I would have embraced Korakda or Binoyda in a flower-strewn bed!

There is the drowsy moon today in the sky. My elder sisters have gone. The house is empty. Solitary. I felt empty. Actually my elder sisters were my opponents. I used to make up keeping in track with them. I tried to defeat them when Korokda, Binoyda came. Actually I know that if my legs would have perfect, then no one could have beaten me.

From today, there is no war. There is no vow to defeat anyone. I looked at myself in the mirror. Really I am extremely beautiful! I felt depressed. I felt quite suffocating inside the room. I looked through the window and saw the moon floating like a boat in the sky. Am I addicted to the moon? Otherwise why does the moon madden me? Why do I search for fishy smell like the witch who devour fish? Above the head of the moon is floating like a boat! The moon light is sleepy now. Faint! Almost sleepy! The wind is blowing, due to the signal of a call in the night. I feel depressed. Only realize that my back is carrying the wings of fire. They are plunging.

I Came to the garden riding on the wheel chair. A few trees extended their wings like weed.

Strange! I was weeping! I do not know from where those tears came and broken my bones! I do not know! I only embraced the Arjun tree. I cried placing my head in its strong root. And at that very moment an unbearable comfort spread throughout my body! My boobs were pressed into the chest of Arjun. Out of extreme delight I embraced Arjun with my whole body. Out of unfelt glee, my waterspout broke itself. Like a shameless person, I snatched away every bit of happiness, desire! Wonderful! I am moist. Like a shameless person I was uttering the words .....! Just at the point of time a fishy smell floated to me with all its arrogance. I looked slowly to find out the root of the smell. The two eyes were glittering outside the fence. They were offering sharp gazes towards me. I looked as though mesmerized. Is it of a human being? Or of a satan? I do not know. There is a pond on the other side of the fence. A smell of water is coming from the direction of the pond. The two eyes of the other side of fence are spreading sharp smell than that smell. I am heading towards leaving Arjun. For the last time before losing sense I realized that my two eyes were almost burning. The wild civet-cat is coming forward!

Ms. Kaberi Roy Choudhury
183, Jodhpur park,
4th floor,
Kolkata- 700 068
Mobile 9830964044
rckaberi@gmail.com

A Broken Clock

Nilkantha Ghosal

Sikander is walking. On the way there are inscriptions on the stones, countless sounds and seemingly sounds reverberate through his ears. The path is the receptacle of history. It is misty and devoid of light. In that deeper horizon a dot of light shines and reflects on the bright eyes of Sikander. At the call of that of light he is walking on the way as if an ever-moving wayfarer. He carries in hand a stick given by his mother. Handing over the termite-infected stick, his mother has said—'my son, you need to go to that Narora Patia, where they have killed your father by burning and you have to bring a piece of a bone of your father. You shall have to make a search to find out the bone of your father by removing the ashes repeatedly with this stick. I need the bones at any cost.' 'What an impossible task you have given me, O mother!' Sikander failed to utter these words to his mother. His father is one among the ninety one martyrs of Narora Patia. His father could save many lives. But, he could not save himself from the attack alike that of barbarians of the middle ages on him.

'The bone of any martyr is the bone of my father. Perhaps I shall be able to bring those to you. Will you be able to bring the life back to it, mother? Moreover, the oil of religious fanaticism is smeared on the body of the stick. It cannot be depended upon. The stick has to be washed in the water of Sabarmati, and I'll do it.' Sikander uttered those words also in mind like the chanting of holy hymns.

Having arrived at Narora Patia and keeping the stick under a tree Sikander sits down there. The burning smells are coming out from every direction, stains of dried up blood are there. His eyes are burning. His body and mind are going beyond his control. What is up there? Whose cry is this? It is the indistinct cry of a child! It is the cry of an unborn life! Is the death crying itself? Sikander knows the cry of life. But he does not know the cry of death. It seems that someone has just told in a child voice alike the semi-bloomed flower, 'Can you all hear me? I am an unborn child of your Kausar Bibi. I would have stepped into your mother earth within three days. I thought how beautiful might be our green earth; it is filled with how much light of love! So, I was removing the darkness of my mother's womb with my both the hands. Meanwhile, the sword of religion pierced all through my heart. Thereafter, they have drawn me out by tearing my mother's womb in tatters and thrown me into the fire. I hardly have the time to cry. Would you cry a little at least for me.'

Wailing aloud Sikander rushes to like demented one. There are heaps of ashes everywhere. Does it really contain the bony existence of an approaching life! He started rummaging and ransacking the ashes with his stick by both of his hands. It seems to him that the entire world has been covered with ashes. Suddenly the stick stuck somewhere. Sikander moved his hand in the ashes in a circular way. Having picked it up, he notices that it is anything but a wall clock. It has been wrenched and de-shaped. The hands of the clock are broken. It has been made hushed, silent and a non-responsive. Like a static piece of rock, Sikander is standing with the clock in his hand. He is the witness of time. The broken clock is now laid over his body like a rock inscription. With awe and amazement, Sikander notices that the hands of the clock are still moving.

Translated by: Subhajit Bhadra

Black Hole Of The Market

Nilkantha Ghosal

The place had to be vacated again. The scorching sunlight crossed the shoulder and touched the left earlobe. There was a mild pain on his earflap. The hand was raised, the palm covered the earlobe. A dove was sitting in the inner branch of the 'Bakul' tree just alone like him. Did it also escape from the company of his near and dear ones? The bird was strangely still and silent. The shadow was deep there. This is a small park. The middle of it was empty. The shadow looked very dark through the scorching rays of the sun. Was it perhaps a comfortably cool place? The dove had perhaps already slept. Anish's body shivered when he felt the heat on the opposite side of his palm. Having a look at the sunrays peeping through the Nilmani creepers, he moved off a little. This was the heat of the spring, but it became unbearable this time! He thought whether the time was for extreme enjoyment, or of extreme sufferings!

There were four concretized benches in the four sides of the park, where one could sit reclined. Iron pillar had been erected at the back of this bench. An iron sieve was also used on the top of it. The Nilmani creeper plants shot up hugging around the iron pillar. The plant spread out innumerable parts of its body in the iron sieve above. It was the period of the youth of the plant—its body was covered with the purple colour of the spring. Having seen bunches of oscillating flowers in the shadows that looked like small broomsticks, Anish became absent-minded. The rays of the sun would drive him away gradually.

Once he had to leave the whole of the bench. The scorching heat of the sun captured the area there. The sun of light was then like red-eye of the mid-day, it was impossible to look at. Picking up the bag, he sat under the Bakul tree where a dove was also sitting alone. Where was the bird now? He searched repeatedly the thick cover of leaves and branches of the tree, but could not find the bird. He seemed to develop a kind of sympathy for the dove, it was perhaps a fake sympathy, that bird might have felt irritated to find him coming to sit under the tree and so, it flew away silently, he might have created a trouble in its lonely living in a quiet way. How would he feel if someone would stand near him leaning against the other side of the tree? Would he realize how painful and shameful it was to escape and to perch in a tree in broad daylight of the noon? Could Anish talk to him in a plain and candid way that he had been told by the office that his service was no longer required? He could not tell this to his wife, so it was not possible on his part to stay at home, as a result, he would go out every day during the office hours and come back home at proper time. Such small and lonely parks lying at different corners of the city were perfect hiding place escaping from his near and dear ones—could he make a clean breast of it to other?

Anish looked at his watch as usual. It seemed as if he could hear the voice of Mr. Mohanty, the engineer from the cubicle lying next to him—Hello, Mr. Dutta! I can't find any public right now. Who are you building relations with right now? Let us give relative service of the belly. Anish, the P.R.O of the company. Yes, he was.

Anish drew the chain of the bag as usual, his hands slid into the right place, his hand came up with the tiffin box, and put it on his lap. He did not feel the urge to consume it. Ritu would serve the meal exactly at half past eight in the morning; she would sit with Maman next to him. Maman crossed one and a half years of age.

It was about a month. Ritu would say regularly—Darling, what is wrong? You do not seem to eat your food properly! She has said to-day also—what is the matter? I have prepared your favourite item made with tiny prawns and desiccated coconut. You have not given any comment on that, have you?

It was something additional for him to say a few words of praise for her satisfaction. He was not an actor, after all. It had to be artificial. He was unaware of the expressions displayed through his face and eyes. Ritu could catch his artificialities easily if she looked at him with attention—this fear would grip him all the time. The tastes of his favourite and non-favourite items gradually became vague. His throat would choke with the wave that came out of his chest, as he would see Ritu beside him carrying her daughter in her lap. He would drag a glass of water and drink quickly.

Ritu would say—that is you. It is not at all summer, but even when you sit down to eat, you drink water any time you like. You do not say if some items are very hot or not.

Anish had to manage the situation by saying this or that— in the office manner. His voice choked twice while he attempted to talk to- day. Having drunk a little water and savouring quickly the meshed rice, he said—Oh shit! It is late again. I will not take more. After that, having attached his head near Maman's tummy, he would make certain sounds of fondness. It could not be understood whether the sound was of pleasure, or of the dried up cry of him. He rushed to wash his hands.

After coming out and having looked at Ritu's eyes, he could find that her eyes had shrunk. That was an issue of uneasiness for Anish. He could not see Ritu's eyeballs at that moment—he knew these eyes very well. Her glance was now like the invisible light of the pencil torch lying in her grips. She would often spread out her range of vision to understand or catch unintelligible Anish. Ritu would open her eyes when she would be satisfied with the reply or excuses of Anish. At that point of time, Anish had neither the way out nor much time. He made use of the excuse of the paucity of time before the office hours.

Ritu laid a new trap last night. Maman would normally be caused to lie down on the bed between them. Last night he observed that their daughter was on another side of the bed and her mother in the middle. Anish used to watch television after the dinner, and then he would go to bed. Anish received a shock as soon as his hands touched Ritu's body. Leave aside the saree on; she did not have even a nighty on her body. A piece of soft fabric was spread on her, it was her dupatta. When Anish's hands were just moving in surprise on her body, Ritu's hands and feet began to work forthwith like the eight tentacles of the octopus. After having inhaled a pleasant deep breath of satisfaction and exhaling the same with a sound, when he changed his side, Ritu made Anish turn towards her. Thereafter she asked a series of questions to grill him. She asked questions with regard to the parents, brothers and sister, relatives of both the sides one after another, and she asked questions about his almost forgotten girl-friend during the college days that he had once discussed with her, all of a sudden, she started asking meaningless questions even about her. Although Anish got extremely excited at the enjoyment he had, he came back to his senses very fast. He replied in as less words as possible. Anish felt a little strange— Ritu did not say anything about his office. Even then, the news of the mass job dismissal all around the globe was telecast the night before the previous night. From America to China—the hair-raising news of mass dismissal was telecast—the figures were all assumptive and it was like a masthead of a sunken ship. It could be realized that some invisible editing were done in the matter of this news item. In fact, how could the all-powerful capitalists, who were excited about a sudden capture of the market across the globe, tell the people worldwide shamelessly about their sudden helpless unmanageable imbalance in trade! How could they tell the people that the high-end gambling in the world trade had been gradually deteriorating one by one? The devilish lights of the imports and exports of the lighthouses were gradually turning red. A vain attempt was being made to cover this sound pollution of inherent problems with external extravaganza.

Their small company with three to four hundred labourers also showed their colour. At first, the company curtailed the salaries, and it was closely followed by dismissal. On top of the letter of dismissal, it was written in red ink—Top Secret Personal. In the body of the letter, it was clearly written—your services are henceforth not required for an indefinite period with immediate effect from....etc. The catchwords 'your services are no longer required' were not simply told in the letter. A different style was maintained there, just to have an advantage. The main objective was to avoid the immediate payment of all the outstanding dues. They would have more time to utilize the money of the employees' funds. Ten per cent of the new labourers and the staff of the lowest category were dismissed. He was the only officer to get the sack. For this, the hurt was acutely felt. Having completed his degree of M.B.A., he joined the service nine years ago. The company said—none was required in that post for the time being. This was but a trick—it was a way to reduce the cost of production and to maintain the same volume of profit during the depression. They had no other obligation to any one besides maximizing their profit. The government was then neutral, in other words, inactive.

Anish could not divulge the news of the secret dismissal even to his friends, not even to others at home. He did not know why. The ghost of managerial secrecy of the company was still moving within him. The creed of the business world is —to show off extraordinarily to save its bad image in the market. But, why should an ordinary householder like him be such poseur?

There was a negotiation regarding the purchase of an apartment. How excited Ritu was! She disclosed the news to all and sundry of her near and dear ones.

Although it was a vague and some distant dream, Anish was, nevertheless, dreaming it happily—he felt that a job would surely be availed of somewhere

   Delving Into Different Literary Terrains

else by virtue of his brilliant result in Management degree together with his vast experience. By carrying his own bio-data in his pocket, he ran to many company offices lying far and near for the next twenty to twenty five days. In an utter exasperation and illusion, he even went to meet the secretary and the president of the employees' union. With a coarse sarcasm, they said—you are a cadre of the management. How can we fight for you? Who would take account of the amount of sufferings that our people already had?

Anish wanted to say angrily—your wrong estimation may occur quite naturally. You have been chanting the bookish language for long—the destruction of capitalism is imminent. What will you say now? Has the process of destruction started or not? Why the workers of the world cannot get united and cannot dash it extremely? Why can't you shout loudly—give back all the powers of supervision in the hands of the government? You have broken your own waists. How else will you set it right? What is there for you except crying?

Anish thought—Let it be, speaking that out will be devil's pleasure.

Things became unbearable. After returning home, he longed for, what he would do earlier after washing his hands and feet—roaming around taking Maman in his arms, rolling on the bed, singing rhyme songs in full-throated voice. His favourite items were the songs sung by Antara Choudhury during her childhood. He tried to repeat the same defying the challenges. His eyes began to burn badly as he was once fondling Maman and singing a song. He wiped his face on the bed on the plea of caressing Maman for the fear of being caught by Ritu. Maman was born later than usual. What would he do after this? All his money was exhausting thick and fast. It was about the time to hand over the money of monthly expenditure in the hands of Ritu. She will demand for that as soon as the month is ended. The company gave him some extra amount as a show of magnanimity. It is equal to the salary for fifteen days. The money he has in the bank at this time is enough to hide the facts from Ritu temporarily.

What then? There is nothing next to it. There is no guarantee.

Everything looked empty—as far as his eyes could see—a void, a dried up and spread out field....the scorching heat of the sun like a desert...the heat wave in the air...he was producing the high-pitched laughter of the ghosts. The sounds produced by the working populace were similar to that laughter of the people who would move about in trams, buses or even walk on foot. Anish wanted yet to hold hands of any one and say a few words, but he could not.

It seemed as if that dove suddenly cried once beside his ear—kukkurrr-kuk.

In a fit of nervousness Anish got up and sat properly. He sat reclining on the stock of a tree, he could hardly know when he became drowsy.

He looked at his watch. It was the time for his returning home. He was surprised by touching the bag-- the tiffin was not yet consumed. Ritu would demand a thousand explanations for this. He opened the box and had one 'roti' with a piece of sweetmeat. He threw away the remaining two rotis and the curry with it.

Anish was walking. He was watching Kolkata over and again—Kolkata was different. Kolkata was running—running ceaselessly--people were moving about for work, moving in search of jobs. Everyone was busy. Only he was not, he did not have any job to do. Sometime his feet halted unknowingly. Anish was looking at the busy city without blink in his eyes. He heard—Take care! Sir, be careful! Who was saying this!

Anish was standing in the middle of the footpath. People were moving away in front and beside, nobody was standing aimlessly like him.

Suddenly someone cried over his ear—Hello, Sir! What are you doing! Do you want to be injured!

Moving back, Anish got startled and almost sat down on his knees. The big sheets of steel were coming dancing and were about to dash the crown of his head. Two people were carrying those on their heads. Anish was now walking with his head bent and by squeezing his bag tight unnecessarily. A man spoke in a coarse voice—young man, you are new to see the city of Kolkata, is it?

Another one said—yes, he must have lost his senses.

Anish perhaps forgot to board on any bus. He was walking continuously, will he walk all the way from South Kolkata to Kasundia in Howrah! He stopped when he got back his senses. Would he get the bus from here to Babughat? Then he would cross the river by a launch and get on board on the other bank of the river. His office was in Shalimar. Carrying his office bag on his shoulder, he was walking in Southern end of Kolkata. He had no idea why he was doing so. What could be said about this act—to abscond? Was it an act of hiding? Actually, he had been doing such acts during his school or college days. He did so even during his days in an Engineering College. He hid all these to his wife, to his friends—Anish felt that innumerable ants were moving all across his body, and they would immediately bite him together. Anish started rubbing his erect body on a lamp post standing next to him. Some buses went past him speedily; it was not a bus stop after all. His left hand was caressing the hair on his head, suddenly he gripped the hairs on the back of his head, and dragged them. He pressed the temples of his head by right hand on both sides. Was he doing it by chiding himself or by becoming angry at the world?

Anish got off the bus. He became cautious as he stepped into the lane leading to his home with his tired and loose feet. He made his body look a bit more erect than usual—as a regular drunkard would do to hide his drunken stupor. Almost all the people by the doors and windows of the lane knew him well. What was wrong even if they had known him? He had to walk like that, and he had to enter home. Obviously, he was not charged with stealing something.

He bought two mausambi fruits in place of four and some grapes for his daughter that day, which he buy almost regularly. He thought of buying something for Ritu. He went to a nearby stationery shop and said— please supply me four good quality chocolates. Showing two pieces of star chocolates, the shopkeeper said—that is all I have right now. Keeping those inside his pocket, he drew out the currency notes. Hearing the sound of the calling bell, Ritu came near the door with Maman as usual. Putting the daughter in her father's lap, she went inside with Anish's bag. Anish adored Maman more than usual, something unusual would have happened to his throat as he took Maman in his lap, he felt choked.

An irritated voice of Ritu could be heard a little later—ah, did you pay attention to the items you purchased today? The mausambi fruits have dried, grapes are found to be excessively sour. Wherefrom you purchased these? I shall not give those to my daughter, better you will have those. What else can be found in your Shalimar besides all the things made of iron? You need not buy from there. I shall buy from Kalibabu's market.

Anish did not say anything. Taking out two bars of chocolates, he held those just before Ritu's mouth.

---Oh Maman, I am being taken special care of today! Have you seen! What is the matter? Ritu said so taking those in her hands.

This was an obstacle to Anish's anxiety—if he would be caught a little through the sharp eyes of Ritu, then all the hidden walls of secrecy would come down due to her repeated attacks. The result would be—the situation of the day and night would be the same and similar due to Ritu's incoherent talks and tears. The care of his daughter would not be taken properly, he did not know if he would be allowed to go out after that! The situation would be widely unbearable and immense.

Anish said—Take the child. Let me put off my shirt and trousers. Give me lungi. Putting the towel around his waist and carrying a 'lungi' in his hand, he dashed to the bathroom. He willingly took much time to get out of it. He saw that Ritu had prepared his favourite egg-sandwich. Tea was being prepared. Immediately after taking tea, Anish said—I am going out for a little while. He wore pyjamas. He could not stand any longer before the inquisitive eyes of Ritu.

-- Will you get out? Uh—I see. I thought you would manage Maman, I thought I would prepare a special menu today. Uh—Ritu said in fondling voice.

--I mean, I will go just to the club. I have not visited there for a long time. So, let me go.

--Come back quickly, understood?

Nodding his head in obey, Anish went out. Actually, he did not think of visiting the club at all. Did he have the stamina? Coming out of the lane of his house, he got mixed up in crowd in the main road. He felt much relieved to stay away from Ritu and his daughter. He could feel the vibrating sounds of an earthquake when he stayed close to them. It was not simply a matter of his uneasiness; an anxiety of fear seemed to gobble him up. He knew that his face might reflect his anxieties at any point of time. Ritu would see and understand, he could not escape it. He wondered how women could understand their husbands easily. Was it the ultimate success of love! Ritu loved him very much. There was the crisis. His anguish was getting deeper and deeper.

He wished if he could have any information for a job! An overwhelming frustration had been throwing him harshly. They were made to believe that no management degree holder remained unemployed! They would surely get some assignments somewhere. Those were all bogus. Those were the spicy words in this market of gamblers. Everything was uncertain; there was blind approach to everything. His life was like stake in the hands of international gamblers. Now he had been thrown away. The government, on the other hand, had nothing to do with such abrupt dismissals. The government was not meant for the common people, but it was for the big business persons.

Thinking about something Anish halted for a while. After a while, he suddenly moved back and started walking. Now he was walking fast.

Ritu was cooking. Anish entered, and said—Hi, I have many things to tell you.

--Wait a bit, this is the last item, Let me prepare it, Ritu said.

Anish could not endure delay. He said— just you listen to me and cook. By setting a cane stool beside the door of the kitchen firmly, he sat there by leaning. He began to talk about their house at Kalna without any introduction. After listening for a while, Ritu said smilingly—what happened? Why are you suddenly speaking all these right now?

Ritu started gigling.

Anish was let down a little. -- I did as I had wished. Anish threw a furtive glance at Ritu. He said—Did you know everything?

--Yes, I do. I knew it long back. Your mother told me everything. It was long back.

Anish moved with excitement. –what did she say?

--What else? She told me the facts alike. Your ancestors had big business for generations in Kalna town. The trade that spice-merchants normally dealt in—you would have big business of spices. This business made your ancestors a traditional millionaire. Monopoly business --

--No, it was neither monopoly business nor something alike, it was actually a hereditary.

-There was no shop as big as this in the town. Am I right?

Anish nodded.

Ritu said—that big hall-type house with a tin roof on it has been lying in a tattered condition. I don't know why have you kept it? Why? Your father was averse to that business. Then why is it so? He has spent his life with the service happily. Now he is satisfied with his pension. But...if the business could be carried out—

Suddenly Anish spoke out with excitement—that was the matter, I was supposed to discuss with you.

--What? Tell me. Making the gas-oven off, Ritu started arranging things in proper order. After a little pause, having looked at Ritu, Anish said—I thought I would go home. I shall talk to my father. Yes, either by a promoter or with the help of a bank loan— it should be built immediately— Anish paused all of a sudden. Ritu looked at Anish while she was washing and wiping her hands. Anish found the eyes of Ritu to be very sharp. Anish stood up. Turning towards the dining space, he said—I mean, the family tradition needs to be revived. If our tradition of the trade and business is....

--Who will run it after all? Ritu said this standing near the kitchen door.

--I shall, no, I mean, my father, besides, some people will have to be employed.

--What did you say? Your father? Are you crazy? Are you greedy for extra money all of a sudden? Sell the area to a promoter. You will have enough money. Saying so, Ritu came closer to Anish. She said— taking a vow not to run the business and making a wrangle with your grandfather, your father left the place and joined a job. And now -- you—you are thinking in terms of business.

--Yes, I am thinking in terms of a big business. I am thinking in terms of a small business of electronics products. Of course, a deal with maximum profit! Ha—ha—

--What do you mean? Will you leave the job? The job is in Kolkata--

--damn it! Kolkata. There will be five times more money if the business could be....

--I will not be able to live in a village with Maman.

--Is Kalna town a village?

--what else? Leave aside all those crazy ideas. How could the ghost of running a business come into your head? How? You have told that you will join a bigger company once you become experienced. Oh, now you think mere about your poor traditional business!

--Oh, no. I am talking about electronics or some modern trade like that—

--Will you shut up?

Ritu came forward and she pushed Anish's chest by her hands. She said—

Listen carefully; don't do such kind of a crazy act. I am thinking of Maman in Kolkata, with her—I have so many dreams. No, I will not leave

     Delving Into Different Literary Terrains

Kolkata at any cost. I shall not go there—I am telling you—I won't go—I won't. Tears filled in Ritu's eyes. She was sobbing.

Anish became perplexed—Ritu was crying! He became indecisive—what should he say in reply or how he can make her agree—and became restless. Once he went near Ritu. Then on the spur of the moment, he said— No talk about not going there, you will have to. They will compel me to go to the leftover business of my ancestors. We shall have to die of starvation if we don't go.

--What? What did you say? Oh, why did you say like that, dear? Do speak out—why did you tell like that? Tell me--

Suddenly the words seemed to burst out of Anish's throat—otherwise you won't be able to live the life, Ritu. I—I have been sacked. I have been---

Holding the dining table firmly, Anish sat down.

Ritu seemed to turn into a statue of stone. After a while, it could be seen that she was gasping severely, it seemed as if her two eyes would come out. Suddenly she cried out in her broken and coarse voice—Oh, Ma-man! Maman! Hear, do you hear? Maman was crying! Maman was crying at the top of her voice! Where is she crying? Where?—Ma-man! Ma-man!

It seemed that Ritu was on her knees on the floor and crawling in search for her daughter. She was also panting strangely. Anish became extremely puzzled. He hugged Ritu tightly. He dragged her to the bed room.

--There she is! There is Ma-man! Look, Ritu look.

Having seen that, Ritu's head slipped on Anish's shoulder. Anish's hands were holding the body of his wife like the static branch of an immovable tree. Then, their own daughter was absorbed in deep slumber.

Translated by : Subhajit bhadra

An Anthology Of Interviews

Chapter - 1
Bhabani Pegu

INTRODUCTION

Among the contemporary fiction writers of Assameselanguage, Bhabani Pegu is a new name but she has pocketed a prestigious award by writing her debut novel. Her second novel oipulir hoponor dekh has found a place in the bestseller list and has created a ripple in the fictional universe of Assamese language. In this novel, she has used imagination and intellect to create an extremely readable narrative. She has plumbed the depth of psychologically challenged characters to create a subtle and nuanced novel.

CONVERSATION

Question: Childhood as a formative phase of life is always important in the growth of a person. Kindly tell us in detail about your childhood.

Answer: Looking back to my childhood , I recall a house (Chang ghar). I still have vivid memories of the house and the big campus Which was surrounded by mango trees , jack fruits , pomegranate, banana trees and a part that was nearly Kept darkened by bamboo trees . From the verandah of that small house one could see the steep railway track in front . and deep down there was a beautiful stream that flows by . That was the house where I spent most of my childhood period . A house that was small, yet so humble . As the only daughter of the house I was much loved And cared by my father . He was a strict man . A man who had strict rules laid down for his children's. Might be because of his strict and concerned attitude towards us , we did not have many friends during childhood. I specially was not allowed to roam and mingle around freely with people and friends. I grew up almost lonely . And probably this was the reason why I was brought up as a shy , submissive and little reserve child . Though I did not have many friends during my childhood , in actual term I was never that lonely. My parents had decent government job , they had our Responsibilities, Yet they always had time for us . They often took us to the green paddy fields . When they were busy in the field, we used to loiter around indulging ourselves with the scent of mud , rain drizzles and greenery . In the backyard of our house there was a fast flowing river. in that river we often sailed on boats made of banana stems , or in the river bank we often used to make sand houses . Sometimes when our father was out for fishing, we used to run after him with the "khaloi"s in our hands . At the evening hours we used to study together under lamp light . I also love to recall those memories, When after dinner we used to sit outside under bright moonlight . My mother and grandmother used to tell us stories . And at the end of each stories I had endless questions to ask till I get scolding . In the morning hours , when my parents were busy with household works, I used to read newspapers for them loudly. They made me read Ramayana in the same manner . And I remember Completing that in 3 nights .

Que: Every creative writer holds his or her environment of his or her childhood days in great esteem. What do you think about this?

Ans: Our childhood were the days, where there was no internet, no mobile . Living a life away from machines , mobiles and technology , we had enormous time for adventure and exploration. Those were the days where we had only black and white TV , and a scooter as the only luxury . Instead of you tube we had our grandmothers who told us bed time stories . Visiting mama , Mahi and grandparents house during holidays and summer vacations were like our foreign trips . Specially born in a remote village , sometimes a colourful frock and a small "Kajal tema" from the Wednesday market were our only ultimate dream and fashion . Yes , I do consider my own childhood days with great esteem . I often indulge myself in exploring my childhood memories and and I believe, most of my imagination carves out from that period of life . It acts like fresh raw material , which Acts as source of creation for me .

Que: Your novel "oipulir hopunor dekh" has created a sensation. Tell us about the genesis of this novel.

Ans:I recall a woman. Her parental home was located near our school . She had thick long braided hair, and a very beautiful complexion . Whenever she Came out from the house and out in the garden someone would just come out , pull her by hair, and beat her with bamboo sticks . Those incidents were regular affair . Me and my friends were very much curious to learn about her . There were gossips all around . She had a child and a husband . But she was thrown out from her house . People called her "pagoli". I too realised , she actually never sang a song . Those were lullabies with no proper meaning. So, she was mentally ill . I can recall another woman roaming around the market . She looked unclean and untidy . She had Yellowish jute like hair, and dresses that were torn . She did not have a home . Or probably she was thrown out from house . She often carried a bag in her back . She used to eat whatever was offered to her . Later we noticed, her belly was growing big and actually she was pregnant. It made me feel disastrous . who in the earth was/were responsible for that rape and unfortunate pregnancy? There was no answer . Later, she gave birth to a baby . And we noticed how she cared the child singing lullabies for him , begging for foods to feed him . Somebody built a roof for her . Somebody brought clothes for her . I was just at my teenage . whenever I went to market I could only give her a mere biscuit packet or sometime a ten rupee note . Later when I joined the BSc Nursing course, as a part of educational requirement, we got 2 months posting in the psychiatry ward . I also got two times exposure in Lokopriya Gopinath Bordoloi Regional Institute of Mental Health, Tezpur . There I got to meet many other mentally ill patient . We could see and feel the pain of their life . There are endless social stigmas around mental illness. There is hatred and crime over mentally ill patient . So, mental illness and pain of a mentally ill client is one important aspect in the construction of the novel "oipulir hopunor deh" . There were other incidents too . I recall a young child (13/14 years) who delivered a baby in the hospital. Later, the family absconded . And the newborn was found in the backyard of the hospital over cold sand . The neonate was dead . That incident had shaken my heart. During our ward postings, We got to see many other such incidents of teenage pregnancy and child birth . Each were associated with rape . Mostly crime within family members or close associates . All these incidents had one tag in them " illegitimate ". I was not ready to accept the term itself . I felt, " illegitimate" might be the act that is carried out , but the embryo which forms as a result of that act is purely innocent. So, this thought actually led to the origin and construction of the novel "oipulir hopunor deh" . The questions that arose in oipulir hopunor deh , are basically questions asked to the society as a whole .

Que: How far this novel is autobiographical and how far is it fictional autobiography.

Ans: Oipulir hopunor deh is not an autobiographical novel . It is basically a fictional work . I have created the Central plotline and the incidents from my own imagination and understanding of situations centering around real events and problems in our society.

Que: You have also pocketed a prestigious award for your debut novel. Kindly tell us in detail about the genesis of this novel .

Ans: Journey of my writing started in the popular Facebook literary group "Ardha Akah". By reading the Short stories and the series published in Ardha akah , I too got the inner motivation of writing . I started to observe the things around me . My little life experiences , the pent up emotions , and observations made in and around me , I started to pen them down slowly in pages of diary . And later I started to post them regularty in Ardha akah . The central plot line about the novel "ejak dhumuhar pisot" is college, hostel life, love , romance and the risk and problems associated with it . It could Jointly bag the prestigious Dr. Dondinath Choudhury award ,2018. And later the book was published by the bindu prakashan gusthi .

Que: What do you think about the relationship between literature and globalization.

Ans: Rather than as a writer, I would love to answer this question as a reader . If we think of globalisation, social media is the first thing that comes to our mind . Apart from these , Story telling technology too can be a powerful tool for globalisation . As we know Literature is the mirror reflection of a society and culture , by reading world literatures we can understand and connect ourselves with the world around us . The world is full of diverse cultures and languages . And literature still centres around few dominant languages. I feel more And more of literature work should be done in regional languages , displaying the tradition , culture, value and their social system . And these local literature works need to taken seriously , and translated in purest form to other national and global Languages.

Que: Do you think that literature is to be taken more seriously to free individual and social mentality from narrow viewpoints?

Ans:Yes . Through reading literature one can develop better understanding about life, culture,values and society . We can admire the good things, and avoid the bad things . In this way One can restructure his or her own beliefs and imaginations, and thus bring about positive personal changes in himself or herself . When every individual brings about positive changes in them , gradually societal changes will follow , and thus modernity in true terms.

Que: What kind of books you love to read ? Who are your favorite authors and why.

Ans:Starting from fictional, non fictional, autobiographical and historical, I read all kind of books . Among the Assamese writers my favourite authors are - Homen Borgohain , Anuradha Sharma Pujari, Rita Chowdhury, Phanindra Kumar Dev Choudhury, and Arupa Kalita Patangia . I love to indulge myself in their rich understanding about life, love and their philosophies. Their outlook about the society and the surrounding inspires me a lot . Among the new generation writers Sarmistha Pritam and Dr. Mrinal kalita are my favourite . Among the English writers I love to read fictional works of Salman Rushdie , Khalid Hosseini and Jhumpa Lahiri . Crime and thriller writings of Sidney Sheldon are also my favourites. Their understanding about love, culture and problems of society are portrayed in their writing in most aesthetic manner .

Ques: What are your future plannings as a creative writer?

Ans:Currently I am working on two projects . Writing deep romantic fiction was one of my dream . And I am working on it . It is near to completion . The another project for which I am gathering data is over tribal socio cultural issues and superstitions .

Chapter - 2
Bhaskar Thakuria

INTRODUCTION

Bhaskar Thakuria is a medical doctor by profession. He is currently working as an Additional Professor and Head of Microbiology in AIIMS Patna, India. He is a passionate microbe hunter who also works in infection prevention. He also has a parallel identity as a creative writer in Assamese. He has four books to his credit, Jatra, Singhdwar, Satyanusandhan, and Bibartan. He is a recipient of the prestigious Munin Borotoky Litatrary award2016for his Singhdwar.

CONVERSATION

Question: You are basically a writer of short stories. Why did you choose to explore this domain?

Answer: I am still searching for creative forms of expression. I started as a playwright and director way back in the nineties when I was a medical student. Those plays had deep plots, abstract expression. Critiques loved them, but friends who are primarily Bollywood followers could not get them. So I thought I had to connect to my friends, so I explored short stories as a medium of expression.

Que: In your stories you are more interested in experimenting with technique and sometimes it is obsessive. How would you address this issue?

Ans: As the Assamese proverb says about a dog's tail, my traits soon reflected in my stories. But I would like to put it in this way - As an avid reader and a movie watcher, I play the mental game of plot and narrative whenever I read or watch a movie. Once the story becomes predictable, I find it barren and flat, and I can never finish it. Hence in my creative expression, I am conscious of these facts. On the other side creativity is an autonomic act. The idea decides, direct and takes shapes of its own. The creator happens to be a possessed man. It is valid for all forms of creation, be it poetry, prose, pottery or painting or even culinary.

Que: Do you think that writing short stories is more often an aesthetic venture rather than a social responsibility?

Ans: It's not all chalk and cheese phenomenon. No man is free of his surroundings. Not even Alexander Selkirk or Tom Hanks in Castaway! The same is the case with purely aesthetic ventures. For example, In the play Waiting for Godot, nothing happens, nobody comes, nobody goes - is purely an aesthetic one. However, millions of people could relate to it owing to the post-war despair. Similar things are happening even today, and many continue to appreciate the play. On the other hand, many contemporary writers identify with a social cause that primarily reflects their stories. I prefer my stories to become independent so that they can express themselves on their own.

Pure art is losing its meaning due to populist pressure. It wants people to stop thinking at all. Few are falling to the perception; they advocate a different path altogether, plain sadhu Kotha of entertainment value only. Yes, literary expression needs to be diverse but not at the cost of a sole. Twenty years back, a similar argument was there when Bhanbednra Nath Saikia's play Shatabdi had a head-on comparison with Lady Diana. People embraced the populist idea, and the rest is history. I am sure as of today, Assamese short stories are resilient to sustain these kinds of pressures.

Que: Contemporary Assamese short stories reflect a blend of seriousness and jocularity. What is your position in this context?

Ans: Seriousness, yes, of course. Jocularity, I don't think so. We are still living up to Bejbaruah's word that we don't know how to laugh. Satire, witty humour, dark humour are almost missing from the scene. It may be due to the volatile, fragile and hypersensitive atmosphere we live in today.

Que: Your recent collection of stories titled Bibartan shows your consistent awareness as a reflective writer. Kindly let us know about the genesis of this Book.

Ans: It has short stories written from 2009 to 2019. For a change for me, all are a story with a tale to tell. I have lived in various parts of north India for the last fifteen years, many of the stories reflect real-life experiences. Like the Mahut who lost his Elephant in Corbet National Park, The Ban Gujar (a nomadic tribe of Uttarakhand Hills) with an axe confronted in the jungle, or experience of night bus journey with a stranger who turned out to be a hardcore criminal.

 DELVING INTO DIFFERENT LITERARY TERRAINS

On the other hand, few stories explore myths and questions on genesis and humanity. The global, scientific and humanitarian issues have also shaped the plots of some stories. Such diverse themes like the link between my laptop and the civil war in Congo and suicides in China; Or link between comet forecasting the downfall of the Ahom Kingdom and the arrival of three papery white men with hair like that of jute in Rangpur appear in the stories. Few of them are science fiction exploring scientific probability exploring nostalgia and politics. Of course, Assam history and identity have emerged as a central question in many stories. When plotted in a linear time frame, I found that the fifteen stories are telling the story of human evolution. Hence the name Bibartan-from genesis to a dystopian future.

Que: You have also written a few plays which show western influence. How do you construct a play keeping in mind this issue?

Ans: Writing fiction is always the plot and story and the divine push to complete it. It is not the east vs west tale. One of my play successfully staged was German Dream. It is set in second world war Germany, but its genesis was from my Textbook of Surgery, where the Nuremberg trial was referred to, and on exploration, the play happened. My other play Oikyatan was a musical, and I used many Christian iconographies. Though the story part is entirely different, the iconography part, I think, was influenced by a book I was reading at that time, Quo Vadis. But today, I don't remember anything about Quo Vadis. My later plays and writings also explore a lot of Indian/Assamese essence and philosophy. But when I finished writing those plays, our drama group disintegrated into individual professionals across the globe. So we could not stage them as we would have like to do it.

Chapter - 3
Dr Garima Kalita

CONVERSATION

Question: Would you please intorudce yourself?

Answer: I was born In Tezpur but was brought up in Diphu a small hilly town in Karbi Anglong. My father Late Bali ram Kalita was in service In District Council as a school Inspector and he was one of the pioneers of beginning primary school education in the newly formed hill district in the 1950s. He went to then Mikir Pahar to join in service in 1955 from Murara, Rangia. From that time our family has been settled in Diphu and it has been my home town ever since. I consider myself very fortunate being able to pass my childhood years in Karbi angling , a repository of bountiful Nature. So much has changed since those days but still the hills are as beautiful, its verdant green is as pristine and the dense forests are as luscious as ever. What I am as a person , I consider the surroundings to have greatly contributed to the developments of the attributes and faculties in me. In this age of fast paced technology and restlessness, perhaps we have lost the quality and leisure of rumination that is the core of peace of mind . I too don't have time to introspect and reflect, yet when the past flashes like lights of revelation at moments, I begin to see things in proper perspectives.

When we were children, Diphu was a small sleepy town and the silence of the surroundings was broken by the vibrant community in clusters of variety and difference. We used to reside in Council colony quarters and the residents were all from different offices of District Council administration. We the children had a free wild world to live in, nurturing nature around us and it created a sense of freedom and we began to be aware of the beauty of nature and the awesome influence it can cast over human spirit. The council colony was basically two rows of housing facilities founded on a wide hillock with three plains in between. We , the children used to play on these smooth turfs cleft within the slops of the hillock. I still have vivid memories of those playtimes interspersed with our exploring into shrubs for bitter gourds and wild berries.

Que: Environment often shapes an individual. Do you think your environment of childhood shaped you in any way ?

Ans: Yes, I believe wholeheartedly that the circumstances or the environment shape an individual. Whatever I am today , my circumstances have been instrumental for it. Going back to my childhood environment , I was lucky that we had nature around us and I trust that it gave us a sense of uncurtailed freedom and liberty to choose. As a person I am a libertine and a believer in the indomitable human spirit . Growing up in the free wild town of Diphu , I learnt the significance of society and community as this small town was a harmonic cluster of different cultures. It was agog with cultural activities like staging of drama ,plays , music recital etc. a sense of belonging was developed and respect for individual talents was formed. Maybe at that time only we learnt to respect the simple values of life like, integrity, simplicity, respect for others , compassion for the natural world , love for the animals etc.

Que: Kindly tell us about your earliest school life.

Ans: Well, my earliest school life began in Diphu in the early 1960s in Diphu basic school, a primary institute for basic learning. It was an Assamese medium school, and we were from various ethnic communities studied together . Karbis, Nepalis, Bengalis, Sikhs , Dimasas, Asomiyas etc. Maybe from our early bonding together we learnt the importance of social life and community . Life was very happy and carefree for us . During leisure hours, we used to explore the vicinities for wild mulberries and had to face punishment for returning late for class. And Diphu was as it were, (it still is) an epitome of cultural harmony and assimilation. In 1965 perhaps I shifted to Guwahati to join TC Govt Higher Secondary and Multi Purpose School as a student of class IV. I stayed with my Grandparents in Paltanbazar, and then in Chandmari, Pubsarania. My parents were still in Diphu, but they wanted the best of education for me, and TC Girls' School was one of the best at that time. I hailed from a very small town and the ambience was very different here. But I didn't have to face any unease, as in the Entrance test itself I stood first and that gave immense confidence to me. I found very good friends and many of my classmates and schoolmates are still my friends. I did well in my studies and I began to gather life's experiences in Guwahati and this city formed the essences of my personality.

Que: How did you grow as a person along with your higher education ?

Ans: It's rather difficult to say , but I began to feel that added responsibilities were thrust upon me and I had to meet the some high ideals. I was not an extrovert as most of the time I ruminated about the people and surroundings. I loved reading and reading books of all kinds, specially philosophy, literature and psychology became a strong ground for learning for me. Since I took up English literature as my course of study , it has helped me to take keen interest in life, society and human mind . When I was in college and university, a strong inclination towards social activism was growing but I haven't been able to engage in that, maybe because it requires a lot of sacrifice and self will. But be it as it may, History , politics and class still fascinate me and my perspectives on life and people veer towards those aspects.

Que: Did you have any buried desire to become an academician?

Ans: Yes, to be very honest , I was sure that teaching would be the profession for me, . When I was very young , maybe in primary school , I used to play teacher pupil most of the time with my contemporaries . I took it to be my privilege that I would teach all the young children who were with me . So It was very spontaneous and natural and I was certain that one day I would teach may be in a college and university. I am wonderstruck when I think about these reflections and the confidence with which I thought of pursuing my goal. It was very easy, not at all effortful. Of course the ambience in my family was also contributing towards it. My mother was a schoolteacher and my father as a School Inspector was constantly in association of the teachers. I like teaching and the profession of a teacher is one of the most prestigious in this world. Here is what connects people with one another, appreciating the faculties that one possesses and trying constantly to upgrade those faculties by relentless endeavors ! Another factor probably helped me to think in advance about the profession I would be interested in. My father loved books and he taught me to read books of all kinds . Since the time he instilled that interest in me, books began to be my friends at all the stages of my life. So teaching would be my only choice of profession. I wouldn't be anything else if not a teacher.

Que: Kindly tell us about your long stint as a teacher in Cotton College .

Ans: I was associated with Cotton college since the time I joined the Pre university course in 1973. The ambience in Cotton was always charismatic and hearty and cheerful. A responsible aura as it were , was in the air. It seemed to be the same when I joined the College in 1987. It was always with a deep sense of gratitude that I served my duty as a lecturer of English. Because I was aware that we needed to give back substantially what we owed to this premier institute of higher learning. Studying in Cotton College was a very happy phase of mine which marked indelible marks in mind and memory. Teaching here was always a matter of great satisfaction. I taught brilliant students, my colleagues in the department were extraordinary people and I had company of academic stalwarts in different fields.

As a teacher of Cotton College I was witness to so many changes that took place within and outside the campus of the college. The college is now a full fledged University There has been for many years a demand for autonomous status for Cotton College and I was always in the company of people who wanted an upgraded status for the college because we considered that the position of Cotton College in the field of higher education is unique and distinct from everyone else. We needed more freedom in making syllabuses appropriate for the age and more freedom in the administrative structure was also necessary. On official appropriate forums these demands and needs were filed and submitted , but for various administrative and political reasons nothing substantial came up in time. The demand for autonomous status was replaced by the demand for Deemed to be University. That again was another long chapter of research, speculation and apprehension on part of the administration, teaching community and the students. On popular condescension the idea of the Deemed university was given up. Then came the next phase and Cotton College State University was formed with Cotton College as a part of the university with two administrative offices in the helm of affairs, namely the offices of the Principal and the Vice Chancellor.

The dual and ambivalent position of Cotton College in the name of up gradation under the wings of Cotton College State University was to be detrimental for the future of the institute and also for the academic ambience of the North East. The Government of Assam at this juncture intervened and chalked out to enact the Cotton University Act by which Cotton College became a State University. That happened in July, 2016 . By coincidence, I was elected as the President of Cotton College Teachers Association and Dr Arup Kumar Hazarika as the general secretary of teachers' body in 2014. We were proud of the fact that we could be associated in this significant process of transition towards a full fledged

State University with a future of its own. We were excited and hoped earnestly that we would have a developed and mature academic institution of a very high order. My days and years in Cotton College were eventful and I was completely involved in academic duty and other duties designated to me in various capacities and I have learnt immensely from these years. In fact during this period only I learnt diverse perspective of life, the meaning of a true society and the immense joy that teaching a young community of students can give the person. As an academician I began to be conscious of the hurdles and challenges that the system presented before us. I retired from service in January,2018. I still cherish all the fond memories of this great institution .

Que: When and how did you start your writing career?

Ans. I was interested in writing from before and had written quite a few poems and a few short stories. But mostly literary criticism interested me. In early part of 1990s I was asked to present quite a few radio talks in AIR Guwahati in Literary section, English talks and the women's section. During those days I delivered a talk on respected Homen Borgohain's novel Subala. As readers would know, it was one of the most daring Modernist social novels in Assamese. Homen Borgohain , the author had listened to the talk and the next day I got a telephone call from him and he asked me to meet him in his office of Asom Bani. He offered me the opportunity to write book reviews in Asom Bani as they wanted someone else to review along with Late Nalinidhar Bhattacharya, the books sent to the office. I started writing articles, essays, reviews etc since then. Another noted literary person of the day , Late Chandra Prasad Saikia asked me to write for Goriosi and he was also very encouraging .

Que: Apart from literature, you have written extensively on cinema. Do you think they complement each other ?

Ans: Yes, it's true that literature and cinema do complement each other in many ways. Though they are distinct art forms both do work on a basic aesthetic plane. Storytelling too works for both the forms. Though filmic medium is image based and literary text is word based both mediums are engaged in life, society and people. I am interested in good films and this passion of mine is given a very conducive outlet by my association with Gauhati Cine Club for the last twenty years. I am just an admirer in this field. I haven't been able to master any technicality for that matter.

Que: English literature being anti canonical , what's your opinion about it ?

 Delving Into Different Literary Terrains

Ans: Going against canons has been a recent trend and as you have rightly said ,it has entered into academics and syllabus making. What I feel about is that the way deconstruction cannot replace literary criticism, anti canon as a consistent pattern cannot stay. Decentering would give place to marginal literature and in fact all kinds of literary categories are given due recognition now. In this age of advanced and diverse episteme that's a welcome sign . Caribbean literature, African literature, Dalit literature etc have become part of various discourses and more reading and research are going to fully fructify in near future. But ultimately great literatures , canonical or not have to be retained and read. This currency of anti canonical literature can also perhaps be related to " incredulity towards metanarratives ' of Lyotard.

Que: Kindly share your views about contemporary northeast literature.

Ans: Literature of the North east is diverse and fascinating. It's a multicolored prism which flashes its hues to make distinctive and unique patterns. The culture and society with their ethos manifest both universal and topical concerns in the literary outputs. One especial characteristic of this literature of the North east is its close affinity with folk lore and folk life. All the authors and poets of this region are integrated to the collective psyche and cultural ethos of the region. So a sense of regionalism is a part of this literature. Specific geopolitical issues have to become a part and parcel of this literature. Talking about contemporary literary figures emerging , each one speaks of individual literary personality. One mistaken notion shouldn't however blind our opinion and that is , that north east literature is not necessarily English ,it is Asomiya, Bodo, Manipuri, Hindi, Kokborok and any language representing a people here. Because it is our literature we should be more and more involved with its reading, discussion, analyses and research. It should be made an integral part of the college and university syllabuses. More research wings for facilitating North east studies must be taken up in the future. We are happy that we could introduce a compulsory paper on North east literature, in the syllabus , Department of English in Cotton University.

Que: Do you think contemporary Assamese literature is too provincial ?

Ans: No , I don't think so. Because the contemporary literature in Assam is making an attempt at projecting a wider perspective of things, people , society and the world. In fact in case of Short stories much experimentations are now exercised. Many promising story tellers are enriching the genre. Atanu Bhattacharya, Ratna Bharali Talukdar, Daso kalita, Monorama Das Medhi, Dibya Jyoti Bora, Pranjal Sarma Basistha and so many others are writing excellent stories . In other genres of Assamese literature too broad based cosmopolitanism has emerged and it has been a whole new experience for the readers.

Que: Who are your favourite authors and why you like them ?

Ans: Jorge Luis Borges is a favourite author of mine. I like the variety of his stories and the uncertainty which runs through them. Magic realism is a very interesting technique and I like reading such stories by ....Borges's handling of time and space in Garden of the Forking paths is marvelous. Margaret Atwood also strikes me to be a very strong author. Her depiction of female sensibility in an oppressed state is spine chilling. I like to read more about totalitarianism and democracy, the strengths and vulnerabilities of both the systems. I have done my Ph D dissertation on D H Lawrence and I like his liberalism and poetic sensibility. To read his prose with its evocative picturisation and suggestive quality is a really promising proposition. He remains a fond author. Kafka is another author who I can affiliate with. His absurdity, magical realism and the conflict prone human state I can immediately connect to. Metamorphosis is a strange yet candid portrayal of human non human dichotomy. Ibsen and Bertolt Brecht are two other dramatists whose work I like. Among poets Pablo Neruda is a favourite for the magnificent scope he offers through poetry to the people. And at last I am an admirer and avid reader of Sigmund Freud . among Asomiya authors, I must mention Mamoni Raisom Goswami and Dr Hiren Gohain as my favorite.

Que: What are your future projects as a writer?

Ans: I have plans and projects like everyone else. But only time can tell what's in store. Anyway I am bringing out a book in these months , to be published by Evince publication . The title is Culture in Crisis. I am thinking of publishing my Thesis on Lawrence. At present I am working on its revision. Another project I am long speculating – a book on the theory and praxis of Feminism. I am going to publish an anthology of critical essays on literature and culture in Assamese. These are only tentative thoughts and dreams. I don't know how far I can realize them.

Chapter - 4
Ismail Hussain

INTRODUCTION

Ismail Hussain is a familiar name in the literary and cultural horizon of Assam. He is a prolific writer. He never compromises with quality and his works emit fragrance of the soil. He has written novels, poems and socio cultural books. He has specifically concentrated upon Hindu-Muslim amity and such integrating framework has enriched his works. His interests range from the works of Sankardeva to the poetry of laborers living on the bank of the river Brahmaputra. In this candid interview with subhajit bhadra, Ismail Hussain shares his ideas about his works and literary experiences.

CONVERSATION

Question: How and when you entered the realm of Assamese literature.

Answer: I started my study on Assamese literature, specially on poems, short stories, novels etc.. at the age of 15 years within 1979-80. I completed study on 925 Assamese books written by Sankardeva, Lakshminath Bezbaruah, Hem Baruah, Bhabananda Dutta, Homen Borgohain, Syed Abdul Malik, Mahammad Piyar, Kumar Kishor, Nirupama Borgohain, Dr. Hiren Gohain, Dr. Birendra Kr. Bhattacharya etc. I started to write poem in the initial stage; but seriously entered the realm of Assamese literature in the year 1982, when I was a student of Cotton College of Science stream. At that time, I became close to some noted litterateur of Guwahati city and followed them. From my student life I regularly visited to library and readout Assamese books in my spare time.

Que: literature has many genres and you have crisscrossed almost every realm. Tell us in detail about this diverse literary experiences.

Ans.I have crisscrossed poems, articles, novels, criticism, short stories etc.; but my main theme of writings are poems, novels, articles and criticisms. My four books were published by the publishers in the year 1994; these were – (i) Jivon Aru Manuh Bishayak (About Life and Human Beings), (ii) Jivon Pathik Rahul Sankrityayana (Life – traveller Rahul Sankrityayana), (iii) Safdar Hashmi Aru Bator Naat (Safdar Hashmi and Street Theatre), (iv) Hindu– Musalman Prashna : Samannay Aru Sanghat (Hindu-Muslim Questions: Assimilation and Conflict). At that time, I was 29 years young boy. These four books helped me to climb the ladder of Assamese literature. The first book was selected for prestigious Ambikagiri Roychoudhury Award as a best creative Assamese book containing national consciousness and human sense of values in the year 1995-96. The second book was the second biography book on Rahul Sankrityayana in Assamese literature. The third book was the first one on Safdar Hashmi, the pioneer of street theatre in India and also on the history and contexts of street theatre. The fourth was the only Assamese book in details of Hindu-Muslim Relations written in Assamese language.

This book was specially appreciated by renowned historian and then President of All India History Congress Dr. Heramba Kanta Barpujari. After reading these books, maximum unknown readers thought that the writer (myself) may be a senior person i.e. more than sixty years. In different places like Book Fairs, in book stalls, libraries some readers asked me about writer Ismail Hossain and they wished to meet me. It was a strange matter for me that they could not identified me as writer Ismail Hossain due to my young age of 29. Since that time, i.e. 1994 I have passed my 27 years of book-writer life and created more than hundred books and published by thirty seven publishers including Lokayat Prakashan, Sahitya Akademi (Delhi), Cambridge India (Kolkata), Jyoti Prakashan, Banalata, Asam Prakashan Parishad, Chandra Prakash, Samannay Book Stall, Anamika Granthalaya, Asam Sahitya Sabha, Rekha Prakashan, Jagaran Sahitya Prakashan, Asam Book Trust, Bandhab, Arunodoi Prakashan, Panchajanya, N.L. Publications etc. Upto 2021, my published books are as follows – Poems (5), Articles on history, communal harmony, language etc. (20), on tribal and indigenous communities (8), On literature and criticism (4), on Char-Chapori areas people (10), on diversities of Bihu culture and folk literature (11), on Sankaradeva, Satra culture and Vaishnava heritages (19), on life and works of renown writer, legend persons etc. (20), on travelling and self verses (2),children literature (6), novel (3) etc.

Que: You seem to be fascinated by the indigenous cultural root of Assam. Tell us about this.

Ans:Yes, I am deeply associated with indigenous cultural root of Assam, specially the communities like Misings, Bodos, Saraniya Kacharis, Chutias, Ahoms, Koibartas, Morans, Koches, Rabhas, Deuris, Sonowal Kacharis etc. I have writtern books on these communities fully and partly. My writings are colourful by the heritages of these communities. I have tried to adopt the part- culture of indigenous communities. Partly learned their most critical languages also. The main attraction of fascination of these communities are their cultural life is colourful and free from caste difference. I seem to be proudful one of them.

Que: You have edited the Assamese poems of char areas. What propelled you to do that and what are the aesthetic merit of such kind of literature.

Ans:I have edited one poem-book of Char-Chapori areas Assamese poets of last seventy years which is unique in Assamese literature. Renown writer Homen Borgohain commented on this book in his inaugural speech on 25th December, 2020 that the included poems will enrich the life of Assamese literature and language. He also expressed that the emotions of these poems explores the root of exploitations and disregard of some poor peoples. I think that this book will highlight a part of Assamese poems of community contributions. Besides this book, I have written and edited another nine books on Char-Chapori area's Muslim peoples who have adopted Assamese language as their mother-tongue and medium of writings and spelling.

Que: Your magnum opus is your book on Hindu and Muslim amity. What do you think about complex issue in the context of Assam.

Ans: Yes, my magnum opus is two books on Hindu – Muslim amity one is 'Hindu – Musalman prashna : Samannay Aru Sanghat' (1994) and another is 'Asamot Samannayar Oitijya' (The Heritages of Assimilation in Assam). The latest was published by Jyoti Prakashan in 2019. This book covers the integration and assimilation of different communities of Assam irrespective of religion, caste and language, in the field of religion, language, folk-culture, India's freedom movement activities of the locatities, literature, songs, peasant movements etc. It takes thirty two years to complete in the field of research and local investigations. I think that this book will be able to reflect the high village communal harmony of peoples of Assam of different villages, districts, both tribal and non tribals from locality to India and abroad.

Here, same complexity arises time to time from the sides of religious fundamentalists, the racists and a group of political workers. I think that all the complexities and conflicts may be eliminated if one goes through this book.

Que: What are your plans for future and who are the writers whom you admire most.

Ans: My future plans are as follows :

1. One epic novel on Phatobihu, the local cultural heritage of Dhakuakhana where Ahoms, Chutias, Misings, Deuris, Koches, Koibortas, Sonowal Kacharis etc. assembled for trade and commerce and celebrated spring culture of different communities for seven days in the first part of seventeenth centuries.

2. One novel on Char –Chapori area's Muslim peoples.

3. One novel on Srimanta Sankardeva. Already I have written one novel on Chandsai, the one of the main Muslim disciple of Sankardeva, which is running in 'Gariyoshi', the famous literature magazine of Assamese language.

4. One Folk-dictionary, namely 'Asamiya Folk-Dictionary'

5. One book on Sankari Philophy and culture.

6. One book on golden cultural heritages of Assam in English language.

7. One book on contribution of Muslims of Assam in the field of freedom movement of India' etc.

I admire the famous writers of Assamese literature who encouraged me to write are – Late Homen Borgohain, Late Prof. Nalinidhar Bhattacharya, Late Dr. Amalendu Guha Dr. Hiren Gohain, Late Prof. Shashi Sarma, Late Prof. Kheshwar Chetia, Dr. Nagen Saikia, Late Chandra Prasad Saikia, Late Medini Choudhuri, poet Harekrishna Deka, Late Dr. Kabin Phukan, Malayashree Hashmi of Delhi, Late poet Anil Sarkar of Tripura , Dr. Dhrubajyoti Bora, Pradip Barua (editor, Prantik), Late Tilak Chandra Hazarika, Dr. Karabi Deka Hazarika, Dr. Birendra Kumar Dutta etc.

Chapter - 5
Jayanta Madhav Borah

CONVERSATION

Translated by-Jintu Gitarth

Question: Would you please introduce yourself?

Answer: My Childhood was spent in a village. Its a remote place of the present Golaghat district. The river Kakdonga, the Namghar of the village., a primary school, tiny grasslands and vast paddy field- all had created the environment of my childhood.

My adolescence days were spent in tea garden. That was another environment. Only green and green. My youth days were spent in town. In my writings (many short stories and novels) the village of my childhood finds it space. Even, now also, in the core of my heart, you will found the Kakdonga village and the river of my childhood. Every writing having village background contains my childhood's village. It happened during writing the 'Mariahola' also.

I often feel nostalgic reminding my childhood's tea garden. My first novel (published as book) 'Amrit' was written on the plot of a tea garden. The novel was honoured with the Giridhar Sarma Award by Asam Sahita Sabha.

Que: ???

Ans: My adolescence days were spent amidst tea garden and my youth days were in town. May be I am one of those fortune people who rarely get chances to live life in so different environments. Village, tea garden, town- all these have enriched me making familiar with the different problems, pains, dreams and conflicts of each. I think, it has made me able to pen down short stories, novels on the three different backgrounds.

Que: ???

Ans: I was fond of literature since childhood. As a child, I loved to have reading of the tales. Historical episodes had attracted and impacted me. I wrote a story in the school magazine when I was in class eight. At that time, there was no conscious effort, but a spirit like the river of youthfulness. That was the first time that I got to see my name in published letters. After that, another inspiring incident happened when I was in the ninth standard. In our school, an all Assam essay competition was held. I had participated there and it was an wonder for me that my essay bagged the first prize. I can never forget that day of receiving the prize. In college, I was a student of pre-university science stream and concentrated on my academic studies. I had no relation with serious literary practice or what we call activism. But I used to go the library to borrow books of stories and novels. In hostel, it was quite trend-contradictory that being a science student, I used to study novels and stories during my leisure. In case of literary practice, I became serious when I was a student of Jorhat Science College and then of Dibrugarh University. In Jorhat Science College I studied Physics in B.Sc. and in Dibrugarh University, M.Sc. Actually, I had developed the feeling of responsibility towards writing when I was in Dibrugarh University. I got inspiration from my friends and well-wishers there. But more than that, the unstable inner soul had voiced me to write. I had to speak on against the ongoing corruption, de-moralisation in the society. That rebellious spirit energized me to pen down.

Que: ???

Ans: As I have said, I had the kind of habit of writing since my childhood. At that time, I read the Assamese as well as Bengali novels a lot. We were acquainted with the foreign literature through the translated versions. Now I can't mention any specific name that this person or that writer had great impact on me. It was the content, more than the writer which had impacted me.

A writer must struggle. To write well and standard, deep study as well as practice is essential. I am also not exceptional of this cult of struggle. I was containing the story-line of the novel 'Mariahola' for 25 years. For 25 years, I was playing with it. I was collecting data. After that I sat to write. It was same in case of my another novel on Majuli titled 'Namata Kahaya Majuli Sawe'. Those were also one kind of struggle. Another thing is that – I am never satisfied with my writings. When I am writing a story. I think I am writing a very good story. On due course of writing a novel, I think I am writing a strong novel. Even I tell my friends with proud. But after completing, it seem for me like- is it a story? What have I written!- But I don't have that much of patience that I will sit and rewrite. I have never gone for re-writing. I just write and send for publishing. I think this habit is not good. May be, after rewriting, my novels or short stories would become more polished. But this unsatisfactory position is making me to write one after another. So this struggle to write, with own self has brought me to what I am today.

Que: ???.

Ans: I have already said that my childhood was spent in a village. That had enriched my life. Those rituals, people, their thoughts and talks-all are alive in my mind. In my writings, it finds its own spaces spontaneously. In the core of my heart, you will find that village and the river. In every writing with village background, the village of my childhood gets portrayed. Even, in writing Mariahola' also, happened the same. Even after residing in city, I can't forget that village and those sweet days of my life. In the lonely moments amidst the mechanical city life, the village comes silently and makes me nostalgic. This conflict between the feelings of village and city shapes the new stories.

Que: ???

Ans: Not only mine, most of the writers' (except the journalists) occupational field is different. It brings obstacles in writing also. Time does not permit you. When I get time, I write. Whenever the inner voice arise, I am bound to Write.

Life and livelihood are not one. Life is aim. Livelihood is the mean. Life and the field of livelihood may not be same; or may be same for someone. Those, whose are not same, loss the joy, so mine also, sometimes.

Que: ???

Ans: Yes, I write both short stories and novels. The story, jerking in mind decides whether it will be a short story or a novel. Some stories can not be shaped as short story whereas some as novel. I enjoy writing both, But I consider myself more in novel writing.

Que: ???

Ans: Mariahola' 'Azan Phakir', 'Namata Majuli Kahai Sawe' , 'Mayang' – these novels are written in a new technique. Each of these novels is based on historical episodes and events. But these novel are not historical novel. Here, historical episodes have been reconstructed. They are reanalysed from the narrator's view point. An imagined character is plotted in the historical setting and own views are presented. This is my own technique. I am thankful that readers have accepted this technique.

Ans: Planning are there. Now, I am writing a novel titled 'Deul' whic has been being published in Gariyasi serially. The plot of the novel covers up the 19th Century- from the Mans' invasion to 1900. I am working on a child novel also. I have also planned for more novels. I will have to pen down one by one.

Chapter - 6
K. Satchidanandan

CONVERSATION

Question: Sir you hail from Kerala and your state is known for its exquisite natural beauty. Please tell us something about your native land and your upbringing.

Answer: I was in Kerala until I was forty-five when I moved to Delhi, and now at 75, I have moved back to my native state, though my links with Kerala were always intact as I write chiefly in Malayalam and my first readers are Malayalis. Yes, Kerala is blessed by natural beauty. I spent my childhood in a village full of small lanes filled with greenery, ponds, wells, canals and a river close by. The sea was not very far either; we could hear the sounds of the sea during the monsoon. Mine was a lower-middle-class household< I studied in the lower and upper primary schools in the village and in a government high school in the nearby town. I could study further only because I had scholarships for my degree education in another town and post-graduate education in Kochi. My family could hardly afford my higher education; if I did not win scholarships I would have ended up as a clerk in some office. When I look back I can say I had a Wordsworthian childhood as I grew up in the close company of nature, walking many kilometers to my schools, climbing trees, and swimming in the pond in our compound. My sister, brother and I spent our holidays also in the village itself. My village had two public libraries which helped me read first children's books, and later translations of Indian and world classics- Kalidasa, Bhasa, Tagore, Bibhutibhushan, Tarashankar, Manik Banerjee, Yashpal, Jainendrakumar, K A Abbas, Victor Hugo, Thomas Mann, Dostoevsky, Tolstoy, Turgenev, Charles Dickens, etc in Malayalam. I got acquainted with modern writers mostly during my college days -Kafka, Camus, Sartre, Eliot, Auden, Baudelaire, Mallarme, Brecht and others. Of course, I was reading all important Malayalam writers of all genres.

Que: You are basically a poet. When did that sojourn begin and when.

Ans: I began writing poetry when I was thirteen years old. Today I would not call it poetry, but it was verse, inspired either by my personal experience in the village or by the poetry I had read. I used to take part in poetry competitions until I finished my degree; by the time I understood that that kind of poetry is very unnatural, as we are forced to write on a given theme, at a given time, within a given duration. Now I began to take poetry more seriously; it was no more a hobby, it was my deepest self-expression. During my days as a post-graduate student, I also began publishing poems in literary journals. That was the time when modern poetry was emerging in Malayalam as in many other Indian languages. I was also drawn into the new sensibility and we began a journal as the mouthpiece of modern poetry, titled 'Kerala Kavita,' that published poems by new poets, studies of poetry and translations of poetry. I did some of my important translations for that journal- Chairil Anvar (Indonesia), Zbigniew Herbert (Poland) Jeebanananda Das (Bengal) etc. From then on I have been writing as well as translating poetry till this day. I have around 1200 pages of my own poetry and 2000m pages of translations from Indian and foreign poetry. I was also forced to write critical articles on poetry for the journal to introduce the concept of modernism in poetry.

Que: In your poems your ideological mooring often comes out. Why?

Ans: I believe in a just, free and egalitarian society; that is my dream. You can call it an 'ideology' if you like. And because I am committed to this idea, naturally I also raise my voice against injustice, authoritarianism, racism, casteism, communalism, and patriarchy. Environment is another major concern in my poetry. Of course, themes like love, relationships, nature, and death haunt me like any other poet.

Que: You are a thinker about Indian literature. Kindly tell us about this nomenclature and the implications of this term.

Ans: I believe that we should better use the term 'Indian Literatures' as each regional literature has its own specific history and character; but that does not mean we should ignore the shared movements, literary exchanges, and common ideas inspiring many literatures at the same time or at different times. We need to develop a healthy idea of comparative Indian literature, taking into account the similarities as well as differences among different regional literatures, by which I mean also literature in less recognized and marginal languages and dialects.

Que: You have written very powerful prose. Please tell us about that.

Ans: I began writing prose when I started writing poetry. In fact, my first book was a compilation of my studies in modern Malayalam poetry, only my second book was a collection of my early poems. Since then I have written a lot on poets and poetry as also on fiction, theatre, and cinema. I also began writing on literary and social theory in Malayalam as well as English since my late Twenties as I was associated with the People's Cultural Forum in Kerala that made several meaningful interventions in politics, media, health, culture and literature.

Que: You successfully worked as the editor of Indian literature. Kindly tell us about your experience as an editor.

Ans: In sum, what I did was to make the journal more democratic. I changed its size to begin with, increased the number of pages, began to get stories illustrated, updated the lay-out, launched new sections including interviews with outstanding writers, brought out language specials as well as theme specials and genre specials, had special issues on women's writing and dalit writing and introduced a lot of new writers and movements.

Que: You were also a teacher. Did you enjoy that stant.

Ans: Indeed. I taught English language and literature in two colleges for 24 years. I enjoyed talking to the young: I still do. It was also a very productive period for me. I read a lot and wrote too. I worked with students to organise literary forums and bring out literary journals. Teaching generations of students kept me young.

Que: You are a voracious reader of world literature. Who are your favourite writers?

Ans: This is a very difficult question. I have some eternal favourites like Dostoevsky, Thomas Man, Kafka and Marcel Proust besides writers like Borges, Calvino, Marquez, Llosa, Achebe, Ben Okri, Adichie, Murakami etc in fiction and Lorca, Pablo Neruda, Cesar Vallejo, Raul Surita, T S Eliot, Whitman, Sylvia Plath, Szymborska, Brecht, Paul Celan, Mallarme, Rimbaud, Ted Hughes etc in poetry. There are quite a lot of them. Among Indian writers in English, I like Salman Rushdie and Alan Sealy best in fiction and Arun Kolatakar best in poetry; besides there are dozens of writers in the Indian languages , for example Nilmoni Phookan, Navkant Barua , Indira Goswamy, Gopinath Bordoloi, Syed Abdul Malik, Hiren Gohain , Karabi Deka Hazarika, Nirmal Prabha Bordoloi, Arupa Kalita

Patangia, Mitra Phukan and a lot of others from Assamiya_ I know many of them are no more. I am generally familiar with the Assamiya literary scene though I do not know all the younger writers except a few like Nilim Kumar, Jiban Nara, Anubhav Tulasi etc. I think we need more translations of Assamese writers into English and Hindi to begin with.

DELVING INTO DIFFERENT LITERARY TERRAINS

Chapter - 7
Dr. Ratnottama Das Bikram

CONVERSATION

Question: Kindly tell us in detail about your childhood as it is the formative stage of life.

Answer: I was born in Dibrugarh, but brought up in Lakhimpur. The place I grew up is Narayanpur, a very small town in Lakhimpur district. Our home is near to Madhabdev College which is a University now. My place is called Collegepara, named after the 'college'. One can easily assume from the name itself that the place Collegepara is a sort of educational institute hub. So, obviously, environment of the place is still very academic because the college (University) and various schools in the locality. Both my parents were into academics who taught Economics and wrote books on economics. We had heap of books in our home and we were always encouraged to study. Most of our neighbours were teachers in the nearby College or in the any of the surrounding schools. We grew up looking up to many bright students hailing from our area. The whole ambience inside and outside my home was an 'academic' one, where I got the opportunity to shape-up my educational background. This helped me in becoming a part of academia today. But what helped me grow as a creative writer, was my voracious reading habit inherited from my father and the time spent with people and nature. I used to roam around the picturesque tribal villages, stroll amidst the greenery of the nearby muga pam (sericulture farm) and lark around with lots of friends of different age groups from different villages. I spent my holidays in my maternal grandparents' home in Kamarbari, a village situated only five kilometres away from my home. I consider myself very fortunate to be brought up in such an enriching environment where my writer-self germinated.

Que: Do you think your upbringing was responsible to make the person you are.

Ans: Of course. Without an iota of doubt. But my upbringing has nothing to do with the restlessness I carry inside me. I am solely responsible for it, no one else, nothing else.

Que: Can you shed some light on the contemporary situation of Assam when you were growing up.

Ans: Well, it was the nineties, and I grew up in upper Assam. So, you can imagine the situation of then Assam. We have seen the rise and the fall of the ULFA. We, as teenagers, always felt fear and hope from a very different angle. The socio-political scenario was a gloomy one. But surprisingly, the literary scenario was comparatively stable. The birth of the literary magazine Gariyosi during this time is an apt example.

Que: Kindly tell us about your academic life and the medium of your learning.

Ans: As I have already mentioned, I was brought up in Narayanpur of Lakhimpur. My place has always been considered as a place to produce good and successful students. The fertile environment helped me too to grow. Though I had had the taste of failure, I had had the fair share of my success too. It feels great and at the same time stressful, to remain as the apple of the eye of your teachers. I was the teachers' pet. But, yes, I did also disappoint my teachers at times. Medium of my education was Assamese. But after coming to Cotton College, I realised, being a graduate student with major in Assamese, I had no scope to write in English and I didn't like it. So, I volunteered to write my Pass Course papers, which was Philosophy, in English. During my post-graduation in Gauhati University, the medium remained the same as my major was in Assamese (Group-B, Language). It was disappointing to me for not to be in direct touch with English. All I could do was to keep on reading out-books in English. This habit helped me to a great extend when I came to Delhi University for my PhD and wrote my thesis in English.

Que: Did you nurture any ambition to become a writer. If yes then since when.

Ans: Yes, I did. Since my childhood and my early teen days when I started writing in the children magazines and the children's' pages of newspapers.

Que: You have been a student of Cotton college and it is the most esteemed institution of Assam. How did it help you to grow as a person and as a writer?

Ans: Cotton provided me the wonderful platform to fulfil my dream of establishing myself as a writer. It gave me the freedom to taste life and test myself. The cultural and literary group 'Nabin' and the dozens of wall magazines and little magazines during my Cotton days helped me gather my confidence as a writer.

Que: You are both a novelist and short story writer. How do you make a balance?

Ans: I believe, the 'balancing' act not very tough, though not a cake-walk, since both short stories and novels fall under the same genre prose. But yes, 'balance' is required. For instance, most of the times, while writing a short story I feel the urge to expand it to a novel, or at least to a novella, and it affects the storyline sometimes.

Que: Kindly tell us in detail about your published Assamese books.

Ans: I have two published books to my credit till now. My first novel Hariguna kahana najaai was published by 'Banalata', in December, 2013. This novel received a state level recognition by

Jeevan Initiative, Guwahati. My second book, a collection of four novellas, under the title Nakh narakha sowaleebor, was published by PeeGee India (Unique Books) in December, 2015. After that, I have been writing novellas and short stories in the leading literary magazines and the special issues of newspapers regularly. But not yet published any third book.

Que: What is your happiest and saddest moment of life.

Ans: Happiest was the journey of my pregnancy and delivery, in toto, whole the journey of me becoming a mother. The saddest was the moment when came to know that my father was no more. Being a papa's girl all my life, that was the moment of my greatest loss mixed with an emptiness that never filled.

Que: Kindly tell us about your future plans as a writer.

Ans: Margaret Atwood once said, you become a writer by writing, no other way. I add, you remain a writer by writing, no other way. And as I want to remain as a writer, all I can say about my future plan is that I want to keep writing. To be specific, I would love to tell more stories through my stories and novels.

Chapter - 8
Pradipjyoti Mahanta

INTRODUCTION

Pradipjyoti Mahanta is not a new name in the cultural and social realm of Assam. He is an educationist, critic, writer, vaishnavite scholar, and cultural articulator. He has carved a niche for himself in the literary horizon of Assam. His recent book on Sankar Deva is an attempt to understand the aesthetic dimension of Sankar Dev's nuanced writings.

CONVERSATION

Question: You are recognised as a scholar of cultural studies in assume and beyond. How do you contextualise your subject in the present.

Answer:Thank you for your compliments. I would however, love to be called myself a student of Cultural Studies. Although I was a student of English Literature studies during my years in Gauhati University, my interest in Assamese literature drew me nearer to cultural history of Assam with a passionate love for the early age. My years in Tezpur University in the Department of Cultural Studies unfolded before my eyes a new world of understanding and interpretive dimension of studying culture that emerged in the western academics since the sixties of the 20th century.

Cultural Studies, as often misconceived in the common parlance, is not the study of nor aesthetics of diverse cultural traditions and expressions, but looks at the political process and power relations underlying such traditions and practices including institutions. It also looks at their inherent dynamics of contextual significance, meaning and representation of any form of cultural text or practice. Traversing larger areas across disciplines - humanities, science and social sciences and liberal arts - Cultural Studies takes into its web multiplicity of issues and concerns of day to day social relevance and addresses them from its own perspectives, and is thus interdisciplinary, multidisciplinary and even post-disciplinary in nature, spirit and content.

Looking beyond traditional and conservative idea of culture - mostly literary and artistic expressions - and taking its shaping influence on a nation or a community into consideration, Cultural Studies stresses on "the attitudes and values of a community through the examination of its lived cultural processes and the cultural texts (forms, practices and expressions) the people of that community themselves produce and consume." Since its emergence in the Birmingham Centre, UK, Cultural Studies in the years that followed, received new momentum and flourished independently in Europe, USA, Asian and African countries expanding its network and incorporating newer concerns and addressing local issues.

Que:Your academic credentials adds a lot to your intellectual standing. How do you address this equation.

Ans:Neither my academic credentials nor my intellectual standing in the social and academic milieu is that high as you have observed. It is not for the sake of humility that I am saying so, but it is a reality. I am aware of my limitations. Be that as it may, with whatever knowledge and experience I could have from the academia and the social environment through which I grew up to what I am today, I have been trying with a sense of seriousness and purpose to harness the experiences and resources to contribute to the culture and society to which I belong and which has given me a liberal ethos and understanding of my land and culture, the humanity and the world at large.

Que: Do you think that the academic discipline of cultural studies in India is different from its counterpart in abroad.

Ans: India with its diversity and richness in all directions, continuity of a civilizational history over two millenia, offers even a greener pasture for examining its multiplicity of traditions - linguistic and literary, artistic and religious, religio-social institutions and practices, food, social behaviour and environment and so on from Cultural Studies perspectives. The bewildering diversity of Assam and the North-East is also a paradise for the practitioners of Cultural Studies as it is for linguists, anthropologists, ethnographers, folklorists and ethnomusicologists. Orality and treasures of collective and cultural memory, not to speak of issues of environment and unbanization, globalization and its perilous impact on smaller communities and their cultural identities, invite constant attention of Cultural Studies professionals. Considerable amount of work has been done by scholars and young researchers in this direction within and outside academic institutions. As Cultural Studies has grown in many countries in many institutions all over the world taking into its web issues of respective communities and nations, similar initiatives can be undertaken in India too evolving a framework and approach of its own however, without sacrificing the philosophy and rigour of the discipline.

Que: You are also regarded as a vaishnavite scholar. Please tell about your learning in this field.

Ans:Born and brought up in a sattra situated in a rural environment in Sivasagar, I was introduced to the Vaisnavite tradition of learning in diverse spheres since my early childhood. All these learnings - practices, rituals, behaviour, memorization of various texts, reading and recital of such texts in domestic and social congregations - which formed essential part of our daily routines during those years parallel to our school education for the children of our family, remained as ever cherishing memory. With constant social interaction I could see through those lived experiences how and to what extent Vaisnavite culture was embedded in the social mind and contributed to the 'organic growth' of the society, to borrow an expression of the German philosopher Johann Gotfried Herder used in respect of culture. And the Sattra institution was an agency of mediation playing an important role in this direction for centuries. Even after remarkable changes caused by the course of history and brought about by modern developments including the impact of education, science and technology, the pulsating rhythm of that organic harmony created by Vaisnavite culture is felt everywhere in most of the villages of Assam, not alone among the followers of the Vaisnava faith. Perhaps the abiding memory of those formative years of my childhood and my journey through the cultural history of Assam have greatly impacted my academic pursuit.

Que: Your recent book on the Saint sankardeva is a milestone in this field. How and under what circumstances you conceived the genesis of the book.

Ans:As I said earlier, my childhood years of experience, training and social interaction opened before me the vast portal of the Bhakti Movement in Assam and its renaissance bearing, much of it was however, unconsciously. I also felt at the same time the adulating and reverential memory of Srimanta Sankardeva's ideals and teachings at all levels of social and cultural life in Assam. As I tried to perceive the roots of the abiding impact of the Bhakti Movement and the monumental personality of Sankardeva, I found it to be in his social vision and philosophy integrated to that of bhakti imbiud with the ideal of social bonding and fraternity across all hue that he envisioned through the religion of bhakti engendering however no malice and rancour towards those outside the fold. This social vision of togetherness, tolerance and participatoriness at all levels of the pursuit of the faith greatly attracted me not because I happen to be an insider, but as a distant observer and as a student of cultural history. I believe, the liberal and democratic ethos that Sankardeva internalized and put to practice in sync with the pursuit of bhakti was crytallized from his own lived experience as a ruler of the Bhuyan principality, rife with social, political and religious conflicts, in the capacity of 'Shiromani Bhuyan'. With his genius as a thinker and a scholar, he gave it a crystallized form and ideal enshrined in his texts.

With a view to highlighting Sankardeva's prescient social vision as evidenced in his ideals and works, I planned to work for the present book. It is worthwhile to mention in this context that Sankardeva's social vision or role as a social reformer cannot be seen in isolation from his mission of preaching the faith of bhakti as well as his literary and other artistic oeuvre. All of them had a common goal and worked in unison, created a socio-cultural activism resulting in the resurgence unprecedented in the history of Assam.

To add a disclaimer to your point, let me say that the present book is not a milestone in Sankardeva studies. Many other scholars of eminence have greatly contributed towards wider understanding of Sankardeva's works and ideals. My effort is an addition to what has been done so far.

Que: Your book on sankardeva is on the aesthetic discourse of the great saint. How did you chance upon this unique idea.

Ans.:The entire range of Sankardeva's enviably large corpus of creative expressions - poetry, devotional lyrics, drama and theatre, music and dance, painting and sculpture, architecture and crafts, Assamese renderings from the Bhagavata Purana and the Ramayana, canonical treatises on bhakti in Assamese and Sanskrit - were aimed primarily to propound the faith of bhakti and to reach out to the commoners, both lettered and unlettered. But as a gifted poet and composer, he had never let loose the poetic or artistic virtuosity to suffer for the sake of espousing a doctrinaire faith. With his mastery over the language of the people around him he adopted it for his epic compositions and translations. Similarly with his deeper understanding of the great tradition of Indian aesthetics as well as indigenous art traditions, he took an artful middle path by interwebbing of the margi with the lokayata without deviating from the goal of imparting joy and beatitude to the readers, singers, players, viewers and the cognoscenti. In addition to what he achieved as a poet and a composer, Sankardeva also elevated Assamese verse, its music and rhythm to the pedestal of divine pursuit at the sacred space bereft of any political patronage which in itself is a remarkable contribution to Assamese letters.

Besides this, from my early childhood I was exposed to the environment in which each and every text of Sankardeva, Madhavdeva and the later composers was an act of performance. The mellifluosity of those congregational singing, theatrical performances is still live in my memory. The spontaneity and devotion with which the lettered and unlettered sang and continue to sing in congregations in village Namghars and Sattras is a constant reminder of another dimension of Sankardeva's aesthetic vision ingrained in his poetry and plays. Visualization of each text to a performance setting through music, dance and theatre for which too, the composer par excellence evolved a set of melodic modes, rhythmic patterns, and dramaturgy, is an incredible addition to the volume of his creative expressions. Moreover, they left an indelible impact on the collective memory to remain in 'social unconscious' (what T S Eliot referred to as a precondition in his discussion on culture). All these referentials inspired and prompted me to bring the aesthetic vision of Sankardeva complementary or supportive to his social vision. Thus what I believe, the subtleity in integrating the philosophy of the faith that he propounded with aesthetic modes of all arts - literary, visual and performing - and a deeper social conviction that Sankardeva demonstrated all through his life is a rare phenomenon in Indian history.

Que: Tell us something about your conception of the responsibility of intellectuals in difficult contemporary period.

Ans: Although it should be, I am not in the disciplined way of charting a work plan for the future. Often I respond to the needs and demands of the time as well as invitations from various institutions as much as I can. However, I am working on writing two other books on Sankardeva - in English and Assamese, and another book on the life and works of Dr. Birendra Kumar Bhattacharyya. I have also a long cherished dream of writing a book on Sattriya Dance in English incorporating a historical outline of its evolution and development as an intitutionalized form of performance at ritual space and the margi-desi dynamics inherent in this iconic tradition of Assam.

Que: Kindly tell us about your ongoing projects and future plans as a writer.

Ans:Left me to speak, I do not consider intellectuals a class apart. As a conscious citizen of this vast and great country having a multiple cultural setting, everybody has a right as well as an obligation not alone to respond to difficult situations but also to contribute towards amelioration of crises that the nation is facing. The literati has even a greater responsibility in sensitizing the public mind towards evolving a way out in any critical moment in the nation's life. The democratic ethos of the nation and its polity should always and at all cost be respected and preserved.

Chapter - 9
Soumyadip Datta

INTRODUCTION

Soumyadip Datta is not merely and ecological and bio-diversity preserver, he is also a lone crusader in the field of preserving forests, trees and animals. He has given birth to many NGO's that take care of his mission. He is also interested in Buddha and Buddhism and has penned a lot of books on this particular field. His book "Nam chankor anteshpur" was a milestone which got him critical acclaim. His book titled "Axomot Buddha Kirat" has shed new light on this unknown aspect. His work on Patkai civilization is unique. He is an untiring and dynamic personality. In the following interview with Subhajit Bhadra he shares ideas on himself, man, nature, forests and animals.

CONVERSATION

Question: You are basically an ecological conservationist. when and how were you attracted to the domain?

Answer: Basically I am a natural conversationalist. I got attracted to this domain when I was in class V and VI. My father was my inspiration.

Que: What is the difference in the modus operandi of Eastern and western environmentalists?

Ans: Actually whatever we talk about animal and natural conversation stem from our Indian tradition and I believe in this Indian tradition. We need not learn anything about animal and forest conversation from anywhere else. We have this tradition starting from Vaidik era continuing till the Buddhist period, roughly 2500 years ago. Our ecological concern goes back to that period. During that time emphasis was put on natural preservation and forest preservation. Chandragupta Mourya planted the seeds of trees about 2,000 years ago. He planted trees on both sides of roads and pavements. We had a concept of 'Avayaranya' in our vaidic era which, later on, was, denominated as "sanctuary" by the entire world. The trend of animal preservation is a pan Indian tradition. In Indian ecological system we have the concept of "absolute love" for animals and forest. From Europe we can only see or learn the concept of "give and take" I am pointing towards economic conservation of forest and animals. But it is not merely related to the financial aspect. Our relation with forests and animals is the relation of mother and child. Just like a mother takes care of her babies, they also have the moral responsibility to look after her. And we are doing exactly this.

Que: What are the recent environmental issues towards which you are concentrating upon?

Ans: The specific areas where I am working upon are conservation of forest and forest biodiversity. Actually many people think that if we plant many seeds of trees then we can create forests. It is a commendable concept but we cannot create natural forest. If natural forest is destroyed once somehow then we cannot retrieve it. That is why the challenge before us is to preserve natural and virgin forests. If natural forest is preserved then thousands of plants thousands of trees, thousands of mammals will be protected. Entire biodiversity will be protected. That is why emphasis should be put on virgin forests.

Que: You have written about Patkai civilization? How did you get attracted to this domain?

Ans: Its a good question. We roam around Dihing and Patkai region. When I started the movement of preserving Patkai region conservation then we came into intimate contact with the indigenous people of there. Year after year I interacted with them, stayed with them, ate with them, roamed with them. Then only I formed my opinion about them and my wife, who happens to be an anthropologist also helped me. But Patkai as a civilization has not been recognized. You will not find any material on Patkai as a civilization. The inhabitants of Patkai were looked upon as brutes and uncivilized. There have been studies on them but not as a civilization and they have not got their due. The basic inspiration I got was from indigenous people of Patkai.

Que: What do you think about garbage dumping in Chandrapur?

Ans: I am hearing a lot of debate about this issue. There has been dumping on Chandrapur. When garbage was damped on dipor bil I protested as it should be kept free. But it is also true that garbage should have to be damped somewhere and it will be possible if only the issue is scientifically managed. The view regarding Chandrapur is that ultimate opinion will have to be given by the people of Chandrapur itself. The inhabitants of Chandpur should be asked if they have any objection regarding the dumping. These people are nationalists, they understand the whole issue and if only they agree then the dumping mission should go on.

Que: You have written extensively about Buddha and Buddhisim in Assam? How did this idea come to you mind?

Ans: Actually Buddha is Indian. It anybody has respect for Indian culture and civilization then he or she would have respect for Buddha also. Buddha is not merely a preacher of religion. He is also a naturalist and conservationist. I was drawn towards Buddha's teaching since my childhood. Later on when I started writing articles and books on Buddha then readers came to realize that I have interest and curiosity on Buddha. I used to hear a lot about Buddha from my grandmother in my childhood. Later on I took interest in the issue in tibet and met the Holy Dalai Lama a number of times.

Que: In your writing we basically find painstaking research and that is why your books become authentic. Kindly tell us something about this aspect.

Ans: Basically I started to write to strengthen conservation process and environmental preservation is Assam. When I started this venture, there were few rivals. About nature only poems, songs and novels were written regarding "nature" but there was no powerful writing on ecological and animal preservation. My writings are always judged by my readers. That's why I always bow down in respect to my readers. Readers purchase my books. I get a percentage of money from publisher for the selling of my books. I am also grateful to my publishers. But if my readers would not have published my books, then no publisher would have published my book. And the question that you have asked me I leave it for my readers to consider.

     Delving Into Different Literary Terrains

Chapter - 10
Tapan Das

INTRODUCTION

In the cultural horizon of Assam, Tapan Das doesnot require any introduction. He is a brilliant actor of cinema. His cinematic performances have earned him praise and popularity from viewers and critical acclaim from serious cine-critics. He shifted his gear to the domain of mobile commercial theater and he has carved a niche for himself in this domain. True art lies in concealing art and Tapan Das excels in this art. Later, he moved to the domain of short stories which are funny and serious at the same time, ludicrous and intellectually stimulating at the same time.

CONVERSATION

Question: You are an excellent actor. When and how were you drawn to this field?

Answer: In my childhood my father had to move to different places for his transferable job. Thus when I was a child I had exposure to Theater, Jatra (an indigenous from), Opera, Circus, Music show and other such ventures. Seeing this I had the fascination and tendency to perform myself. It happens in case of most of the children. The situation became so when we were in Bilashipara itself. I was then six or seven years old. After that I had to stand on the dais and recite poetry at the age of eight. After that in school we started one act plays. The seeds were swoon at the school itself. Most of the children and adolescents undergo such experience. I got the praise from spectators. My enthusiasm rose. I continued, did not leave and hence my courage grew.

Que: Right now you are more comfortable in theatre. Why?

Ans: This is for livelihood. Commercial theater means mobile theater. I did not venture into this realm for pleasure. Neither did I joined for aesthetic or technical pleasure; I also did not want to do experiments. This is just livelihood or profession to earn bread and butter. Actually I am not comfortable in any fixed domain. Acting is a craft for me and it is a matter of extreme pain. In this sojourn there is pain and melancholy, but there is also enough space for release.

Que: Do you think that Assamese cinema and theatre are capable of competing with the best of Indian cinema or drama?

Ans: Assamese cinema has reached the heights of national cinema though the number is lesser. It has even reached international standard. Example is not required. And theater is also moving ahead gradually. Theater of Assam has also reached to the national standard. Some attractive and mesmerizing performances have been delivered. But in order to comprehensibly reach to the international standard it requires a syncretic and combined effort from play wrights, producers, actors, necessary budget etc. But it is completely my personal opinion. Even in the midst of such crisis a number of play groups, actors, and workers have been able to put up good show by fighting the hostile situations. In this way Baharul Bhagirathi's Seagul, Robijit Gogoi's jirsung, Anup Pakiraj's Bah, Gunakar Dev Goswami Himansu Prasad Das, Vinod Sarma, Niranjan Bhuyan, Manik Roy, Pabitra Rabha and others have done a commendable job. We have been busy with commercial theater for the last few years. That is why many group names or personal names might have been missing due to my ignorance. For this I seek forgiveness.

Que: Very few people know that you are an excellent short story writer. Kindly tell us about your literary journey.

Ans: I feel a sense of discomfort to declare myself as a writer. I tried to write those sorts of writings which I most enjoyed in my school days. When those writings were published I felt happiness when I got remuneration I felt twice glad. Most of those writings were ghost writings, adventures, thrillers and detective tales. Thus I started writing initially in the school magazines and after that the writings were published in the recreational magazines like Bishmoy, Kuwali, Rahashya, Atanka, Shiharan, etc. I got pleasure in the matter and that is why I wrote. I did not write for the demand of the readers or for the sake of only getting readership. I did those on my mind. After writing I put these in envelope, put post office ticket and sent these to the magazines. With that I attached a letter to the editors and asked them to publish my items only if they were up to the mark. Actually it was a hobby or favorite pleasure. During leisure time if something clicked in the mind, I penned it down. And then one day I stopped writing these abruptly.

Que: You have always experimented with the theme and technique of your stories. Please shed light on that.

Ans: Afterwards I took pen again in my hands due to the enthusiasm and response I got from people like cinema critic Utpal Datta, Shashi Phukan, Gunjan Phukan, Debabrata Das and a few others. But this time not purely mystery stories, but something different. Some small incidents crowded in the mind. I tried to give that thinking a shape which was pleasant. There was no serious intention behind that. It was just fun. Thus when I am called a writer I suffer from a sense of hesitation. But afterwards due to the praise from Prashanta Kumar Das, Imran Husain and others I again stated to write a few serious stories.

Que: Who are your favorite writers and actors.

Ans: I am a very ordinary reader. I, in fact, do not dare to go near any world famous serious book. I like the writings of Saurav Kumar Chaliha, Shilabhadra, Bhabendra Nath Saikia, Sunil Ganguly, Shirshendu Mukharjee, Abul Bashar, Mahim Bora, Arupa Patangia kalita, Anuradha Sarma Pujari, Prashanta Kumar Das, Mrinal Kalita, Monoj Kumar Goswami, Atanu Bhattacharjee and Imran Hussain . but this would be a long list. I also like the writings of Mrinal Talukdar, Soumadip Dutta, Arnab Saikia and Deben Dutta.

But it is difficult to talk about actors. It is actually a medium of directors and editors. Many weak actors have occasionally rendered splendid performance. Some weak actors have performed majestically under the guidance of brilliant directors. We know of many national and international movies like this. Still we think that it is difficult for a non-actor to perform splendidly always under such circumstances. Looked at from that angle in the context of Assam a few talented and trained actors have acted well and have earned international fame, amongst which two names I would like to take and they are Adil Hussain and Seema Biswas. Their acting is stupendous. After that I am reminded of Bishnu Khargaria who has also provided acting of international standard.

My Life My Writing Says Nagen Saikia

INTRODUCTION

Charles Lamb, better known as an esajist, went back to his childhood to say In my days of childhood, in my joyfull school days mates play I have had my pleymates, I have had companions,

All are gone, the old familiar feces. So to me now at this age of mine.

I was born on 11 February, 1939 in a village, named Hatiakhuwa at a distance about ten kilometers from the Golaghat town, now the district Head quarter. Our joint family was a lower middle class agriculturist family and my father Umaram Saikia was the first to be qualified a matrienlate of the Calcatta University.

There are tea gardens in the surrounding areas. My father joined as an assistant in the office of the Borkathoni tea Estate. But, as there was no school to teach English as a subject within an area of about ten Kilometers radius, he lift the Tea garden job and opened a Middle English school in the village road side under the name Borkathoni M. E. School and appointed two other teachers to assist him.

We came out of the joint family and my father built a house of his own next to his brothers. We had enough landed property and all the agricultural land was allowed to be cultivated by others on conditions agreeable. Therefore, I did not get the opportunity of ploughing or working in the cultivable fields.

Everyone has got a time-frame of one's life. I am also living within time-frame, the end of which is not known to me. " Who knows the world may end tonight! I can't cross that unknown limit. But my writings, however insignificant they may be, have no demarcated time frame as such in comparison to my life.

Of course time is infinite. Nobody knows what is time. It has got no beginning, neither middle, nor end. But not only the human life, the whole universe has got its beginning, middle and end. We live in this limited time-frame. But the human mind dose not live within this limitation. It crosses the border of life. Since time immemorial the human mind has been expanding in such a way that it has been continuously covering new areas keeping its earlier areas intact. It has been carrying of its physical and mental experiences, and its thought and feeling and imaginations with it, through the ages. Even existing in a temporal and transitory body in a limited time-frame, it possesses a universal character of unlimited time. So, the human mind, though it works within a physique of an individual in a limited time-frame, Is partially filled with the universality of human mind. From this point of view, it is limited, and at the same time unlimited, in its own individual character. A writer, however small or big he\ she may be works within the time-frame of his\her life with a 'timeless time frame' of universal human mind. He\she writes on the basis of the working of his\ her own mind.

I am a humble writer holding on to the rim of a circle accommodating the noble writers. Even then I feel, my mind works beyond the physical reality of my life and experience.

Let me look back to my life. My father owned a middle English school, and it was the only school of the kind within the radius of ten to fifteen kilometers. I was born in 1939 in a village in Assam in a lower-middle-class agriculturist family. People of my village are of the so called higher caste of the Hindus, next to the Brahmins; and all of them are followers of the Vaishnava religion propagated by Sankaradeva (1449-1568), the great saint-poet- artist-philosopher of medieval Assam, nay of medieval India. So, I grew up in an atmosphere governed by the spiritual, moral, social and cultural values generated by the neo-Vaishnavite movement which is still at work in Assamese society. I had the opportunity of going through and listening to the poetical and musical work and of the theatrical works of Sankaradeva and Madhavadeva, and also of other writers of the age. The Namghosha of Madhavadeva put indelible print in my mind. And he is one of the three most favourite poets of mine, the other two being kahalil Gibran and Jibanananda Das.

My father maintained a home library besides his school library. He brought both Assamese and Bengali books by placing postal orders. Along with the ordered books the Calcutta publishers sent free-gift books life Sishu Bodhok, Barnoparichoy, Kavitahar, Aguner Parashmoni, Thakumar Juli, Swami- Srreer Gopan Katha etc. In the absence of my father I even went through the books prohibited for children.

I also had the opportunity of going through Assamese translations of the novels of Bankimchandra and Saratchandra, published by Chapala Book Stall of Shillong. The Assamese novels of Lakshminath Bezbaroa, Dandinath Kalita, Padmanath Gohain Barua and Rajanikanta Bordoloi also become a feast for me in my early school days. I think, then I was a boy of ten-eleven years. It was quite natural for a boy of that age not to be able to grasp the essence of the writings; but the boy tried to eat the stories ravenously.

I now recollect three events that contributed in moulding my thoughts. The first was the Second World War, and I was just a little child at that time. But even than I saw American and Negro soldiers, digging trenche in the football filed of the village and heard the irritating sound of the fighter planes flew over the sky. Secondly, the non-cooperation movement, launched by Gandhiji also reached its peak at that time. The Congrees volunteers singing the glories of Bharat Mata and Gandhiji sometimes passed through our village. The third was the CPI movement that was banned after Independence. Two CPI activists, college mates of an older brother of our family, came to our home also, and I could gather some vague ideas about the communist movement form the cyclostyled bulletins that they left with us. That they wanted all men to be equal in economic and social status appealed unconsciously to me and I tried to write the first story of my life which had not come to light under the title Sombarar Deutak (Somber's Father) on the hard life of Bhaiyai, father of Sombar, who was engaged as an agricultural labourer by an elder brother of my father. That was the beginning.

I had also the opportunity of going through the poetical works of Chandra Kumar Agarwalla, Lakshminath Bezbaroa, Chandradhar Barua, Dandinath Kalita, Binandachandra Barua, Sailadhar Rajkhua and others. The rhythm of Binandra Chandra Baru's and Sailadhar Rajkhowa's poems an the humorous vein of Dandinath Kalita and Chandradhar Barua's poem attracted me much. The dramatic pieces of Alexandar and the Dasyu, the drama of Ganesh Gogoi and Atulchandra Hazarika, also made some place in my sensitive adolescent mind.

That cosmic-human-social self accompanied me visibly though the early collections Kuber Hati Barua, Chabi Aru Frame and Matir Chakir jui. Their literary excellence apart, the self and the consciousness were consistent and they have not deserted me yet.

Gradually my self delved into a deep source of pain and I imagined myself an agent that delivers that pain, that human suffering. I know not how far I have communicated it, but I had to look for new form—I tried Galpangkika combining the short-story with the one-act play patng away all grammatical signs to approximate the inner workings of the mind with the mode of expression. The critics thought that I was experimenting with the forms of Virginia Woolf. Kafka and James Joyce. I am acquainted to some extent with great modern writers, but I do not think they influenced me at all. I had to announce in a foreword to Astitvar Sikali (Chain of Existence) that I was not writing short-stories to experiment with a form.

I believe there is a poet in each writer and artist and indeed in all men. Emotional understanding of this poet is at the source of all creations. I cannot write without it and neither can I read those written without it. I do not have any target audience at the time of writing My first self writes to record the emotional understanding and my second self watches out. I believe in this dual self in each writer—like the existence of the two birds— Suparna and Sajuja, In the case of a writer one watches out while the other creates.

I feel that the creative self is egoistic. It stands no criticism; the second self sobers it. I fight with the first self, sometime to win and at other times to lose the battle.

A sense of pain may have acquired an extra dimension in my latest short stories without myself being fully aware of it. Have they? They may have. It has almost become an obsession and deep source of pain in me that I will have to pass away from the world full of hopes and this bodily existence of flesh and blood. I have been painfully aware of my non-existence in a mighty universe. Looking for a new form to communicate this feeling, I have been writing 'Mitabhash' without the 'objective correlative' of the situation, character or events. I call it 'Short Expression' in English. I communicate very briefly in prose with an image; and call it 'Mita-Bhash'. Some people have asked me to find an alternative to 'Short Expression', but a father's affection is a constant quantity free from the name given, Let 'Short Expression' remain so.

My short stories Silpir Chakulu (Sorrows of an Artist) written and published during my school days, began with sorrow. That approach stands vindicated now that I feel that the sorrows of life are a constant quantity. We encounter it, get scared and try to escape into the rush and hectic activities of the world of flux and change.

The self of an individual is dual. Family, society and the world are related to the outher self; the other self is confined exclusively to the world that belongs to him only. The writer in the world of the mind is all alone. Each writer carries within him an inner silence and loneliness. The jostling crowd cannot break in upon the loneliness and noise its silence.

I feel love is accompanied by pain. Life is so brief that one cannot help loving it, but the thought that it slips away gives you immense pain. In many of my short stories I talk to myself and interface with myself. I make no complaint even if they are not accepted as short stories. My 'Mita-Bhash' may be kept aside. I do not grumble. I know I am very much present in them. Moreover, I also know the readers of the same mental wavelength can only appreciate the work of a writer. Therefore, why should I expect that everybody would like my short stories and 'Mita-Bhash'?

Though the ultimate test of literature is aesthetic expression of the sui generic, it is firmly rooted to time, place and tradition. Globalization cannot break down barriers that differentiate attitude to an acceptance of life peculiar to to climatic conditions in different countries. What is sui generis in national literature comes out through distinctive national features.

Lovelessness and hatred do not buttress any art and literature. Belching out poison and hatred against a class in a class society also cannot create anything abiding. The class enemy is also a man and a writer is prompted by love. I love man and see the best beauty in men also. Through my life I can feel the life of others. My life has a smell of its own, a taste of its own, a frame of its own. I feel the life of others through my life.

In my Short Story collection Andharat Nijar Mukh is a selected collection of four stages of my own development of Short Story. In the first stage I may be without knowingly I tried to portray the characters with their inner small conflict. Then at one time I to some extent became concerned to the class differences in the society. My second collection "Chabi Aru Frame" contains a few stories of the kind. At the same time gradually my mind become more sympathetic to the 'man' within the man. In the third stage I think I, without nullifying my previous stages I tried to vitualise the 'man' in its broader perspective of the totality of the man and the Universe. And in my last stage I have tried to feel the inner man through myself. I do not know how much I could succeed.

When I go through a creative work, if I feel that it dose not carry an inner poetic feeling in its base rather it carries the ariter's statement about something. I feel bored. I believe in every work of creative Art the feeling of the artist tries to express itself with the help of some subject matter. Even a thought also is to be transformed to a deep feeling. I do not take myself to be a critic but to some extent a reader in search of aesthetic joy. Of course in some cases I am to play the role of a critic which my profession demands.

The aim of the 'History of the Assamese' is people to find out the genesis of the growth and development of the Assamese Nationality touching all prob able aspects without being biased.

I love my state at first with my mother tongue, culture its natural beauty with hills and rivers, its greenery with varities of trees and creepers, then I love my country which possesses its manyfold heritage of philosophy and scientific outlook towards life and the Universe, its languages and cultures, and the humanity at large. I belive Gandhijis view that India is one in many and many in one. In spite of so many verities the Indians share the same values of life and the same outlook towards life and the Universe.

Love for my language since my childhood drew my attraction to Asam Sahitya Sabha. In 1954 I first had the privilege of withnessing the session of the Sabha at garhat presided by the famous poet Nalinibala Devi. I remember of the faces of the great writers of Assam of the time. In 1959, I with my friends formed a branch of the sahitya Sabha in our village. Since then I attended the sessions as a delegate. In 1966 I was selected to be the Assistant Secretary attached to the central office of the Sabha at gorhat to In 1972, I left the D.C.B College of Jorhat and joined Dibrugarh University In 1973 I was elected General Secretary of the Sabha and it was the time I tried to expand the activities with new planes and projects In 1997 and 1998 I was elected the President of the Sabha for two terms. Now, Of course I maintain a distance from organizational work.

In 1985 I joined the RjyaSabha and had the opportunity to witness the Parliamentary Democracy of our country from inside and to take part in it. I was also selected to be in the panel of the Vice Chairman of the Rajya Sabha.

AS a reader I have been always trying to be acquainted with the great writers though the numbers is not a big one. Of Course some of the western writers of England, France, America have put indelible marks in my mind. English is the only medium for me to go near to the Frence writers of importance.

In case of Indian writers the English and the Bangali language both I undustand to taste translated and original works. Of course many books have been translated in to Assamese also. Whenever for nothing I feel lonely and sad I take out from the almiral as mentioned above.

At this age of mine I cannot dream of taking big projects. But even then a book on Lakshminath Bezbaroa, a book on Aesthetios, both in Assamese ect. Contemporary Assamese Literature is taking new avenues in poetry, short story and novel also. Woman writers are prominently coming ahead not only in numbers even sometimes in quality also. The numbers even sometimes in quality also. The number of poets is bigger in the case of 'man writers'. I foresee good days of Assamese literature in near future.

CONVERSATION

1. Question : Tell us about your childhood and upbringing.

Answer: I consider myself to be fortunate to be born and brought up in a mufussil town Raha, in the Nagaon district of Assam, where my father worked. Within the periphery of 3-5 kms of the town history was and is still vivid. As a child I walked through the Raha chowki – a post established by Ahom kings, walked by the side of Singh Gaon – a village of Assamese Sikhs and had afternoon walks on the ridges of Jongal Balahu Garh. I heard the stories of those places and the people and never realised till I grew up what a great impact on me was there due to historicity attached to those places and the people.

My primary education was in a Balika School, where most of the students were balak (boys). It was not far from the Basic Center for training women for primary education. I visited the center often with my sisters – two of whom were trainees in that center - and attended and participated in the cultural programmes there. Visiting the secured hostel widened my mental horizon in those formative years of life as I met Bodo, Kachari, Naga, Khasi Jayantiya, Garo and sisters from other communities of Assam at one place. Most of them were fair complexioned with chubby faces and communicate with broken but lovely Assamese words uttered with unfathomable sweetness that still rings in my ears. They presented songs and cultural dances with their colourful attires on. I was also encouraged to take part in the various cultural functions in singing, dancing and acting.

All – the trainees, students, instructors and teachers – were introduced to Gandhian ideals in the center by two Wardha trained teachers and had to participate in Sutra Jajnya – a programme of spinning thread from cotton with a spinning wheel.

After my father's retirement, our family left Raha and moved to our ancestral village near Nagaon town. By then I was nine years old and was privileged once again to see the village life from a close quarter till I graduated.

These exposures of my early life helped immensely in my writings.

2. Question : Living away from Assam , what was the experience.

Answer: I left Assam for my job, but Assam did not leave me. I carried its memories, language and culture. Staying in the hill station like Aizawl gave me a chance to ponder over my experiences of my childhood and youth. I worked in an Institution, where I met people from all parts of the country and from all kinds of social and religious backgrounds. My experiences gave me the realisation that we ought to learn something or the other from all of them including the local Mizo people. Tlawmngaihna – though a Mizo word, but a concept associated with the culture of self sacrifice for others, that cannot be translated into English - is unique.

3. Question : You lived and saw troubled time in Mizoram. Tell us about that.

Answer: The 'troubled time' for security and administration was peaceful to me. I did not hear or see any problem faced by any doctor or a teacher.

4. Question : Tell us about your intellectual and creative world.

Answer: I do not have the luxury to call myself intellectual. Of course, as I said, staying in a hill station like Aizawl gave me a chance to ponder over my experiences that I gathered over the years and found some to be delightful. My imaginations moulded the experiences and came up with themes to share my happiness and sorrow with my readers through my writings. I live momentarily with my characters at different places in my creative world to dispel boredom.

5. Question : Tell us about your novels and their genesis.

Answer: My first novel Diktawn was on the Mizo society and its people. I was impressed

to see them realising quickly that they are more secured with a great nation like India and

within twenty years of armed struggle they came to terms with the Government – surrendered - mingled with common men - work together and even formed government to serve people. When one reads their stories of the last one century one will be impressed to see how dynamic the people are and how fast were the paces of development. Through Diktawn I made an attempt to depict the advent of Christianity to the region, the decaying role of the Chiefs due to abolition of Chieftainship, changing of food habits, life style, dress code and even vocabulary due to their interaction first with the British and then with the army personnel. The novel has been translated into English as The Highlanders.

I wrote novels on such subjects of social transitions of Assamese society as well through Kolong Paror Itikotha, Unmilito Upoon and others.

My decision to stay in Aizawl came supportive when I read on the lives of Christian missionaries and the difficulties they faced leaving behind the comforts of their motherlands. That prompted me to write Udbhasito Upokul on the lives of Nathan Brown and Miles Bronson, who worked in Assam in adverse situation of the second quarter of the nineteenth century relentlessly to protect the Assamese society.

My frequent journey by train and bus through Barak valley gave me an opportunity to see and hear the plights of the displaced people from the erstwhile East Pakistan. Some of them are so pathetic that those touched my heart. Many of them had to leave the one time cultural center of Bengal. But political situation forced other communities also to leave their ancestral land and it had great impact on the NE region – particularly Assam. This is the genesis of Upotyakar Pora Upotyakaloi and is translated into English as From Valley to Valley. Its Bengali translation is Sthanantar.

After reformation and openness in USSR, in 1989, a particular case of Tolstoyans staging resistance to Stalin's forceful occupation of lands from farmers by means of Gandhian ideals of non-violence came to light in an archive in St Petersburg. This was published in The Assam Tribune in 1997. As I was influenced by Gandhian ideals at an early stage, going through the story as reported in the newspaper, moved me greatly. So, I wrote Mahanogoror Najon Nibashi. It was all about the nine Tolstoyan's love for Tolstoy, Gandhi and Gandhian principle of non-violence, by adopting which they made an attempt to resist the government in 1932 and became victim of Stalin's government. The novel is my tribute to Gandhi on 150th years of his birth anniversary.

We live in a land far from the place where we were evolved millions of years ago. Over the years, in the process of migration, we came across 'surrogated' lands. That way we all are related and the whole world is our kin. The concept led me to write my novella Veronia Matri.

I have completed another novel on our great Indian cultural heritage based on certain events of 11-12th century.

     Delving Into Different Literary Terrains

These are the genesis of some of my novels.

6. Question : Do you see any difference between the writings of your generation and younger generation of Assamese writers.

Answer: Younger generation is more exposed to the different theories of literature and have the means to access anything at their finger tips. So definitely they have the opportunity to explore the world at a faster rate. Some of them are good and promising.

7. Question : Your works have been translated into English. As a creative writer what is your view about translation.

Answer: English translations of our works definitely help to cross the barrier and reach a greater audience – I mean, readership. That is how I see translation work effective and the process should be a movement.

My translator Mrs Gayatri Bhattacharyya did justice to my themes.

8. Question : Who are your favourite writers and why?

Answer: During my schooldays , I read some of the works of Thakazhi Sivsankar Pillai, Kalindi Charan Panigrahi, Khwaja Ahmad Abbas, Premchand, Rabindra Nath Tagore and many others, including novels of world literature in Assamese. With my limited readings, my international novelists Milan Kundera, Gabriel Garcia Marquez, Leo Tolstoy and Boris Pesternek had impressed me. Tagor's Gora, Kundera's The Joke, Marquez's One Hundred Years of Solitude, Tolstoy's Anna Karenina and Pesternek's Dr.Zhibhago are my favourite

novels. I liked the national authors because they depict a society I grew up in. I like the foreign authors because their novels expanded the horizon of my imaginations enormously.

Among my favourite novelists in Assamese Birendra Kumar Bhattacharya tops the list. His Iyaruingam impressed me so much so that while I was a student of class VII (1960) I wrote an essay on it as my favourite book , which I consider to be my most original work in those days, and kept that ready for my school examination. I liked the novel because it gave me the flavour, charm, excitement and a plot of a society different from that of ours and opened the window to a different imaginary world. I still consider Dr Bhattacharya to be the source of my inspiration to write novels.

My favourite short story writers and poets are not many, but the lists include Saurabh Kumar Chaliha and Hiren Bhattacharyya.

Ashok Bhowmick

Ashok bhowmick is recognised as a painter both in india and outside India. Many exhibitions of his paintings have received warm response from abroad and india. His paintings are natural and landscape oriented but he also experiments with various forms abstract painting. He is also a writer fiction and an art critic.

Q1.You are one of the major painters of our country. When and how were you drawn to the world of colour.

I was drawn to painting at a very early age and it was my mother who taught me the first lesson of drawing . My mother was a self taught artist and very fluent in sketching. I got attracted to the patterns she used to create in her stitchings and alpanas . While copying her, I was introduced to the world of lines and colour.

Q2. You just had an exhibition at Sidney. Tell us about the event in detail.

In fact in 2017, Mr Shahid Malik, the owner of the Gallery One62 invited me to participate in a group show in Sydney. Two of my works were on the display in this show and they attracted the attention of local art lovers. The gallery decided to have my one man show in early 2020 but because of the Covid restrictions the plan had to be postponed for December 2021. This year also everything was far from normal but it was the courage of Shahid Bhai who decided to mount my show. 31 of my works were included in the show and Mr Shahid took all care to mount them beautifully in his gallery . Sydney has a large number of art loving population and those who visited my show amid the present situation , liked my work very much. Looking into the response of this show , Mr. Shahid has decided to have a big show of my paintings in December 2022 in his gallery.

Q3. How are you going to respond to your forthcoming painting exhibition in Karachi?

I had a major exhibition of my paintings at Hamail Art Gallery, Lahore in 2005. This show was a big success and coming back from Lahore I did not look back . The Lahore show was attended by many art lovers from Karachi and many newspapers and magazines carried reviews of my show. So, I am not a stranger to a large number of art lovers of Karachi and Lahore . When Mr Shahid decided to exhibit my work in his Karachi gallery, I was naturally excited as I knew that my paintings would be well received there.

Q4.you are also an art critic. How do you feel about it?

Like any artist , be it a musician or a writer or an actor I also subject my paintings to an intense and constant analysis. This analysis is not always expressed in written words but an artist always evaluates his position among the fellow artists of his time and also looks back to the tradition which he belongs to. This is usually a silent process but in my case I decided to put these in words .I am critical about many aspects of Indian art and I think we talk too much while attempting to 'explain' our paintings . I believe that art can only progresses in a society where and artist is a dumb and a viewer deaf. History of our art is largely the history of illustrations that only tells you about gods and goddesses , kings and queens . This tradition still continues and an artist who can 'explain' the concept of his paintings and its social or historical contexts. Such explanations are always in a language that sounds philosophical, mystical and difficult . As Tagore said , a painting should be 'felt' and not 'understood' , I believe that in post-independence India art has been made a stuff that is very exclusive and understandable only to the elites living in few metros only. Painting has been made a thing that moves in the hands of artists, art dealers and the buyers or investors, where an art lover without enough money has no role . As a result of this, today art is no longer a priority for a large section of society.

You may call me an art critic but I write, because I disagree with this trend. I believe that in deciding the merits of a work of art , the verdict of a common art lover should be considered as of ultimate importance as the choice of the investors and buyers are quite often driven by greed for profits only . For a common art lover while a painting is an artistic creation, for the market it is just a 'commodity'.

Q5. You have written both fiction and nonfiction. Kindly tell us about your experience as a writer.

Yes , I have good numbers of fiction and non-fiction to my credit but I do not write for any pleasure or prize . For me writing is a mission to question the things that are not good in society and also in the art. I have also written on the life and works of Zainul Abedin, Chittoprasad, Debabrat Mukhopadhyay , Sadequain, Kamrul Hasan and many such artists who did not get what they deserved.

Q6. What is your perspective about the prospect of painting in India keeping in mind the global context.

It is a very serious question and disturbing as well. In an effort to promote Indian art the government did founded many academies and cultural bodies neither with a clear understanding about the people nor about the art . Further this was allowed to be controlled by politicians and cadres of administrative services. The executives of the cultural department and those who were assigned to head these organisations exercised their personal likings or dislikings in promoting art and eventually this shaped the distorted face of present day India art . Today, there is nothing which can be called Indian art, instead it is Bengal art , Bihar art , Delhi art , Mumbai art etc. In managing our folk art too, they tried and succeeded in limiting folk art forms such as Madhubani for Bihar , Gond for Madhya Pradesh, Warli for Maharashtra etc. While discussing art we always refer to our illustrious past and attempt to revive it or draw inspiration from the same and we draw a strange pleasure in claiming Indian art tradition as the oldest thus best one which is far more superior than art tradition of other countries. Painting as an art form exists and grows only when we rise above the limitations and narrowness of nationalism . As an artist or art lover when we talk about Picasso or Van Gogh we don't consider their nationalities but in India we talk about Bengali, Assamese , Bihari artists . With such regional consideration in practice it is even more difficult to claim our entry into the global art scene .

Further , a large number of our recognised and famous artists proved themselves in the hands of the market and to meet the market demand they simply repeated themselves and thus making 'repetition' as the single most distinguishable aspect of Modern Indian Art . If a horse was in demand the artists painted a thousand horses and if a 'Bindu' was in demand thousand paintings on 'Bindu' were created . In India , only repetition can guarantee the survival and success of an artist whereas repetition is not considered creative elsewhere .

Unfortunately, the rest of the world may appreciate Indian art for its historic or archaeological values ; modern Indian art still remains far from being worth noticing .

Interview Of Jitumoni Bora

Q1. Kindly let us know about your childhood and upbringing.

A. I was born in a small village called Deuri Goan approximately two and half km from Tezpur Town , as a result I found the atmosphere of the both the town and village life.Our childhood was golden. We went to the jungle to play hide and seek and come back tired to lie down on my grandma's lap and doze if listing to her stories . Our childhood was diverse and rich with experience . The stories of childhood burglary that we now read in the pages of novels were realities in our childhood.

I was born in an educated family and did my initial studies under the guidance of my parents . We had a legacy of teaching in our family . My grandfather late Manik Bora was a popular school teacher and a Gayan of Namghar. My father and my uncle were also teachers .The name of my village has a history associated with it. A large number of people from our village were involved as deouri bilaniyas of the historic Bhairavi temple located in Tezpur and there is. Even today the main priest of Bhairavi temple is from our village. From Deori Bilania, They day the name of our village became Deouri Gaon because of this lineage .

Q2. You are basically a creative writer. What prompted you to become a creative writer.

A. I have been finding peace of mind through creative writing even though journalism is my life and livelihood. My first book was on travelling "Themsor Parot . People appreciated the book . Earlier I wrote the story of the popular full length Assamese film 'Surjasta'. I then wrote 'Sesh Pristha', which is a result of the belief in me of friends and well wishers.

Generally away from the mathematics and grammar of writing novels, 'Sesh Pristha', 'Chiyahir Rong', I have written 'Bikul' and 'Janani'. In this case Dr. Lakshminandan Bora wrote that literature does not change if it is within certain mathematics and ranges. To create a new trend in literature, it is away from traditional ideas and genres. Experiments should be done. He brought this reference to the paper by praising the 'Sesh Pristha' and 'Chiyahir Rong'. I wrote novels in my own way away from the traditional genre.

If katha kabita, mitabhash can be created in Assamese literature, my novel can be a new genre of literature written independently by cutting a little away from some traditional ideas. I have written the novels in my way. Apart from this, two travel stories and three political books published are the result of my social responsibility.

Some stories and events in the society make me hurt. In my view, these extraordinary stories constantly haunt me. The tranquility that the mind gets after decorating these stories and making it a novel, that happiness is not comparable to anything. I have also tried to write down the important time that the recently written novel is lost from the political history of Assam in the form of novels. Things I have not got the medium to say but are important. I have tried to write those things as novels.

As my well wishers especially my social media followers, some of the new generation of young people of Assam are now interested in every book I am writing, The young people and College-Universities students' who want to know from me what I am writing. It has been inspiring me to write new books and novels. For these young people, I am 'Bikul', 'Janani', 'Chiyahir Rong' just as I have written 'Sesh Pristha', Ihave also written a political book titled 'Moi Asomiya Hoiyei Thakim' with a assamesemind. The new generation of Assamese literature and the young generation associated with assamese life are the first and main source of my inspiration.

Q3. You have written about yellow journalism. Please shed light on this aspect.

A. Dr. Hiren Gohain once wrote a sentence while presenting me the book 'Asom Andolan Pratisruti aru Falasruti' edited by him. The sentence was a writer should never deviate from this sentence, Careful about that. The wise man said that journalists should play the role of opponents in democracy. What role has a soldier journalist like us been playing in this regard? The people of Assam have seen.

Recently, there has been a buzz about yellow journalism across the country. One of my novels, 'Chiyahir Rong', challenging yellow journalism, has already been published. This novel has also been filmed by Pradyut Kumar Deka. I was arrested and imprisoned in 1997 for taking up a pen against corruption and certain government works. We have that experience.

In 'Chiyahir Rong', We try to keep the time of assam's media world tied up. This novel is an visitor to my journalist life and founder editor of the

'Dainik Asom', late Kirtinath Hazarika. I have also raised a huge reaction among the younger generation as a result of Indian journalism. There is no dearth of journalists who have given their lives in India because of the tradition of good journalism against allegations that an editor like a public relations officer of the government is working.

Q4. You have written about the period of Assam agitation in Bikul. Kindly tell us about the genesis of this novel.

A. Assam movement is a turning point in the social and political life of Assam. This movement was discussed all over the world. The movement which saw 855 martyrs and thousands of Assamese turned around for life. This movement changed the political landscape of Assam. Signing of Assam Accord, Illegal foreign expulsion slipped into power and a new regional party AGPdid not fully meet. There was no change in the lives of Assamese people. Instead, there were new challenges in the lives of Assamese people. The result of Assam Movement became a huge void. Illegal foreign nationals have not been expelled. The death of 855 people, the loss of an academic year and the cheating of Assamese people again after the agitating leader sat in power can be termed as an accident in Assam history.

Many books have been published about the Assam movement. I had not read any such book or novel before Writing 'Bikul'. My mother Mrs. Binu Bora was an active activist of the Assam movement. We were students of the lower class of high school at that time. Mother saw her getting up early in the morning to agitate, being beaten up by the police, imprisoned. Every person in my village was involved in the Assam Movement. On the day of the signing of the Assam Accord, Village People took out a procession on the streets of the village by playing dhol-khol, barkanh.

It can only be felt how much joy the people of Assam enjoyed! From 1979 to 2019, from the day the Assam Movement started, the Assamese people, from the day the Assam movement started, to the anti-CAB movement, the leadership has cheated even after being involved in the larger interests of the nation in every mass struggle. 'Bikul' not the history of the Assam Movement. My mother and I have many such characters, The 'Bikul' leaves that exist. The story of the struggle for the rights of Assamese people and the cheating of Assamese people is the main seed of 'Bikul'.

Q5. Your latest novel Janani has also become a successful novel. How did you formulate the seed of this novel.

A. 'Janani' started from where 'Bikul' ended. Assamese people protested against the attempt to impose a special law, That is the basis of 'Janani'. 'Janani' is a social and political novel. Critics have commented that the idea of the kind that comes to our mind when called a novel is broken in 'Bikul' and 'Janani'. However, new versions of these novels would have been published but for the pandemic it has got delayed .

Contrary to the struggle to protect the rights of Assamese people and the supreme sacrifice, the character of some Assamese politicians forced me to write 'Janani'. The novel is reported to be the most popular among the younger generation of Assam. This is an inspiration and blessing for me. Which made me interested in writing another novel.

Q6. Do you think that journalists are more socially attuned.

A. I have spent 29 years in active journalism. Am Still learning. Journalists are called the most ardent guard of society. Moreover, journalism exists because of a society. That's where We're involved in creative literature. As a journalist, I've always taken a position among people. I have sometimes taken people, especially the happiness and sorrow of the society around us, as a matter of news or reporting. Moreover, the journalist cannot be separated from the society. Journalists are also citizens. The collective movement of Assamese people will be my only goal and purpose of journalism. I considered it a matter of security of political leaders and the people who have become spokespersons of political leaders. Today's generation does not consider this type of journalists. Society wants journalists to be fully partners in the society

   DELVING INTO DIFFERENT LITERARY TERRAINS

Dipak Kumar Barkakati

QUESTIONS & ANSWERS

1. Question : Tell us about your childhood and upbringing.

Answer: I consider myself to be fortunate to be born and brought up in a mufussil town Raha, in the Nagaon district of Assam, where my father worked. Within the periphery of 3-5 kms of the town history was and is still vivid. As a child I walked through the Raha chowki – a post established by Ahom kings, walked by the side of Singh Gaon – a village of Assamese Sikhs and had afternoon walks on the ridges of Jongal BalahuGarh. I heard the stories of those places and the people and never realised till I grew up what a great impact on me was there due to historicity attached to those places and the people.

My primary education was in a Balika School, where most of the students were balak (boys). It was not far from the Basic Center for training women for primary education. I visited the center often with my sisters – two of whom were trainees in that center - and attended and participated in the cultural programmes there. Visiting the secured hostel widened my mental horizon in those formative years of life as I met Bodo, Kachari, Naga, Khasi Jayantiya, Garo and sisters from other communities of Assam at one place. Most of them were fair complexioned with chubby faces and communicate with broken but lovely Assamese words uttered with unfathomable sweetness that still rings in my ears. They presented songs and cultural dances with their colourful attires on. I was also encouraged to take part in the various cultural functions in singing, dancing and acting.

All – the trainees, students, instructors and teachers – were introduced to Gandhian ideals in the center by two Wardha trained teachers and had to participate in Sutra Jajnya – a programme of spinning thread from cotton with a spinning wheel.

After my father's retirement, our family left Raha and moved to our ancestral village near Nagaon town. By then I was nine years old and was privileged once again to see the village life from a close quarter till I graduated.

These exposures of my early life helped immensely in my writings.

2. Question : Living away from Assam , what was the experience.

Answer: I left Assam for my job, but Assam did not leave me. I carried its memories, language and culture. Staying in the hill station like Aizawl gave me a chance to ponder over my experiences of my childhood and youth. I worked in an Institution, where I met people from all parts of the country and from all kinds of social and religious backgrounds. My experiences gave me the realisation that we ought to learn something or the other from all of them including the local Mizo people. Tlawmngaihna – though a Mizo word, but a concept associated with the culture of self sacrifice for others, that cannot be translated into English - is unique.

3. Question : You lived and saw troubled time in Mizoram. Tell us about that.

Answer: The 'troubled time' for security and administration was peaceful to me. I did not hear or see any problem faced by any doctor or a teacher.

4. Question : Tell us about your intellectual and creative world.

Answer: I do not have the luxury to call myself intellectual. Of course, as I said, staying in a hill station like Aizawl gave me a chance to ponder over my experiencesthat I gathered over the years and found some to be delightful. My imaginations moulded the experiences and came up with themes to share my happiness and sorrow with my readers through my writings. I live momentarily with my characters at different places in my creative world to dispel boredom.

5.Question : Tell us about your novels and their genesis.

Answer: My first novel Diktawn was on the Mizo society and its people. I was impressed

to see them realising quickly that they are more secured with a great nation like India and

within twenty years of armed struggle they came to terms with the Government – surrendered-mingled with common men- work together and even formed government to serve people. When one reads their stories of the last one century one will be impressed to see how dynamic the people are and how fast were the paces of development. Through Diktawn I made an attempt to depict the advent of Christianity to the region, the decaying role of the Chiefs due to abolition of Chieftainship, changing of food habits, life style, dress code and even vocabulary due to their interaction first with the British and then with the army personnel. The novel has been translated into English as The Highlanders.

I wrote novels on such subjects of social transitions of Assamese society as well through Kolong Paror Itikotha, Unmilito Upoon and others.

My decision to stay in Aizawl came supportive when I read on the lives of Christian missionaries and the difficulties they faced leaving behind the comforts of their motherlands. That prompted me to write Udbhasito Upokul on the lives of Nathan Brown and Miles Bronson, who worked in Assam in adverse situation of the second quarter of the nineteenth century relentlessly to protect the Assamese society.

My frequent journey by train and bus through Barak valley gave me an opportunity to see and hear the plights of the displaced people from the erstwhile East Pakistan. Some of them are so pathetic that those touched my heart. Many of them had to leave the one time cultural center of Bengal. But political situation forced other communities also to leave their ancestral land and it had great impact on the NE region – particularly Assam. This is the genesis of Upotyakar Pora Upotyakaloi and is translated into English as From Valley to Valley. Its Bengali translation is Sthanantar.

After reformation and openness in USSR, in 1989, a particular case of Tolstoyans staging resistance to Stalin's forceful occupation of lands from farmers by means of Gandhian ideals of non-violence came to light in an archive in St Petersburg. This was published in The Assam Tribune in 1997. As I was influenced by Gandhian ideals at an early stage, going through the story as reported in the newspaper, moved me greatly. So, I wrote Mahanogoror Najon Nibashi. It was all about the nine Tolstoyan's love for Tolstoy, Gandhi and Gandhian principle of non-violence, by adopting which they made an attempt to resist the government in 1932 and became victim of Stalin's government. The novel is my tribute to Gandhi on 150th years of his birth anniversary.

We live in a land far from the place where we were evolved millions of years ago. Over the years, in the process of migration, we came across 'surrogated' lands. That way we all are related and the whole world is our kin. The concept led me to write my novella Veronia Matri.

I have completed another novel on our great Indian cultural heritage based on certain events of 11-12th century.

These are the genesis of some of my novels.

6. Question : Do you see any difference between the writings of your generation and younger generation of Assamese writers.

Answer: Younger generation is more exposed to the different theories of literature and have the means to access anything at their finger tips. So definitely they have the opportunity to explore the world at a faster rate. Some of them are good and promising.

7. Question : Your works have been translated into English. As a creative writer what is your view about translation.

Answer: English translations of our works definitely help to cross the barrier and reach a greater audience – I mean, readership. That is how I see translation work effective and the process should be a movement.

My translator Mrs Gayatri Bhattacharyya did justice to my themes.

8. Question : Who are your favourite writers and why?

Answer: During my schooldays , I read some of the works of Thakazhi Sivsankar Pillai, Kalindi Charan Panigrahi, Khwaja Ahmad Abbas, Premchand, Rabindra Nath Tagore and many others, including novels of world literature in Assamese. With my limited readings, my international novelists Milan Kundera, Gabriel Garcia Marquez, Leo Tolstoy andBoris Pesternek had impressed me. Tagor's Gora, Kundera's The Joke, Marquez's One Hundred Years ofSolitude,Tolstoy's Anna Karenina and Pesternek's Dr.Zhibhago are my favourite novels. I liked the national authors because they depict a society I grew up in. I like the foreign authors because their novels expanded the horizon of my imaginations enormously.

Among my favourite novelists in Assamese Birendra Kumar Bhattacharya tops the list. His Iyaruingam impressed me so much so that while I was a student of class VII (1960) I wrote an essay on it as my favourite book , which I consider to be my most original work in those days, and kept that ready for my school examination. I liked the novel because it gave me the flavour, charm, excitement and a plot of a society different from that of ours and opened the window to a different imaginary world. I still consider Dr Bhattacharya to be the source of my inspiration to write novels.

My favourite short story writers and poets are not many, but the lists include Saurabh Kumar Chaliha and Hiren Bhattacharyya

     Delving Into Different Literary Terrains

Interview Of Laxminandan Bora

1. Sir childhood is a very important phase in the life of an individual. Kindly tell us about your childhood.

2. Childhood is more important in the life of a creative writer. How would you recollect those experiences.

3. You must have gone through a different youth as a student and researcher. Kindly share your experiences.

4. You had an illustrious professional life in many academic institutions. Kindly tell us something about those days.

5. You also had a stint in abroad. Please tell us about that phase.

6. When how and under which circumstances you first responded to your creative call.

7. Your earlier short stories magically revealed the nuances of rural life in provincial dialect in evocative ways. Kindly tell us in detail about your experiences of those writings.

8. You have written novels based on sankardeva madhbdevas lives. How did you work out these novels.

9. You got sahitya akademi award for patal bhairavi in which you dealt with the under world life. Kindly tell us something about the conception of that novel.

10. You had written kaykalpa which fetched ypu the prestigious saraswati samman . The english translation of this novel also followed. Please shed light on this important novel.

11. You had been the president of assam sahitya sabha and your tenure was marked by a positive gesture. Kindly shed light on those days.

12. Your lengthy aubiography is soul searching and a retrospective reconstruction of your past. Kindly give your opinion on this observation.

13. you are presently the editor of a prestigious monthly magazine. What is your idea of being a good editor.

14. Who are your favourite indian and western writers and why.

15. What is your future plan as a creative writer. Do you have any regret.

Looking Back Nagen Saikia

1. Sir kindly tell us about your academic and creative sojourn.

Ans : My informal primary education began at my home under the guidance of my father Umaram Saikia (1904-1999) who after he matriculated from Calcutta University, having felt the need of a school to teach English within the radius of about ten miles centering our village. started an M.E. School by the roadside of the village, appointed two more teachers to assist him. After twenty years he donated the school to a society the whole school. Of course he continued teaching in.

In the meantime I completed the lessons for pre-primary and the class I and had been admitted in a nearby L. P. School to appear in the final examination of class III. I completed by primary education and again admitted to class III in the M. E. school founded by my father. After completing my education up to class VI. I had to take admission in Dhekial H. E. School in class VII.

Till VI since the days of my primary School I had the to be familiar with some parts of the writings of Assamese Vaishnavite literature and of the Assamese literature of the romantic period. At the same time I had the opportunity of being acquainted with Bengali language and a small part of the Bengali literature too. My father baught some books from Kolkata through postal service. Most of the publishers of that time, besides the ordered books sent free of charge some children literature like Agner Parashmoni, Thakumar Julee, Sishu Bodhak etc. Moreover my father was a subscriber of the Assamese weekly 'Asomiya'.

All these small experiences perhaps pushed me to write when I was a student of class VII, for our annual school magazine 'Prabah'--- one poem, one story and an article under the title "Asamiya Bhasha aru Sahitya". That was the beginning. Then from class VIII I started writing poem and also short dramatic scene with a tone of criticism in the Saptahik Asamiya'. I wrote the first short story "silpir Chakulo" (Tears of a painter) in class X for the school magazine.

I was a subscriber of 'Asom Bani' from its first issue. When I was studying in J.B College, Jorhat for my college education I started writing short stories. I received the first Prize in the college week competition. My stories gradually published in the Asom-Bani, Amar pratinidhi and in some short lived magazines too of Assam.

I started writing articles both academic and Journalistic also. My first story collection "Kuber HatiBaruah" was published by Assam Book Depo of Kolkata in 1967. My stories had started taking a changed character both in subject matters and form later on. Gradually, now I feel, instead of telling story I rather started to find out the actions and reactions of the human mind under certain circumstances. My 7th and till now collection last "Hemanta Kalar Eta Godhulit" was published in 2001. Later on I wrote only two stories.

1. You have created a new genre of poetry called mitavash. Please tell us about the genesis of this form.

Ans : The Question of the life and death has been after me since my youth. I feel the journey of life is a tragic one. I do not know for what I am born and my life is meant what for. I tried to understand the The Vedantic philosophy about life and death. But I feel there is no other theoretical way to find out the meaning of life and death. Now, Physics is also going near to the some theory. Yes this knowledge can help me to live the life of an ascetic. But when I try to find out my existence in this unexplainable Universe, I feel my existence to be a non existing one. Moreover when I try to find out the man within me of flesh and blood, I feel a deep sadness which I cannot overcome. At such a moment of my life, I, instead of writing stories, I started to read my feelings of different momements. But I felt that the words with their actual meanings failed to express my feelings. Therefore I tried to hear the inner voice with the related pictures with a few words for my own self. I mamed such writings 'Mitabhash'--- feelings in brief.

2. Your book asomiya manuhor itihash is a ground breaking work. How did you conceive the idea.

Ans : In 1964 whom Dr. Birinchi Boruah Suddenly breathed his last I wrote, "Dr. Baruah was the scholar who could write a history of the Assamese people". I think I heard about prof. Nihar Ranjan Rai, a scholar par excellence, who wrote the 'Bangalir Itihas'. Later on I acquired the book. But I did not even think of writing a history of the Assamese people.

When I was elected president of the Sahitya Sabha. I contacted Prof. Bhuban Mohan Das formally and personally too take up such a project for the Sabha. After few days Prof. Das very politely said a 'No'. I could not find second person at that time. After two years when Chandra Prasad Saikia elected the President of the Sabha, in the first meeting of the Executive Body, he raised the point and thrust upon me the responsibility to take up the project against my repeated protest. I did not take myself to take up the right person to do such a project.

As there was no way out for me, I prepared a plan in detail. Then I proposed that I would try to write monthly a chapter and send the same to 'Goriyoshi', the monthly Magazine edited by Chandraprasad Saikia himself. He agreed to my proposal. I had to go through books and journals and went on writing. When the work had been completed Sri Sonit Bijoy Das, a poet and a serious reader as well as the owner of the 'Katha Pablication' came forward to publish the book 'Asamiya Manuhar Itihas'.

3. You got sahitya akademi award for your stories. Do you feel writing stories is difficult and did you enjoy that.

Ans : I have not asked this question to me myself. Because, when an idea comes into the mind, sometimes it takes many days, even months, to come out as a story. Sometimes the idea dose not take much time. Until I am warmed inside with an expressive from of the idea I do not write down a story. Certainly, if I myself become satisfied I enjoy the story. I think the stories of my later period carry this character. Moreover I believe, whether it is a story or a Mitabhash or a novel, behind every creative work a poetic feeling and imagination become active to warm up the mind. I do not think that any theoretical knowledge can create a creative work in the true sense of the term.

4. Kindly tell us about your intellectual autobiography.

Ans : I do not take myself to be on intellectual. I am a man with sincere love for man irrespective of cast, creed, language, religion and country. I can't support doganati view that can cause harm to man and society. I also love my mother tongue, my state, my country. I take myself to be an Indian writer writing in my mother tongue. I am Indian because my out look towards life and the Universe is Indian. Otherwise I am an Assamese in my language and in my culture. I take India to be a continent from its colorful natural properties, with its languages and cultures with own characteristics. Therefore I believe the words of Gandhiji that "India is one in many and many in one".

In my autobiography 'Playing with Dust' (Dhulir Dhemali), I have tried to look back to my life with its rights and wrongs for which I am responsible, and I tried to be true to my own self. I am not hangkering after praise and prize for my work, but at the same time, I can't bear even a small strike to my self respect for no fault of mine. In my autobiography I am speaking out my experiences and feelings without hatred and malice. When I go through sometime, I find my own self with the background of my life.

5. You wrote a thought provoking book titled background of modern Assamese literature. What prompted you to write that book.

Ans : In my 'Background of Modern Assamese Literature", I tried to find out both the social and intellectual background of the 19th century Assamese literature, that was responsible for the growth of new trends and tendencies in language and literature. I do not claim that my work is flawless and faultless. Only I can claim that this work of mine is first of its kind regarding the study of Assamese language and literature.

6. Who are your favorite writers and why.

Ans : In my Child hood I had the opportunity of meeting Mitradev Mahanta, one of the important writers, who composed the song "Chira Chenehi Mor Bhasha Janani". He taught me to reaite poems. I met during my school days syed Abdul Malik whom I later on met as my teacher in the college days. Moreover, he visited our home also. I had the opportunity of going through some works of Lakshminath Bezbaroa, Gunabhiram Boraooah, Rajanikanta Bordoloi, Dandinath Kalita, Padmanath Gohain Barua and others of the time. Later on, I was also impressed by the writings of Chandrakumar Agarwalla, Nalinibala Devi, Ratnakanta Borkakoti, Atul Chandra Hazarika Suryya Kumar Bhuyan etc. These writers along with his translated novels Saratchandra became my favourites during the early period of my life. I was subscriber of 'Ramdhenu' since 1954. I too a little bit became acquainted with the new trends of literature. Though I could not continue later on Sanskrit was a favourite subject for me.

From the English romantic poets, along with shakespear few plays, and Rabindranath, I gradualy became acquainted with the modern writers of the post World War II. Later on Albert Camus and the writers of the absurd trend became close to my mind to some extent. I feel Madhavdeva with his 'Namghosha', Kahalil Zibran with his writings and Jibananada Das still move me. There are so many writers that it is difficult to write in a short space.

7. What do you think about contemporary Assamese literature.

Ans : I feel contemporary poets like Nilim Kumar, Anis Uz Zaman, Sananta Tanti, Samir Tanti, Anubhav Tulasi and other, and novelists like Anuradha Sharma Puzari, Dhurbajyoti Bora, Jayanta Madhav Bora, Monikuntala Bhattacharyya and more others have been enriching the Assamese Literature of today. In the domain of short story also a good number of young writers are coming forward with their own voice different from their seniors. But, I feel the absence of a single dominating view of human life and society during this period. This is an age of plurality as such. Let us hope that with this characterstics this age would be able stand with its own vigour.

Interview Of Prabhat Goswami

Q1). You are basically a great dramatist in the domain of Assamese literature. When and how did you venture into this field?

Ans: My journey in the world of drama have started in the year 1964,after getting the 2nd best actor award in the drama competition which was held at school week of Dibrugarh Government H.S,I got many awards in the school till I left the school, after appearing in the Higher Secondary Final Exam.

Career of drama was parallel running with my studies at D.H.S.K College Dibrugarh and collection of prizes I have received. I became a popular actor in the town. Then I have to leave Dibrugarh and settled at Jorhat in the due to my job at Assam Agricultural University, during the same time I started writing drama at that time.

After that I have to stay in different places of Assam for my job. Finally I have settled in Guwahati in the year 1991.

Till then I have established myself as a dramatist, director and actor. Many of my drama was regularly staged at Guwahati and other places of Assam and outside Assam.

I was awarded National Award in 1995-1996as the best radios play named "Sesh Upahaar". Still I staged drama in Guwahati with script and Direction.

Lastly a drama was staged at Rabindra Bhawan on 6th of May 2022 named "Bakrukgir Bishnu PrasadRabha" written by me.

I wrote more than hundred dramas, directed around sixty numbers and acted around thirty numbers.

My world of drama not only consists of stage and radio drama but also in T.V and Cinema.

Serials based on my scripts were telecasted for D.D.K Guwahati, D.D.K, Delhi, Tura and in private T.V channels of Assam. Till date around one thousand episodes were telecasted already. Short film, documentary, V.C.D films based on my script in uncountable. I have written the story of scripts of eight feature films in Assamese language. I am writing radio play and script for T.V serials till date.

Q2).Your plays have appealed to elitist and common people .What is the reason for that?

Ans: My plays have appreciated by every class of people of the society from common class of people to elitist classes.

My plays are always realistic. It always reflects the society and the problems of the common people.

I try to establish deep philosophical thought through a moral story with conflicts which is related to the common people.

Q3).Your most recent novel "Canceror Kelenderot Tumi,"is about the this deadly disease. How did you get the impetus to write the novel. Please also tell us about the genesis of the novel.

Ans:"Cancer Calenderot Tumi" is my latest creation planned to write this novel after death of mywife.Deepa Goswami suffering from Cancer in 2013.We can win the battle when we know everything about the enemy. So,I start writing the novel in this subject. My aim is to make awareness to the commonpeople and to make them free from the dread of the disease. There are two aspects of the story line in the novel. One is Sujata a young girl with conflicts in her life. Another is Agastya the boy from a foreign country who narrates the history of cancer till the latest treatment and research by the doctors and scientists of the world. At the end of two story lines meet together and also the characters . It also consists of hidden facts about the world of medicine and treatment which were not yet disclosed. It narrates how the people play with the life of a patient. The novel also consists the food which creates cancer and what is the proper food which resists Cancer and about the treatment where it is effective is also mentioned.

The main aim of the novel is to create awareness for the society to prepare to fight against cancer.

Q4.)Your novel on cancer is full of details about the deadly disease. How did you balance between data and imagination?

Ans:I tried to create awareness on information related to Cancer treatment and its cure. But only information related to cancer is not enough for all class of people. So, I tried to bring this information by the medium of story. Just like icing on a cake. But the information is so interesting that while writing it I gave the flavor of a novel. Therein imaginational aspect and realism have been taken by the audience.

Q5.) Kindly tell us about the genesis of your novel "Hukula Hatir Khoj" which is also an aesthetic document of an important phase of Assamese culture.

Ans: "Sukula Hatir Khoj",was published in the year 2012.The amount of appreciation which I gotfrom this novel is more than any other novels I have written. There are two aspects in this novel; one aspect is after arrival of British in 21st centaury beginning in relation to Assam's socio-cultural and political historicaldocument. In the beginning of the civilization how elephants have played a vital role in lives of the people of Assam, the novel is about that. The practice of elephant trapping is banned by the Government. But from the ancient times elephant trapping was being practiced. Taming and selling of elephants were done.Alongwith there is mythological and modern medical treatment. In the end this novel is all about human and elephant history which have been described.

Q6).Please shares your experiences about the genesis of your novel "Antarjudha".

Ans: The main theme of the novel "Antarjudha"is Rhino. There are two parallel to the story.

In this novel there is detailing of a Rhinoceros and a beautiful story of a relationship.

In this novel historical animal Rhinoceros all aspects are embedded by the means of the story. How one thief became a Rhinoceros poacher and a simple village woman became the leader of a criminal organization the novel is all about. In this novel there is history of Assam forests and many unwritten stories.

Q7).You has also proved to be an avid satirist. Please shed light on the aspect of your writing.

Ans: For me satirical literature for me as a rebellion. The wrongdoings of social and political are being portrayed by satirical ways. More than thousand satirical literaturesare being published in leading Assamese news papers and magazines. Presently Dainik Janam Janambhumi, Girijonit regular writing is being published. The stories related to contemporary times are loved by readers.

Q8).Who is your favorite writers and what future plan you foresee for yourself as a write-in breaking some ground again?

Ans: My favorite writer is Lakshminath Bezborua .In English it is Arthur Hailey. In my novels I have both facts and story. My future projects includes a novel in magical literature, one children novel, one book related to facts about drama and from time to time dramas. Till health permits my pen will never stop.

Interview Of Prakalapranjan Bhagwati

Answers Q1. Your latest book of 38 poems is not only perceptive but also thought provoking. What is your view regarding this statement? A. As you have said, my poems have been received well by the reading public and critics. Some of the readers and a few learned critics shared their opinion with me. It is upto the readers and critics to judge what my poems are worth but I have tried to communicate to my readers. I have tried to express my thoughts and experience in poetic terms. I shall be very happy if my poems make my readers think and feel what I have tried to say. Q2. This is also your maiden collection of poems. There is a long gap between your early poems and later poems. Why such slapdash approach? A. I do not call it a break as such as I continued to write but upto 2020 I could not develop friendship and rapport with poetry. I wrote poetry but I was not happy with what I wrote. I felt I was an outsider to the world of poetry. I groped for a way into the world. In 2020, a group of poets and writers headed by the critic Dr Ananda Bormudoi published a manifesto on poetry from Dibrugarh University campus titled Parbantarar Padya. The objective was to consider and re-consider some of the major issues in contemporary Assamese poetry. The manifesto raised certain questions, especially regarding poetic language. The issues we raised out of dissatisfaction with certain features in contemporary poetry invited the attention of poets, critic and the poetry reading public alike. My association with this movement brought me closer to poetry and the door opened. What we proposed in the manifesto in a group, I began to practice in my poems. In my collection of poems you have mentioned, I have included only six poems written before the publication of the manifesto, and the rest are written after. Q3. Your images and symbols are very complex. Is it just a technique or cultivated effort? A. Yes, I admit difficulty in one or two poems and that was in the pre-manifesto period. In the post-manifesto period, I have been trying to write poems in as simple a language as possible. In a few poems I have, however experimented with style, e.g., I tried writing visual poems. But I do not think that such experiments will make poetry difficult. Q4. You are a critic in your own right and a translator. How do you balance this dichotomy? A. I do not consider myself a critic. Sometimes I write critical articles and book reviews on request. My translation is also like that. On request I translate. So far, two

   DELVING INTO DIFFERENT LITERARY TERRAINS

of my translated books have been published. One is a collection of folktales for children and the other is an autobiographical book titled Siksha authored by Mr. Manish Sisodia, Deputy CM and Education Minister of Delhi. Currently I have been working on two books. Q5. What prompts you to write poetry and do you think that the poets are the unacknowledged legislators of the world? A. I always carry within me an obligation to express in poetic terms my reactions to the everyday situation, events and happenings and my experience. I write poems to express such experience. Shelly's statement made in 'A Defense of Poetry' in 1821 that the poets are the unacknowledged legislators of the world might sound exaggerated when taken literally but there is vital truth in it. The poets can rouse the consciousness of man. They can charge language with meaning. Q6. What do you think about contemporary Assamese poetry and its future direction? A. There is second flood of romanticism in contemporary Assamese poetry. Love of nature and folk life is a striking feature in it. These poets do not see in nature the glory of God revealed but it is nature which is a part of daily existence. The voice of protest heard in the poetry in the seventies of the last Century is no longer the voice of the main stream poets now. But I do not believe in art for art's sake. The poets should address the major social issues. The poets should not confine themselves to nature and countryside. They should take urban life also with equal seriousness to make poetry relevant to one and all. Q7. You have launched a web magazine of bilingual poetry titled Poetry without Fear along with some other reputed scholar. What is your view regarding this venture? A. The issues raised in our manifesto are at root of the publication of the bilingual magazine Poetry without Fear. We need a platform for a discussion of the issues. We want to help people to get rid of their fear for modern poetry. This objective has been suggested by the title itself. The Editor-in-Chief, Dr Ananda Bormudoi has engaged himself in the criticism of poetry for a long time. We have been helped in different ways by poets and critics like Harekrishna Deka, Dr. Kalyan Bhuyan, Munin Bayan, Pranay Phukan, Sarifa Khatoon Chowdhury, Dr. Mridul Bordoloi, Rajib Bora, Dr. Binod Borah and Dr. Gunadeep Chetia. Q8. Who are your favourite poets and why? A. As time advances taste also goes on changing. I do not like today so much the poems I liked a decade or so ago. Now I can name as my favourite the poets like Chandra Kumar Agarwala, Durgeswar Sarma, Navakanta Barua, Kabin Phukan, Arun Kolatkar, K. Satchidanandan, Kedarnath Singh, Kunwar Narayan, Shankha Ghosh, Emily Dickinson, T.S. Eliot, Sylvia Plath, Pablo Neruda, Charles Bukowski, Robert Hass and many more. From among the contemporary Assamese poets, I enjoy reading the poems of Harekrishna Deka, Cheniram Gogoi, Nilim Kumar and Anubhav Tulasi.

Interview Of Ajit Singner

1. Kindly tell us in details about your childhood.

Ans:- I was born in a village named Palasaguri gaon on 27th January, 1965 under Nagaon District and I spent my childhood in rural areas. I played marble, coins etc with my friends. I often went for tending grazing cattle. Sometimes I went to forest with elders and friends to bring firewood.

2. Please give us an accurate description about your place of origin.

Ans:- The village where I born is surrounded by paddy fields. There are some villages in some distance apart from which are linked some small roads. In the North direction about one Km from our village there is Kapili river. Sometimes the flood of Kapili river touches our village. In South direction about 2 km from our village there is a forest where we went for firewood.

3. It seems you hail from rural background. How did it effect in your future life.

Ans:- As I spent half part of my life in rural areas obviously its effects are on me today also. I enjoyed the natural beauty of rural areas, culture and customs of various peoples. These are in my mind and these reflects in my writings also.

4. Kindly tell us in details about your academy life.

Ans:- I read in 1) Niz Chahari L P School, Niz Chahari 2) Amsoi High School, Amsoi 3) Nagaon College, Nagaon and 4) Assam Engineering College, Jalukbari. I passed HSLC in 1982 from Amsoi High School, PU in 1984 from Nagaon College and BE (Civil) in 1989 from Assam Engineering College.

5. Please tell us your professional life.

Ans:- My service life started in 1992 as an Asstt Engineer in the office of The Executive Engineer, PWD Diphu Roads Division, Diphu. In 2004 I was promoted to Asstt Executive Engineer and 2019 I was promoted to

Executive Engineer. Now I am working as an Executive Engineer in the office of The Addl. Chief Engineer, PWD (R&B) Hills Assam, Diphu.

6. When did you get the inspiration to dabble with words?

Ans:- In class X.

7. What was your fist literary output and how did it shape your future writer life?

Ans:- For a function in our school we were asked to write short story, article and poem. I wrote a short story named "Tetiya Rati Puwaisil. At that time I was in Class X. The short story was selected for reading in the function. After a long time gap I started to write and a short story was published in the magazine Bornamala (Poruwai Powa Manuh) in 2004, in Prantik "Abansita" (1st Dec, 2009), in Goriyasi "Mohan banhi" (May, 2011) etc. My first novel "Longri Atoman" was published in serial in "Satsari" from April, 2012 to Dec,2013, third novel "Ser Hongthom" in "Mahekiya Anubhuti" from July, 2014 to June, 2015 etc.

8. You and Rongbong Terang are the two Karbi individuals who are writing in Assamese. Why did you choose Assamese as the medium of your creative expression?

Ans:- I was born in a place where Tiwa, Koch, Bengali peoples also are there. We usually use the Assamese language in conversations. More over I read in Assamese medium and I am more comfortable in the Assamese language than other languages. So I write in Assamese.

9. You have basically written about tribal culture, ritual and history. Why?

Ans:- Even now there are a few books on the tribal of Assam. Their history, culture and other activity are not fully unfolded. There are many writers to write about non tribal

peoples in Assam. But a few writers working on Tribal. For this reason I write on tribal.

10. In your works there is evidence of rigorous research. What riggers that?

Ans:- When I write a short story or a novel I always concentrate the possibilities of situations, culture and behavior of people, language used (mainly in dialogs) and names used for peoples such that I can focus the actual picture of peoples as per time and place. For example, if I write a historical novel my mind goes to that time, place and people where the historical event took place. I visit the place and search everything as possible as required. I take some interviews also. I think whether it is present or past without a research a novel may not be fruitful.

11. Kindly tell us in details about each of your novel till now.

Ans:- I have written till now six novels. Those are "Long Atoman"(2014, Ank-Baak Publication), "Sandhya Belar Sokgatha" (2016, Astha Publication), "Ser Hongthom" (2016, Astha, Second Edition 2019, Angik Publication), "Barshadevir Malita" (2019, Angik Publication. Moreover two novels are in the pages of Asam bani Bihu Sangkhya issues. Those are "Aranyat herowa Geet" (2017) and "Bot Tolor Rati" (2020). These novels are not yet in Book Form. My first novel "Longri Atoman" is based on the events of creation a district and autonomous council for the Karbi people. The story of the novel covers the events from 1938 to 1952. Time to time Karbi people demanded for a district for them. They placed memorandums to Governors of Assam in Shillong,Mohongdijuwa, Dengaon and other places when and where it was possible to meet the Governor. The district demanding team was led by MLC Khorsing Terang and School Inspector Semsonsing Engti. In 1945 one organization was formed by named "Karbi Adorbar" for the purpose. In the effort of Karbi Adorbar and MLC Khorsing terang a district was formed on 17th November, 1951 and an autonomous council on 23rd June, 1952. To create a story for the novel I read many books and took some interviews. In a note Dr. Hiren Gohain comments 'Examining many documents and taking interviews of persons of that time the writer has done a work as a historian.' The novel bears not only historical events but also imaginary situations, characters including Karbi culture, belief, social and customary administration etc.

My second novel, "Sandhya Belar Sokgatha" is based on the revolution led by Veer Shambhudhan Plonglo against British. Shambhudhan Plonglo tried to save the Dimasa Kingdom from the British. The novel has been written on the works done by Shambhudhan and his followers. Dimasa culture, customs and village administration also present in the novel.

My third novel "Ser Hongthom" is based on the life and works of Karbi legend Waisong Terang who was able to create a new Karbi Kingdom. Some miscreants of Jayantiya did oppression on Karbi people in the border area of Karbi Kingdom and Jayantiya Kingdom. Waisong with the help of this people fought against Jayantiya. At that time Ahom also attacked Jayantiya Kingdom. It indirectly helped Waisong to create a new Kingdom. He made

   Delving Into Different Literary Terrains

friendship with Jayantiya King Jaynarayan, Kasari King Tamradhwaj and Ahom king Rudra Singha. He got three gold ring from these three king for why waisong's another name became "Ser Hongthom". Ser means gold and Hongthom means three pieces. The novel covers Karbi and Jayantiya's history, culture, society and the events of attack by Ahom .

My fourth novel "Barsadevir Malita" is based on the myth of Haii. The myth is found in different forms in different places. The myth analyzed and a believable story made in the novel. Karbi culture, custom and administration are also in the novel.

My two novels which are not in book form are "Aranyat Herowa Geet" and "Bot Tolor Rati". The novel "Aranyat herowa Geet" is with a imaginary story. But there is some activity of politics occured during the year 1999-2000 in Karbi Anglong. The novel "Bot Tolor Rati" is a imaginary story on Tiwa Community. There are Tiwa cultures, myths etc in the novel.

12. You have also written many evocative short stories. Tell us about your experience as a writer of short stories.

Ans:- As a creative writer I started at first short story writing. The art of short story writing is critical but very enjoyable. To write a good short story every writer should know the common rules of short story writing. The rules control the structure of the story and the language of the writer.

13. As a writer what is your ideology?

Ans:- I write for man. If my writing gives something needed to somebody then I think my writing is fruitful.

14. What is your thinking about local languages being threatened by English as a global language?

Ans:- It is upon us whether our language will exist or not. We are already under globalization. But languages of every country is running parallel to English.

15. Kindly tell us about your future plans as a writer.

Ans:- I will write some novels and short stories to reflect our society.

The Indian Partition: Its Residues

In the civilizational history of the subcontinent, the partition of India still remains a black spot which claimed the lives of many innocent people and displaced a mammoth mass of population from their indigenous roots. It is not an unjust comparison when the partition of India is equated with the Holocaust in terms of the magnitude of its victimization. It is not only that both the Holocaust and the partition claimed the lives of many but it is also an established fact by now that both these historical events left tortuous scars in the minds of the survivors. It is also to be taken into account that both these historical events were manufactured by the power hunters and political opportunists. The Indian partition shattered the great dream of the larger Hindustan forever and since then the political and geographical turmoil with Pakistan has hardly ever subsided.

The creative writers of India and Pakistan have tried to deal with the issue of partition in their own ways and because of obvious reasons most of the partition literature is available in Urdu and Hindi languages respectively. Since Punjab and Bengal were the directly and immediately affected victims of the Indian partition thus it is no coincidence that the writes of these geographical regions have been more concerned with the theme of partition. However, it is also a huge irony to note that Bengali literature has been more or less silent on the issue of partition which is often linked to the writes reluctance to trigger further communal violence by writing on an already volatile issue. But literary and cultural historians like Dipesh Chakraborty, Ashrukumar Shikdar and Shemanti Ghosh are busy finding out the various layers associated with such silence. Sunil Gangopadhaya's Purba Pashchim, Prafulla Ray's Keya Patar Nauko and Atin Bondopadhaya's Neel Kantha Pakhir Khoje are notable exceptions in this regard – all these novels paint the pain of partition in terms of the huge human miseries it entailed.

The celebrated Urdu writer Sahadat Hassan Monto could not come to terms with the massacre and loss that partition caused and his fictional creation Tobatek Singh dies in no man's land unable to decide which his own motherland is. Monto's evocative story **Khol Do** (translated into

English as **Open it**) captures the trauma of a girl who has been brutally raped by a mass of people during the partition and who keeps on uttering "open it" because of the psychological scar and fear that the rape caused her Bishma Sahni's **Tamas** is a landmark creation in the entire domain of Indian literature as it given a very bleak but superbly authentic picture of the suffering, genocide, political opportunism, erosion of human values, religious bigotry and distrust in social and individual lives which the partition caused. Sahni's story **Amritsar Aa Gaya Hein** (translated into English as **We have Arrived in Amritsar**) exhibits the violent bloodshed caused by partition and the havoc it created in the minds of the survivors. Amarkant's powerful story **Maut ka Shahar (**translated into English as **The City Of Death)** provides a vivid but touching picture of the distrust, fear, panic and anxiety that ensued between the Hindus and Muslims because of partition.

The Indian English novelists have also dealt with the theme of partition in their fictions which can be cited as a proof that they are equally concerned about the Pan-Indian issue like their counterparts in Bhasha literatures. Khushwant Singh's **Train to Pakistan**, Shauna Singh Baldwin's **What The Body Remembers**, Siddharta Dev's **The point of Return** and Amitav Ghosh's **The Shadow Lines** make an attempt to understand and acknowledge the significance of the partition in their own terms.

Because of the magnitude of pain and suffering which the partition entailed, it is often observed that the writers dealing with the theme of partition exhibit a struggle between speech and silence in their creations. Since pain is related to remembering a certain incident or an event, there is often an attempt in the factious of Indian partition to willingly forget this incident in order in order to lessen the pain. But this act of forgetting is essentially embedded in the narrative act of fictions dealing with partition as a theme and this is borne out by the unnamed narrator of **The Shadow Lines** who proclaims –

"Every word I utter about these events... is a product of the struggle with silence"

Partition was not merely a passing historical event as it residues are still felt both at the personal and socio political levels. Scholars working as partition must take into account both the political and the human cross-currents associated with it.

Subhajit Bhadra

The Politics Of The Intellect

The role of the public intellectual has been an important concern in every civilized society where ordinary citizens often find it quite difficult to fathom the larger intricacies of power controlled and unleashed by the state. It is precisely in this context that the role of the public intellectual becomes one of paramount importance that cannot only question policies and power dynamics of the state, but also can arrest various myths of development and success propagated by the political mouth piece of the state. Any civilized society accords great value to the beauty strength and power of the intellect that acts as both the conscience and rational morale of the people at large.

The public intellectuals of any nation should understand the value of their intellect and the exercise of such intellect in the contemporary world cannot be innocuous. The public intellectual must engage with the contemporary power dynamics of the state in an active and nonchalant manner. The late American intellectual Edward said in his famous Reith Memorial Lecture underlined the importance that a public intellectual has within his / her nation. Said emphasized the necessity of questioning the autocracy of power by the public intellectual staying away from the center of power. When Said advocates the need to be away from the center of power, he does not actually mean a passive or disinterested engagement with state policies formulated by the government at tenterhooks. The public intellectual must critically question the idea of the national interest that often acts as a detrimental force for the larger interest of the nation. The late British playwright Harold Pinter disparaged both George W. Bush and Tony Blair for unjustly attacking and destroying Iraq in his famous Nobel Prize Lecture in 2005. When George W. Bush menacingly and arbitrarily proceeded towards Iraq with big missiles and tanks, public intellectuals like Noam Chomsky and Gore Vidal warned about the possible and probable consequence of such genocidal onslaught. And this is where exactly the public intellectual's exercise of intellect should always be politically motivated, the definition of which is naturally different from the self- centered and power- mongering politics of the nation state.

India is sold in the global market as an exotic commodity and unjust and often myopic representation of India often earns big accolades from the western world as exemplified by the awarding of Oscar to Slum Dog Millionaire and Booker Prize to Arvind Adiger's The White Tiger. Public intellectuals in India have exhibited a remarkable critical inertia in their failure to question the authenticity of such representation. The public intellectuals in India have always shown a tendency to act as the mouth piece of state power rather than questioning and even arresting the nation of such myths of progress development and national interest when the BJP Government was singing the purchasable tune of "Feel Good Factor" during the beginning of this decade, very few public intellectuals in India dared not to dance according to that tune. In a country like India's where millions of people still live below poverty line it is a disgrace to propagate myth of large scale progress and development. It is also an affront to the intellect of the so called public intellectuals when they simply nod their head in front of political power gymnasticians. The verbal rhetoric of the Public intellectuals in a country like India often remains locked within the easy comfort of big air conditioned hotel rooms where lakhs of public money is spent in the name of seminars and conferences. The bitter irony is that a self proclaimed feminist like Sobha Dey has no knowledge or concern regarding the oppressed women in villages as the filthy wall of glass, glamour and lucre where always stands as an unbridgeable gap.

During the notoriously bleak phase of Indian History when Indira Gandhi autocratically declared emergency in 1975 that still remains the blot on our democracy, almost all public intellectuals surrendered pathetically to her ruthless power. The public intellectuals not only notoriously sided with her, but also showered rhetorical garlands and praises on the Prime Minister. The famous and renowned Public intellectual of Assam Devkanta Baruah went to the extent of declaring "India is Indira and Indira is India" that saw him consolidating his self interest in the power corridors of Delhi. Even our most acclaimed and dynamic octogenarian public intellectual Khushwant Singh could not resist the temptation to sleep and sideline with the irreresistable lust of power. The only exceptional public intellectual who dared to raise his voice against Indian emergency was writer Nirmal Verma who wrote a brilliant and provocative article in Seminar edited by Karan Thapar who matched Verma's courage by publishing it without censoring its content.

In the contemporary context of India where the country is threatened with not only thousands of internal and external jeopardizes, but also with the burden of accommodating a hugely multiplying population, the role of the public intellectual like Shashi Tharoor into the inner corridor of state power politics can be an asset if he understands and effectively manipulate his own intellect to bend power to meet real interests of the state. The public intellectuals of India should shake off their complacency and wake up from inertia to effectively and meaningfully intervene in the larger power domain. And this can become a reality only when the intellect is politicalized itself to contest, question and arrest the larger power dynamics of the nation state.

Krishna Sobti, Jnanpith Award
And Assamese Literature

By Subhajit Bhadra
Asst Professor. PG Department of English
Bongaigaon College, Assam

Only very recently the Jnanpith prize for the year 2017 has been bestowed upon the nonagenarian Hindi Writer Krishna Sobti who has already carved a niche for herself in the domain of contemporary Hindi literature through her outstanding themes chosen for fictional works and by dint of intellectual and artistic integrity which have been her constant companions. Getting the prize at the fag end of her life may not animate the writer herself, but it is bound to be a literature's privilege to have a writer like Sobti on its lap. I have been a tentative and enthusiast follower of Hindi literary world which is so vast because writers belonging to very different geographical locations have enriched and continue to enrich the domain quite nicely. The prestigious honour coming to the way of Sobti at such a ripe age remains me of the Noble prize for literature being awarded to the writer Dorris Lessing who was an octogenarian when she was bestowed with the most covetous award. If a writer is influential and makes impact through his/her writings, she/he can prove it within a short time indeed. What matters most in the domain of literature is the acceptance of the readers, not prizes and accolades which followed naturally with the passage of time. The Jnanpith prize offered to Sobti at the age of more than ninety raises a few question about India's prize policy raises itselt. This year veterian Assamese writer Laxminandar Bora was also in the shortlist of the Jananpith award but failed to make it to the winner. Laxminandar Bora is definitely a good/great writer but one of the disadvantage of judging his works turns out to be the fact that Bora's Works have not been extensively translated into English and Hindi. While Bora's later novel Kaya Kalpa has been translated into English by Biman Anandhara and published by the esteemed publication house Niyogi books, but the translated version failed to make any impact because seasoned readers throughout the world failed to find in the work any merit which could have contributed to the global acceptance of such a veteran writer. However it should be noted that Laxminandan Bora got the prestigious Saraswati Samman for the aforementioned novel. However it must be remembered that Indira Goswami and Birendra Bhattacharjee were awarded the prestigious Jnanpith award through the intrinsic artistic quality of their writings, not because of any literary politics on lobby. It is really unfortunate to realize and accept the fact that great treasures of Assamese literature are not available in English translation which could have gone a long way to create a general consensus about Assamese literature in a global context. If Laxminandan Bora would have been awarded the prestigious Saraswati Samman for his novel like Gonga Chilonir Pakhi, on Jakir Nahike Upam or Hehi Gunanidhi then it would have been justified and as a common reader I am sure that if these novel were translated into English, they would have   surely earned global recognition.

However coming back to the issue of the recent Jananpth award declaration one question nags me persistently and it is this fact that makes me more perturbed. Within the short span of last ten years at least four hindi writer were bestowed with the Jananpith award and; is it because Hindi is the most dominating language in India? Or Hindi rules the literary world because who are at the helm of power are Hindi speaking themselves? Writers from Assamese and Bengali literature fail to make a mark in the midst of hullabaloo created by prizes and accolades Krishna Sobti is a great writer indeed because she has made an assault on the ordinary perception of readers through her bold theme and candid expression. In this context I am reminded of Sobti's work Mitro Marijini which is a bold work as it highlights the fact of sexual right of a girl child within the domain of a tradition patriarchal society. Mitro is a brave girl who does not hesitate to assert her sexual right and she reminds one educated reader of the character of the Wife of Bath in Chaucer's The Cantubury Tales who is equally bold as one who comes out of the closet of patriarchal framework. In traditional Indian societies marriage is regarded as the ultimate goal of a girl and Mitro reacts against this traditional scheme Sobti uses slang language and the other so-called taboo words in Mitro Margani and a bold girl in a bold manner catches the attention of the readers and it is this precise fact that had jolted the traditional Hindi readers when the novel was published during the first half of the 1960s. The work that fetched the prestigious Sahitya Akaademy Award to Sobti was her magnum opus Zindaginama which is a pan-Indian Literary tour-de-force. However this novel poses some threat to the non-hindi readers of Hindi literature (which I am) because of its colloquial Punjabi dialects and seemingly complex structure. In this work Sobti has exposed all her artistic strokes positively and bears some resemblance with Dilo Danish and Aye Ladki (Translated into English as Listen Girl). Krishna Sobti is a very erudite person and she sweeps the reader with her narrative power and breathtaking themes. As a person in her own life she has never compromised with her ethics and this fact also has cemented her place in the domain of not only of Hindi literature but Indian literature as a whole. Ayi Ladki (Listen Girl) is a poignant work that bring to light the pathos of a tortured relation between a dying mother and her daughter who share a love - hate relationship between them. This novel remind one of Leo Tolstoy's famous story the Death of Ivan Iych which also deals with the trauma of a dying person. Sobti's novel have often been adapted to the stage with equal success and aplomb. Her memoir Hum Hashmat is a great work that is a pean to the   life lived by her. Marfat Dilli is a great work which is a tribute to the city of Delhi and common readers as well as seasoned reader are awestruck by the originality of the theme and delightful descriptions which trigger memories. As one feels that this award must have come to her many years back but it is better late than never.

The contemporary literary scenario of India is quite optimistic because in the recent years this has been a conscious effort by the reputed publisher and academician to make the English translation of Indian Literary classic available for the perusal of the reader and acceptance of our writer at the global level. Hindi will continue to be the aggressive language in the coming years but what could decide factor will be the quality of the translation of the indigenous literary works of India into English. the politics of prices is a universal phenomenon and one can still wonder over the fact the writer like Milan Kundera, Philip Roth, Borges and Achebe have not been considered fit for the Nobel prize while Kazu Ishiguro, a much smaller entity compared to the aforementioned stalwarts has pocketed the prestigious price in 2017.

Prizes and accolades will count but what will survive the onslaught of time is first rate creative writing with sensitivity and compassion. Krishna Sobti will be remembered even after her demise as the fictional oeuvre will continue to provoke and scintillate readers. The avowed scholar of Assamese literature and academician and the translators of Assam should concentrate on quality translation which alone will clinch a global status for the rich treasures of Assamese literature.

Postcolonialism And Globalisation

In the last three decades post colonialism has emerged as a major critical theory and it has comfortably sealed its position within the academic realm throughout the world. Post colonialism, in its contemporary shape, appears to be stale and seems like a catch phrase because of its overuse and abuse by many so-called First World and Third world intellectuals. Postcolonialism, as an academic and theoretical paradigm and critical canon, can be approached from two distinctly different perspectives-one is temporal and the other is thematic. The periodic approach to postcolonialism implies the period after the end of the formal colonialization in the occupied territories and the thematic consideration would take into account the socio-political, historical and economic point of view or reconsideration and analysis of the erstwhile colonized countries. Edward W. Said's seminal book titled Orientalism enabled a generation of researchers, critics, historians and readers by opening a new door to rethink the giant efforts of the orientalists anew. Said, a displaced intellectual from the Arab-world who lived in America and taught in Columbia University was influenced by the French Cultural historian Michael Foecault and argued in his book Orientalism that knowledge was never a disinterested endeavour for the orientalists and most of them were simply paid agents to strengthen the British Empire on which the sun never supposed set. Saids's main contention in Orientlaism was to prove how knowledge became a discursive practice and his analysis became more sharp in his subsequent book Culture and Imperialism where he argued about the interesting link between our perceived notions of culture and the British imperial mission throughout the world that reached its peak during the Victorian period. Homi K. Bhabha is another major name in this field and his path-breaking books like The Location of Culture and Nation and Narration came up with a new angle of postcolonial theoreization and a few relevant and interesting coinages like 'hybridity', 'liminality' etc. Gayetri Chakravarty Spivak, a seminal intellectual from India who became a professor in a first grade University of the so-called First World provided a mind-boggling mixture of post-structrualism and feminism, of which her canonical essay "Can the subaltern speak"? remains a glaring example.

The Marxist intellectuals and sub-altern historians have always begged to differ with the postcolonial theorists on the ground that the latter group of thinkers ignore issues of class-conflict.

Thinkers like Eijaj Ahmed, Ranjit Guha, Partho Chatterjee, Shahid Amin and others have analysed Indian history from a sub-altern perspective and during the early 1980s they gave birth to a new genre of writings crucial to the growth of another intellectual discipline popular throughout the academic domain of the world, namely the sub-altern studies.

Neo-colonialism is a monster that persists even after the demise of the formal colonialization all over the so-called Third World. Neo-colonialism refers to the subtle cultural domination of the so-called Third World countries by the so-called First World countries. Thinkers and writers like Chinua Achebee and Ngui Wa'Thiongo warned against the ill-effects of neo-colonialism long back and Wa'Thingo's revolutionary rhetoric of doing away with English Departments from the African Universities and his plea for decoloniation were not merely novel concepts, but also practically viable ways to resist neo-colonialism. In the wake of globalization, neo-colonialism has gained more currency and the entire world is transformed into a potential and practical market by the U.S.A. Globalization is not merely a concept or an interdisciplinary paradigm, it is another monster that strengthens its claim on the daily basis to take away our liberties and make us economically and culturally dependent on the wish-making policies of a few and handful of people. Joseph Stiglitz, the Nobel Laureate in Economics argues about the catastrophic effects of globalization in his path-breaking book Gloablization and its Discontents. The twin efforts of neo-colonialism and globalization have given birth to the rise of popular culture and there is an attempt to homogenize cultures all across the world. The market is now seen anywhere and everywhere and in a so-called Third World Country like India, the market has now reached the villages but due to be inability of the villagers to avail that market, a disoriented, social psyche is born which is equally dangerous and harmful. In the euphoria of globalization and in the wake of cultural homogenization the grand-narrative of which Lyotard spoke of is returning again to subdue, submerge and swallow the hundreds of mini-narratives fighting against the death-knell of neo-imperialism and neo-colonialism. One must not accept globalization innocently and it is only by being aware of the subtle and multiple menaces of this phenomenon that one can both accept and resist it at the same time.

Demystifying The Stereotype

By Subhajit Bhadra

The North Eastern part of India has always been represented as an exotic land and the writers who have represented this part of India have shown biased attitude. If the East was configured by the Orientalistists as stereotypical and exotic, than India's North- East has suffered the same fate. If the orientalists represented the East as Exotic (in this case the waster orientalists) then the mainland of Indian treated the North- East with neglect and disdain. Apart from a few benevolent and understanding souls, India's North East has not received any sympathy from the center. The North East has not only been neglect, it has also been configured as an "Imagined Community" (a term used by Benedict Anderson). The politics of representation regarding India's North East has not been well documented except a few scattered observations by scholars and academician belonging to different fields. The North Eastern part of India has been stereotypically represented in fictions and non- fictional works also. Kishalay Bhattacharjee's non-fictional book titled Che in Paona Bazaar is an exception in this context. This book demystifies the stereotypical representation of North- East and the aim of this paper is to highlight how the author has attempted to do that. The North- East is not merely a hot-bed of insurgency, there are other realities as well- of forbidden love, weddings, cuisine, childhood memories, and other 'unimportant stories' that never made it to our newspaper and television screens. Bhattacharjee tries to present an alternative and private vision of North East in Che in paona Bazaar and I have attempted to document and highlight the process through which Bhattacharjee tried to achieve his goal. I have consciously avoided critical jargons though at places a few theoretical assumptions have been added. This paper basically concentrates on the test and I have not attempted to go beyond the text by being too speculative.

Buri Ma lives near a place which is besides the cremation ground. She lives a simple life but has noble ambitions. She nurtures cultural heritage and rituals but she also gives shelter to infants. Bhat begins with an invocation to terrorism but says that people live normal lives also. Like Lyotard, Bhat gives importance to mini- narrative of small statured people against the construction of grand narrative of bomb and terrorism. Bhat goes back and forth in time to tell his tale. Bhat gives importance to those stories which are seemingly unimportant but pregnant with deep human reality. There are the mini- narratives which do not find a place in the mainstream news. Bhat does not like the stereotypical representation of North East, he wants to tell the reader something different and he is against is against the so- called condescending outlook of North East India. If the orientalists had represented India in a stereotypical manner during the days of colonialism, then India's mainstream had looked at the North East with the same outlook. If Delhi has been the centre then the North East has been relegated to the level of a margin on periphery.

Bhat remembers his formative years in Shillong which has been idyllic and full of fun, not of fear and frustration. According to him, there is no single narrative that can reveal the complexities of North East that is inhabited by people belonging to different ethnic classes or communities or groups. Bhat however remembers the agitation against the non- tribals by the tribals in Shillong during the period of 1979. The tribals felt insecured and reacted against particularly the Bengalies, who according to the tribal were usurping the economy of the regions. Bhat tells how that incident went somehow escaped the attention of the media. But having said that, Bhat does not tell that the North- East is a hot bed of insurgency. Bhat talks about post- conflict literature which is not a testament of collective pain. Bhat recollects the memories of India's North East through various sources and in this connection he makes a personal sojourn. Bhat invents a fictional character named Eshei who turns out to be the story teller and navigates through 'Youth Love and loss in the backdrop of the conflict but is also faced with the universal trails of everyday reality.' Bhat also wants to showcase an outsider's view of North- East but through sympathy and compassion, debunking the stereotypical representation. He does not follow a linear pattern, but has used a mixture of genres combing the text with personal correspondences. Bhat is against the old patterns of representation of North East as he says-

"It is a personal rendering of a people who are perceived as a single entity, wrongfully identified as a single entity and have been trapped in images that mark them as xenophobic, militant, aggressive and different from the rest of us."

If the orientalists represented the Non- West as their 'others', then India's mainstream has also treated it as its 'civilizational others'. The people of North East India could not utter the realities of their experience nor could they make themselves heard in front of the mainstream media and this text informs the reader about this fact.

There is an attempt to make a direct connection between the readers and the real people and not 'imagined communities' (term first used by Benedict Anderson in his ground breaking book of the same title) Bhat tires to prove his thesis through concentration upon three important places of North East- Manipur, Guwahati and Shillong. He has used the metaphor of food that can weave together the taste of a community and a generation of writers like Anita Desai uses the theme of food in her novel Fasting Feasting.

In spite of Bhat's scrutiny on other areas of North- East it is basically the tale of Manipur that forms the foreground and background of the book. We find matters other than stereotypical image of North East, we come to know about its culture, folklore, heritage etc. However Bhat says that he deliberately avoids the idea of polygamy in urban Manipur or the genocide by terror groups as he wants to tell an alternative tale of love, bonhomie and peace.

Bhat narrates the grim situation of North East and the often volatile condition of the region but he places stress on the narrative of ordinary people who form the backbone of the region. But he suffers from a sense of uncertainty as he says that-

" In spite of my effort, I fear that my narrative can only offer a modest glimpse into their lives and I hope that I have been able to capture their real- life experiences, their stories in their voices and often, in their words."

The process of stereotypical formation of the North East takes place at a dual level. People living within the North East also stereotype it and people living out the North East also stereotype it. Thus the North East becomes an unreal place. The exoticization also takes place at several places. The North-East has been described as a place of uncanny incidents and happenings. What Edward W. Said tried to expostulate in his ground breaking book Orientalism (1978) can ne applied to the context of the North East. Said showed how the so- called oriental scholar mystified the orient.

Similarly the North-East is also sought to by mystified by the so- called mainstream and center of power. The North- East, as Elwin Wrote in his essay titled My Impressions about Assam has been configured as an exotic land, full of unearthly charm when we mention the name of Jim Corbett we are remaineded of his so called exoticization of remote forest places of India. He was hailed as a savior of people as he killed the man-eaters and similarly the North- East becomes a microscope within the macrocosm of India. The North East is also regarded as a dangerous place where terrorists are always waiting with arms to kill the outsiders. Kishlay Bhattachrjee demystifies the process of stereotypical configuration of the North East in his book and he succeeds because he writes from an insiders' point of view. He has shown the ground reality of Manipur, Particularly Imphal in his book Che in Paona Bazaar. What has struck him as major factor that the North East has always been looked at from the particular viewpoint. The book under discussion attempts to discard many such illusions and conceptions which are contrary to truth.

The Sense of exile also pervades the narrative as Bhattacharjee tries to show how the people of the North- East feel exile in their own land. It is sought to be established in the book that how a group of people with their distinctive culture and ritual feel alien in their own land. The title Che in Paona Bazaar becomes significant from the perspective that Imphal has become a place which has been pervaded by western modes of behavior. The sense of belonging comes only when the people of the land feel affinity with the rest of the country. But Kishlay Bhatacharjee shows how the people of the north east do not feel any sense of belonging because they do not have that kind of affinity with rest of the country as the mainstream not only ignores them but also gives an exhibits a step- motherly attitude towards them. Bhatacharjee shows how the people of the North- East feel alienated and cut off from the rest of the country. Life in the north east has a rhythm of its own a cultural mosaic and unique socio- political structure. Bhatacharjee writes with a sense of anguish and utter chagrin regarding why the inhabitants of the North- East had to feel a sense of isolation.

Bhatacharjee does not write without any factual base or authentic point of view. He is not one of those foreigners who looks at the North- East with exotic eye. He represents what he has experienced and demystifies whatever is stereotypical. For that he takes recourse to witness literature and as he meets local people and hears their stories, he becomes both sympathetic and compassionate towards them. It is not untrue that the North East witness terrorism but Bhattacharjee goes beyond that as he tells us nice stories about daily life of the people of North East. He writes aptly-

"I've collected anecdotes from those street fighting years, stories told to me by the solders... some of them are silly but witty as well. Documentation of Assam and for that matter, the regions contemporary history is grossly inadequate. I felt stories of the people who have witnessed the turbulence and disillusionment can never be replaced by any alternate fiction or narrative. I have tried to retain much of the flavor of these stories."

Bhattacharjee does exactly what he proclaims and that is why his representation of the North East does not become stereotypical.

In the conclusion we can say that Bhattacharjee represents the North-East with all its different hues and colors. He does not want to sell sensational tales to the western world or to the mainstream power center. His representation is not biased but authentic and he laces his narrative with several heart-felt anecdotes. The readers become convinced that Che is Paona Bazaar is not just another book about the North-East which sells false stories. It is a book that contest and demystifies the stereotypical representation of the North- Eat and this is exactly why the book will be remembered for a long time.

Works Cited:

Bhattacharjee, Kishalaya. "Che in Paona Bazaar: Tales of Exile and belonging from India's North East" Pan Macmillan (2013) Print

You The Target

A bizarre sultry weather prevailed all over the house. But there happened nothing such thing as any quarrel or misunderstanding in this family. People think the same. Everyone found Satyabrata as usual as daily. Serious. Worried. And little bit embittered.

Satyabrata looked usual yesterday, when he was leaving his office. After returning from his office he had hardly any talk with Manika. It is now his daily habit to talk little with Manika. For an hour he taught math to Parmitha. Perhaps, no talk happened between Satyabrata and Anshuman.

Satyabrata is not much a cheerful man or a merry man. That is true. He is little bit disturbed and reserved. This is not the first time that he turns so silent in this manner. There is a little madness in him. Manika is sometimes afraid that he might turn complete mad. She could not share all this things to others. This apprehension did rise in the minds of Parmita and Anshuman too.

A little before Anshu had asked—'any quarrel with your husband last night?'

This year Anshu reached his twelve Class. Maybe, his question is innocent. Yet Manika comes up with the reply—'no, there is no misunderstanding'. Anshu did not advance his talk as he sensed some wrong in the house.

Satyabrata went to the pond to take his bath. He returned now. He was spreading his towel. Then, Parmita asked—'why you so silent, Baba?'

What could be its answer? Satyabrata thinks upon this. This is also true that he has no mind to talk. But why? This is not clear to him. But he has to reply something. He said—'I am in thought'.

While he sat eating his lunch he shared a few words with Manika—white rice—Miniket—'how much rice do we eat a month, Manika?'

--'Almost fifty kilograms?'

He once looked at the ceiling of the kitchen and said—'the kitchen room needs to be repaired...'

After that he sank into deep thought.

Satyabrata was moving towards the railway station to catch the 8:21 train. Something is written in front and back side of his ganzi shirt: a misuse of death.

Murder and death all around. Satyabrata often reacted while reading the newspaper—'people should not be killed this way'.

They all are young men of around twenty years. When satyabrata talked to others about all this things, he found that some of them agreed upon his views—but some would react by saying—'that was destined to take place. Those who are dying are all downtrodden people'.

Something like that was written on the T-shirt of Satyabrata—

It was Anshu who wrote all this. Red coloured. Blood seems to be oozing from the letter 'y' and 'g' of 'dying'....

After a long time, the T-shirt has finally got its place—on Satyabrata's body. The letters of the writing are shining in the morning sun of 8 a.m.

The local train is entering the station blowing the dust of the platform. His attention is fixed on a target compartment. He threw himself into the train to get the first seat.

Roy Da was seated on the first seat toward Howrah. He was reading a newspaper spreading it across his lap. Satu turned his attention to the paper. A headline with bold letter is highlighted: the Middle Class is itself a danger.

Some of the passengers put their eyes on the back of Satyabrata to investigate the letters on his ganji. Some unusual thing often can be seen on the T-shirt—the flag of USA, Titanic Love, Bruce Lee or and many other things.

Then Satu asked himself—which class do I belong?

I am a man who sees no single dream in his life fulfilled, occasionally purchase one or two poetry book over all my poverty.

My wife possesses only one bra. I have a single under pant. We couldn't make the life of our two kids more delightful. 'what's the matter, Satu,?' asked Kesto da, 'Why so upset?'

--no, nothing happened! just reading the newspaper.

The caption of the newspaper shows some news: hike in ration prices of Wheat and rice-- subsidy Cuts on fertilizer—

White rice—Miniket—50 kg a month.

Could we touch white rice any more?

The ration sugar cannot be the privilege of an income tax payer. Public sectors that are dying will be closed off. His eyes unconsciously turn to Dutt Da. The family sector of Dutt da is also in dying condition.

Three children—two of them are daughters—none of them could be married off yet. The son may be in tenth class.

A long deep sigh is struggling to come out in Satu's chest.

Increase of budget in the Defense Sector.

Suddenly Satu's mind stops working.

The caption of the newspaper burns the eyes:

The employee community is quite upset; angered—war

surcharges—the World Bank affected: the Chief Minister

in worry about what will happen to the dying sectors. Frustration in the whole state.

Satu closes his eyes. A heavy tiredness comes upon his body. It may be Bhaat ghum. A ease on the eyes.

'Satu da', asked Kunal, 'what are you thinking so serious?'

Satu opened his eyes and looked on—'no, nothing serious'.

After saying this he turned his eyes towards the face of Dutt da—quite thoughtless. Does man turns thoughtless after a long-term living in anxiety. His eyes turn again to the newspaper. A cartoon of the Finance Minister— good humored. The budget under his arm. Yesterday, he was sitting in the office canteen and watching the budget session in the television. Members of the ruling party was clapping against the tables—at such point his mind could do nothing—he was watching on the screen but noticed a terrible scene before his eyes—people, walking or sitting, were dropping dead on the earth.

Death! Is it because of this that he put on the T-shirt today?

'Roy da, could you leave the paper?' Kesto da throws this request that makes Satu little bit disturbed. Something echoes at his ear...but that does not get disclosed.

'How was the budget', asked Kunal—

'Fantastic! It was the war that was wanted', Roy da replied—

Satu thought that there was an intense mock in Roy da's reply. Yet, he had wanted to say—no, everyone doesn't want war. But he could not gather courage to express that. He is afraid to be attacked. He saw how voices against the war were overwhelmed by the gleeful chorus of patriots.

'Dada, are you mocking?' said one of them—

Satu turned to look on. Unknown person. Roy da too noticed this.

'No, bhai', he replied—

'There is no mockery in it.' replied Kesto da, 'The forever enemies are there on the borders—we need to be more alert than before.'

This time Satu really gets moored.

Satyabrata did not notice any special difference or any reaction in the office. Everything appeared normal to him. Some of them are, of course, upset about the income tax. This was determined to happen—the patriotic sentiment reached its height during the war, its impact is still felt—making jokes and funs in the office time are usual as daily habit—only Satyabrata could not respond.

Ram Babu comes close to the table and says, 'Satta, are you getting all right?'

--Why did you ask so?

--you look some changed.

Satyabrata stared at him for a moment and replied: 'nothing in this world happened according to the will of the common people like us, didn't it?'

Ram Babu could not come up with any explanation about the statement. Looking back to his past experience, he answered: 'all this are upto the will of the Almighty'.

'--Ram da, do you ever realize, I might be killed any day.'

--it is the hallucination of your mind.

--the war preparation is going to be much strong, Ram da.

Ram Babu intends to say now—are you gone mad?

Satu got a seat during his return trip. Kunal kept this seat for him. The compartment is quite dark. They couldn't see one another's face. Just after boarding the train some talks were echoing in his ears—these discussions develop from their talking about the price decrease of different equipment and particles of computer and internet. The language they are talking in was incomprehensible to him. Yet he was listening. While listening the discussion, he suddenly breaks his silence in exclamation--my lord, dinosaurs!

All turned silent. The wheels of the train were moving fast on the rail—its sounds echoing in the silent. After a little moment, Satu broke the silence—'I mean, the world will run mad like the dinosaurs of ancient times.'

'Why did you say it will run mad? It is already gone mad', replied Dutt da—

'Dutt, I have heard', said Roy da, 'there are some inventions that the computer now writes poetry, songs, isn't it?'

Just after Dutt da's reply, Kunal said—'oh, is it really so! We are sensing poetry.

Satu is clear that Kunal wants to tease him. He used to be silent when he realizes this. Sometimes, he took this poking very serious. This time he gave a normal reply—'yet, a lack of rhetoric will be there in it.

--'why?'

Do you think we are the people who can possess such e-tech? We could no become people of that height who have pockets always full.

There creates a gap of understanding.

'Whatever it is, internet is much like modern poetry', replied Prabeer—

Prabeer often threw comments on poetry. Target—to nag Satu. Satu came to be known as a poet in his daily travelling. Of course, he once tried to write poems—all my songs targeting at you—this sort of thing. But this thing was not to be disclosed before them. It is true that he loves poetry very much. Often he quoted from poetry, proverbs while talking to others—all these made him a poet to others. While discussing and debating on the poetry, he took the side of modern poetry. Above all he is a poet. It is the habit of Prabeer to mock the poet-Satu. And Satu is quite determined to make Prabeer understand modern poetry.

Is it suitable to create a compare between internet and modern poetry—that is different matter. Satu, in connection to the present discussion, said, 'now you understand, Prabeer, if you are not much in good thought and mutual understanding, you can never be a man of knowledge. Dutt da can understand what you cannot understand; I can understand the poetry you cannot understand.

--'whatever it is, no need to understand too much. To understand excessive is dangerous. I may become a talker like you and may throw comment everywhere.'

'But', replied Kunal, 'Satu da remains silent almost all the time.'

--that is true. Today also he was silent—suddenly Dinosaurs...

Satu intends to reply, within the Dinosuar itself, the seed of success is hidden.

In any time and in any moment, I might be killed like the incidents in the newspaper—bullets or printer—something like that is racing towards me—

You are also the target—

You too, you too—

All my songs targeting at you, the thong, the bullet is racing—

The bullet is racing, targeting at you—

Satyabrata returned to a room. He was lying awake late night. He was trying to write a poem with that line. Finally, he decided to send the line to a poet and slept.

Today morning everyone is happy. A freshness in Satyabrata's lips! An amazing song. Parmita woke up in the song. She looked at her father with her drowsy eyes and said, 'you are so happy!'

'Happy!' replied Satyabrata—

Anshuman was standing at the door.

Another song in the lips of Satyabrata.

'You the man of yesterday and you the man of today—unbelievable.' Said Anshuman, 'happy, why'

'Eureka', answered Satyabrata —

In this time, Manika came out of the kitchen and stood and said, 'what did you get'.

Again another song. Standing in front of Manika he replied-- 'dream'.

Satyabrata realized the demeaning light of the family. They face much trouble in their family.

After two days more, as Satyabrata sees himself in the dream, others notice the same thing; he is marked with the letters on his back and front sides: a bullet is tearing—you the target.

Title : Woman As The Victim Of Racial Violence : A Critical Reading Of J.M. Coetzee's Disgrace

Subhajit Bhadra
Assistant Professor
Deptt. of English
Bongaigaon College
E-mail : subhajit.bhadra@gmail.com
6001171042

Abstract

Women have passively accepted the terms and conditions imposed by men on them over the ages. They have often been silent and mute. They (women) have attempted to clinch equal rights along with men over the years. But that has not become a reality yet. Women have been subgugated by patriarchy and patriarchy has been responsible for the marginalization, oppression and even construction of women. The body of the women has been a potential site for male violence. Traditionally the body of the women has been a male destination but with the onslaught of feminism women's body has been her own destination. Women have tried to articulate their needs, desires and angst and it has given them a tough rhetoric. Women cannot afford to be passive objects of male violence; rather women have to inculcate the habit of subverting the structure of patriarchal violence. Without women no society or nation can run and it must be noted that a world bereft of women would be anything but a world. Women should also realize their own potential and try to be vocal about the torture, humiliation and oppression they have received over the years.

The aim of this paper is to provide a critical analysis of the character of Lucy, a woman, from the Nobel Prize Winning author J.M. Coetzee's novel Disgrace. Lucy has been a victim of sexual and racial violence and she articulates her protest to such violence through silence. In this context it is important to note that Lucy is a white woman who has been a victim of multiple rape by Black thugs who try to change the equations by challenging the existing reality. Lucy is not a coward but unlike her father David Lurie she is practical. Disgrace shows the limits of woman's tolerance, patience and even breakdown, but not extinction. That Lucy overcomes the post-trauma condition attests to her agility. Lucy is not a toy to play with but lioness to be afraid of because of her stern attitude. She knows how to cope up with reality and it gives her strength. She remains alone in her fight even thought she tries to take a protector. But the rhetoric of protest that Lucy shows in the novel is really astounding. The aim of this paper is to situated all those complex tropes 8in the context of the development (the response and attitude) of the character of Lucy and to show how to fights patriarchal oppression¬¬¬¬¬

Keywords : Social, Violence, Body, Black and white, Patriarchy, Rhetoric, protest.

J.M. Coetzee is an extremely important writer from the African continent who has penned many important novel and essays. He hail s from South African but due to the extreme controversy after the publication of his best selling and readable novel Disgrace Coetzee had to leave South African and settle down eventually in Australia. In fact Coetzee was compelled to hide behind the glare and glamour of publicity and anyone familiar with Coetzee life knows that he does not like to be visible in public domain much. South Africa has produced novelist like Alan Paton, Nadine Gordimer and indeed J.M. Coetzee, all of whom have reached a certain goal-the goal of depicting racial segregation, racial violence, sexual oppression and political unrest.

J.M. Coetzee is often compared with his fellow white Nadine Gordimer whose writing is explicitly political. Coetzee has always depicted the plight of the helpless black people who have received bad treatment from their white oppressors. Coetzee writing are not explicitly political but subversive indeed. There is an undercurrent of political overtone in his novel but he is not aggressive in such matter True art lies in concealing art and Coetzee is a master of this. He does not waver from his own point of view and that is why his previous novel before Disgrace attempted to show the psychopathology between the colonizer and the colonized.

Having written Disgrace Coetzee found himself at a false position in South Africa because in this specific novel he had shown how the white people are oppressed by black people in port-apartheid South Africa whereas his earlier novel showed how the black people were oppressed by the white people, Disgrace showed how the black people started repressing the white people. We know that formal colonization haven happened in South Africa but three where as the policy of apartheid which meant a kind of racial segregation between the whites meant a kind of racial segregation between the whites and the blacks Alan Paton's cry the beloved country became a seminal text from South Africa and it had also made a huge impact in term of racial discrimination Coetzee's text Disgrace is important because here he show revenge historiography works at a certain level but three will be many question which would be addressed through this paper. Disgrace is a postcolonial novel both periodically and thematically and it would not be exaggeration to say that it is a novel with explicit political overtone. Disgrace is both Coetzee's swansong and masterpiece.

The plot of Disgrace revolves around the fate of a literature professor at a technical university at Cape Town named David Lurie who supposedly seduces a black girl Melanie and who is also a compulsive womanize. When David Lurie sexual relation or rather sexual deduction is brought to the light and Melanie and his boyfriend along will the family lodge a formal complain against Lurie to the university committee Lurie is asked to seek forgiveness but to the utter surprise of everyone he refuse to do so. He say that women's beauty exist for the enjoyment and entertainment of all. Lurie's womaning halite is brought to the fore in the following lines-

"He existed in an anxious flurry of promiscuity.

He had affairs with the wives of the colleagues;

he picked up tourists in bars on the waterfront

or at the club Ilalia; he slept with whores."

(Disgrace, Page 7)

Now we would critically analyze how David Lurie daughter Lucy become a victim of racial and sexual violence. When Lurie loses his job by referring to apologize formally he retreats to the farmhouse of his daughter Lucy. There one day Lucy is gang-raped and one of the perpetrators is Petrels who actually is a worker at Lucy's farm house. A woman should exist in the world will dignity and proper space should be given to her for the advancement of her life. But how Coetzee show how Lucy becomes a victim of racial and sexual violence because she happen to be a minority complain but Lucy retest in a different way. Lucy articulates her protest through silence she is even ready to marry to peters and give her son would not mind even becoming the whore of Peter. Such a rhetoric of protest is uncommon and it would not be out of place here to mention that Lucy is a Lesbian. Lucy says at one point in the novel that she had to alone for the crime of her forefathers. Earlier the white males raped black women but now in a changed and charged political scenario black males are raping white women. Lucy is not aggressive but she is firm, she is not valuable but determined, she is not well-armed but resolute. That Lucy has negated her father's point of view itself is a sign of her feminist stand point. She is not an egotistical like her father but she strongly believes that a women's identity can be established only when she decides to assert her independence.

Lucy would not mind undergoing a change of identity but it must be through the protection of a black person. That she aggress to marry petrels is not a sign of cowardice but a strategic measure adopted which is also pragmatic. One can also say that she is a radical feminist because she is a lesbian. One can think in this context of Simon De Bourvur's comment –

"One is not born, but becomes a women"
(The Second Sex, Simon de Bourver)

Lucy articulates her protest also by deciding to live alone if everyone abandons her. That is sign of great cowage under such a changed political situation.

Lucy is adamant to give birth to the child that would arrive in this world because of the result of the gang rape. And this decision itself is a mark of protest against patriarchal hegemony. Patriarchy wants to subjugate women through cultural conditioning but Lucy retorts against such conditioning. Feminist critics like Helen cixous talked about a diffluent rhetoric for women and it would not be out of place to mention a remark by her –

"It is impossible to define a feminine practice of
writing, and this is an impossibility which
will remain, for this practice can never be
theorized, enclosed, coded.....it will always
surpass the discourse that regulate the
phalocentric (male dominated) system."

Thus we find that a woman's body is a site of potential male violence and it is through their bodies that women can resist racial / sexual oppression or assault.

Lucy is a brave character, she does not depend upon fate and she can manage her business alone. She becomes the victim of male and racial atrocity but it is none other than she who overcomes her problem without becoming a burden on anyone else. Disgrace is a powerful text that shows the limits of racial / sexual tolerance and the text also attests to the issue of women empowerment through well-calculated rhetoric of protest. Lucy becomes an emblem of that and that is her success.

Expanding The Possibilities Of Contemporary Assamese Fiction: A Critical Reading Of Leena Sarma's Krishnadhara

Subhajit Bhadra
Assistant Professor,
Department Of English, Bongaigaon College
Email- subhajit.bhadra@gmail.com.
Mob No-9957858903

The aim of this paper is to show how Leena Sarma has expanded the possibilities of contemporary Assamese fiction in and through her novel Krishnadhara. The comingling of fact and fiction has been Leena Sarma's forte and her latest novel Krishnadhara takes it forward. In this novel Leena Sarma has taken a different trajectory as it is the experience of various so-called criminals, freedom fighters and revolutionaries in Andaman Islands. The writer has carefully liberated Assamese fiction from provincialism as her locale is not Assam. Earlier Mamoni Roisam Goswami has done it in novels like Chenabor Srot, Tej Aru Dhulire Dhusarit Pristha and Pages Stained with Blood. A contemporary example is Purabi Baruahs Ashwin Villa and a well read reader can remember the Bengali writer Prafulla Roy who wrote Shindhu Parer Pakhi based on life on Andaman. But Krishnadhara is different in the sense that it is not merely a historical record of life lived in a particular place, but also a life lived through passage of time where different major and minor characters of history appear as Sarma makes it vibrant with imaginative hue. The language is very poetic and Sarma evokes the natural landscape successfully looked at not merely from the point of view of cellular jail but also through love, boredom, death and she does it both historically and imaginatively Sarma's art of characterization impresses the reader as it is subtle. The sense of claustrophobia evoked is sought to be compensated by the emotional warmth of the captives for each other. But we also encounter a hardcore criminal who doesn't think twice before murdering his own friend.

Ultimately love and grace elevate the novel to a higher plane. Both pre-independence and post-independence India is captured but the focus is the microcosm. The clash of civilizations between Indians and the Britishers is also drawn as a narrative focus. Andaman becomes the specific geographical location where human destiny is played out in the larger gamut of life of a segment of people belonging to different class, caste, religion, language and culture. But it is human beings who occupy pivotal place in the novel. In this novel Sarma uses conventional narrative but she meticulously travels through time to achieve authenticity. Krishnadhara can be termed as a historical imaginative fiction.

In Assamese fiction there has been a tendency to depict incidents of Assam and that is why critics often have been compelled to label the charge of provincialism against the writers of those fictions. Leena Sarma is one of those few writers who has expanded the possibilities of Assamese fiction in and through her novel Krishnadhara. The novel deals with the lives of a group of convicts and freedom fighters who were deported to the Andamaan Islands because of anti-British activities. The group of victims consisted of freedom-fighters, revolutionaries, thieves and dacoits and various other law breakers. The writer brings to light the fact how the Japanese sodiers had burned the library of Andaman just before leaving the place. The time span of the novel happens to be 1857 to 1947 and the novelist confesses that historical characters appear in the novel and yet there is also a colour of imagination. There is a blending of history and imagination in this novel which can be found in many Assamese novels but Leena Sarmas Krishnadhara is unique because of its locale, plot, context and humane appeal. There is a character called Pratap Singh who has been deported to Andamaan because he took part in the Sepoy Mutiny and there are many of his companions who have been punished by the Britishers because of the same. A group of soldiers rebelled against the British as they came to know that cartridge made of pigs and cows had been used which ultimately infuriated both the Hindus and Muslims. Pratap Singhs companion Madhusudan Sen who expresses his strangeness because they are taken to the Andamaan island and he says that the mythical character from the Ramayana Hanuman went to fetch Sita and that is why it has been named Andaman. Leena Sarma goes to the extent of demythologizes many aspects and makes the boundary of her novel broad.

There is Mr. Stuart who only knows how to physically torture the convicts and he wiggles out a peculiar sound from his mouth because he detests the

Indians and it is also connected to his past which is shrouded in mystery. The convicts are not given proper food and drinking water as they languish in jail. One of the characters says, "This hunger is a bad entity. Hunger resists anger and resentment and becomes an over whelming patriarch and a overpowering existence.".[Krishnadhara 4] There is a stereotypical representation of India and it has been shown how India is configured as a land of disease and death. The oriental outlook of the Britishers has been brought to the fore and it is precisely this outlook which becomes a matter of disgrace. The interrelationship between the Indians and Brititishers has always been a relation of superiority and inferiority complex, darkness and enlightenment and the oppressor and the oppressed. The Indians have been always regarded as a bunch of inferior people by their counterparts and the Western people have called them brutes, uncivilized, barbarians and even reduced them to the status of animals. The character called Pratap has a troubled history in the narrative as his aunt was once abducted by a British Sahab who was ultimately responsible for her wretched condition. This particular hatred for one British officer materialized into hatred towards the entire British people. As soon as Pratap got job in a British company he came into contact with many white officers. Some of them happened to be cruel while others were soft-hearted. When Prataps aunt Pramila became a concubine of Mr. Malcolm she became inferior to a dog as there was insurance money against everyone's name accept any formidable sum for Pramila.

One aspect of the novel is that the author has not romanticized the locale that is Andaaman as the following words suggest, "There are five revolutionaries who have been exiled after fighting against the British. They have no idea about the place of exile. They will have to prepare themselves for staying through the rest of their lives in an unknown island or a bunch of islands named Andaaman."[Krishnadhara, 15] They have been brought here to experience death in life. Some characters felt it was worse than death. The author also provides historical information about Andaaman island as sea pirates attacked the ships passing through the route of the Indian ocean and The bay of Bengal going towards China and Malaya island. The island is full of animal-like men. The author has brought about a myth where it is believed that Hanuman once ravaged Andaaman in search of Sita but the giant himself could not stay here for long. The author has used historical characters as well as mythical characters in this novel to accentuate the narrative appeal. This co-mingling of history and myth adds to the novel a special dimension and makes it more interesting.

The historical Sepoy Mutiny and the reference to the Ramayana appeal both to the historical time and fabricated time.

References:

1. Sarma, Leena. Krishnadhara. Guwahati: Bhabani Publishers, 2017.

2. Goswami, Mamoni Roisam. Chinavar Shrot, 1972.

3. Barua, Hem, Assamese Literature, National Book Trust of India, New Delhi, 1970.

4. Sarma, S.N. Asamiya Uponysar Gotidhara. Gauhati: Bani Prakahsan, 1976.

The Portrayal Of Modern Anxiety, Individual, Familial And Social In Suresh Chakravarty's Short Stories

Subhajit Bhadra
Assistant Professor,
Post-Graduate Department of English,
Bongaigaon College, Bongaigaon, Assam

Abstract: This research paper introduces some of the most touching short stories of Suresh Chakravarty and explores how the writer portrays diverse modern anxieties of today's people at the individual, familial and social level in his short stories. Being a psychiatrist medical practitioner by profession, Suresh Chakravarty got a chance to listen and observe diverse human urges of modern society and fictionalize them in his short stories. His short stories are the results of his own observations and experiences of various anxieties faced by his patients. The writer finds and treats people who are living a world full of disorder, abnormity and anxiety which he vividly reproduces in his fictional writing. The present essay reads some of his best stories like "Astorag", "Aquarium", "Atmaja", "Naishorgik", "Bhuikop", "Golok", "Kritagya", "Maram", "Praloy", "Polatok", "Nigari", "Dhushar" and analyses them from a modern point of view.

Keywords: Anxiety, abnormity, disorder, modern society, modernism, short stories.

Writers of the present century are striving to catch up with the problems of modern society and their writing are always found to be filled with anxiety and depression of modern people. Apart from novel and drama, short story has also become among the most effective artifact to reflect upon the human emotion and urges of modern society. West comments that as a microscope focuses on the unseen nature, and short stories capture with unnoticed human impulses,

Such a method has its limits, in science as well as in fiction, so that when the miscroscope and the X-r revealed to scientists a universe of being beyond the limits of man's ordinary perception and when psychologists came forward with their claims of an hitherto unknown existence within the mind, fiction, too, shifted its method and its aim, discovering a means of focussing its attention upon those inward motives and impulses, even as a microscope focusses upon the unseen world of outer nature. (West 534)

And modern short stories vividly capture human emotion and urges today's people are experiencing. Mehta writes,

The short story is like a visible nucleus, where the protons, neutrons and electrons surround it but are not visible. There is a rich plethora of meanings that the short story encodes within itself. It invites us to an expansion of the meaning from the essence rather than from the meaning to the essence. The feelings of our experiences, our subjectivities do not flow out in one huge volcanic outpour but in little splintered bursts of stories. Every story is filigreed with something special, something indestructible. It becomes like a form of energy which cannot be destroyed—is there like us and our consciousness. We link to each other, the outside world and the world within, through stories. (Mehta 152)

In almost all the short stories of Suresh Chakravarty, we find reflections of various moderns concerns like frustrations with personal life, unsatisfaction with family, unrest with society.

"Astorag" is one of the stories that deal with love, death, regret, loss, despair, hope, dejection, and above all, the cruelties of life. Astorag reminds us of the famous Assamese writer Homen Borgohains novel with the same title. Throughout the story by Chakravarty a sense of death overwhelms the readers. The story opens with reference to a cricket match and it also refers to the historical India versus South Africa series. The reference to Praveen Amre father makes it more authentic. The story is narrated from the point of view of Niren Dutta an ordinary clerk in an Ordinary office and it revolves around his dreams, aspiration, gloom, a consciousness of death, feeling of unease, and above, his gradual deterioration. The story time and again refers to sexual imageries which adds a voluptuous dimension to it. One morning he walks out of his home and finds that the street is devoid of people except, a few cars and newspaper hawkers and in that same morning, he witnesses a dead body being carried through to the graveyard. He suddenly becomes gloomy and thinks that the day might not go well for him as a dead body is an omen in Indian culture. He is overpowered by a sense of despondency which knows no limits. He feels like severing ties with his family and thinks of going to an unknown place where nobody would recognise him. But immediately he is transported back into the realm of responsibility as he has to fend for his mother and two unmarried sisters. He thinks of Committing suicide but the same thought pulls him back. Niren Dutta's elder brother Mrigen Dutta got a high-paid job and left home and started living together with a woman without marriage. Niren Dulta's father disowned his elder son on this ground and he did not live long to see further moral depravity. Niren Dutta suffers from insomnia and has to take recourse to sleeping pills. He wants to repair the old and dilapidated house and it is beyond his earning but still he has done something to prevent water leakage. After his father's death, Mrigen started coming to his mother and sister frequently and he also left his share of the property for Niren. Some people advised Niren to construct a few rooms and to let those. But because of the extremist problem and rising political unrest he desists from doing so - Niren Dutta loves a woman named Arunima and after some close interaction, Niren decides to bring her home one day when nobody would be then at home. Here also Niren's suppressed sexual desire manifests itself and there one can bring about the concept of the male gaze and female body. On the day Niren Dutta is supposed to bring Anurima to his home taking advantage of the fact when nobody will be there at home he suddenly comes to know that his employer is admitted to a hospital in a serious condition which makes them jittery. But he goes to his home along with Arunima and the story reaches its climax when Niren suddenly finds that from his empty house an unknown man comes out followed by his sister. Niren Dutta feels as though his body is turning into a dead body. The story thus ends with a tone that matches with the life and problem of the present society and it is a story that finds a place in the arena of modern literature with all the touches of modern life. Isvaran writes,

The short story inevitably tries to bring home some lesson, but in a quiet, unobtrusive manner. Ho real author ever appears to teach, but all great authors have been leaders of epochs (ix)

Being a psychiatrist, the writer could bring himself close to the people are the most sufferer of the curses of modernism. He observes, experiences and treats people who are struggling to survive and adjust the modern society and sometimes failing to adapt to it. "Golok" is a story that deals with a person fails to adjust and adapt the society. The story is a portrayal of the life of the mind of the narrator who suffers from severe mental depression which is conveyed by the author through the protagonists growing isolation both within and outside the family. The story begins with a sense of nostalgia, as he contemplates upon few lost habits which he had in his childhood like looking over the open sky, watching the flora and fauna of the natural world, listening to the chirping of birds, thinking of ponds or lakes, etc. He nostalgically feels that he has not laid bare his heart to his own friends for a long time who are now few. The story takes a different turn when the readers are made to travel through the workings of his new dead parents at the village when he was a child. His father was a hard-working farmer and he regarded the bullocks as his friends. When his father used to have breakfast in the morning his mother had to serve and at that moment the mother of the narrator appeared to be a goddess. The protagonist's household affairs were taken care of by regular servants but still when other people used to come to the protagonist's father he did not disappoint them and he knew how to preserve these poor people s pride and dignity. The protagonist's mother was also a kind-hearted woman and both his parent's regarded guests as Gods. Though they unlettered still they knew the deeper secret of life. To the protagonists, his parents were like great books which one could not finish regarding. The narrator's elder brother was not interested in studies and became a traditional farmer. The narrator however came to the city to study and his father used to send him hard earned money. One day he study came to an end he married a city-raised girl named Aruna. Gradually the narrator lost connection with home. His parents died in quick succession and he became aware of the fact how much his parents loved one another. Gradually he lost all touch with his elder brothers who however did not deprive him of her share in parental land. On many occasions he felt like giving away his share of his property to his elder brothers ..but his wife Aruna went again such an idea. One day the narrator feels unease and consults the doctor who thinks that the protagonist is suffering more mentally than physically. He took rest for a few days from office but nobody came to enquire about his health which makes him feel more lonely. At his home everybody including his wife is busy and each has a life of his or her own. The narrator feels that he never desired such a life. One evening as the narrator sits over ruminating upon his life he feels a heaviness in his chest and breathing difficulty. He felt as though a giant is dancing upon his chest and he also felt a sense of unease along with giddiness. The story ends abruptly when the narrator in his worse situation calls the name of his wife and leaves multiple layers of meanings for the reader to explore turning the story a modern one.

"Praloy" is another story that brings to light the modern human fear and paranoia regarding the natural disaster. In this story the writer has shown how economy of expression can bring about elegance create an excellent story. In this story the writer has not taken recourse to hyperbole but the response of human beings towards natural disasters is exaggerated for maximum effect. Being a Psychiatrist, the author knows the lurking panic and dread within human psyche. The protagonist of the story happens to be a humble and timid fellow who has always lived according to social norms. The story begins when the protagonist's son returns one day from his school before time and when he asked what happened the boy said that they were given training by the disaster management team that has come to their school regarding the impending earthquake. The story then immediately refers to the episode of the impending doom of the world which had been predicted thousand years ago by people of a certain civilisation who had prepared a calendar which did not show any further date after specific one. This has been interpreted as a doomsday for the world by general people and television and news channel have made it a business-like affair and has created panic among ordinary people devoid of normal rationality. The protagonist however thinks that it might have been an incidental mistake on part of one particular race or civilization to end the calendar on a specific time or date and hence all the panic and paranoia of people are misplaced. But he also feels jittery when some scientists proclaimed that the earth might be burnt to ashes due to the fall of comets.

The story shows how people of the present society are suffering from some strange fear. One day as the Protagonist opens the television he finds that in the environment channel it is shown how the glacier of the Himalaya is melting because of global warming which would sooner or later destroy the earth . He notices that the world is passing through a phase of anarchy as many American's have died in tornado and many people have lost their lives due to earthquakes in Philipines. One morning when he was walking with his neighbour Mr. Mahanta he was briefed about a Hollywood movie ehichpotrayed the end of the world realistically and it has been reported to Mahanta by his son. Gradually the protagonist also anticipates some impending doom and after that the story takes a different turn where a long chronicle of his entire life is sketched by the author. The story wonderfully portrays how a rumor can spread due to several modes of communication in the contemporary world. The knee jerk reaction of people while anticipating natural disaster and the gradual deterioration of social mores bring to light how realistically the writer can create fictional space which is both effective and eloquent .in this story Chakravarty has shown how ordinary people everywhere behave in the same way and gap between fictional character s superstitious and the author's rational attitude makes a perfect story.

In "Polatok", Chakravarty has shown how a suddenly human being can face unforeseen circumstances and how under these circumstances they are bound to react irrationally. It is a story where disease operates both as a metaphor and motif and a minimum number of characters present in the story makes it more compact. This is also a story where the author has shown how neglecting physical troubles initially can lead to major ailments in the future. The story setting is basically the hospital where the narrator's friend's brother-in-law has been admitted for treatment after suffering from a brain stroke. We also get the information that the patient did not abide by the rule of the doctor as he had been diagnosed with hypertension and sugar or diabetes. The patient ate everything even items that would aggravate his physical condition. The narrator of the story works in a hospital and hence has got connections with all the doctors. He helps whoever approaches him and this quality has made him popular. Sometimes he helps the poor patients who cannot afford to be admitted in the hospital because of poor financial conditions and these patients are helped by the narrator who requests the concerned doctors to prescribe medicines for them. One day his school mate Haren called him and explained that his brother in law would be brought to the hospital where the narrator works and hence he urged the narrator to help him as much as he can .the patient was always irresponsible and had no control over mouth and on the day of the accident he fell down on the ground of the hospital. The report of the C.T scan revealed that this had been bleeding within the brain. Hence started the narrators daily visit to the intensive care unit of the hospital where the patient had been kept. On each of such occasion the narrator met Haren's sister and she regularly asked him how far her husband had improved or deteriorated. She requested the narrator to come daily and the narrator agreed. The narrator turns out to be nostalgic when he remembers his school days when he had Haren were intimate friends and how Bina was younger than them and how she used to wear a frock and later on it becomes clear that the narrator loved Bina from the core of his heart. When the narrator and Haren were in higher secondary classes Bina got married at an early age. The narrator did not attend the meeting citing some pretests. Again the narrator comes back to the present And readers get to know that Haren brother in laws condition was worsening. Gradually the narrator's daily routine was hampered and he was struggling to be normal and he made many mistakes on daily basis which were unwanted. The story reflects the suffering of people from different diseases which are also problems of modern society.

"Nigari" is also a modern story that talks about self -hatred, self narcicism, love, life, and the pathos of existence. The author picks up a first person narrator's in the form of a male protagonist who narrates his life up to certain point and the disappointment he had to find in his life is described immensely powerful description. Character in control but same character are allowed to act out their sentimental and emotional life. The narrator begins with the proposition that a man like him is not worthy to live and he makes it clear that this assertion is not coming out of emotion. After that the narrator asks a few rhetorical questions to the readers and has there is an attempt by the writer to minimise the gap between central character and the ready of the story. After that the narrator nostalgically reminds himself of his escapades and free life in the village. We gradually come to know that the protagonist is called named by others or he is I'll treaded by others but his weakness is that he cannot protest. When he reached a higher class in a different school one day he borrowed a history book from the school library and on the due that he comes to school accompanied by the book but it was stolen by one of his classmates during leisure hour. He could identify the thief but did not say a single word and had to pay the entire amount for the last book after two months. He is the youngest at home and that is why he did not have new books till he crossed high school and he had to manage with old books of his elder brother and sister. He was not ever given any dress for many years and had to wear the cloth of his elder brother. Whenever he requested his father to fetch new books and copies for him he even told her father to wait since he was the youngest. And regarding this when he stopped going to school his mother intervened and provided him new copy books and he resumed going to school. The protagonist confesses that he is very timid and shy and gives reference to a particular reference to a marriage ceremony where he was not served with an egg which was served to everyone else but when another person intervened and he was subsequently served the egg curry he felt like dying and shame. He had suffered in life because he took the headache of others and here the readers get another reference to his dwindling confidence. He received the bicycle of his elder brother as an inheritance when the farmer entered college but her also another boy took hold of the bicycle through cunning plan and again he was a mate spectator. In spite of good result he could not go to other places and because of financial security admission the local college. Here he met his classmate Krishna who always complained about her family. And then there were lots of problems in her family which she used to disclose to the narrator. After passing pre- University they drifted and after many years during the puja they met again. Krishna started talking about older days and she expressed her grief over the fact that she still remained unmarried even though some others were married. The narrator was always trying for a job in the intervening years and he gets a job when he was past his youth? His friends tried to direct his attention towards the fact that if he remained eternally unmarried than nobody would look after in his old days. And some of his friends is suggested that he could easily marry Krishna who also remained unmarried. The Narrator was reminded of Krishna's face after many years and he felt that all her candid assertion about the torture meted out to her at home, anger and accusations ever but substance of love. Now when the narrator proposes to Krishna to marry her she candidly says that she would be unable to fulfill his desire. The narrator replied that he understands certain happening of life quite late but once he has understood he does not want to delay. Krishna then says that she has another younger sister and she cannot leave her to which the narrator finds a solution. He requests his friends to find a suitable groom for Krishna's younger sister which they did and thus both the marriage were solemnised on a single date. Within one year of her marriage Krishna'sister become pregnant and Krishna enjoyed the information. Krishna circulated this news to the neighbours of the village and they, in turn, ask her about her own probable and possible pregnancy. She becomes embarrassed and explained everything to the narrator. Finding no other alternative the narrator decided to take Krishna along with him to the town by abandoning his own mother in the village home cared Krishna for everything Krishna reacted in a very hostile way to his mother but the narrator told that his mother is too old to keep any grudge against them. Once they started living together in the town Krishna becomes more angry and more volatile. She does not have to do much at home and during leisure hours thinks about all irrational things. He gets trapped in her past and can hardly look forward to the future. She suffers from mental agony and out of suffering cares her own family as well

     Delving Into Different Literary Terrains

as her husband's family members. They were married socially and nobody at the narrator's home knew the fact that he knew Krishna from earlier days. The narrator's elder sister tells him that the bride would be of the same age of the narrator. But the narrator cuts her short and tells that the prospective bride is an orphan and hence age does not matter. When the narrator's sister mentioned this to Krishna she could not tolerate and started curing her husband's entire family. All the pent-up frustration, often. Vindictiveness and sorrow are transferred to an easy target Krishna husband who some how compromises with all these. The narrator is sad regarding the fact that he could not convince Krishna's about his nature. Krishna still accesses him that the marriage could have been solemnised earlier had he been Frank enough. And then the otherwise peace loving narrator also becomes angry. He also tells Krishna that being the youngest offspring to the family he could not do according to his own wish. But Krishna's anger aggravates and she breaks things of home which the narrator can handly tolerate and it is at these moments that he feels like withdrawing to the Himalayas. He cannot weep as he is a man and he regret's over the fact that his hand- earned objects are so easily destroyed by his wife. He thinks that he is an unfortunate person, even if he dies, nobody would be affected. He then remembers Krishna and thinks what would happen to her if he dies suddenly. She has always sought love but gets hatred as her family members exploited her on her weak point. She doesn't have any kid, with whom would she pass her remaining days if she loses her husband now? One evening after returning home the narrator marks that Krishna is sleeping pointing her face towards the fence. The narrator enters the kitchen and starts slicing of vegetables and prepares to cook some items and suddenly he sees that Krishna is standing near him. She inquires if he thought that she has died to which the narrator replies that he thought she was sleeping. The narrator insists that he would cook this evening and find to his utter chagrin that Krishna has buried her body inside his chest like a baby. He did not object and felt that something was passing through his chest and coming down. The narrator did not try to dry up Krishna's tears and he felt that the tears drops would enter his heart. This is an extremely emotional story which reminds many of Indian stories pained about Indian tragic life. Anand writes,

I should like to think that these and other stories bring to life some of the beautiful and tragic characters from the lanes and alleys of India, from the bazaars of small towns and the wide streets of the big cities" (06)

Like many other Indian writer, Suresh exposes and unveils the vulnerability of modern society. The short story writer asserts V.K. Gokak says that Indian short stories

expose the hypocrisy of our daily lives, the hollowness of our pretensions and the vulnerability of our social, political and religious institutions. (116)

"Dhushar" is a very unusual story as it deals with the fear, anxiety and emotion of a transgendered fellow who being apparently a boy likes to behave and live like a girl. Being a doctor himself the author knows the imperatives of such characters and in this story he reveals the identity of the protagonist only towards the ends. The author is able to arrest the attention of the readers at the very outset and sustains it till the very end. Isvaran writes,

A short story can he a fable or a parable, real or fantasy, a true presentation or a parody, sentimental or satirical; serious in intent, or a light-hearted diversion; it can be any of these, but to be memorable, it must catch the eternal in the casual, invest a moment with the immensity of time. (ix)

In the story, the protagonist is marked by his do normal behaviour throughout the story and his different aviators create confusion in the mind of the readers. The so-called male protagonist happens to be a college teacher who feels uncomfortable in his classroom as he can hardly concentrate on study and teaching. It is a girl's college and he became more unnerved when he thinks that he is being watched by his girl's students. Whenever he asks in the class whether his teaching is understood by the girl's students, he does not get any answer. This has created anxiety in his mind and he discusses with his friends the probable outcome of his decision to leave the college job. His friends taunt him by telling that he is an ass and he cannot enjoy the fragrance of the girls. Sometimes he feels that every girl of the class is looking at him from head to toe. The girls gate rattle through his body and then he arranges his hair.Somehow he sweats it out and finishes his class- after that goes to the washroom where he washes his hand and face and combs his hairs. After returning to home he again entertains the idea that he is being watched. When he was I class eight his classmate Anamita told him after gifting him a shirt "if you study well and do a good result, then you will in my heart". Last few years he attention to concentrate on studies because of Anamita but her face kept on disturbing him. However when the results come out he was legging for behind Anamita and she told him point blank that she no longer was interested in him. But he was encouraged by his teaches and passed matriculation examination getting an equal number with Anamita. Letter on he again thought that he was watched by other people and for a few days he went to village to stay with his grandfather and grandmother where he met a girl called Rina who he re-energised him. She blamed him for being an escapist and the protagonist felt like posting lipstick on his fingers that would put him but at the pen with Anamita. Rina tried to give him confidence but he felt more like a girl than boy. When he took honours one madam like him a lot because of white nature. In every discussion madam took his side which infuriated others. In the main time a new lecturer had come out to his college who had just past out from university and was very restless. She made him the but of her ridicule and shattered his confidence in a seminar. A time consciously started taking care of his body without being aware of it. He started takings special care of his hands and feet, he boiled water, made it hot and pot his fit in the hot water, rubbed oil also. Gradually his fit also becomes soft like his hands. He took care of his hair and arrange it accordingly. He passed much of his time in front of glass- mirror. He became bothered if this was any pimple in his cheeks and thought that he had to be presentable in front of others. When he passed out from university he felt bore at home and his decided to learn something interesting. He had a weakness for learning violin since his school days but one day his companions teased him by telling that all his co-music learners are girls, he is the only boy. Since that day he decided to leave music class even though he loved the violin. But he ultimately went to complete his half-learn music course and one day he found that one of his girlfriends has cut her long hair. He objected to it but the girl said that it was very annoying for her. The boy said that others would have liked her more with her long hair but the girl replied that she was not bothered about others. She had done what was comfortable to her and since that day he was afraid of girls and left his music class. Now a days Parash, the protagonist, the transgender fellow does not go out of the home but takes evening walks and goes for a long distance. He chooses a thinly populated place and takes a cup of tea and if he sees any known person he searches alternative way. He does not know about his behaviour which does normal and escapist in nature. Suddenly he becomes nostalgic &reminds himself of puja days which was followed by the festival of Dusshera when he played the role of Sita. His madam always gave him the role and ask him to bring Saree, hair, nail polish, lipstick. He used to take the items from his mother and handed them over to the madam. The same madam said that he looked more like a girl and less like a boy.One day after watching television he came to know specific things about transgendered fellows.When there is no college he usually remains at home as he thinks that someone is watching him & he someone wants to visit his room he feels uncomfortable. On a Sunday when he is relaxing with a cup of tea he suddenly hears knock at the door. He opens the door and finds the maid standing at the door who expresses her discomfort regarding when the protagonist is well dressed and sitting on the bed so early in the morning. She accuses that he haves like a newly married bride which creates problem for her. Being angry the protagonist shouts at his mother and warns her not to clean his room which he would do himself. His mother asks him to go to her room and in spite of his unwillingness he enter his mother's room . He closes the room and stretches his hand and legs on the bed. He finds the glass mirror in the front side where he locates his mother's cold cream, lipstick, combs etc. He finds well placed sarees and mekhelas which appear like a rainbow to him. He goes near the mirror stand in front of it for long and then gradually starts undressing. He did that secretly hiding from everyone's glance and unconsciously his hands and legs move towards his mother's wardrobe. Here the story ends suggesting the transgender identity of the protagonist and it can be even interpreted in the mode of modern queen theory. This story captures with one of the most difficult situations of human minds. Mehta writes,

The tone of a short story is at once close to that of shared confidence, even occasionally confession, as if the moments we recall from certain short stories arise from our own experience. The short story can express the most difficult, paradoxical unparaphrasable truths of life as it is actually lived. It is through stories that we have a variety of human perceptions about our world and reality (Mehta 152)

To conclude, it can be said that all the stories discussed above are representative modern short stories that vehemently fictionalize the modern society and its people and show how these people are struggling to fit themselves to the changing social values. Astorag, Golok, Praloy, Polatok, Nigari, Dhushar are stories that successfully portrayed the life of characters Niren Dutta, Haren, Krishna, Anamita, Parash and their sufferings at the individual, familial and social level, which in turn reflects the problems of our own society. Thus, the stories help us understand the modern life in a better way so that we could make way to a better future. Because "the story teller, today, cannot abstract himself from the contemporary world; he cannot also absolve himself of the role of the seer

- one who sees truth and the inner harmony on which things are strung together" (Isvaran x).

Works Cited

Anand, Mulk Raj. Preface to Selected Stones. Penguin Books, 2006.

Bhatnagar, K. Manmohan. Indian Writing in English. New Delhi: Atlantic Publishers, 1999.

Isvaran, 'By Way of Preface,' A Madras Admiral, 2011.

Mehta, Tania. "The Changing Configurations of the Indian Short Story: Sites, Space and Semantics". Vol. 48, No. 2 (220) (March-April 2004), pp. 151-160. Stable URL: https://www.jstor.org/stable/23341275

V.K. Gokak. "Kannada literature." Contemporary Indian Literature, 2001.

West, Ray B. "The Modern Short Story and the Highest Forms of Art". The English Journal. Vol. 46, No. 9 (Dec., 1957), pp. 531-539 Stable URL: https://www.jstor.org/stable/809657

Fractured Identities And Quest For Self In Suresh Chakravarty's Short Stories

Subhajit Bhadra
Assistant Professor,
Post-Graduate Department of English,
Bongaigaon College, Bongaigaon, Assam

Abstract: The search for identity is the cornerstone of modern literature and it emerges as a major concern not only in the mainstream Indian literature but also in the Northeast literature. Another aspect of Northeast literature is the search for roots and it becomes an overriding concern in the Northeast literature of postcolonial India. Northeast, still suffering from colonial hangover and ethnicity crisis, has always been swamped by the mainstream Indian politics and governance. This political dominance has forced the Northeast writers to explore their distinctive identity and give shape in their writing.

Suresh Chakravarty delves deep into the hearts of Northeast people and digs out some of the most intensive crises of modern times and thus constructs each of his short stories depicting specific human sufferings and problems. He shows how the people of modern Northeast society are struggling with their dismantled identities fractured by the colonial legacy and mainstream political domination and how they are searching for their distinctive identities. The present essay discusses the above-mentioned concerns and explores how the writer successfully cultivates some of the most valid issues of modern Northeast people.

Keywords: identity, modern, political dominance, Northeast, colonial legacy

The quest for order and identity is remarkable in the writings of Suresh Chakravarty. Though he is not the first to deal with the crisis of identity, yet he is quite unique in his writing in several ways. Many postcolonial writers have explicitly explored the theme of the individual's predicament in the form identity crisis. Chakravarty's short stories witness the experience of

 Delving Into Different Literary Terrains

a minority culture adapting to a mainstream society, the changing value systems. The theme of identity crisis runs in almost all of his short stories.

'Identity' simply means the distinguishing character or personality of an individual. Identity is what a person is and always has been. It is also a mark of individualism and identity. It assures one's life and career in the face of overwhelming odds. A crisis in one's identity arises when one is unstable and unbalanced in one's self and in relation to his / her own surroundings. The Webster's Dictionary defines identity crisis as a

Psychological confusion and maladjustment that arises especially in adolescents when unable to alter psychological identification because of conflicting demands and pressures. (563)

"Debabroto Bhishmo Nohol" is a story by Suresh Chakravarty that deals with the "Psychological confusion and maladjustment" by drawing heavily upon mythical characters and episodes. The link between mythical and real character sought to be negotiated by the first person narrator's behaviour and conduct of life. Just like Debobrata, the son of Ganges promised to his father Shantanu that he would never become king, similarly the protagonist of the story scarifies his own benefits for the wellbeing of others. However, he could not be transformed into the mythical character of Bhishma because of his human limitation. It is not an easy story to understand though apparently the narrative appears to be plain enough. It demands repeated readings from the realise to understand its multilayered subtle nuances. When the story begins we find that the narrator has a dreadful dream at the dead of the night and when he comes to his senses from deep slumber he reaches reality. He sips a glass of water and comes back to his bed but cannot sleep. He saw his dead grandmother in his dream who has now become an old historical character. He does not want to disturb others by switching on the lights as he finds that other members of the family are sleeping. His beloved wife is sleeping near him, she could have been a college teacher, she had that capacity and qualification but the narrator did not give her the permission. His wife happens to be the eldest daughter-in-law of the family and the narrator has other six brother and sisters. The narrator had to shoulder the responsibility of everyone as he looked after their career, education, job and marriage. He thinks he has turned to be Debobrata of Mahabharata and the only difference was that while the son of ganga was unmarried, the narrator was married. Since last few days the narrator constantly wakes up mid night after seeing bizarre dreams. He philosophically muses over the fact that while a teacher teaches first and then takes exam but life takes exam first and then teaches lessons. The narrator confesses that he could not learn lessons from history and he also tells that Bhishmo is his favourite character, his idol. But he could not accept Bhishma's idol, Karna. He did everything to his brothers and sisters and made stand on their feet. His wife has also sacrificed her wishes for the well fare of others. The narrator and his wife only went to Shillong for one night after their marriage and his wife never asked him to take her to somewhere again. The protagonist has always sacrificed his own happiness for others since his childhood. He cites a few examples where he was the catalyst of success. After his brothers and sisters stood on their own feet they forgot the narrator's contribution in their lives. On each occasion he is approached by his parents and is asked by them to help others which he has always done. After many years his wife becomes vocal and tried to alert her husband to stop providing physical help and financial help to other. The narrator gradually comes to know about his parents' selfishness and he remembers how many times he has helped them through everything. Whenever the narrator's father is put in crisis he rushes to help him. If his father needs medicine the narrator provides it as though only he is bound to discharge his filial responsibility. On the occasion of his youngest sister's marriage he has to offer all the gold ornaments. The narrator takes everything seriously and that is why he is dignified and can be trusted. The author again refers to the mythical figures as the narrator says that he never wanted to become Bhishmo, even the son of Ganga himself never thought that he would ever become Bhishmo. The transformation from Debabrototo to Bhishmo is a planned phenomenon. Again the narrator comes to the present as he informs the reader his daughter's result is not upto the mark. His wife accused him that if he would have cared a bit about their own daughter, keeping aside the responsibility of the other then they would have been in a better position now. The mythical figure of Bhishmo could die according to his wish but the narrator cannot do so as his family members would be crushed by life if he commits suicide. Now a day the narrator does not want to go for morning walk and one day when his father requests him over the telephone to take care of his son in law who is ill and is admitted in a hospital, the narrator makes an outburst and reminds his father that he is a fifty years old person and he can no longer help them. His wife Swagata was standing near him and she switched off her husband's mobile before he turned out to be Bhishmo. Chakravarty writes about the disintegrating influence of religion and myth on an individual. He conveys the experience of a transplanted Indian whose identity is surrounded by confusion.

 Delving Into Different Literary Terrains

In "Antarnad", Chakravarty portrays the lost, rootless, homeless and alienated individual. His characters are divided people, they are the people with a receding past and an anguished Northeast presence. The cultural clash, the clash between the new and the old, past and present, tradition and modernity and the clash between an individual's aspirations and environments, between an important island and a world of opportunities lead to the identity crisis. It is a multi-layered story where the protagonist Avagya Das finds himself trapped into the workings of his destiny. Sometimes human beings can only act, the outcome of their decisions may be good or bad but there is no escape possible as long as one lives in this world. The story brings to light the trauma of the protagonist who has committed a blunder by going to help a female friend of his wife. The story is divided into different segments and employs a flashback technique, the narrative is the third person omniscient one. It is a story about one man's pain and suffering and the ultimate disgrace and helplessness. As the story begins we find the protagonist sitting near the river and he is so engrossed that many poetic descriptions are provided by the author. As he looks at the river Avagya Das expresses a sigh as the once-powerful river has now aged and has become bankrupt like him. After a long time Das has come to visit his maternal uncle and when evening descends he decides to go back to the house. His uncle has got a habit of helping others- he would go to the market and would purchase food items with an exorbitant rate while he can get the same items by sitting at home in half the price. Both the protagonist and his uncle happen to be the people who help others without any self-interest. The story then turns into a different episode where we find that Das is talking with his wife. They are discussing the death of Rumi's husband Mriganka and Rumi is a long time friend of Das's wife. The protagonist accuses his wife of being self as she only thinks about her well being. The protagonist confesses that his outlook and thinking do not match with his wife Anushikha's thinking. After the post-mortem of Mriganka's body who died in a car accident, Rumi was bound or rather forced to live along with her two daughters. All her near and dear ones abandoned her and Rumi now needs help and support from her friends. The protagonist cannot convince his wife that Rumi needs help but she does not seem to care. Gradually through the sympathy and helping hand of the small town Mriganka's initial official matter was almost settled. But the problem that sprang up was related to the accident as a case was filed and this frightened Rumi. Rumi had to go to Guwahati and she was a woman of more than thirty years, gradually Das also get involved into the matter. The money that Rumi was supposed to get involved lots of law related matter and Das would never have known such intricacies if he would not have been involved in this matter. The protagonist was fed up, became angry, lost his patience, became angrier when he often missed the last bus that goes to his town, the situation worsens when Rumi accompanies him, he suffers for because of her, they change one vehicle after another, reaches home at midnight, finding no other alternative the protagonist express his anger to his wife. When Rumi gets the money, she brought sweets to Das's home and when rejoiced over the fact that he would be free from now then Rumi tells him she always wants him. One day Rumi told das that since she already has a job, that is why she could not claim her dead husband's pension. Das said that the children can get and Rumi asked Das to go to the clerk and investigate the matter. Accordingly he went to the clerk who told him that if the mother marries for the second time, then only her offspring would get the pension. Das tries to convince Rumi that these are difficult matters and since she herself has a job, there would be no freedom. But Rumi says that if one of her daughters can have a fixed amount then her worries would be over. Suddenly there was a bolt from the blue as Ruma gave the proposal of marriage to das. Das is surprised beyond measure and tells that he cannot be so great as he has got a happy family. Rumi said that only two of them would share the secret and they should care about society. The episode changes again and the protagonist was found with his uncle. When being asked where the protagonist went, he replied that he went to see the river. His uncle said that after leisure they can talk but das was almost ready to go. Then his uncle asked him the reason for his arrival to which das replied that he came to see his elder. However the uncle noticed that his nephew was not looking well and after forcing him the truth came out. Das told his uncle that he has married for the second time to which his uncle rewarded by telling that he was not a characterless man. The uncle then ruminates over the death of das' mother and how after all the ceremonies he carried his nephew to home on his shoulder. After the death of Das's mother his father married again and das explained everything to his uncle. The narrator informs his uncle how due to guilt feeling he has told everything to his wife who cannot tolerate even Das's shadow now. Then uncle said that das should live with Rumi and the protagonist informed that Rumi has also changed her stance as she is not ready to live with him now considering the future of her children. The narrator now tells that he has on another way rather than committing suicide to which his uncle responds with both anger and sympathy. The

     DELVING INTO DIFFERENT LITERARY TERRAINS

uncle said that there is nobody in this world to shed tears for Das and as he said this his childless uncle started shedding tears for Das. The narrator got hold of the neck of his uncle like a child of three years his scream reverberated through coconut tree and reached the river. Jhumpa Lahiri expresses about the question of identity:

the problem of cultural identity involves the question of the self and of culture. In other words, this means reflecting on the essence of culture itself and the implication that there is a reasonable motive of self-questioning... Understanding of identity was a result of the romantic interpretation of the self as the inner reality of a given subject. It revealed in itself the concept of the subject as an absolute and autonomous being and denied any decisive or obligatory references outside itself. It denied transcendence outside oneself and identified itself only with its immanent reality or with its own immanent validity. (2)

Astoron is a clinical description of a bereaved woman's loneliness and her gradual degradation to a state of mental depression because of lack of companion. Man cannot live by bread alone, human beings always crave for accompaniment and that is why the institution of family has been created on earth. It is a heart-rending and social-wrenching story of a woman who has lost her husband and father. Her only son is well settled in life, wants to take her along with him, she refuses, he does not force her and leaves for abroad where he works. The story is narrated from the perspective of a first-person narrator, a woman who leads a solitary life full of boredom. The story reminds one of the absurdity of human life on earth and one can also remember the line of Gaiting For Godot "Nothing happens, nobody comes, nobody goes, it's awful". During their youth, her husband Rupam chooses a plot of land for them and they made a nice home with the money they had saved. But Rupam suddenly died one day and after the rituals were over the narrator's son wanted to take her with him but she refused and her son did not insist. She said that the memory of last twenty-five years was enough to make her stay alone in the house. She remembers the older days when Rupam used to pick her up from the Office gate where she worked. After the death of the Rupam the narrator went to Guwahati and her father did not let her go to Jorhat again and he even managed her transfer. One day she sold the home that was so fondly built by Rupam and she got lots of money in the form of Rupam's gratuity, provident fund, his sudden death and also the amount she got by selling the home. Her father insisted that she must purchase a home for herself at the new place even though she felt lonely. After that she really purchased a wide and well maid flat and her father came to live with her permanently. Her father started taking care of her in a way she suggested as though she was a kid. Her father's presence eradicated her loneliness to a considerable extent, she felt as though she has returned to the heavenly days of her childhood. When she was a child, she used to sleep with her father who was a judge in court. Her father used to tell them about the many criminals who had been punished because of his verdict. She suffered from paranoia that her father would be murdered by some criminal one day. When her father used to fondle her hair in her childhood she fell into sleep. She was always overprotected by her father and even her husband Rupam did the same. in absence of Rupam, she again wanted to be protected by her father which eventually became a reality. But one day her father was hospitalised and during these days she took all care of her ill father as though other siblings were none. Now she lives with a maid servant, her father is dead. She thinks that if God is really looking after the wellbeing of humans on earth then why does that omnipotent entity bring curse to his devotees. Sometimes she feels like rebelling and even her son tells her point-blank that if she re-marries he would not become unhappy nor he would object to it. The narrator could not even see her husband when he was dying and her father surrendered against age. She cannot find any dependable person whom she can trust but there is none like that. In moments like these, she eyes her various long sarees, brings more bottles of finale than is required, looks at the passing train from the backyard of her home, looks at the night train. All these suggest obliquely that she might commit suicide but she resists the idea. As the mobile rings, she looks at the familiar number and responds immediately and it is her son on the other side of the phone. He tells her mother" I felt like knowing what the little child is doing at this moment. Have you taken your dinner"? and these words from Rupam's son bring tears to her eyes like the rain during the monsoon. This is an extremely sensitive story that shows pathos and the frightening aspect of alienation. The story can be interpreted from the point of philosophical existentialism.

Gandhari is a rich text that brings to light the pathetic plight of an almost naked girl who is running through the city and she is being chased by a group of the wild man. But the most surprising aspect is that nobody in this great city is coming out of the home and trying to protect her. In this story the Chakravarty has revealed how middle-class human beings behave like Voyeur. The story refers again to one of the greatest characters of the

Indian epic Mahabharata named Gandhari who willingly lived a blind life in order to sympathise with her husband, the king of the Hastinapur, named Dhristarashtra. As the story begins we find that an almost naked girl is chased away by a group of wild hooligans and everybody's she called is shutting his or her Window's to avoid eye contact. At the very outset the author describes the body of the unfortunate girl in such a way that arouses sexual feeling in the mind of the readers. But the author does this in order to suggest the helplessness of the running girl, he does not write any pornography. Rather he provides a detailed sexual description in order to suggest the voyeuristic tendency of the middle class people. Suddenly someone threw a piece of cloth for the semi naked girl and she was still short of enough to prevent her bare body. In the next episode we find two characters named Sadhana and Hamid helping each other out of respect and affection respectively. Sadhana's day begins with an active session till he prepares breakfast for her daughter and husband and sees them go to school and office respectively. Hamid sometimes wants to present a piece of chadar or shawl to Sadhna but she refuses by telling that he should sell it at an appropriate price in the market. Hamid works in an office as a fourth-grade employee and finds it difficult to make both ends meet and this is the reason why he sells cloth after the end of the office hours. Hamid draws the attention of Sadhna regarding the incident of the girl and after switching on the television. She sees the heart rending and frightening footage prepared by the media. The author lashes out at the social media who wants only sensationalism and they only rum after money without any human concern. The male gaze and female body that feminism emphasis upon is brought to the fore here. Sadhna feels uncomfortable and switches off the television. Arunav (her husband) and Atri (her daughter) arrived on the appropriate time to their home and in the night Sadhna cannot sleep. When on the next day Sadhna sees the footage again she feels like she becoming the mythical Gandhari who willingly chose blindness for her. As she read the newspaper and find how the media people exaggerate everything for heavy sail and profit. Suddenly she feels that her Atri is also running in an almost naked manner through the streets of the city followed by a group of civilized men who are looking at her bare body and saving the pictures in their mobile and camera screen. The story ends here where the author shows how beastly human beings can be and in this context, one can remember William Golding's comment "As bee produces honey so man produces evil".

Even after going to America Himadri did not forget his beloved's birthday as once he called his wife and mother in law to Calcutta to celebrate his wife's birthday and he returned by the early morning's flight to America. The protagonist is gradually reminded of many episodes in her life as she had lost her memory after death of Himadri and their only son Rahul in a car accident on way from Dibrugarh to Guwahati. The female narrator earlier used to boast of her strong memory, she regarded herself with a gifted memory as could exactly recollect every small detail of her life. But now her parents are with him as shadows and they remind her of her loneliness. The doctor tried to bring back her memory but she was not cured and she also was not sure about her disease. She becomes exasperated and thinks how her parents have surrendered to God by clinging to their ultimate support and her future. The story end in a touching manner when the female protagonist is reminded of her birthday by her parents and the pain of the parents is optimum.

Gagori is a heart-rending story about an aged man's grief who has gradually lost the enthusiasm of life. As the story starts we are introduced to the principal protagonist of the story titled Agasta Chaudhary who is still sitting upon a chair placed in his broad veranda. Unknowingly he crept into sleep and when suddenly woke up he saw that evening was descending upon the horizon. He came into consciousness when his stick (which he used as a support)fell on the ground making a sound and he picks up the stick from the ground. He also felt helpless as he thinks that he has grown old because of an untimely nap. After sometime Chaudhary opens the gate of his house and stepped into the road. He is very depressed since the last few days, the reason of which is revealed by the third person omniscient narrator only towards the end of the story. Chaudhary still remembers that he suffered from similar helplessness a few years back when he and his wife Priyamvada were shocked by the sudden marriage of their only son Jon who was a doctor and who decided to remain in a different state after the marriage. The son did not back to his home, a fact which still depresses Chaudhary. He never was a miser regarding the education of his only son and two daughters. After that the Chaudhary couple pined their hope upon their daughter Panchami and Priyamvada decided that the ornaments which were supposed to be given to their daughter-in-law would now be given top their daughter Panchami when here marriage would be fixed. There is a saying that man proposes and God disposes of but the irony of the Choudhary couple's fate was that Panchami too betrayed them and went away with a different person chosen by herself without thinking about the shock that such decision would give to her parents. After that Chaudhary became very guarded regarding their third and younger daughter. She was admitted in a local college and after doing result from the university she herself became a permanent lecturer in that college. After all these flashback Chaudhary comes back to the present and he sits on a Calvert to take a rest and he also wanted to chalk out a plan for the future. The letter given by Abhishek has created a new would in his heart and he never thought that such disturbances could ever be created. While going to the University the youngest daughter vowed that she would return to her home after the end of her education and she kept her promise. One day Abhishek proposed to her for marriage but Bandana said that for that he would have to meet his would-be father-in-law. But after knowing the details of the Chaudhary family, Abhishek rejected Bandana. Chaudhary again comes out of the past memory and starts moving towards his home. After reaching home, Chaudhary was served a cup of tea by Bandana would then sought permission of asking a question to her father. Chaudhary said yes in fear and Bandana asked her father, "even if I do not get married, wont you allow me to live in this house". This is a very poignant story that brings to the light the theme of filial obligation and old age suffering.

To conclude, though identity crisis is a typical theme in Indian or Northeast literature, it has been dealt with new dimension in postmodern context. Earlier it was in context with social, political, and economic background. In the postmodern context it has become more complex. In postmodern context it is in the case of individual being struggling in his own world to find out space and scope.

Suresh Chakravarty deals with the theme of identity crisis in the postmodern context. All characters from his short stories are on interior journey. They struggle to find out new patterns of life or new orders of life. They attempt for the self- assertion. They get swayed by the problems of loneliness, pessimism. Their conflict arises from self's craving for fulfillment. Though they are self-conscious about the reality around them, they carry a sense of loneliness within them.

Works Cited

Merriam-Webster. Merriam-Webster.com., 2011. Web. 8 May 2011.

Iyengar, K.R. S. (1995). Indian Writing in English. 1962, Delhi: Sterling.

Lahiri, Jhumpa. The Namesake. London: Fourth Estate, 2009.

•Mahatma Gandhi (1921). "English Learning." Young India, 3(6)